SANDY JOHNSON
8/14/91

D1165329

360
MOST GUARDED
SECRETS
of
EXECUTIVE
SUCCESS

NATIONAL INSTITUTE OF BUSINESS MANAGEMENT, INC.
1328 Broadway, New York, NY 10001

Reprinted May 1991   ISBN 1-880024-00-4
Copyright July 1990 by National Institute of Business Management, Inc.
1328 Broadway, New York, NY 10001

CREDITS

MANAGING EDITOR
Sally Scanlon

CONTRIBUTING WRITERS/RESEARCHERS
*The Professional Staff of National Institute
of Business Management*

COPY EDITORS
Marquita Guerra
Linda Lehrer

EDITORIAL ASSISTANTS
Arlene Connolly
Barbara Young

MANAGER, DESKTOP PUBLISHING
Marie Mularczyk

DESKTOP/EDITORIAL PRODUCTION
Brian T. Ehrlich

MANAGER, TYPESETTING SERVICES
Patricia Spieler

ART DIRECTOR/DESIGNER
John Kwong

MARKETING DIRECTOR
Lawrence E. Galcher

EDITOR & PUBLISHER
Brian W. Smith

TABLE OF CONTENTS

SECTION • 1

MANAGING YOUR PEOPLE

3 MEETINGS

4 RECRUITING/HIRING

5 | SALES MANAGEMENT

S E C T I O N • 2

MANAGING YOUR BUSINESS

1 | BUSINESS STRATEGIES/TACTICS

10 TAX ISSUES

SECTION • 3

MANAGING YOUR CAREER

1 CAREER DEVELOPMENT

2 FITNESS

3 INTERPERSONAL RELATIONS

4 JOB HUNTING

5 LEADERSHIP/COMMUNICATIONS

6 OFFICE POLITICS

7 PRESENTATIONS

8 SELF-DEVELOPMENT

SECTION · 4

Managing Your Finances

1 ESTATE PLANNING

2 FINANCIAL PLANNING

3 INSURANCE

4 INVESTMENTS

5 PERSONAL FINANCE ISSUES

6 REAL ESTATE

7 RETIREMENT/PENSIONS

8 TAXES/TAX STRATEGIES

MANAGING
your
PEOPLE

Chapter 1

EMPLOYEE RELATIONS

COMMUNICATION: OPEN OR CLOSED?

■   ■   ■   ■   ■

Twenty years ago, organizational theorists advocated "closed" behavior—strictly separating one's personal and business lives, feelings and actions. Then, recommended management styles did an about-face. Open communication was advocated as a general style.

Now, research by communications specialist Eric Eisenberg of the University of Southern California and others question both positions as absolutes.

DETERMINING HOW OPEN YOU SHOULD BE

How much is appropriate, these specialists suggest, depends on five factors.

■ **Content of the message.** This is the most obvious determinant: Some organizational activities, particularly those having safety or legal implications, require clear, complete communication, the experts observe. But, in many cases, they advocate the "strategic use of ambiguity." When expressing opinions about others or taking a stand on policy, for example, ask yourself:

• *Is what I have to say unexceptionable or possibly controversial?*

• *Do I firmly believe what I want to say, or might I change my mind?*

• *Is what I am saying a fact or an opinion?*

• *Would I say this to anyone, or only to this audience?*

■ **Individual characteristics.** Personal motives, preferences and styles affect communicative choices, state Eisenberg and others. It's important to analyze your own preferences, since they may run counter to

1

your organization's climate. If this is the case, you may have to consider how adaptable you are willing to be. Ask yourself:

• *Do I place a higher value on privacy or sociability?*

• *Am I basically shy or gregarious?*

• *Am I generally guarded or trusting?*

• *Do I tend toward cooperativeness or competitiveness?*

■ **Closeness of the relationship.** People in a group with a long history can communicate less explicitly without compromising understanding, report Eisenberg and his colleagues. Usually, the decision by an individual to reveal highly personal information to another employee depends on the degree of trust and respect in the relationship.

• *Do I have a long or short relationship with this person?*

• *Have this person and I historically been forthright or cautious with each other?*

• *Do I know how badly or well this person has reacted to the openness of others?*

• *Do I want to maintain the relationship as it is or deepen it?*

■ **Perceptions of the organization's best interests.** A decision not to reveal company secrets or to hold back information from employees about a tentative plan may be justified because it furthers or protects organizational interests. Alternatively, a decision to share information about the big picture with employees can be viewed as one way of promoting more participative decision making, according to the experts.

Ask yourself if saying this would be in keeping with, or contrary to, the usual style of communication in the organization.

• *Do I want to follow the norm, or should I risk trying to change the organizational climate?*

• *Do I think saying this would simply further my own goals or also help the organization?*

■ **Environmental realities.** Factors outside the organization itself sometimes help determine how open you can or should be. The more competitive and publicly visible your industry and company are, the more guarded you must be about trade secrets and leaks of potentially sensitive information. Ask yourself what groups outside your organization watch it, and what impact your words might have on them.

• *Is your organization regulated by the government?*

• *Is your organization vital to the community in which it operates?*

• *Is what you have to say of potential benefit to competitors?*

OBSERVATION:

In most cases, you probably ask yourself these questions before you talk to your employees or write a memo. But when you're not sure how to broach a subject, it can be helpful to analyze your message against this checklist to give you some general ideas and point you in the right direction.

A NEW WAY TO DISCIPLINE EMPLOYEES
· ■ ■ ■ ·

The next time you have problems with an employee who is uncooperative, frequently absent or habitually late for work, give the person a day off—with pay.

If that sounds preposterous, consider this: It's the essence of the positive discipline technique that has been used successfully by a number of companies, including AT&T and General Electric, for at least 20 years.

POSITIVE DISCIPLINE

The idea of nonpunitive discipline, introduced by Canadian industrial psychologist John Huberman, is based on the belief that punishment is solely for criminals and misbehaving children—not employees. It's an approach that places the burden for improving undesirable job behavior where it belongs—on the shoulders of the worker.

Positive discipline requires a radical change in traditional company procedures for dealing with improper or inadequate job performance. When counseling an employee who is habitually late for work, for instance, a supervisor decides it is better not to argue with the employee's feeble excuses, however lame they may seem. Instead, he or she accepts the excuse ("Yes, I can see that's a problem"), but then immediately shifts the solution to the problem back onto the worker's shoulders ("What are you going to do to be sure you get to work on time?").

Because no one is punished, the approach is more acceptable than conventional disciplinary procedures—not only to employees, but also to supervisors. Many companies using the approach believe it is more effective than punitive procedures for that very reason, because supervisors are less reluctant to use it when an employee breaks the rules.

HOW TO SET UP
YOUR OWN PROGRAM

• **Oral reminder.** The supervisor meets periodically with the employee to discuss a specific work problem, with the objective of getting the employee's agreement to solve it as soon as possible. Rather than warning the employee of the serious consequences that will result if the problem persists, the manager reminds the individual of his or her obligation to meet company requirements. No record of this meeting is placed in the employee's personnel file, although the manager does make a note that the reminder was given.

• **Written reminder.** If a similar incident happens within, say, a year of the first occurrence, the manager again meets with the employee to discuss his or her failure to abide by the original agreement. The manager also tries to get the employee's cooperation once more, and a record of this meeting is given to the employee and placed in his or her personnel file. Normally, this memo is removed from the file after a year has passed, and if there are no further incidents, the employee's slate is wiped clean.

• **Decision-making leave.** If the previous two discussions don't produce the desired results, the individual is asked to take a day off with pay, to decide whether or not to comply. Now, the employee is expected to decide either to make the commitment and remain with the organization or resign.

• **Follow-through.** Upon returning, the employee announces his or her decision. If he or she agrees to stay, the supervisor places a formal memo in the record stating what the employee has agreed to do—and that subsequent failure to stick to the agreement will result in the employee's termination.

OBSERVATION:

In actual practice, positive discipline seldom reaches the day-off-with-pay stage. Yet, it usually brings significant improvements in employee attendance, morale, and performance.

HOLD ONTO EMPLOYEES WITHOUT INCREASING SALARY

■   ■   ■   ■   ■

Fatter paychecks are not the only way to hold on to veteran workers who have reached budgetary pay ceilings. There are other appealing, less costly ways to entice people to stay, says David Schreiber, professor of management at the Management Institute of the University of Wisconsin at Madison.

ALTERNATIVE INDUCEMENTS

• **Educational opportunities.** College courses that teach job-related skills are one option. The organization may be willing to pay the tab. Alternatively, the organization could absorb part of the cost for courses for the person's own enjoyment (studying literature, art or music, for example), or for those that lead to a second career.

• **Time.** You can offer more vacation time (two to four extra weeks a year) or allow the person to work half-days on Fridays. A sabbatical type of leave where you offer time off (two to three months, for example) at half pay is another possibility.

"Many people will jump at the opportunity to take extra time," says Schreiber. "It means time to yourself to do whatever you want. For some, it's the opportunity of a lifetime to launch a part-time business, or get a second career off the ground." Alternate work schedules, such as flextime, can make working parents' lives, for example, a lot easier.

PLAY IT STRAIGHT

Be honest with valued workers who have reached pay ceilings, advises Schreiber.

"Tell them that they are at the top of the range and there is nothing that can be done about it. Before you offer enticing incentives, find out how they feel about the job. Ask them what it would take to keep them happy and motivated.

"You may be surprised to find that they don't want the world, just some simple changes in their day-to-day routines. Some people don't want more money, but would be content with new job functions, for example. They would welcome the opportunity to test an idea or project they may have been thinking about, but didn't have the time or support to get off the ground. Together, you may be able to arrive at a doable solution."

SOME ON-THE-JOB INCENTIVES

• **Expanded job functions.** Many workers welcome new challenges. You can take advantage of a person's experience and knowledge in many ways.

Or this person could be valuable in the field as a roving ambassador, traveling to different offices around the country to assist them or keep them abreast of what the home office is doing.

Other assignments could involve having this individual write reports or head special projects that call upon the person's unique perspective of the field.

• **New job.** The employee can be a valuable source as an internal consultant who troubleshoots difficult problems or spearheads and coordinates complex projects.

• **More internal support.** Many nonprofit organizations are understaffed. If you can't offer this employee his or her own secretary or assistant, a shared one is an alternative. A personal computer or memory typewriter might also make this worker's life easier.

HOW TO KEEP A GOOD SECRETARY
. . . . .

For most of this century, many office secretaries and clerical personnel have been relegated to undertaking low-paying, dead-end career tracks that have been a cause of constant personnel turnover and low office productivity.

Companies are now changing their thinking. Some Fortune 500 firms are offering secretaries and clerical personnel greater opportunities for training and placement on management career tracks.

NEW AWARENESS FOR THE '90s

One big reason for the change in attitude is the personnel crisis the nation will face in the next decade. The Bureau of Labor Statistics (BLS), for instance, projects a 45% increase in the demand for secretaries through 1995. Employers will be looking for 305,000 secretaries within the next 10 years, according to BLS estimates.

• **The personnel shortage problem—along with an office productivity problem—**has prodded employers into action. The Commerce Department says industrial productivity grew 90% during the last decade, compared to only 4% for office productivity, forcing many to create new job incentives for their office staffs.

• **The increasing value of computers** to business productivity is another impor-tant reason why firms must pay more attention to their clerical employees, since it's these workers who are often responsible for the operation of computers. Statistics show that trained and experienced secretaries and clerical workers give their companies a competitive edge.

OBSERVATION:
Experts say improving career tracks is the answer to upgrading and keeping these most valuable personnel.

IMPROVING THE CAREER TRACK

• **Opportunities.** Provide management career opportunities as an incentive for secretaries. Note that the number of women in management in the U.S. doubled between 1974 and 1984, and 90% of those women began their business careers as secretaries.

• **Training.** Make sure that secretaries and your better clerical employees are given the same amount of personnel and organiza-tional-development training as executives. Current surveys indicate that secretaries, receptionists and clerical personnel still receive 50% less training than other employees in most companies.

WHAT SOME FIRMS ARE DOING NOW

• IBM sets a personal career objective for all staff members, including secretaries, and pays tuition for any outside education they may need.

• Texas Instruments encourages secretaries to apply for any posted jobs that interest them.

• The Mitre Corporation has organized

a secretarial training council to shape the support-staff training programs. The council consists of secretaries who meet regularly to evaluate training courses.

• McGraw-Hill has designed a workshop in proofreading skills called "Proofmatics" that can lead to editorial job opportunities. The workshop also is valuable because it can be conducted by non-professional trainers, i.e., staff members. McGraw-Hill also has designed four other do-it-yourself training packages for secretaries.

OBSERVATION:

When providing additional training and opportunities for your office staff, don't forget your full-time and part-time receptionists. These workers are generally the lowest paid in the firm, but they provide the first contact between the company and the public, as well as prospective customers.

BEAT RELOCATION RESISTANCE
■ ■ ■ ■ ■

Resistance by an executive's spouse and other family members is a major reason why many managers refuse their company's request to relocate. But by paying attention to family concerns, a company can often skew an executive's decision in favor of moving.

WHY THEY WON'T MOVE

Most often, resistance from family members centers around the often severe stress of leaving friends and familiar surroundings. Andrew Starck, president of Relo, a Chicago-based nationwide network of real estate agencies, notes that studies have shown that moving is the third most upsetting experience in life—after the death of a loved one and divorce.

That puts it ahead of being fired, which is fourth on the list of life's most traumatic experiences, Starck notes. And it explains why many executives would prefer not to move, even if it means losing their job or a promotion.

MAKE IT EASIER TO GO

There are a number of gambits employers can use to reduce spousal and family resistance.

■ **Use a real-estate network.** With 1,400 member agencies, it can provide a number of services to smooth a move, in addition to helping a family sell its old home and buy a new one. Among them: job-hunting assistance for the spouse, financial counseling and help in finding new family doctors and dentists. All this makes the move less traumatic.

■ **Offer financial assistance.** Some large companies will buy and sell an executive's old home if it is not sold within a given period, taking over one of the biggest headaches of a move. Today, however, employers will only do this after giving the executive a chance to sell the home, which is both cheaper and easier for the employer. Typically, companies buy the home only if it has been on the market for four months or longer; a few years ago, they would do so after only one or two months, Starck observes.

• *Smaller employers* may offer to pay for appraisals, minor fix-ups to make the home easier to sell, or broker fees and closing costs.

When an executive is asked to move into

an area with higher living costs, companies often provide pay differentials.

■ **Identify special needs.** Have the spouse talk to a relocation service to uncover his or her basic concerns (special medical or educational needs and entertainment or religious interests, for example).

• *Children* may want to know about sports and recreational facilities. A young athlete will be concerned, for instance, about whether the local high school has a winning football team and if it has any openings. In several cases, According to Starck, Relo agents have arranged for local teachers and coaches to make conference calls to the relocating family, to answer their questions about the quality of schools and athletic facilities.

■ **Arrange for a visit to the locale.** Have a local real estate agent plan a company-paid weekend tour of the area, including a look at houses that fit the family's specifications. If the spouse and children can't go along for such a visit, some agencies can furnish them with a videotape that shows off local schools, recreational facilities and homes.

■ **Urge the executive to negotiate with his or her own family.** In the long run, the transferred employee will probably have to make some concessions to family members to make the move more attractive. You might suggest, for instance, that the executive purchase a newly built home or one under construction; or a home with other attractive features, such as a large family room, a swimming pool, an ample lot or close proximity to job, school, shopping, sports and entertainment facilities.

• *Typical spousal concerns* include climate, personal security and whether the new home can be resold at a good price later on. Increasingly, Starck hears worries about

possible radon contamination in ground soil as well. Often, too, there are questions about the "image" of a community; for egotistic reasons, some executives want to live in a higher-status neighborhood than most of their peers. Offering to help find a house in the boss's community may also be a means of an effective inducement.

OBSERVATION:

A surprising finding reported by Relo agencies is that when the wife rather than the husband is offered a transfer, spousal resistance is not as often a problem.

PREPARE YOUR FIRM FOR THE '90s
■ ■ ■ ■ ■

Are you on top of issues affecting customers and workers in the 1990s? If not, you may be in for high job turnover and zero company loyalty.

• *Set up a public policy group* or committee to track issues and activist groups' activities relative to your operation. Stay informed, in other words, and stay ahead of the activists.

• *Keep the lines of communication open* with the leaders of those activist groups at all times. Find out what makes them tick and what they really want.

• *Don't underestimate the seriousness of activists* or how well they can communicate an issue to the media and public. Pick someone in your policy group to deal with newspeople. In case of activist demonstrations against your company or product or an accident that affects your people or the environment, make this individual your sole company spokesperson. One voice or one set of views should emanate from your firm during a crisis.

• *Finally, try to set your own agenda* for change. Don't be pressured into reacting to the activists' agenda.

HOW TO WORK OUT WORKING AT HOME
. . . . .

Although its arrival has been slower in coming than many had predicted, working at home a couple of days a week is now on the verge of becoming a major employment practice.

Factors fueling this trend include frequent traffic congestion during peak travel time and the high cost of commuting, along with the realization that the concept actually calls for less high technology than was originally believed.

TELECOMMUTING

A pilot program for the state of California has about 150 state employees of all kinds testing the potential of "telecommuting," as this arrangement is often dubbed because the worker is connected to the office via the telephone. Dave Fleming, who hatched the program, says the key to making telecommuting work is flexibility. At-home days can be rotated. Perhaps some people could telecommute for six months, then work on an office-only basis the rest of the year.

CHARACTERISTICS

• *Most telecommuters work about three days a week in the office.*

• *Telecommuters have proven to be more ef-*

fective than office-only workers.

• *A computer is not required, but a telephone is needed.*

DISADVANTAGES

Some employees may not want to work at home because they miss the social aspects of the office environment. Others may not have a trusting relationship with their boss, which is needed to make telecommuting work. Also, there may be resentment among those in the office, who may feel the at-home worker escapes most of the daily work problems.

KEEPING WORKPLACE STRESS UNDER CONTROL
. . . . .

Some 25% of the U.S. work force may suffer from various work-related problems, such as anxiety disorders or stress-related illness, while 13% suffer depression, a symptom of stress. These findings are according to a study conducted by the Gallup Organization for the New York Business Group on Health.

The nationwide survey of company medical directors, personnel managers and employee assistance program directors estimates that occupational disability related to anxiety, depression and stress costs employers about $8,000 a case in terms of worker's compensation.

▲ F A C T :

The average employee loses about 16 days a year because of stress, anxiety and depression.

STRESS AT WORK

• More than 80% of the respondents report that fear that their company would be taken over was the major cause of their stress.

• Other reasons for anxiety include career or job burnout and working under various job conditions, such as having to deal with a new boss or do night shift work.

• Stress disorders, associated 20 years ago with middle-aged and older workers, now strike people in their twenties and thirties, at the height of their productivity.

• Stress seems more prevalent among larger firms than smaller ones; some 65% of those in large corporations with more than 15,000 employees said that stress-related problems were fairly pervasive.

RECOMMENDATION: Review the amount of stress-related illness among your employees and the days lost due to this illness. If they're growing by more than 10% a year, take that as a warning that you should try to determine what stress factors may be present in your company and how you can relieve them.

SELF-HELP TIPS

Here are a few tips about how to manage your own stress and keep it under control:

• When scheduling anticipated stress situations, give yourself time to cope. In other words, don't schedule two or three high-pressure meetings or tasks in a row, or even on the same day.

• Find a place where you can have complete privacy and spend five to 10 minutes there during the workday, clearing the mind and perhaps using a relaxation technique to relieve the pressure.

• Maintain control of your mental processes. In other words, don't allow insignificant events to upset you.

• Don't procrastinate. Stressful situations get worse the longer you put them off.

• Maintain and use a support system of friends, family and colleagues to let off steam.

• Make decisions based on your actual needs, rather than what others expect your needs to be.

DEALING WITH EXCUSES

■ ■ ■ ■ ■

Valid or weak, reasonable or absurd, excuses are not a substitute for getting the job done. When deadlines are missed or a job is botched, the boss almost has to accept reasonable explanations; but how can you do that without seeming like a patsy for a "snow job"?

HOW TO CUT DOWN ON EMPLOYEE ALIBIS

• **Don't argue with the excuse.** Even if you're sure an employee is using an excuse to evade responsibility, there are good reasons to ignore it. For one thing, you could be wrong about the validity of the excuse. For another, it can't hurt to allow the individual to save face; you don't need to humiliate the employee to get results.

• **Don't always be sympathetic.** Certainly, you'll want to express condolences if the failure is a result of the employee's personal problems, such as an illness or death in the family. But if the alleged illness is just one of a long list of alibis you've heard from this same person, it may be time to stop responding to the rationalizing and start holding the employee accountable.

• **Reiterate your need.** Explain why the work you've assigned is crucial for you or your company, and impress on the individual his or her key role in getting it done. Make it clear that you don't want a detailed explanation, but that you do need to know when you can expect completion. If you speak in a friendly way, no one can take offense at your position, no matter how legitimate or phony the alibi is.

• **If excuses are chronic, start to record incidents.** Employees who have a seemingly infinite supply of explanations for their failures may be convinced that they can't possibly be blamed for the problems they run into. To prove to them that they may not be blameless, start writing down details of these incidents, including dates, what you requested, and what the response was. You can use these records later to confront the employee with the fact that he or she has a problem. If you can't convince the employee to reform in the face of such evidence, you'll at least have documented your case for dismissal or other appropriate action.

• **Make the alternative clear.** If you've finally had it up to the chin with excuses from the same individual, point out that you and others can't get their work done without his or her cooperation. Stress that the continual letdowns are unacceptable and that you'll be forced to let the individual go if he or she continues.

Don't make light of the excuses, but your position should ultimately be along these lines: "I won't argue that you've had bad luck. But other employees haven't had as many problems as you have. If you continue to come up short, I'm going to have to find someone else to do your job."

OBSERVATION:
Often, employees' excuse-making is a defensive reaction to the boss's harsh response to their past mistakes. Look at the way you react when employees foul up. If you tend to blow up at bloopers, try to ignore the blunders and focus instead on how they can be fixed or avoided. This will usually reduce the number of mistakes—and the excuses employees invent to explain them.

WHAT TO DO WHEN EMPLOYEES LIE TO YOU

■　■　■　■　■

You probably have one or two employees working for you who seem to fabricate outlandish excuses for being late or absent. Often, that's a personality flaw you can't correct, short of dismissal. But if too many people constantly lie to you, do some self-examination.

A lie is often a kind of conspiracy between the liar and the one lied to. Some executives unwittingly lead subordinates into untruths by reacting to *honest* statements with anger.

For example, an employee arrives 10 minutes late for work apologizing about some "car trouble." If she gets a harsh look from the boss, then the next time she's late, that excuse may have blossomed into, "I had to take my kid to the doctor." Little by little, what start out as innocent lies quickly become insidious.

Let the occasional story about "car trouble" pass with forbearance. But in a continuous pattern of falsehood, tell the employee that tardiness is an unacceptable excuse and will not be tolerated. Stress that the late arrivals hurt you and others in your department.

YOUR MOVE IF YOU CATCH AN EMPLOYEE IN A SERIOUS LIE

Many managers would simply fire the individual on the spot. But you could discount the deception and make at least one determined effort to end it once and for all in a constructive way by helping to look for solutions.

EXAMPLE:
A worker tells you he's all caught up, but you discover that he has been keeping incomplete work in a desk drawer and is falling farther and farther behind, not realizing that he probably won't ever catch up.

■ **Questions to ask yourself:** Is it still early enough to catch up on the work? Could the workload have been too heavy for one person? If so, a short but stiff lecture, followed promptly by a new work-sharing arrangement, may solve the problem, end the lying and leave you with a grateful, loyal employee.

OBSERVATION:
You also have to make sure that your own dealings with your superiors are as straightforward as possible. If employees see you hide information from upper management for obviously self-serving reasons, your ability to maintain their respect—and their truthfulness—will be hampered.

DON'T PROMISE MORE THAN YOU CAN DELIVER

In today's turbulent economy, you may have to adjust a sales program in midstream or staff up or down quickly to protect your bottom line. Under such changing pressures, you inevitably make many formal and informal comments and "offers" to employees, dealers and distributors. Some could cause you legal troubles later, experts warn.

AVOID POTENTIAL PROBLEMS

• **When building a staff, don't build false expectations.** Don't take on obligations you didn't bargain for. "Employment-at-will law is being eroded," says Boonton, NJ attorney James H. Walzer, a specialist in business law. That means it's becoming increasingly harder to hire and fire people when you want to. Not only are employees crying foul more often, but "case law has given employees new due-process rights," according to Walzer. And in borderline situations, the employee now tends to win in court.

EXAMPLE:
Suppose you whip up a sales candidate's enthusiasm by pointing to the great, unlimited potential of your new product and implying that you want him or her to stay with you forever. If your product bombs can you summarily drop the new person?

Not without courting legal action, warns

Walzer. "After being fired or not promoted, more and more employees are going to court. Even when the employer wins, it's costly in time and money."

- **Think twice before saying anything that could be construed as a promise:** "If you do well, the sky's the limit," for example, or "We want you to be a permanent member of our team." One employer casually offered a new employee a Cadillac if sales reached a certain level in three years' time. They did, and the employee threatened suit when the boss said he'd only been kidding.

▲ I M P O R T A N T :

To be on the safe side, put promises in writing so there will be no disagreement later on.

- **Take care in dealing with non-employees, too.** Your words or actions may create an obligation you do not intend. For instance, it's easy to run afoul of the law when making agreements with distributors, according to Philadelphia attorney Steven S. Raab, a specialist in the legal aspects of franchising.

As one example, "If you appoint distributors and require them to make you some sort of payment, you may be illegally franchising without knowing it," he says. A court might interpret even a nonrefundable deposit in this light.

- **Build "change" into all agreements.** It is no longer practical to promise sales representatives or distributors, for example, a specific level of compensation. Competitive forces will play havoc with your best-laid intentions. So work with your lawyer to insert contingency clauses into all contracts. Say you'll do X; but reserve the right to do Y if Z happens.

E X A M P L E :

Don't promise distributors perpetual service on a product you may have to discontinue. And don't tell your salespeople they'll make a set amount per sale when you may have to cut prices to meet competition. Qualify your agreements, and use percentages instead of fixed numbers.

- **Take care of what you promise when assigning territories.** You don't want representatives to think they "own" their turf. That's what IBM led its people to believe. As a result, it is currently having to pay its salespeople commissions on sales made in their territories by independent distributors.

HOLIDAY GIFT GIVING
■ ■ ■ ■ ■

Here are some good rules of thumb to follow if your employees are likely to give you gifts:

- Put a dollar limit on what you will accept as a gift. Don't accept anything with more than a $10 value, or $50 to $75 if it comes from a group of your employees.
- Make sure that no gift is perceived by others as earning your favor or establishing some kind of trade-off.
- Return an expensive gift to the employee's home at once by registered mail. Enclose a note thanking the person and point out that you cannot accept it because of your position, not for personal reasons. Make your note neutral and businesslike.
- Never publicly acknowledge the receipt of a gift from an employee.

OBSERVATION

When you are the giver: The gifts you give to your employees can range from a basket of fruit to a holiday lunch. Avoid giving individual gifts, unless everyone receives the same thing, such as a turkey or tickets to a ball game.

HAVE A HAPPY— AND PRODUCTIVE— HOLIDAY SEASON

Shopping and partying can put a crimp in employee productivity around the holiday season. Here are some suggestions for keeping your staff happy and working:

• Be flexible if your employees spend a few extra minutes for shopping and other holiday errands at lunch time, but keep productivity up by making sure that too many aren't away from the job at the same time.

• Don't announce when planned holiday bonuses will be distributed. If it is feasible, wait until Christmas week to distribute bonus checks.

• Don't allow those in a supervisory role to duck their production responsibilities in honor of the season.

• Dismiss employees early on the last workday before Christmas and New Year's Day to boost morale.

BRINGING STRIKERS BACK TO WORK

Animosity between employers and strikers will most likely linger after a strike ends. Many times, employers will be reluctant to take back all the strikers.

CAUTION

Although strikers lose protection under the National Labor Relations Act through serious misconduct or the unlawfulness of their strike, they do retain job reinstatement rights that are either very extensive (in an economic strike over wages, work rules or conditions) or close to absolute (in an unfair labor practice strike, where the employer commits violations).

LEGAL RIGHTS

• **Employees' rights regarding reinstatement.** When the strike ends, you must reinstate strikers to their jobs if: they make unconditional requests for reinstatement within a reasonable time; they have not been permanently replaced; they have not found a "regular and substantially equivalent" job elsewhere; their jobs have not been eliminated for justifiable business reasons; and they have not been guilty of serious strike misconduct.

"If you're out on strike and your employer decides to permanently replace you, your place isn't taken until somebody is actually hired," explains James Holzhauer, a Chicago labor lawyer with Mayer, Brown & Platt. "The employer can't just announce, 'I'm going to fire you,' but he can replace you. If you are replaced, you lose your right to reinstatement, though you might very well have a right to a job when one becomes open."

• **Strikers' rights in an unfair labor practice strike.** If you, as the employer, have perpetrated unfair labor practices, through refusal to bargain, bad faith, or blatant anti-union animosity, the consequences can be costly. Even if an ordinary economic strike occurs, if the employer transgresses after it starts, it can be construed as an unfair labor strike. You must take back the strikers, even if you have no choice but to discharge permanent replacements to make room. If you fail to meet reinstatement obligations, the National Labor Relations Board (NLRB) can require you to take them back and reimburse them from the time they submitted their unconditional-return request until the time they actually return to the job.

• **Employers' rights regarding reinstatement.** An employer is permitted to hire temporary workers in order to keep the business operating satisfactorily during a strike. The NLRB does not ensure permanent positions for replacement workers after a strike settlement, but management can negotiate such an option into the new contract.

● N O T E :

If you promise the replacement a permanent position, that employee, under the common law contract, has grounds for a lawsuit if you fire him or her after the strike ends.

"The right to retain replacements will, of course, come up in the settlement negotiation between the union and company," points out Holzhauer. "The union will often seek to have the employer discharge permanent replacements and rehire the strikers. More and more employers are not willing to do that because, in order to get people to cross the picket lines and get outsiders to take these jobs, they have to agree to keep them permanently."

▲ I M P O R T A N T :
When hiring replacement workers, keep in mind the risks of management-labor friction and ill will in a community that sympathizes with the strikers.

SMOOTHING THE RETURN

Greet returning workers cheerfully and avoid talk of the strike. If the union failed to reach its objectives, don't gloat. Treat returning strikers and those who continued working impartially. Minimize disciplinary action, even toward those who practiced intimidating behavior toward strike breakers, since human emotions should be taken into account. Be prepared to maintain order if strikers refuse to work with nonstrikers. Keep yourself open to hear grievances.

WORKER VIOLENCE: LEARN THE EARLY WARNING SIGNS

■ ■ ■ ■ ■

There are some basic guidelines that firms can follow to avoid possible rampages by disgruntled employees. Neil Livingston, a Washington-based security consultant and author of *The Complete Security Guide for Executives*, advises the following:

• *Get to know your workers.* Conduct lengthy background checks of all employees when they are first hired. Make sure a personal background is screened for the use of alcohol or drugs, any history of mental illness or violence, and a criminal record.

• *Show sensitivity.* Create a humane termination policy for all employees; for example, provide counseling and outplacement service, and make generous severance and pension benefits available.

• *Encourage close supervisor-employee relations.* While you don't want to encourage employees to report everything they hear co-workers say, they should report any threats against the company or management made over a period of time.

• *Beef up security* in terms of access to the premises during and after work hours.

IMPROVE YOUR SUGGESTION PROGRAMS
■ ■ ■ ■ ■

Although many companies have employee suggestion programs, few embrace more ideas from the rank-and-file than Philip Morris USA, Richmond, VA. The company's adoption rate is 45% of suggestions submitted, compared to a national average of 29%, according to the National Association of Suggestion Systems (NASS).

William Arey, president of NASS in 1989 and cost-reduction administrator for Philip Morris, says his company adopted 1,100 employee suggestions in 1988, for a total of almost $26 million in savings. And the company provides no direct cash awards for winning proposals.

HOW TO KEEP IDEAS COMING

• **Demonstrate serious support.** Top management at Philip Morris provides special commendations, including special and unique plaques and membership in the company's Idea Club, reserved for those who submit five or more suggestions. And

while there are no immediate cash awards, successful suggestions are taken into account when an employee is considered for a pay raise or promotion. In addition, management emphasizes to employees the lucrative impact that cost-saving ideas can have on the company's profit-sharing plan.

• **Set specific cost-cutting goals.** Arey sets cost-reduction objectives with each department head, then lets managers pass these goals on to employees, who then take "ownership" of the cost objective. This helps to focus managers' and employees' attention on savings opportunities.

• **Ensure that ideas will be given serious consideration.** Suggestion boxes (which the company prefers to call "idea centers") are used, but are not central to the program. Instead, Arey and members of his Action Cost Team (ACT) go directly to employees to solicit their ideas. Arey himself reads every suggestion, and then refers each one to company experts for review and further follow-up.

• **Give supervisors the tools to work with.** Arey and his ACT staff make special creativity training programs available to department heads to teach employees how to generate useful suggestions. The programs teach workers not to self-censor suggestions that seem obvious; to seek simple, everyday ideas; to concentrate on their own work areas as sources of profitable hunches; and to explain how an idea can save the company money.

OBSERVATION:
NASS members reported average net savings of $7,662 per adopted suggestion in 1988. One apparent key to a successful suggestion program: designating an administrator to act as a liaison between employees and higher management.

SET UP A GOOD PROGRAM TO TAP EMPLOYEES' IDEAS

■ ■ ■ ■ ■

If you need a low-cost way to involve employees in improving customer service, an off-the-shelf program offered by the Advanced Management Group (AMG) may be just what you're looking for. The company's "GOOD Idea Campaign," has achieved 60% to 80%, and sometimes 100%, employee participation.

SOME GOOD IMPROVEMENTS

• As a result of an employee's suggestion, a Philadelphia bank provided plastic holders for its automatic teller machine cards, greatly reducing damage to the cards that caused snarls at the machines.

• Another bank in New Jersey launched a campaign to convince mortgage holders to use the bank's checking account services. The idea was suggested by a teller who noted that most mortgage customers were paying with checks drawn on other banks.

• A hospital in Troy, NY saw a highly favorable patient reaction when it followed an employee's simple suggestion to move its admissions clerk closer to the emergency room. The maneuver provided faster human contact with patients awaiting treatment, reducing their anxiety.

• Five percent of GOOD suggestions at one food-product manufacturer involved ideas for new products, several of which are being actively considered by management.

HOW IT WORKS

GOOD (not an acronym) is an outgrowth of AMG's BAD (Buck a Day) program, which is aimed primarily at garnering employees' ideas for cost reductions. Like BAD, it is designed as a 30-day special event to spur employees to look at their own jobs or work areas to find ways of improving customer satisfaction or quality of service. But it also has fostered practical employee suggestions for improving internal operations, generating new revenue and improving on-time performance. Company departments can modify the program to fit their own areas of greatest need.

• Low-cost incentives—such as specially printed coffee mugs—are offered to employees who provide workable suggestions. Communications materials and incentives are included with the program, along with an operational plan.

• Supervisors responsible for running the program in their company can consult with the AMG staff via the telephone. Users also get a microcomputer software program to help managers analyze, categorize and keep track of submitted suggestions.

AMG says the GOOD campaign is designed for use by companies with at least 100 employees, including supervisors and managers, who participate with rank-and-file employers. Groups without direct contacts with customers are encouraged to talk to their "internal" customers—those from other departments in the company—to find ways to work better with them.

▲ C O S T S :

About $35 per employee, with discounts for larger users.

FOR MORE INFORMATION:

Contact Advanced Management Group, 101 Larkspur Landing Circle, Larkspur, GA 94939; 1-800-223-2402 or 415-461-6870.

Chapter 2

MANAGEMENT METHODS

PUT TOGETHER AN OUTSTANDING STAFF

· · · · ·

Analyze how successful managers get good results from their staffs, and you'll find that there's nothing intrinsically Japanese or American in their methods. They've learned basic management strategies that can work for you.

• *Setting an example.* Do you work efficiently? Set deadlines? Prioritize your duties? Do you anticipate problems or try to correct them once they're a threat? You can encourage these skills in employees by developing them yourself.

• *Giving clear, precise instructions.* Hasty, unclear directions result in sloppy, incomplete work. The time you spend thinking about an assignment and explaining it to your staff is time saved in correcting mistakes.

• *Setting time limits.* Work gets done more quickly when a deadline is set.

• BEST APPROACH:

Let employees have input in drafting deadlines, so that everyone agrees upon and understands the importance of a project.

• *Maintaining priorities.* Let employees know which projects are most important and should receive the most time and attention. Keep your staff updated as priorities change over time.

• *Delegating responsibility, not just work.* People work harder and more effectively when they share responsibility for the final product. Besides freeing up your time for other projects, delegating this way develops your staff's judgment in setting priorities and solving problems.

■ R E S U L T :

They work faster and more efficiently, and interrupt you less with problems that need your attention.

• *Leaving employees alone to do their jobs.* Respect your workers' time. One of the biggest time-wasters for most employees is the boss. Don't constantly interrupt employees with unimportant matters or keep them waiting for meetings or instructions.

• *Encouraging feedback.* If an employee is having trouble with an assignment or deadline, he or she should be able to come to you for help. On the other hand, if an employee finds a quicker or more effective way to do a job, he or she should feel that you are willing to consider it.

• *Rewarding effort as well as achievement.* An employee who feels appreciated will be encouraged to keep improving. You can offer incentives for good work, such as pay raises or promotions. However, something as simple as a "thank you" along the way can inspire an employee to strive to fulfill his or her full potential.

LOW-COST WAYS TO BOOST PRODUCTIVITY
· · · · ·

Employers must constantly look for ways to streamline their operations and cut costs if they want to remain competitive. Increased productivity leads to efficiency and profits. Consider these pointers in your efforts to boost productivity:

• *Computerized inventory control.* When you already have a computer system installed for other purposes, an automatic inventory management system can increase its returns substantially. For maximum effectiveness, be sure the software you purchase provides improved efficiency in determining purchasing requirements, scheduling deliveries, keeping track of demand for various parts and materials and planning production work.

• *Improved training.* If you have high costs resulting from equipment downtime, excessive scrap or lengthy job setup times, strengthening your production and maintenance training can improve productivity 10% to 20%.

• *Concentrated cost-reduction programs.* Efforts to harness employees' cost-cutting ideas, such as suggestion programs or quality circles, have achieved dramatic savings for many companies. You can also achieve significant results by requiring departmental managers to develop cost-reducing ideas—and basing part of their merit raises on their effectiveness in this area.

• *Job rotation.* When workers perform narrow tasks, they can become isolated from the total procedure. By having each one learn all the jobs of an operation, your organization will become more flexible and less vulnerable to delays due to absences, emergencies and so on.

• *Work measurement.* Develop ways to measure indirect labor output as well as direct labor. It is equally important to post this data where workers and supervisors can see it; you can't expect them to improve if they don't know how their work measures up against your expectations. Hold supervisors accountable for any deviations from expected results.

OBSERVATION:

Work measurement can be done in a number of useful ways, such as a ratio of sales-to-labor costs or the average amount of time it takes to perform a specific task. To avoid employee resentment of your work measurement, let individual workers keep track of their own performance, with occasional checking by supervisors. They can compile individual data to determine departmentwide productivity.

FINDING TIME TO DO ALL THE WORK

■ ■ ■ ■ ■

When business is booming—but doesn't justify your having an assistant or hiring additional staff—you can handle the extra work with a little planning and evaluation.

WHERE TO BEGIN

■ **Tackle the routine paperwork problem first,** since that's generally what eats into an executive's valuable daily ration of time. Moreover, paperwork problems are generally the easiest to solve.

Take a look at the volume of paper that is flowing across your desk. Can some be cut out? Insist on quarterly instead of monthly reports, for example, and use the computer to store what was previously put on paper.

■ **Then look for the less conspicuous tasks.** These are just as much an obstacle to getting things done as excessive paperwork is, but they're usually less obvious. Check yourself in the following areas:

• *Excessive follow-up.* If you often check up on your employees to make sure

that various projects are being carried out on schedule, look into the nature of the problem. If there is one person whose competence you doubt, decide if you should relieve the responsibilities that seem to be more than he or she can handle.

CURE YOURSELF OF OVERCONTROL

But if you rarely find anything wrong when you check up, try to cure yourself of this time-wasting exercise. Get into the habit of asking yourself, "What's the worst thing that could happen if I don't check up on them?" In most cases, a serious problem is unlikely to occur. Besides, most employees would inform you if there was one.

• *Multiple handling.* Don't put off decisions that could be concluded the first time the situation is presented to you. If you're in the habit of saying, "Let me get back to you," on routine matters brought to you by your employees, you may wind up considering the same issue two or three times. Clear up matters, as far as possible, in one discussion. If you often find that you lack enough information to make a sound decision, train your staff to both research the matter thoroughly and develop two or three alternative solutions before bringing any problems to your attention.

• *Too many decisions.* If you feel that you have to rule on every small matter affecting your company or department, you're robbing yourself of time. And you are also depriving your staff of the job satisfaction that comes from making decisions on their own. By providing training, authority and policy guidelines to these employees, you can make your days, and their jobs, far more enjoyable.

■ **Delegating.** Decide between the work you must do yourself and the responsibilities that can be delegated safely. Never assign to another a task you should handle.

• Before you delegate, consult your organization chart or any other formal arrangement that sets out the hierarchy of jobs under yours. Don't assign new responsibility that conflicts with the existing structure—unless you intentionally and clearly make a change in the old order of things.

• Choose the person to handle a new responsibility carefully, objectively and deliberately. Don't be swayed by personal likes or dislikes.

• Once you've picked someone, give him or her all the authority needed to do the job. Make it clear to everybody else that the chosen person will stand in for you and have your power to act in this instance.

• Don't interfere. Otherwise, you are not truly delegating, and the person you choose will not take the task seriously or be taken seriously by others.

• Finally, take full responsibility for anything that goes wrong. You made the choice, and if you want to retain respect, you can't afford to make excuses or try to shift the blame to your subordinate.

PERSONNEL SHORTAGES IN THE 1990s

■ ■ ■ ■ ■

Labor shortages are upon us and will almost surely worsen throughout this decade. Particularly hard hit: small business.

THE '90s SCENARIO

While the work force has been growing annually by 3%, it will only be increasing at a 1% rate in 90s, the lowest level since the 1930s. At the same time, the economy through the 1990s is expected to generate nearly 20 million jobs in the service sector, while resulting in a loss of 300,000 jobs in the goods-producing industries.

• *The structure of the work force* also will certainly change. Some 85% of new workers will be minorities and women, with only 15% being white males. The total number of women in the work force will increase from 55 million to 66 million by the year 2000.

• *Shortages are already emerging* in certain industries and locations around the country. Experiencing a crunch, for example, are the garment and resort industries, fast food operations, retail trade, household domestic contractors, and health-care service firms. Among locales suffering labor shortages are Boston; Providence; Atlanta; Poughkeepsie, NY; Rochester, MN; Madison, WI; Los Angeles; northern New Jersey; Greensboro, NC; and Richmond, VA.

• *Not only are workers in short supply, but many continue to be unprepared* to join the work force, especially at the entry level position. Surveys show, for example, that three out of five 20-year-olds cannot add up a lunch bill or determine their correct change. Many lack education and training at the same time that jobs require ever higher levels of skills.

• *Small business will feel the impact* of the labor shortage more than big firms. Small firms already employ eight out of every 10 workers over age 60, and hire more women and entry level workers proportionately than big business. So, it's the small firms that must meet the problem of the new work force head on.

WHAT YOU CAN DO
NOW TO PREPARE

• **Restructure some of your benefits.**
Since small companies are hard-pressed to
compete with big firms when it comes to
compensation, they can somewhat overcome that disadvantage by shaping the
workplace to fit employee needs. Add
child-care options to accommodate the increasing number of women in the labor
force, for example. Surveys show that
benefits are proving to be a greater attrac-
tion to workers than wages.

• **Add automation.** This will not only
speed up worker productivity but also could
lead to a decrease in the number of workers
needed for your operation. Get the most out
of entry-level positions, such as retail clerks,
for example, by automating operations such
as customer checkout activities.

• **Upgrade your present work force
through education and training.** This
doesn't have to be expensive if you use
technology such as video disks and
videocassettes. One pizza outlet, for instance, has developed a quality control formula to produce pizza dough, thereby
eliminating guesswork by trainees.

Have your entry level employees participate in vocational education or community college training programs or
consortiums. A small business consortium
of dry cleaning stores in South Carolina, for
instance, prepares entry-level workers
through programs of remedial reading and
writing.

McDonald's has developed an extensive
program that prepares or trains older
employees by letting them work alongside
younger people.

• **Reduce worker turnover.** Hang on to
your present work force by devoting extra

care and attention to the handling of employees. This means anticipating family
problems that could be cured through programs of flexible work hours and child care.

A KIND WORD COUNTS

In trucking, a high turnover industry, one
company has instituted a program requiring
dispatchers, known for their sharp treatment of drivers, to show a bit more sensitivity. The dispatchers are required to
praise drivers four times more than they
criticize them and to keep a log of their
behavior. The program has been instrumental in lowering the company's high
turnover rate considerably.

WHAT TO DO WHEN
KEY PEOPLE LEAVE
■ ■ ■ ■ ■

There is one person in your group who
always comes up with the answers to current
problems that stump the rest of the staff. He
knows everybody in and around your industry who matters; is a walking en-
cyclopedia of company marketing history;
has the respect, and therefore the ear, of top
management; is an indefatigable and cheerful contributor to the workload—and has
just told you he's retiring next month.

When you've recovered sufficiently to be
able to think, how should you respond?

HOLD ON TO
THE KNOWLEDGE

• **Set up a brainstorming session** that
includes you and the one or two of your
people—other than the "walking en-
cyclopedia"—who make the most use of

their minds. Try to think of everything that the person who's leaving knows more about than anyone else. You don't want him there at this point, because you know better than he which matters worry you most about his departure.

One of you needs to stand at a flip chart and write down everything that is said, because seeing and hearing an idea triggers other ideas that hearing alone might not. Ask one person to review the list, delete duplicate items and organize the rest under topical headings. Than pass around the summary and add whatever else it brings to mind.

• **Appoint a Siamese twin.** Select someone who is bright, knows your business, and has a good relationship with the retiring person. Your choice will need an ego that won't crumble while he or she plays shadow to the other person all day and every day during the transition period. He or she watches, listens, asks questions—and questions and questions—taping them and the answers. In addition, the two will lunch with as many as possible of the departing hero's contacts, and the shadow will be introduced as the heir apparent. The objective is to create a "clone"of the person, as well as a repository of as much of his knowledge as the clone can soak in. At night, the "copy"goes home and studies what he or she has learned. And what has been taped during the day is transcribed and organized for everyone whom it can benefit.

• **Hold debriefing sessions.** The product of your brainstorming session will be the basis for one or more meetings in which the departing expert responds to the questions you bring in, as well as those that arise as the discussion proceeds. The person you are developing as the replacement sits in too. The proceedings should be taped—videotaped if practical—and carefully saved

as an irreplaceable resource for the group.

• **Keep the umbilical cord intact** for as long as you can. A person this rare, this devoted to the company and probably to all of you as well, is likely to be willing to be accessible, at least by phone, wherever he lands. He or she should probably be compensated generously as a consultant—since this person is the consultant of a lifetime for you.

OBSERVATION:

All of this will not be the same as having the person on staff, but it will go a long way in that direction. Over time, most of his "indispensable" knowledge will be recaptured—and be held less exclusively than before.

HOW TO START A JOB SHARING PROGRAM

· · · · ·

Job sharing—splitting a full-time position between two part-timers—can be part of a successful solution to labor shortages for certain types of work. It's a good way for an employer to attract well-qualified people who are unable to work full time because they are young parents or are attending school, or to hold on to retiring workers who no longer want to work full time.

HOW AND WHEN TO SPLIT A JOB

• **Don't split jobs that can't be shared easily.** If it's not clear to you how a job can be shared without causing confusion, the position may not be a good candidate for a shared arrangement. Job sharing in positions that pay by commission, for example, could easily cause friction. You may also want to rule out spots that require handling many clients or customers with fast-changing needs.

- **Evaluate the incumbent.** Begin by assessing how cooperative and mature your potential job sharer is. Evaluate, too, how committed the current full timer is to making the new arrangement work and how skilled he or she is at communicating.

- **Interview the potential partner.** In many job-sharing arrangements, the current incumbent initiates the idea of job sharing, then interviews and chooses a suitable partner. But make sure you or the appropriate department manager screens proposed partners, just as you would a full timer, to ensure that the arrangement will work. Interviewing both partners together to weigh how well the two communicate with each other is also advisable.

- **Ask how the partners plan to divide the assignment.** Assess the system they propose to ensure that work doesn't fall between the cracks. For instance, they should use joint filing and reminder systems, written logs of tasks and telephone conversations to keep their work coordinated. Ask, too, how they'd handle specific problems and how these employees feel about dealing with their partner's mistakes.

In a number of job-sharing arrangements, both partners work three full days a week, so that they are in the office together one day a week—say, every Wednesday. This arrangement allows them to clear up any misunderstandings they may have and determine who is to do what in the week ahead.

- **Explain the details.** You'll have to decide what benefits you'd provide for the two part-timers, such as vacations and holidays. Generally, salary and benefits will be prorated.

- **Prepare other employees.** Inform them of the job sharers' schedule, so that they understand that the position will still be a full-time assignment, even though staffed by part-timers.

- **Consider a trial period.** If you're not sure the arrangement will work out, set a six-month trial period, with the understanding that the arrangement will be canceled if its results prove to be unsatisfactory. You may then either ask the former full timer to return to a full workweek or hire another employee to take over the position—if the previous incumbent is unable to resume full-time status.

EMPLOYERS BENEFIT, TOO

Although job sharing is usually thought of as an employee benefit, it holds several advantages for employers as well:

- It lets you hold on to valuable employees who are no longer able to work full time.

- It provides the position with a backup, in case one of the partners becomes ill, goes on vacation or resigns.

- It reduces training costs, because the new job sharer is usually coached by the experienced partner.

- It can reduce recruiting costs, because the employee who wants to share his or her job will often take the responsibility for finding a suitable partner.

HOW TO LISTEN TO EMPLOYEES

· · · · ·

To be truly adept at hearing and understanding what others are saying, you have to sharpen your ears to pick up the often-hidden messages behind their words and learn to interpret body language as well. This is particularly true in a boss-employee relationship where employees may be nervous talking to you, their boss. Workers are often reluctant to express doubt or other feelings directly to someone in authority. If you're attentive to their hidden statements, however, you can glean a lot of important information you might otherwise miss.

WHAT THEY'RE REALLY SAYING OR DOING

To decipher all of what you hear, learn how to pick up on the unspoken nuances of meaning tucked into everyday business conversations. Examples:

■ **Buying time.** An executive tells a supervisor, "I'd like you to take over the scheduling operation." The supervisor responds, "What does the job involve?"

The supervisor isn't just looking for information. By responding with a question, he or she is buying time to think before committing himself or herself and possibly accepting an undesirable promotion.

When you recognize a buying-time response on the part of someone who comes to consult with you, take it as a signal to ease up. Supply the details the other person is seeking before pushing any further.

■ **Evading responsibility.** One day, as you pass by the service department, you hear a rep talking on the phone to a customer: "The company has a new rule. They tell me not to accept any more credit orders unless they're for over $1,000." The rep should have said something along these lines: "I'm enforcing a new rule: No credit on orders under $1,000. We think this will help us serve all our customers more quickly."

Instead, the rep is evading responsibility

by shifting to the third person ("they"), a tip-off that he does not identify with what he is saying. This individual may not enforce the rule strictly and is certainly not helping you to convince customers of the need for the requirement. You'll probably have to do a better job of selling this rep on the new rule before he'll back it up with your customers.

■ **Deflection.** You caution an employee: "You've been late three times this month." The response: "Has Ann been complaining that I'm not doing a good job?"

The employee is trying to evade the tardiness issue and divert attention to another, less threatening matter. When you pick up on a deflection, head it off with a response that returns to the issue you wish to discuss.

You might say: "Ann has nothing to do with this, and neither does the quality of your work. I want to discuss the problem of your tardiness."

■ **Concession.** There are times when a particular turn of phrase signals that a person is willing to bend. For instance, you ask your employee: "Could you finish the project by Friday?" The response: "Well, Friday would be difficult. Could we make it next Monday instead?"

The employee has not completely ruled out the possibility of meeting a deadline by Friday. With a little coaxing, he or she may be able to accommodate your request. In a situation such as yours, where you must press people to produce but don't want to appear unreasonable, it's important to be able to spot refusals with some "give" to them.

■ **Incomplete answer.** Listen for this type of response when you're asking an employee about an assignment you've given. For instance, you've asked a supervisor to write a major report on market conditions. Then, a couple of weeks later, you inquire about how the assignment is going. The person's response: "All in all, the report is coming along very well."

While the sentence seems to express overall satisfaction, it doesn't. The "all in all" suggests the employee isn't totally satisfied with his or her progress.

◆ A D V I C E :

This response calls for follow-up questioning, to find out what's missing from the person's reply and to identify possible trouble spots. Failure to spot such incomplete answers is the source of many misunderstandings.

In this case, the boss who overlooks the individual's doubts would be likely to complain later, "I can't understand it. A week ago, my supervisor said the report was going well. Now he or she says it won't be finished on time."

Keeping in tune with verbal clues to the need for follow-up will help you to expose employees' hidden reservations, boost morale and save you a lot of aggravation.

IT'S IMPORTANT
HOW YOU SAY IT

∎ ∎ ∎ ∎ ∎

If a company often slips up with grammar, it could damage a carefully nurtured image of competence and class.

◆ D A N G E R :

You may have the problem and not realize it. Clients are not likely to call you to complain about the grammatical errors in your last piece of correspondence. But that doesn't mean they didn't notice.

COMMON ERRORS

Here's a list of the 10 most common grammatical problems, compiled by the Grammar Group, a Chicago-based consulting firm. Watch for them in your staff's written and spoken words—and in your own.

1. Please call my secretary or myself (should be me). The rule is that myself is only used for emphasis or clarity.

2. Just between you and I (should be me). Use me after any preposition, such as between, to, or at.

3. Less than 12 items (should be fewer than). If it can be counted, use fewer; otherwise, use less.

4. Irregardless (should be regardless). Irregardless is substandard English.

5. Feel badly (should be bad). Only use badly when feeling or touching with fingers or feet.

6. February 12th (should be February 12). When the day follows the month, do not use the th ending.

7. Capitol or capital. Capitol always refers to a building. All else is capital.

8. Stationery or stationary. Letter and envelope have e's, so they're stationery. If it can't move, it's stationary.

9. Do you mean to infer that (should be imply). To imply is to send a message, and to infer is to receive one.

10. A group of employees are (should be is). The verb refers to a single thing (group).

R E C O M M E N D A T I O N :
Conduct spot checks of outgoing correspondence, and pay attention when you hear your staff speaking to clients on the phone. If your secretary makes grammatical errors when speaking, he or she probably makes them in correspondence.

If you recognize this problem, don't ignore it—change it. Grammar can be learned, even self-taught, with the right educational materials.

CHOOSE WORDS CAREFULLY WHEN CRITICIZING

∎ ∎ ∎ ∎ ∎

If you have good but temperamental people working for you, you know the problem: They work hard and well, but can be so involved in their work that they take criticism as a personal attack.

HOW TO OFFER SUGGESTIONS WITHOUT RUFFLING FEATHERS

• **Talk about the work, not the person.** Make even more of an effort than usual to say what's necessary in terms that are explicit and objective. For example, don't say, "You could get these orders out faster if you were better organized." Instead say, "These orders might be easier to do if they were sorted by location."

• **Keep it short.** Sticking to the point indicates your confidence in the person's intelligence and capability—and you don't sound as though you're nagging.

• **Make positive statements.** Focus on what needs to be done, rather than on what the person is failing to do. For example, "Let's figure out a system for recording these deliveries."

• **Accept the person's feelings.** If he or she reacts defensively, acknowledge it. But don't reinforce it by apologizing or sympathizing. Say something like, "I understand, but remember this isn't personal."

• **Stress the benefits.** Sell your assignments as thoughtfully as you sell your products or services to customers.

• **Make acceptance conditional.** If a subordinate continues to resist your suggestions, don't insist on a complete change immediately. Instead, say something like, "All I'm asking is that you give it a try. Start it, and see how it goes. If you still have problems with it, maybe we can come up with another idea."

ADVICE FOR YOUNGER MANAGERS

∎ ∎ ∎ ∎ ∎

If you're asked to supervise older employees, proceed cautiously. To prevent your job from turning into a no-win situation, you have to adopt appropriate strategies.

DON'T GET DEFENSIVE

When a young person steps into a top slot, older employees often resent being passed over for a promotion. So it's only natural that they react with some hostility at first.

Don't take these feelings personally. You have to give your people time to get to know you and respect your professional experience and abilities.

Whatever you do, don't try to counter animosity with an "I'll show them who's boss" attitude. You're far better off letting people know that you understand how they feel and that you're willing to earn respect gradually—not demand it at once.

INNOVATE CAUTIOUSLY

Because superiors expect the young manager to take control fast, he or she often feels a strong need to introduce new programs or procedures quickly. But coming on like gangbusters often riles veteran staffers. If you find yourself in this situation, proceed with extreme caution. You're being pulled in two directions.

• Solicit the advice of subordinates about changes you're planning, but don't go through the exercise just to make them feel good. "If you never implement the suggestions they make," warns Susan MacKrell, professor of counseling at the University of Rochester, "they'll see right through your ruse and, eventually, end up feeling used."

• It is also important to keep your superiors informed about any staff resistance you encounter.

ACT YOUR AGE

Some young bosses try to appear older by adopting a more sophisticated hairstyle, growing a beard, or altering their style of dress. These tactics don't work. The generational contrast between your middle-aged style and your youthful face only ends up making you look even younger and calling attention to your insecurities. The end result is that you undermine the legitimate power you've already been given.

● BETTER APPROACH:

Act naturally and put your energies into doing your job well.

CONFRONT RESISTANCE

If an older staffer is trying to trip you up, don't ignore the problem. Ms. MacKrell suggests you take the person aside and say: "I have a strong feeling you're doing this to test me. What is it you would like to see happen? I can't help you unless I know what

it is you want." Then, if the disruptive behavior continues, you may have no choice but to complain to upper management or seek the person's transfer.

In most cases, you won't have to resort to such measures. You can usually overcome the negative attitudes—eventually, if not right away—by encouraging an atmosphere of collaboration and teamwork.

GETTING PEOPLE MOVING
■ ■ ■ ■ ■

How can you tactfully and effectively get people to move more quickly when you need a timely response? Peter Turla, president of National Management Institute, a Fort Worth consulting firm, and co-author with Kathleen Hawkins of *Time Management Made Easy* (E.P. Dutton, Inc., 375 Hudson Street, New York, NY 10014; $14.95), offers some do's and don'ts.

• *Do* tell employees how much authority they have in performing a project. This cuts down on time spent coming back to you with unnecessary questions and requests for approval.

• *Do* take extra time up front for explanations. Ask people to repeat your instructions so that you are sure that they know what you expect.

• *Do* clarify your priorities so that employees don't waste time working on the least urgent part first. This is especially important when everything seems top priority.

• *Do* explain why urgent items are so pressing, and give background information on the larger picture so that people will see why their own contribution is so important.

• *Do* team up a slow worker with some-

27

one who is fast-paced so that he or she can learn by example.

- *Don't* nag or berate people when they are too slow. This will ultimately lead to rebellion.

- *Don't* give fake deadlines or sound false alarms. People will eventually see through this tactic and resent you and stop taking you seriously.

- *Don't* overload employees. When you set a tight deadline on one project, remove something else from the to-do list to even out the load.

- *Don't* convey a perpetual state of crisis and panic. If everything is always an emergency, people will feel overwhelmed and frustrated, and performance will suffer.

- *Don't* forget to give positive reinforcement and show your appreciation for work well done.

WHAT TO DO WHEN DELEGATION BACKFIRES

■ · · · ·

You've expanded the job of someone you know to be competent, but the person hasn't handled it effectively. Should you give some of the new duties to someone else? Should you encourage the employee to do better?

■ **Delegation can backfire for several reasons:**

- Lack of readiness. The employee may lack needed skills or may already be overloaded with work.

- Personality/task mismatch. Even excellent employees are sometimes unsuited to certain tasks.

- Resentment. He or she may think the new responsibility is work that no one else wants to do.

- Overcontrol or undercontrol. You may be giving the person too little—or too much—supervision.

WHEN IT DOESN'T WORK

"Delegation is a collaborative process, and when it fails, the manager has to look at what he or she did or didn't do that may have caused failure," says Dr. Steve Strasser, associate professor of management at Ohio State and author of *Working It Out: Sanity and Success in the Workplace* (Prentice Hall, Route 9W, Englewood Cliffs, NJ 07675; $24.95).

- **Once a problem becomes apparent,** talk to your employee and ask if it is due to anything you did—an approach that makes it easier for the employee to own up to mistakes. However, don't be surprised to learn that you may also have made mistakes without realizing it.

- **Decide what can be done to repair the damage** and to prevent the situation from worsening. Removing the new responsibilities will be counterproductive—like vetoing a vote of confidence. "It's critical for the employee to know that he or she is still valued," says Dr. Strasser.

OBSERVATION:
Your employee isn't likely to do a good job with a bruised ego. If you are confident that he or she is capable of growth, give him or her new assignments quickly.

- **Take extra care when you assign duties to other staff members.** If you award a plum assignment to someone else, explain why you did so. Then tell the troubled employee that he or she will receive fair consideration for assignments that arise in the future.

HOW TO AVOID DELEGATION PROBLEMS

• **Prepare the way.** Make sure the employee feels prepared to take on any new tasks. Encourage him or her to ask questions and discuss how to handle a job before you assign it.

• **Structure your supervision.** Explain that you'll check frequently to be sure the project gets off to a good start. State that you'll supervise less as work progresses, but will remain available to help with any problems, if necessary.

DOCUMENTING EMPLOYEE PERFORMANCE
· · · · ·

Given growing EEOC intrusion into the workplace, managers should pay far more attention to performance appraisals than they do. Defenses against bias charges are often made or broken by their quality and documentation.

Don't count on your memory. If you do, you'll overlook important incidents and behaviors. Keep a notebook in which you can jot down incidents, or maintain a file on each worker and any distinguishing behavioral patterns. It's an easy way to review examples of excellent and flawed conduct during one-on-one appraisal sessions.

Likewise, saying that an employee is "under emotional stress" or "uncooperative" is opinion. Reporting that she "blew up at customers on three different occasions" or "volunteered twice to work late when we were short-handed" are well-founded facts.

HOW TO GIVE EFFECTIVE PERFORMANCE REVIEWS
· · · · ·

Most people in authority dislike the annual or semiannual performance review almost as much as firing someone—and most employees agree.

■ R E A S O N :

Few of us know how to evaluate a staff properly or have a clear idea of what can reasonably be expected from the individual employees we review.

Yet the stigma that attaches to the reviews has robbed business people of a valuable tool for improving productivity and nurturing their best workers.

IMPROVING THE PROCESS

To maximize performance reviews and yield win-win results for you and your staff, don't make the review an isolated routine to be performed once or twice a year. Rather, it should be part of a continuing program that includes the following steps:

• *Set goals.* Start by making each employee's job objectives crystal clear. Let them know what they are expected to accomplish and when.

Encourage them to participate in setting these goals and objectives. In that way, the worker regards them as a contract and is psychologically more committed to achieving them.

• *Make sure employees are coached regularly.* Try to have daily or at least weekly contact with each employee to ask how a job is progressing, to answer questions and to offer suggestions if asked. Use this opportunity to take brief notes on individual employees throughout the year, rather than trusting to memory. This is an aid to objectivity. The notes will come in handy when filling out your performance review form and conducting the formal performance interview at the end of six months or a year.

• *Reward those who reach specific goals.* This can take the form of a verbal pat on the back or even a financial bonus. Make sure, however, that a merit system is part of the ongoing review process.

• *Carry out your semiannual or annual performance review.* If you follow the first three steps, this phase of the continuing performance review is made easier. It can even be coordinated with the third step, in which you reward the employee based on his or her periodic performance review.

CONDUCTING REVIEWS

• **Develop** a simply written performance review form as a permanent record of the appraisal.

• **Divide the discussion** part of the review into three distinct sections: an introductory time for creating a comfortable atmosphere, your explanation of the employee's overall performance and your future expectations, and the employee's reaction to what you have said.

• **Criticize performance** in the areas where it's necessary, not the employee personally. This prevents the person from becoming defensive and ensures your objectivity. Also, make sure that your praise is sincere.

This is where your notes come in particularly handy, since you can recall specific situations or projects during the year in which the employee may have excelled. Citing particulars about an employee's performance, rather than generalities, is much more effective in boosting morale.

People appreciate specific praise. The more specific the criticism, the less likely that the employee will argue with it.

• **Report what you see.** It's unfair to include critical remarks made by other supervisors, unless you have no other way to reasonably judge an employee. If you must depend on others' views because you seldom work directly with the person, seek additional opinions.

• **Strive for consistency.** A common mistake: noting negative incidents involving one employee while ignoring similar behavior from other, more favored individuals.

CAUTION

Don't ever use the review itself to fire someone, or you will never drain the "high stress" potential from the process. Instead, focus on the future and on new goals.

Put all of these steps together and the performance review process becomes a worthwhile exchange of information instead of a "verdict," which often leaves the employee demoralized or angry.

RECOMMENDATION:

Before an evaluation meeting, review your appraisal with these questions in mind: Does it show exactly why the individual's performance is good or bad? Does it mention specific strengths and weaknesses? Does it identify exactly what improvements are needed? And does it include a plan for advancing the person's career?

OBSERVATION:

A good performance review system not only helps you boost productivity and employee morale, but also allows you to build a better and more consistent paper trail, should you need one to counter a disgruntled employee's taking you or your company to court over a real or fancied grievance.

WHAT YOU SHOULD KNOW BEFORE FIRING ANYBODY

■   ■   ■   ■   ■

Avoid time-consuming and costly lawsuits by making sure that dismissals are handled fairly. Any manager can likewise reduce risks by taking the following steps:

HOW TO AVOID GOING TO COURT

• **Be honest in your performance reviews.** Too often, managers sugarcoat bad news because they dislike confrontation. But telling an employee that you're dissatisfied is as important as noting it in a written appraisal. Otherwise, he or she won't realize what's going on.

• **If there's a problem, put an employee on notice right away.** Don't wait until it's performance review time.

Be as specific as possible in describing how you want the person to correct the problem. Spell out the consequences of failure to comply with your wishes.

• **Build a solid paper trail.** It's smart to document the behavior or problem, and the conversations you have with the employee.

A written record can help any discussions along because it puts the facts of the case at your fingertips. It's also useful for any lawsuit that may arise, especially one filed years after the event.

Be as specific as you can in your notes and include dates, times and descriptions of what was said or done.

● SAFEGUARD:

Have the employee sign a summary of any conversation.

• **Have a neutral person review your decision.** If there is no improvement after several warnings, talk to your boss, the head of personnel or a company lawyer. Explain your firing decision.

• **Deliver the news privately.** Don't hurry things. Take time to explain.

If your company has an appeals process, explain how it works. If it doesn't, suggest that the employee talk to personnel or to your boss if he or she feels the firing is unwarranted. Workers whose cases are evaluated by a neutral party are more likely to feel they've been treated fairly, even if the decision is the same.

If you can offer benefits such as severance or outplacement, consider asking for a signed release stating that reasons for dismissal are understood and won't be contested in future. This is not an ironclad safeguard, but it helps.

CAUTION

Failure to follow these steps, and making the employee's life miserable instead by changing responsibilities or assigning a dead-end job, is known as constructive firing. It is a legitimate basis for charges of wrongful discharge and intentional infliction of emotional distress.

OBSERVATION:

Fair treatment through a period of poor performance and dismissal is good management, and good preparation for trial if the situation deteriorates to the point of inefficient work ethics.

BE CLEAR ON YOUR SEVERANCE PAY POLICY

∎ ∎ ∎ ∎ ∎

Many employers provide employees with severance pay benefits not only to compensate them for dedicated service, but also to ease their financial burden between jobs. You should, however, be aware of the legal pitfalls you can run into.

BACKGROUND

A recent Bureau of National Affairs survey found that 65% of large companies and 54% of small companies maintain a formal severance pay plan, and that 58% of the respondents extended eligibility to all employee groups. However, the terms of eligibility vary by industry and status as a union or nonunion employer. Most companies base eligibility on years of service, with the majority requiring one year of service. Standard payment amounts vary considerably from firm to firm, but most companies offer one week's pay per year of service.

ADVANTAGES OF A SEVERANCE PAY POLICY

"You can treat everyone the same; the availability of pay makes employees feel better, and a policy increases the incentive for managers to terminate someone and reduces the anxiety," says James Brennan, president of Brennan Thomsen Associates, Inc., a Chesterfield, MO, consulting firm that specializes in personnel and pay practices, summing up the benefits of having a severance policy. "It also has a major effect on community relations," he adds. "If someone is let go gracefully, that makes the person a disciple of the company—and people talk."

THINGS TO CONSIDER WHEN SETTING UP A PROGRAM

• Severance pay policies generally fall into the categories of "payroll practices" or a pension or welfare plan, subject to Employee Retirement Income Security Act (ERISA) regulations. Under "payroll practices," companies, at management's discretion, determine payment to employees for specific purposes.

EXAMPLE:

In the case of *Blau v. Del Monte*, the employer was found to be arbitrary and capricious when it denied severance benefits to employees who were terminated when the employer sold the subsidiary for which the employees worked, but who continued to work for the same company under its new ownership.

The employer had kept its severance plan confidential and argued that it was intended to provide severance pay only to those employees completely without jobs after termination. The court held that the employer had flagrantly violated ERISA's reporting and disclosure requirements.

● N O T E :

Severance pay policies falling under the "payroll practices" category have spawned a number of employee lawsuits because of ambiguity or improper disclosure to employees.

■ R E S U L T:

Courts frequently rule that severance pay policies, even though they fall under the "payroll practices" category, are subject to ERISA's disclosure rules.

• In addition to ERISA rules, you may have to face state regulations on severance pay policies. Maine has a plant-closing law that guarantees severance pay to most workers. Although that law was challenged, it was found that the law's provisions are not preempted by ERISA. This means that if any other state decides to have similar legislation, it could use the Maine law as a model and employers could be required to provide severance pay benefits to employees under specific guidelines.

R E C O M M E N D A T I O N :

Proceed cautiously when creating your severance pay program and make sure it doesn't violate ERISA rules, no matter what you end up calling your policy.

DEALING WITH EMPLOYEE FRAUD

■　■　■　■

Employee fraud—now estimated to cost U.S. companies an average $200 billion a year—is the result of three forces interacting: situational pressures, opportunity and a breakdown in personal integrity.

At least that's what a team of CPAs and psychologists concluded after a three-year study of employee fraud (*How to Detect and Prevent Business Fraud*, W. Steve Albrecht, et. al., Prentice-Hall, Englewood Cliffs, NJ 07675; $60). They recommend ways of dealing with each of these forces.

SITUATIONAL PRESSURES

High personal debts, an inclination to live beyond their means, and undue family, social or corporate expectations rank high as contributing factors in white-collar crime. However, the experts point out, employees who commit fraud seldom do it compulsively so alert managers have time to pick up on signs of financial desperation and can offer help before a crime is committed.

To reduce the pressures on financially strapped employees, companies can:
• Give financial help to employees whose wages are garnisheed.
• Advance cash loans to employees caught in emergencies. Some employers, for example, will advance a month's salary, interest free, and spread out repayment over a 12-month period.
• Offer financial planning and investment advice to employees.
• To take performance pressure off employees, involve them in setting performance standards and goals for their work so that they are part of the evaluation process and not victims of it.

CONTROLLING OPPORTUNITIES

There are two situations in which trusted employees can take personal advantage of their position in a company. The first is when an individual is probably more familiar than anyone with the total operation of the business. The other is when an employee has a close—and almost exclusive—association with suppliers or other key people. Since many acts of fraud require a kind of expertise that can only come from years of training and/or experience, the cover-ups tend to be equally skillful.

■ S O L U T I O N :

Rotation of jobs is the best defense. It is dangerous for one person to exercise total control over any function in the business.

NO SPECIAL PROFILE

Studies of people imprisoned for fraud reveal no distinctive criminal traits. These individuals' backgrounds and personalities seem to match the general population more than the criminal population.

Although some companies do use lie detector tests to screen potential employees, there are state restrictions and controversy about their value. Background checks can reveal poor credit ratings, financial stress and similar red flags. A questionnaire called the Reid Report, cited in the study, is designed to measure the embezzlement potential of candidates for positions of trust.

DEALING WITH FRAUDULENT JOB-RELATED CLAIMS

■ ■ ■ ■ ■

Fraudulent claims of on-the-job injuries are sometimes difficult to disprove. But they can drive you, and your workers' compensation insurance premiums, up the wall.

If your company self-insures workers' comp, or even if you use an outside insurance carrier to cover this risk, you might be interested in a service that can reduce your vulnerability to fraudulent claims.

InPhoto Surveillance, based in Naperville, IL, with offices throughout the U.S., specializes in using hidden cameras to videotape allegedly injured workers who are suspected of malingering on the job. Using its cameras, it has caught employees working at outside jobs who were supposed to be virtually crippled by injuries for which they were receiving costly workers' comp payments.

Bill Kizorek, president of InPhoto, says that his company respects individuals' privacy and will not shoot tape through the doors or windows of workers' homes, nor will it try to trick them into incriminating activities. Phony claimants "do enough all by themselves," he says. "You don't have to set them up."

Kizorek says that in up to 40% of the cases his firm is called in on, tapes show that workers' claims of disability are inconsistent with the taped physical activity.

▲ C O S T S :

InPhoto charges $60 an hour for its surveillance and often gets sufficient evidence in only a few days—at a cost usually ranging from $1,500 to $2,000, plus expenses. Often, InPhoto doesn't charge for travel and incidental expenses until it has actually arrived on the scene, Kizorek says.

R E C O M M E N D A T I O N :

If you don't self-insure workers' comp, your insurance carrier would be the logical party to hire a surveillance firm like

InPhoto. Yet, insurance companies aren't always aggressive in investigating suspicious workers' comp claims. So you may have to take the initiative in suggesting that it use this type of service to get the goods on a phony claimant.

HOW DO YOU KNOW IF A CLAIM IS FRAUDULENT?

• There doesn't seem to be any physical basis for the claimed injury, or the subject appears to have made a full recovery.

• The supposedly injured claimant is tanned or has callouses on his or her hands and dirt or grease under the fingernails.

• The individual is in line for early retirement.

• The worker is known to have a history of self-employment as a carpenter or electrician or in another trade, and might work for cash while feigning injury.

• The worker is making excessive demands or is claiming a disability not normally associated with the injury claimed.

For more information, write for the free pamphlets, *Using Surveillance Videotapes as Evidence* and *Surveillance: Doing It Legally and Staying Out of Trouble*, from InPhoto, 1163 E. Ogden, Suite 705-360, Naperville, IL 60563; or call 1-800-822-8220.

WAYS TO THWART THE EXPENSE-ACCOUNT CHEAT

· · · · ·

While it's difficult to catch cheating employees who are on the road, you can at least keep them in check with a few simple precautions.

WHAT TO WATCH FOR

■ **Ticket conversion and other ploys.** Employees issued first-class or special coach-class tickets may simply change them for lower-priced tickets. They'll pocket the difference, then turn in the original passenger ticket with their expense report.

■ A N T I D O T E :

Require that all tickets, including exchanges, be charged to a corporate card. Set a policy that the card must be used whenever travel plans are changed, giving you a chance to see all alterations in employees' travel plans.

• When travelers get bumped, they may cheat another way: by pocketing the "denied boarding" compensation (up to $200) that is refunded by the airline for the inconvenience. Travelers may rationalize their dishonesty by the fact that they had to go through the trouble of waiting for another flight, forgetting that their company was the one that paid for the ticket. To discourage this, offer to split the rebate, which may encourage travelers to do the honest thing.

• What to do with frequent-flyer bonuses is another area where you should issue a written policy. Many bonus miles are available by taking higher-cost flights on a preferred airline, rather than lower-cost options. Some may even take unnecessary side trips to accumulate the extra miles. If you decide that those bonus travel miles should go to your company, then it's wise to have expense reports checked for deviations from the lowest reasonable fare, and to challenge travelers who deviate from their planned itinerary.

■ **Bloated hotel bills.** Some dishonest

employees will give kickbacks to hotel clerks who agree to add some false expenditures onto a phony hotel bill. If you require that employees pay all hotel bills with the company charge card, this practice will be discouraged. If, in addition, you stipulate that hotel staff gratuities be charged to that card, you'll deter the common practice of inflating the amount of tips reported.

■ **Charge card gimmicks.** Although requiring employees to use the company charge card helps to reduce fraud, determined cheaters will often plot with vendors, such as restauranteurs, to overcharge the company. In return for submitting the inflated bill, the dishonest vendor reimburses the employee for all or part of the difference between the bill submitted to the company and what the employee actually paid. Establishing daily meal allowances helps reduce this type of fraud.

RECOMMENDATION:

Other steps that discourage cheating include establishing per-diem allowances; publishing cost guides for tips and meals; and requiring receipts for virtually all expenses, including ground transportation.

AVOID COSTLY WORKERS' COMP CASES

Take the time to examine your workplace for potential shortcomings in what your firm does to prevent employee injuries and your emergency-care capabilities. Both have an impact on work-related accidents and future workers' compensation claims.

EXAMPLE:
In the case of computer keyboard operators it may mean changing the height or shape of their chairs, giving them extra breaks from their chore, or improving the lighting at their stations to cut down on glare.

MAKE YOUR OCCUPATIONAL HEALTH PROGRAM MORE EFFECTIVE

Begin by asking yourself the following questions:

• Is one employee responsible for the day-to-day supervision of your occupational health program? Generally speaking, companies need at least 250 employees before they can afford a full-time health specialist. As a result, smaller operations need to designate an employee to contact, say, the office or benefits manager, if there is a preventive-medicine or emergency-care problem.

• Do we help troubled employees to find assistance? Since an employee who is physically or emotionally troubled is more likely to be injured on the job, your program coordinator should have a referral list of psychiatric, social, marital, alcohol and drug abuse centers in your area. This person's role is to help the employee in need to make the first call.

• Is top management informed about all potential workplace hazards? They should be informed if employees who face special danger, such as operating heavy equipment, fall into the category mentioned above. Also, make certain that your equipment maintenance program is effective, and find a physician trained in occupational health to act as your preventive medicine consultant.

• Are job applicants screened adequately? A pre-employment physical or doctor's verification will determine if they can perform the work without risking injury or damaging their health. Periodic medical exams should also be required for those who do strenuous work.

• How are health claims assessed? With a proper system in place, you will know when and if a worker can return to the job.

• Do we maintain first-class medical records? Thoroughness is the key, because any work-related injuries and certain ongoing health problems that arise are potential workers' comp cases.

A PERSONAL PROBLEM IN THE WORKPLACE: DIVORCE

■　■　■　■　■

Divorce is usually seen as strictly a personal matter, not a concern for business associates. But sometimes, that view can be a mistake. There are times when an employee's failed marriage becomes a legitimate concern for higher-level managers.

WHAT YOU CAN DO

• **Keep an eye out for performance problems.** If any do arise, don't hesitate to call in the employee for a talk. Point out the performance shortfalls that gave rise to your concern, whether it be careless dress habits, frequent lateness, a failure to keep appointments or other potentially self-destructive behavior. Try not to be the first one to raise the divorce issue, however; give the employee a chance to broach the subject voluntarily.

• **Offer whatever help you can.** Unless you've been close to the employee, it's usually best to avoid offering personal advice; this is best left to professionals. You can, however, lend a sympathetic ear. And you can urge the individual to seek counseling. If he or she had been seeing a marriage counselor prior to the divorce, for instance, suggest that the employee continue to seek guidance from that same professional, who is closest to his or her problems.

• **Be patient and understanding.** Point out that a lot of other good people have been through the same experience and survived. If you feel it's appropriate, suggest a brief vacation or leave of absence. On the other hand, perhaps the individual will be open to new assignments that can take his or her mind off personal problems.

• **Consider a new career track.** Don't hesitate to discuss any changes in the individual's plans that affect his work for your company. If, for instance, the employee is now reluctant to move or work long hours for the sake of his children, you both may need to agree that this change means fewer promotion opportunities for him. At the same time, you may want to urge the employee to let you know when that situation changes, so that you may once again include him in your promotion decisions.

• **Keep in mind that a divorce may open up new opportunities** for him, because the end of a worrisome marriage allows him to concentrate on the job. Some divorced persons, in fact, throw themselves into their work with renewed vigor, as a way to help them forget. Be prepared to discuss the impact of any such changes on the individual's job growth.

OBSERVATION:

In some divorces, an employee's devotion to the job is a direct contributor to the downfall of the marriage. If you know that's the case, there's no reason for you to feel guilty as the employee's boss; after all, you didn't force the individual to choose job over marriage.

HOW TO MANAGE GRIEF

Whether you manage five people or 50, you are the head of a "family" that looks to you for emotional stability in times of joy and sorrow. This is especially true when death strikes. Your reactions will be crucial to those you supervise. If you are cold and unfeeling, they may try to match your "businesslike" way, but will think less of you for it. If you are too emotional, their respect for you may be jeopardized.

ADVICE FROM EXPERTS

Here are some suggestions from University of Virginia psychiatrist Vamik Volkan and Dr. Henry Seiden, co-author of *Silent Grief: Living in the Wake of Suicide* (Charles Scribner's Sons, New York City, 1987; $19.95):

• *Acknowledge the death.* It's important to recognize the psychological wound death inflicts and to face the grief. Express sympathy directly to the bereaved with a few tactful words.

• *Ask the mourner about his or her feelings* and how she or he would like to be treated. What may seem healing to you could seem condescending to another. Ask what the company and co-workers can do; reaffirm what the employee tells you by rephrasing what you think he or she wants. And be sure to check up periodically on how the person is doing.

• *Expect latent and overt anger from a mourner.* Anger at being "abandoned" is an almost universal response to the death of a loved one, and it is often displaced onto an authority figure—in this case you, the manager. Be sympathetic, but set limits so that grief doesn't disrupt the department's work process.

• *Watch for signs of abnormal reactions to grief* that indicate the need for professional help. They include immediate recovery from mourning or denial of death; obsession with death or dying; severe depression; passive anger exhibited by habitual lateness; a marked personality change; sleep disturbances or nightmares.

FENDING OFF UNION ORGANIZERS

If your group is a nonunion shop and you would like it to remain that way, it would be nice to know what sort of working environment leads to the successful entry of labor organizations into firms.

A confidential in-house AFL-CIO survey of the National Labor Relations Board (NLRB) election results shows the factors leading to union-organizing losses, and the tactics labor groups will need if they want to turn the tide.

OBSERVATION:

Union membership has been declining, going from a high of 35% of the nation's work force just after World War II to the current 16.8% of the work force.

The study indicates that the promise of higher wages is not the key to organizing success. The survey examined the factors surrounding 189 elections between 1985 and 1988, and found that unions won only a third of the campaigns when pay was the No. 1 issue. Unions were much more successful when the issues involved work conditions, grievances and dignity on the job.

FACTORS THAT LEAD TO UNION VICTORIES

• A key factor to a successful organizational attempt is having a rank-and-file union committee firmly established within the company. When the committee became involved in active campaigning, the success rate was 62%. This fell to a mere 10% success rate when such a committee wasn't present.

• To be victorious, unions need a large initial sign-up of interested workers. To secure an election, 30% of the workers need to sign an authorization card. When the initial sign-up totaled 75% of the work force, unions won more than 50% of the elections. They won only 8% of the time when 40% signed the cards.

• Face-to-face contact between union organizers and workers is critical for success. When house calls were made on 60% to 75% of the employees, the success rate was 73%. When organizers used only the telephone, mailings and videotape to contact workers, it dropped to 40%.

• Good worker attendance is needed at initial meetings. When 60% of the work force showed up, the success rate was 73%; when 25% showed up, the rate of union victories dropped to 29%.

• Union success is greatest among those who earn the lowest-paid salaries, minorities and women. Unions won 58% of the elections in cases where workers earned $5 or less an hour. The success rate was 57% when women made up 75% of the work force, and 65% when minorities made up 75% of the voting unit.

• Second tries at organizing work units are rarely, if ever, successful. When unions had a previous membership campaign without an election, they won only 30% of the time in a second attempt. When there was a previous election, this number rose to just 36%.

The union success rate has improved, reaching 48.6%, up from the 45.9% in 1985. And yet, there were 15% fewer elections, while the number of new units that labor organization won fell from 1,900 to 1,700 within a three-year period.

■ L E S S O N :

Unions need to organize themselves in larger units, rather than spreading their resources thin over numerous, small groups of workers.

• The time period between a union petition for an election and the election itself is critical for unions. When the election took place within 15 days, the win rate was 55%, but only 33% when the election came six months after the petition.

O B S E R V A T I O N :

Besides using this survey to refocus their organizing efforts, unions will constantly push for legislation to speed up NLRB elections after the organization petition is filed.

WHY YOU MAY NEED TO CREATE AN AIDS POLICY

· · · · ·

When an employee contracts Acquired Immune Deficiency Syndrome (AIDS), myths about the disease often overwhelm the facts. The fact that AIDS can't be spread by casual contact hasn't prevented unfounded fears among workers.

IRRATIONAL REACTIONS

• Some New England Telephone employees refused to work in the same area as a co-worker who had contracted AIDS. They walked off the job, as TV news cameras filmed the whole sorry episode.

• In some localities, police officers assigned to "gay rights" demonstrations wear gloves to "protect" themselves. And, on some highways, a few toll collectors have also been wearing gloves, out of fear of contracting the disease from a passing infected driver.

• In one company, a female employee who suspected a co-worker was a homosexual demanded either a change of partner or a reassignment.

Irrational reactions like those put the employer in a bind. Legally, AIDS should be treated as a handicap that you can't discriminate against. This means that if an employee contracts the disease, you can't mollify other employees' fears by firing the individual, even if you want to.

The best approach is to assume that you will eventually be confronted with at least one case in the workplace, and develop a policy that will help your people deal with it wisely.

HOW SOME COMPANIES ARE HANDLING THE PROBLEM

■ **Establishing a specific AIDS policy.** A law firm, Morrison & Foerster, developed a policy stating that "employees with AIDS or any of its related conditions may continue to work, and the firm will provide them with reasonable accommodation, as long as they are medically able to perform the duties of their position. Stricken employees will be treated with compassion and understanding," the policy goes on.

■ **Establishing a policy covering all life-threatening illnesses.** When a BankAmerica employee contracted AIDS, a pregnant co-worker threatened to charge the company with not maintaining a safe work environment under the regulations of the Occupational Safety and Health Administration (OSHA) unless it removed the employee from her work area. Ultimately, she dropped the threat of legal action, after the bank did the following:

• *Issued a policy statement* that said, among other things:

"BankAmerica recognizes that employees with life-threatening illness, including, but not limited to, cancer, heart disease and AIDS, may wish to engage in as many of their normal pursuits as their condition allows, including work. . .

"At the same time, BankAmerica has an obligation to provide a safe work environment for all employees and customers. Every precaution should be taken to ensure that an employee's condition does not present a health or safety threat to other employees or to customers. . ."

• *Equipped its personnel relations department* to provide employees with education and information on specific life-threatening illnesses, including AIDS.

• *Provided managers with guidelines* for dealing with situations involving employees with AIDS and other potentially fatal illnesses. The guidelines urged managers to: take precautions to protect information regarding an employee's health as personal and confidential; make reasonable accommodations for employees with life-threatening illnesses; and make a reasonable attempt to transfer employees with such illnesses, if they request a move because of "undue emotional stress."

The guidelines also instructed managers to "be sensitive and responsive to co-workers' concerns and emphasize employee education available through personnel relations." Workers who feel threatened by a co-workers illness can make a "normal" transfer request, but will get no special consideration.

■ **The do-nothing approach.** Some companies, such as Pacific Bell, have intentionally refrained from developing a policy for AIDS. Far from hiding their heads in the sand, however, these companies do have general policies regarding illnesses—and believe that it would be inappropriate to single out AIDS.

◆ W A R N I N G :

Bear in mind that having no specific policy regarding AIDS is not the same as being apathetic on the subject. If an existing company policy about employee illness provides for reasonable accommodations in the workplace and offers counseling or other assistance to ailing employees while prohibiting discrimination, no additional policy is required. If there is no such policy, however, it's advisable to either develop one or provide AIDS-specific guidelines.

DEALING WITH DRUG PROBLEMS

■ ■ ■ ■ ■

The Bush Administration is putting the heat on American business to make the workplace a "drug-free zone"—and this responsibility is a heavy one.

Drug czar William Bennett is putting the message out loud and clear: No drugs are to be allowed on or off the job. Also, drug users who are presently employed must either agree to treatment or face dismissal.

HOW TO WEED OUT THOSE WHO ARE ABUSING DRUGS

• **Check your employee manual.** If a no-drug policy isn't clearly defined there, develop one at once. If your business is too small to warrant a full-fledged manual, distribute and post a special notice in regard to this problem. You also might consider administering drug tests to new hires. They're legal, quick and relatively inexpensive.

• **Monitor the behavior of your employees consistently.** The signs of probable drug abuse are fairly easy to spot: dilated pupils, sudden fatigue, a slower output of work, frequent absenteeism, a recurring headache, unexplainable irritability and excessive trips to the rest room. Take action on your suspicions after you have compiled a substantial body of evidence.

• **Confront the troublesome person diplomatically.** If this individual cannot give you any explanation for his or her objectionable behavior, or admits to using drugs, suggest that he or she seek help. In most areas, community services are provided and other referrals can be made, and you should be prepared to supply this information.

• Don't threaten anyone with dismissal or some other punishment—unless you are certain that the person is a substance abuser and he or she refuses to seek help. Otherwise, your company could face costly litigation.

TESTING

Test current employees only if the evidence is clear cut. At present, the courts tend to uphold random testing for cause, or for individuals in a sensitive position.

The problem of drugs in the workplace is far more serious than most people in key positions realize. About 15%–20% of all Americans use drugs, and the total cost of drug and alcohol abuse to business is $60 billion a year. So you have a vested interest in making your plant a drug-free zone.

To receive extra help with work-place drug problems, call the National Institute on Drug Abuse (1-800-843-4971) from 9:00 a.m. to 8:00 p.m., Eastern Standard Time, Monday through Friday. The agency can advise you on how to spot addicted workers, indicate what action to take when you do and guide you to other informational sources.

PROTECTING VITAL RECORDS DURING DISASTERS

■　■　■　■　■

Businesses throughout the U.S. that are exposed to misfortune from hurricanes, floods, tornadoes and other disasters would do well to learn the lessons of the earthquake that hit San Francisco's Bay area in 1989. One area in which disaster-recovery planning paid off for many companies hit by the quake: Vital records were largely protected, thanks to precautions taken to protect computer operations.

PLANNING HELPS

• **Uninterruptible power supplies.** Only a few Bay area companies had backup generators to keep computer operations going, but many reported that their standby batteries helped avert a major loss of data. The batteries, designed to keep computers running for only about 15 minutes, provided enough time for operators to save data and bring computers to a "soft" landing, averting damage to fragile drive heads.

• **Recovery services.** Disaster-recovery services like Comdisco and Alicomp provided computing sites to dozens of Bay area businesses, enabling the firms to shift computer operations to alternate data processing centers as far away as Chicago. Companies whose computers were inoperative sent their data tapes to these centers, along with crews from their data processing staffs.

• **Backup centers.** A number of banks and credit companies had redundant data processing facilities in other areas of the state or nation to serve as backup. By maintaining duplicate facilities, the firms were able to keep automatic teller machines and retail services operating in areas that did not lose electricity or phone service.

• **Indexing systems.** To some companies, it wasn't the loss of computers that caused the worst problems, but the physical problem of putting spilled tapes and disks back in order. The quake toppled many filing cabinets and shelves to the floor, pitching magnetic storage media in the process. Companies that used clear, simple procedures for indexing and labeling tapes and disks had the easiest time putting the mess back in order.

OBSERVATION:

The biggest problem for some companies was getting staff to and from work, due to the earthquake's disruption of highway and transit systems. To make it easier, many companies temporarily adopted flexible work hours to permit employees to avoid commuting during the busiest hours.

MASTERING RENEWAL
■　　■　　■　　■　　■

Change and renewal are crucial for both corporate and personal vitality.

- *Habit breaking* is a prerequisite for change, and change, in turn, lubricates renewal.
- *Information* is a tool. It's always needed for strategic advantage.
- *Everyone around you* is a source of creative input.
- *Change* breeds opportunity.

RETHINK YOUR ROLE

The first step towards understanding the importance of renewal is to rethink your role as a manager. The renewing manager is usually engaged in a daily effort to fight corporate entropy, to welcome change, to uproot tired habits and to use renewal to build the future.

- *Ask yourself how much your managerial mind-set empowers others.* By empowering others, you're giving up tight control in order to achieve better results from your employees. Define the boundaries and let your subordinates figure out the best way to do the job within them.
- *Treat your people as the main creative engine for your organization.* When we think about the creative element of organizational change, we erroneously look to top management, the research department, marketing, etc. We are too prone to leap to the conclusion that creativity is the realm of a relative few. Instead, look to each person as a wellspring of renewal.
- *Look for ways to speed up the process of getting things done.* The risk is overlap, confusion, and duplication as the program lunges forward. The benefit is that the project in total moves faster and is less prone to mistakes. Learn as you go with thousands of small and overlapping feedback loops.
- *Start thinking about the implementation of a decision at the moment the decision arises as an issue.* A decision and the ability to implement it go hand in hand. What counts is results.
- *Ask, explain, communicate.* The way to empower people is to let them know what you are trying to accomplish. Ask for their ideas, reach mutual understanding. Consensus would be nice but probably is not possible; understanding is what you're looking for. You cannot force involvement, but you can get good ideas from everywhere on what would make implementation easier.
- *Do not give a lot of thought to boundaries.* Try them. When people get outside the boundaries ask yourself whether the boundary was wrong. If so, change it. If not, nudge them back into the solution space. Keep monitoring the process. Don't be afraid to step in and create a new boundary if something is not working. Look for ways to widen the boundaries for people who can operate effectively within broader limits.
- *Keep pushing for lean organizational*

structures in terms both of smaller staffs and fewer layers. But think about the implications for the people; more responsibility, less direction. Understand your own unique strengths and build on those. Get yourself into jobs that are the most natural fit with your own personal strengths, skills and inclinations.

RENEWAL FOR CAREER ENHANCEMENT TOO

Too many people worry about the precise strategy for their career, just as companies worry about the precise direction of their company. Instead, structure your career around the principle of informed optimism. Know yourself well.

Know what is out there so you can make good moves and be flexible. Have a general sense of direction but don't try to be too specific.

Opportunity knocks frequently, but it will knock softly and in unpredictable ways. Be ready to take advantage of it when it does.

BLACK-BELT MANAGEMENT
· · · · ·

As a manager striving for excellence, you can learn valuable lessons from the Asian martial arts. Consider the following thought: Great executives and masters of the martial arts both possess the same qualities: courage; the ability to make change work for (and not against) them; calmness under extreme pressure; focus and self-discipline; and the efficient use of energy and power to attain goals.

Robert Pater, author of *Martial Arts and the Art of Management* (Destiny Books, $16.95), explains that to fully develop the above qualities there are three stages a manager must undergo:

SELF-MASTERY

"You must develop real self-honesty—not only knowing your own strengths and limitations, but also developing courage," Pater says.

• *Invite colleagues, family and friends to give you candid feedback on your strengths and problems.* Watch how you receive their input. Defensiveness is a danger sign. You should be looking for ways to improve your performance, not for stroking and approval.

• *Part of self-honesty involves viewing your organization realistically.* It's great to be for the team—but not by blinding yourself to its weaknesses. Without seeing weaknesses, you can't bring about needed change.

MANAGING PEOPLE

One key martial arts concept is leverage—using minimal force to get maximum returns. Managers can employ it too. "Using leverage is critical in times of staff cutbacks when managers must achieve more with fewer resources," says Pater. Here are more examples:

• *To use minimal force, get close to your people.* "Closeness creates power," explains Pater. Take the small amount of time needed to establish human ties.

◆ M I S T A K E :

You walk into a subordinate's office and gives orders right away. Instead, take the time to ask how that person or his or her family is doing. And listen to the answer. The few seconds spent establishing a human rapport will be handsomely repaid in heightened morale and renewed commitment to shared goals.

• *To know your staff's concerns, keep your supervisory antennae working.* Then have the courage to face problems when they are first cropping up. One way to avoid crises is to head them off early through the use of intuition and emotions as well as intellect.

• *To gain power by giving up power, reduce unnecessary controls and learn how to delegate intelligently.* Avoid delegating tasks you don't understand and performing the ones that you do. This leaves you unable to guide your subordinates when they come to you for help and appraisals of their work.

● BEST METHOD:

Delegate the tasks you know best and save the challenges for yourself. This way, both you and your subordinates will grow and learn the most.

• *To work through disagreements, recognize that "there are four forms of conflict—over facts, methods, goals and values.* And they get more difficult to deal with as you move down the list. Don't fall into the trap that snares many managers— looking at conflict on only an intellectual level. You can't defuse the conflict by focusing on facts and methods when the problem really reflects differences in goals and values.

MASTERING CHANGE

Understand that people need change. Many managers believe simplistically that people oppose the idea of change.

▲ REALITY:

The endless shifts in fashions and fads show that this is not true. What subordinates do resist is change that is implemented too quickly or that makes them feel that they lack control.

Therefore, respect your people's needs regarding change. Give them whatever warning you can about changes that are coming, downplaying the negatives of the new situation and emphasizing the positives.

A DIFFICULT, WORTHWHILE PROCESS

Becoming a black-belt manager requires continual practice and self-appraisal.

◆ CRITICAL:

Determine when things are working well, why they are doing so; and when things go wrong, pinpoint why they are out of kilter. Develop the ability to see the principles at work. Otherwise, you waste learning opportunities.

ADVANTAGES OF AN OPEN-DOOR POLICY
■ ■ ■ ■ ■

One of the toughest decisions a new manager has to make is whether to place a welcome mat outside the new office. On one hand, a manager should be responsive to the concerns of all employees; on the other, there's a real danger of undercutting supervisors when workers know they can always go over their heads "right to the boss."

A BALANCING ACT

Experienced managers agree, however, that their office doors should be kept ajar. Certainly there are dangers involved, but the benefits outweigh the risks.

• Everett P. Suters, chairman of three Atlanta-based companies, commented in an *INC.* article (January 1987) that an open-door policy had been both an "ongoing challenge" and an "indispensable management tool" in his 28 years of running companies.

• One open-door enthusiast who heads a federal agency was so committed that he replaced his office door with two swinging saloon doors. Like others, he's found that an open door is one of the best early-warning systems yet devised for managers. When trouble is brewing, the manager who sits behind an open door is likely to get loud and clear signals right from the start. One manager got an early clue from an employee that one of his supervisors was on the verge of a nervous breakdown. He was able to take early and supportive action.

• An open door is also a useful means of keeping subordinates on their supervisory toes. It reminds them that if they don't treat their people fairly, employees do have a recourse—one that may come back to haunt a supervisor.

• "Perhaps the greatest benefit of an open-door policy," says Suters, "is that people throughout the company feel they have an ally at the top." When employees are backed into a corner and know that they have someone they can turn to without fear of firing, the pluses in morale and motivation are everywhere in evidence.

◆ R I S K :

Undermining the morale and effectiveness of your fellow supervisors. Any supervisor is going to be troubled when he sees one of his people walking into the office of their mutual boss.

■ A N S W E R :

Convince your supervisors that you will not cut the ground from under them. Do this by always keeping them informed of your visitors and their concerns and by briefing your fellow managers thoroughly before any meetings with complaining employees, making sure that they understand your position. Because your supervisors have proved themselves time and again over the long haul, chances are that your open-door policy is going to reaffirm, rather than weaken, their authority.

DON'T STAFF A COMPLAINT DESK

Never let your open door become an invitation to vent personal antagonisms and trivial gripes. You could end up losing valuable time handling problems that should never have reached you. Set a high standard for issues in which you will become involved. When you intuitively know that you shouldn't be involved, don't hesitate to send a complaining employee back to an immediate supervisor.

HOW TO MAKE AN OPEN DOOR WORK

• **You have to mean it.** Don't open that door if you have any reservations about who might walk in. The worst mistake you can make is to present yourself as a manager who is accessible to all people, all the time, and then wave off the first visitor who tampers with your privacy or challenges your understanding.

• **You have to be ready to go the route.** Most complaints or queries that come through the open door are routine matters for a sharp manager. But there are occasionally the zingers: when, for example, an employee and a supervisor are clashing, and you are the last court of appeal. But the employee is tying your hands, insisting that there be no confrontation. At that point, you have to be ready to step in and say, "I can't solve this if you won't let me. Something will have to give: my manager or you. Someone will go. Are you ready to put your job on the line?"

ADVICE ON GIVING ADVICE
■ ■ ■ ■ ■

If you feel uncomfortable when an employee comes to you for advice about some type of personal problem, consider this: Employees who turn to you for counsel are showing that they trust you and value your opinion. It's a sign you're a good manager.

On the other hand, you're probably better off not getting too involved in employees' private concerns. There's always the possibility that your advice won't work out. If so, your attempt at being helpful can backfire.

To keep your role as counselor on track, follow this advice:

• *Don't upstage.* Start off by listening, not talking. Even if you've had a similar experience, keep it to yourself until you've heard out the employee's problem completely. Later, you may want to bring your own experience into the picture to shed light on the situation.

• *Keep the talk flowing.* Maintain eye contact throughout the conversation, nodding occasionally or saying "uh-huh," "yes, go on," and so forth. Ask questions if the person bogs down: "How did you feel about that?" The point is to help the individual express feelings.

• *Don't assume you're expected to give advice.* Often, people who come to you with problems are only looking for sympathy. After all, if your secretary complains about her boyfriend, you can be fairly sure she doesn't want you to suggest she break off with him. In this case, the best response might be something like "You certainly have to put up with a lot from him. I don't know how you do it."

• *Suggest, don't direct.* Help the person make the decision for himself or herself. Ask such questions as "What do you want to do?" or "What have you considered doing?"

If the person has hit a dead end, you might suggest a few alternatives. Be careful not to sound like you're endorsing any particular approach. Don't say "You ought to. . .," but rather, "Have you considered. . .?"

To bring the discussion to an end, you might want to make your suggestion sound more conclusive. A good approach might be: "If I were in your position, I think it would help if you were to sit down with your wife (creditor, friend, etc.) and explain how you felt."

RECOMMENDATION:

If the advice seeker is taking up too much of your time, refer him or her to others—including any professional counselors your organization may have provided for such situations—who are trained with the expertise to deal with employees' personal problems.

HOW TO ENFORCE A DRESS CODE

∎ ∎ ∎ ∎ ∎

As a manager, you are within your right to enforce a dress code for your employees. The courts have stated that a reasonable dress and grooming code is a proper exercise of management authority, as long as the policy is uniformly applied to all workers. In addition, different regulations for male and female employees are allowed, just as long as they are based on the same general standard.

• Each employee should be given a copy of these regulations, which you may want to review first to make sure that they are specific and easy to understand.

• If you have a problem with an employee, talk to him or her privately, and explain how the individual's style of dress can hurt the company's image through loss of business or even complaints. (The person may also be creating an image that he or she doesn't want to project, due to poor judgment.) Allow the employee to voice his or her opinion, but be prepared to back up your company policy.

Avoid any emphasis on your own tastes and preferences. If you don't, the employee may focus on that immediately and miss the main message that you are trying to convey. Other employees who have begun to "bend" the rules will probably become more cooperative once they see this individual dressing more appropriately. If not, you should take appropriate action later on by firmly reminding them of the company dress code.

Chapter 3

MEETINGS

WHEN TO CALL A MEETING

· · · · ·

Much of the business transacted at meetings is better done in writing. Convene people only when you need individual and group reactions.

REASONS TO MEET

• Delivery of messages with a personal and/or emotional content, such as good or bad news. A meeting is the place to tell sales staff heads will roll if orders don't improve dramatically or to single out a top performer for public praise to inspire the group.

• Announcement of important company news—creation of a new division whose mission everyone must understand; the introduction of a new senior executive.

• Explanation of new procedures, such as automation of support functions, introduction of new equipment or discussion of a new, aggressive sales strategy.

• Brainstorming to develop ideas or concepts through group discussions that play one person's thoughts off another's.

REASONS NOT TO MEET

• To transmit straightforward information, such as changes in payroll procedures, vacation schedules or a switch from time cards to time sheets.

• To conduct routine business, such as regularly scheduled update meetings on sales curves.

• To explain how a new product works.

OBSERVATION:

Tersely written summaries get these kinds of messages of across more effectively.

PICK THE RIGHT MEETING SITE
■ ■ ■ ■ ■

Even the most carefully crafted meeting can be ruined by breakdowns in audio-visual equipment, poor meal service, too few chairs available for plenary and workshop sessions or shoddy recreational facilities.

BEGIN PLANNING EARLY

• **Tap the experts for information.** Once you've selected the exact city—or are considering a couple—get in touch with the local Chamber(s) of Commerce or convention bureau(s). A phone call should be all that's required to bring you all the brochures and literature you need from these sources. And they are impartial about competing hotels and resorts.

Then write out all your unanswered questions and use the phone again. You might want to check on whether there will be any big conventions in town coincidental with your meeting—and perhaps plan around them.

• **Consider a small establishment.** Many small hotels will go to great lengths in the price and service areas to get your business. You're also less likely to find yourself competing for attention with a bigger group.

• **Make your inspection unannounced.** If you pay your look-see visit without making an appointment, you have a much better chance of seeing life there as it is. There will be no red carpet treatment to soften the impact of any shortcomings in food, service, attitudes of the working staff, etc., that you pick up.

• **Get it all in writing.** Once you've decided on the place, be sure that your contract includes details ranging from the precise kinds of sweet rolls to be served at breaks and whether you pay for coffee by the cup or by the pot, to specific meeting rooms and A-V equipment.

• **Meet the staff.** You want to get a feel for the individuals who will be responsible for the myriad needs of your meeting. Question staffers closely about those things that most concern you. Do not accept "Don't worry about it" as an adequate response to any query.

• **Be a real nuisance.** Look at every projector, mike and lectern that you will require to be sure that they work. Inspect the various meeting rooms to be sure they're not too small—or even too big—for the groups that will use them. Check the illumination and ventilation in every room. Examine the location of electric outlets in relation to your plans for the way the equipment in the rooms will be set up.

RECOMMENDATION:
Be sure to consider the kinds and amounts of play you plan to include on your agenda, as well as the requirements of your working sessions, when selecting your meeting site.

USE GROUP DYNAMICS TO IMPROVE MEETINGS
■ ■ ■ ■ ■

In his research, Robert B. Morton, a pioneer in group dynamics at Ohio State University, zeroed in on the question of effective leadership in small groups. Morton developed a series of roles that managers can play to keep decision-making meetings productive and targeted.

NINE LEADERSHIP RESPONSIBILITIES

1. State the position. Do this in writing before the meeting, so people will have time to think about it before they convene. Be sure you don't foreclose options in your memo. "How can we get our products to the West Coast competitively?" may suggest that you are not willing to manufacture or license your product locally. A better summary would be "How can we sell profitably in the West Coast?"

2. Clarify the position. During the meeting, you may have to redefine the problem as the issue changes under scrutiny. The competitive disadvantage on the West Coast, for example, may begin to show itself in other places as well. Or the product life cycle may be declining, and the problem may become whether to modify it or replace it.

3. Develop alternatives. Groups often tend to pick a solution early in the discussion and ride with it—to the exclusion of other options. You must see that no reasonable option is ignored.

4. Keep the discussion on track. When a meeting loses focus, participants become confused. Don't cut off anyone before you get the gist of the thought, but be prepared to challenge the relevancy of certain approaches. Ask the speaker to justify his or her direction, or ask other members of the group if they think the discussion has strayed.

5. Summarize. Too many ideas or too heated a conflict can blur the issues in a meeting. When you say, "It seems to me that this is a fair summary of what's been said so far," you clarify positions and give everyone a welcome breathing space. Your summary may also reassure everyone that, despite the confusion, you are making progress.

6. Define the consequences of choices. A group may decide on a bonus program to boost productivity on one line. How will that affect productivity on other products? What will the impact be on employees? Discuss all the possible effects, direct and indirect, now and in the future.

7. Test commitment to the decision. After a full discussion of consequences, is the group still committed to its choice? If you suspect that there are some second thoughts that individuals are hesitant to express, draw them out.

8. Make the decision. Push for a firm statement that reflects the thoughts and feelings of everyone around the table. Express the statement out loud and confirm that everyone subscribes to it. No one should leave the room with a question about what has been decided.

9. Create a plan of action. You must define individual responsibilities clearly and get agreement on future deadlines before the meeting is adjourned. Later, you can distribute a written summary.

CONTROLLING A MEETING

A meeting in which people get loud, excited, even border on the disorderly, has something going for it. The participants care about what is being discussed. Since that alone makes it unusual, the trick is to put some order into the chaos without dampening the spirits of those present:

• *Let the tempo build for a while.* After you open the meeting and ask for opinions, don't step in too fast when people start interacting and interrupting each other. Let the hubbub go on long enough to get as many participants into it as possible.

◆ A D V I C E :

If you want to manage it, not inhibit it, just bring the noise down slowly," advises William Korn, president of Marketing Communications Systems, Inc., Ivyland, PA.

• *Step in as the facilitator.* When the noise approaches a roar, take charge in a low-key way. Make a vertical line down the center of a flip chart or a blackboard and say, for example, "OK, everyone who thinks the big annual sales contest is the way to go hold up your hand, and I'll list the reasons here. Then I'll do the same for those of you who are opposed."

After the ideas are all listed, open the floor to discussing them one at a time. That will force every person in the room to listen to both sides—or to all sides—without your seeming to take control of the meeting.

• *Create referees from among the participants.* When two vociferous advocates of opposing points of view start getting red in the face, you want to cool things down; but you don't want to seem too directive. "Pick out a person in the crowd whom you know the others respect," advises Korn. "Ask his or her opinion: 'Judy, what was our experience when we offered a car as first prize five years ago? Do you remember how well we sustained interest through the whole campaign?' That way, Judy has the floor, the yellers are quieted, other people will get a chance to participate and you haven't put anybody down."

• *Give hairsplitters their moment.* You can almost count on someone raising a point

that is at best inconsequential, at worst irrelevant. It is equally certain that someone else will disagree. Let them go at it for a bit, and then say—in very soft tones—"Since most of you don't seem involved in this, why don't we table it for now, OK?"

"*Now* lasts forever," says someone who uses this technique. "But the nit-pickers stay in the game. And they may have something to say that's useful later on."

• *When you must get in, be sure you don't dominate.* Whether it's because things are getting out of hand again, or they're not going anywhere, move in like a gentle giant. "OK, looking at this list, we seem to be stuck on these two points. Let's begin with number one. Who can briefly defend this position?" Says Korn, "You're getting back to the agenda, getting people to think instead of argue, and you've refocused the discussion—all without being the heavy."

O B S E R V A T I O N :

It is a little like directing a dance ensemble. You want everybody in it, but you don't want them changing your choreography or refusing to join one another in the finale. That's what managing is all about—directing without browbeating to get the best from everyone.

'STORYBOARDING': A NEW WAY TO BRAINSTORM
■ ■ ■ ■ ■ ■

"Storyboarding"—which takes its name from the posting of idea notes on boards—sparks individual innovation, and cross-fertilizes the ideas of a group. The method is deceptively simple.

HOW IT WORKS

Prior to an idea meeting, a problem is defined and broken down into subtopics or questions. Bulletin board stations—usually two to five—are placed in different spots in the meeting room. Participants are divided into subgroups, one per station. A facilitator asks the members of each group to read the sub-problem and write possible solutions on slips of paper or Post-it™ notes—one idea per note. Members attach the ideas to the bulletin board for group members to see. This sparks additional ideas.

After a few minutes, the facilitator asks the groups to move on to the next bulletin board station and offer ideas for solving the next subproblem. When each group has visited each station, the process is complete.

IDEAS APLENTY

More than 100 solutions may be generated by a typical group of managers in a single hour, according to practitioners of storyboarding. This compares to hashing over just a handful of ideas during a typical business meeting and not coming up with concrete suggestions.

During a recent session with 25 employees of a pump manufacturer, Yankee Ingenuity's Clark collected over 250 ideas, none of which were duplicates. Many were readily implementable.

When asked how the company's pump sales reps could make more money, one participant suggested getting an 800 number. This would speed up orders by expediting communication between reps and distributors. When asked what methods could be used to recruit new distributors in underdeveloped markets, a participant wrote, "Show them a product video." The

video would not only illustrate the product line, but also offer tips on how the potential distributor might sell it profitably.

OTHER BENEFITS

Patrick J. Farrell, Director of Training for Pizza Hut, says storyboarding has not only generated numerous solutions to problems, such as how to keep restaurants clean, it has also brought intangible benefits. "By focusing attention on all dimensions of a situation," he says, "we're much more likely to surface attitude problems." Once identified, these problems can be dealt with.

"One of the pitfalls of conventional brainstorming," says Farrell, "is that there may not be equal participation." One person can dominate a group while others remain silent. With storyboarding, everybody contributes at least one idea per station.

HOW TO SET IT UP

• For easy display of ideas, use 3″ × 5″ Post-it™ notes.

• Use foam-core boards for idea stations. Post-it™ notes stick well to the surface.

• Use color felt-tip pens, which produce notes that are easy to read from a distance.

• At each station, post the question attractively, in large type.

• Keep the process moving. After 10 to 12 minutes, or when groups run out of ideas, guide them to the next station.

OBSERVATION:

A properly run storyboarding session temporarily suspends criticism and judgment so as to encourage the free flow of ideas. Such a meeting is filled with activity, excitement and accomplishment for the participants.

GIVING EFFECTIVE PRESENTATIONS

■   ■   ■   ■   ■

If you want to make a presentation that comes on strong, you have to finish just as strong.

PLAN A POWERFUL FINISH

■ **Write your ending first.** To make the conclusion the most vivid part of your talk, write it first. Use it to sum up the main points of your talk as cogently and dramatically as possible.

Be prepared to spend a lengthy amount of time choosing your concluding words. That time will pay off later when writing the bulk of your talk by helping you to structure the whole presentation to build toward that memorable close. You'll find it much easier to focus your whole presentation on the point you want to get across.

■ **Emphasize a few main ideas.** To keep your conclusion brisk and snappy, avoid using any anecdotes, examples, jokes and minor points in this part of your talk. Those details belong in the body of your presentation.

■ **Don't announce the conclusion.** Avoid leading into your final remarks with obvious phrases such as, "In conclusion. . ." or, "I have tried to demonstrate. . ." If you've been clear about the purpose of your presentation up to that point, they're really unnecessary.

■ **Use fresh phrases.** By all means, use the conclusion to remind the audience of your main points, but don't be obvious about it. Avoid simply restating these objectives for the audience; instead, try to rephrase them as colorfully as you can.

> **EXAMPLE:**
> At the end of his presentation to senior executives on a new advertising campaign, one marketing manager summed up his dominant themes this way: "It will turn the traditional media strategy on its head, confound the competition and put this company on the map."

■ **Keep the tempo up.** Make the conclusion build in energy by progressively increasing its forcefulness. A good principle to apply is incremental repetition, in which the same phrasing is repeated, but more intensely each time, much as Abe Lincoln spoke of "government of the people, by the people, and for the people. . ."

■ **Let your conviction show.** If your conclusion sounds hollow and shows lack of interest, your whole talk will appear unpersuasive. Even if you're not the demonstrative type, display a little emotion during your closing statement through gestures (jabbing a finger into the air, thumping gently on the table or lectern) and a rising tone of voice.

■ **Choose an appropriate close:**

• Ask for action on the part of your listeners: "So on your very next call, put these ideas to work. . ."

• Summarize what you have said briefly: "If you do nothing else, remember these three principles. . ."

• Try to challenge the audience in some way: "Do we have what it takes to put this project over the top?"

• Appeal to people's sense of history: "Joe Jackson believed this when he founded this company. And his son Frank believed it when he rebuilt the plant after the fire 20 years ago. . ."

• Give some choices: "We can do nothing and continue to watch fine young managers leave to work for other companies. Or we can..."

HOW TO HANDLE TOUGH AUDIENCE QUESTIONS

■ ■ ■ ■ ■

The question period following an oral presentation can prove intimidating, even for experienced public speakers.

HOW TO COME UP WITH A STRONG RESPONSE

• **Preparation.** When preparing your speech, try to anticipate tricky or aggressive questions that your speech might elicit, and frame brief answers for each one. Writing down those answers will help you remember later, when you're on the spot. You might also rehearse your potential response aloud, to build up your poise.

In framing your answers, keep in mind the perspective of the vocal dissenters in your organization, and be prepared to address their concerns while remaining true to your mission. Your ability to respond effectively under gunfire is essential to ensure a persuasive presentation.

• **Delivery.** Once you've prepared your speech, present it with conviction. A speech given in a conversational, anecdotal tone, even if it's read, will be more easily absorbed by your listeners. You'll find that the audience will tend to be "with" you, not "against" you. This will help to cut the risk of aggressive or hostile queries when it's your audience's turn to speak.

CAUTION

"Watch your expression," warns Franklin C. Ashby, vice president, Department of Instruction, Dale Carnegie Institute. "Maintain a pleasant demeanor and don't take on a defensive mode."

• **Rephrase the question.** Assume that your speech is delivered, and here come the "stumpers" from the audience. "The first step is to rephrase the question to buy yourself thinking time," advises Kevin R. Daley, president of Communispond, a New York-based company that offers communications-skills training for managers and corporate officers. In other words, reframe the question so that you understand it better. Instead of looking at the person asking the question, "break visually from that person and rephrase it to the rest of the audience," says Daley. "If you direct your restatement back to the person asking, he might disagree and get into a one-on-one discussion, and you're not interested in that."

• **"Direct your answer to the entire group,** not just the person who asked," Daley adds. "Since you rephrased the question to the entire group, you have a right to answer to the entire group." It's no longer just the individual's question; it belongs to the entire audience. This reduces the leverage the questioner has over the speaker.

Once you have given your response, don't ask the questioner, "Does that answer your question?" because he may respond, "Not really," and begin taking over the forum from you, the speaker. "You don't want to relinquish your authority to a hostile member of the audience," says Daley.

• **When you have completed your answer,** raise your hand and ask for another question. "By raising your hand you are showing that this is the modus operandi as opposed to shouting randomly from the floor, taking away the advantage from the heckler," says Daley. "If the hostile person raises his hand, you don't have to recognize him."

• **Pass the question on.** If you find yourself among a panel of speakers and someone hits you with a difficult question, consider passing it on to a co-panelist. You're "passing the buck," but that might be a better defense than fudging an answer.

• **Tie the questions back into the talk.** If you're hit with far-reaching questions not entirely related to your speech, respond to them, but then tie the answers back to the theme of your speech to reinforce your main point. "In this way, the question-and-answer session becomes an extension of the talk, rather than a random set of unconnected questions," says Daley.

RECOMMENDATION:
If you run into a question you feel you cannot answer perceptively or completely, ask the questioner for time to research the answer. Ask the person to meet with you afterward so you can take his or her name and get back with the information. "That closes the issue from the audience's point of view, and it's no longer a public forum," says Daley.

Chapter   4

RECRUITING/HIRING

FINDING WORKERS IN A SHRINKING LABOR POOL
· · · · ·

With competition increasing for the services of skilled and technical employees, companies have to be shrewd in searching for suitable candidates. Here are some of the astute recruiting tactics recently developed by some organizations to attract hard-to-find managers and workers:

• *Active recruitment.* Rather than waiting for experienced people to answer ads, more companies are applying aggressive tactics borrowed from professional headhunters.

● ONE APPROACH:

Reading technical publications with an eye on the credentials of authors, then calling promising candidates to invite them to interviews.

• *Keeping track of layoffs.* Large firms that have announced layoffs are often eager to have recruiters from other companies interview their terminated workers. Don't overlook far-off companies that have recently laid off employees whose skills you can use. Unemployed workers are often willing to relocate.

• *Job-search help for spouses.* Some high-tech firms offer to help the spouses of relocated new employees find new jobs. In Ohio, several such firms have banded together in a network, to share job openings for displaced spouses of their new employees.

• *Voice-mail job hotlines.* Voice-mail systems, which let callers leave recorded phone messages, can be easily adapted to serve as job hotlines for recruitment campaigns.

EXAMPLE:

One computer service bureau established a 24-hour, seven-days-a-week hotline, supported by an extensive newspaper advertising recruitment effort. Callers with push-button phones could learn about specific types of jobs by punching in certain numbers (such as "1" for full-time jobs, "2" for part-time), then would hear a recorded listing of available types of jobs.

To get further information about a specific job, the caller would then punch in a second number. Pressing still another number enabled callers to leave their name, address and phone number, for follow-up by a personnel specialist.

• *Refresher training.* To attract applicants who have been out of the work force for some time, some organizations offer to bring rusty skills up to speed. One hospital offers such a refresher course on a no-obligation basis, to attract nurses who are returning to the field after several years' absence. It has been able to hire 20% to 50% of those who take the training.

• *'Quality of life' perks.* One hospital offers company-paid personal maid services to clean the homes of nurses living within a 20-mile radius of the institution. The perk was added when a study showed that housecleaning was a major concern of many staff nurses.

● ANOTHER BENEFIT:

Travel reimbursements for nurses living beyond the 20-mile limit.

• *Early engagement.* If you need college graduates for certain positions, it may not be too soon to approach nearby high schools with your recruiting message. Be present on career days sponsored by the schools. Identify outstanding students in advance, and prearrange with them to talk with a company executive.

It may take years for such an effort to pay off, but bear in mind that labor shortages are expected to worsen in the next decade.

OBSERVATION:

One company in Cleveland offers scholarships, with amounts based on the academic performance of high school students it hopes to recruit eventually. The idea is to encourage the students to maintain good grades, while getting them to think of the company as a potential employer, once they've completed college.

RECRUITING RECENT GRADUATES
· · · · ·

Effective recruiting of the best new graduates is not difficult. Most of them have strong feelings about the kind of employer they want to work for. By building the right kind of image for yourself and your company, you stand a good chance of attracting the best and the brightest from this year's class.

SUCCESSFUL RECRUITMENT TECHNIQUES

• **Take a personal interest in the candidate.** You may have other, more important tasks that you should be doing instead of chatting with a prospective hire, but it's well worth your effort to come across as someone who cares. Note that talking about campus life, subjects studied, and so on, is a good place to open conversation because these subjects are close to the applicant's recent experience and concerns.

• **Keep interruptions to a minimum.** Have your calls held, and close your door so that staff members don't keep popping in. Such simple steps communicate something important to the candidate: You value his or her time and interest in joining the company. That can make a difference in the decision on whether to accept your job offer.

• **Talk about the future.** According to Roper Campus Reports (the educational wing of The Roper Organization, a major polling organization based in New York), recent graduates care most about long-range opportunities with a company, including such benefits as promotion possibilities and income potential. So find out what a candidate's aspirations are, and describe how you see them fitting into your organization's goals.

CAUTION

Don't paint too rosy a picture—you may lose your recruitment and training investment if the candidate comes on board and is later disillusioned.

• **Get the candidate's ideas.** Ask how an applicant would solve a theoretical problem. You'll find out if the person will bring initiative and creativity to the job, and he or she will respond favorably to being asked. Judge the creativity and enthusiasm of the answer, not the practicality. Don't brush off an idea by thinking "that would never work here." Remember, this person knows nothing about your company yet. You want an answer that shows logic, reason, and good problem-solving skills.

• **NOTE:**
Opportunities to contribute ideas are very important to 61% of first-job seekers, according to Roper Campus Reports.

• **Make sure the candidate is shown around.** If you have the time, do it yourself. If that's not possible, have a staff member who will make a good impression do it for you. Taking the time to introduce the candidate to potential future co-workers or superiors is crucial.

This introductory process helps the graduate decide whether he or she fits into the organization. It also provides the opportunity to have your choice corroborated by the people who will be in contact with the candidate if he or she is hired.

CLASSIFIED ADS SHOULD SELL YOUR JOB OPENING

For an opening in sales, customer service, and other areas where you must appeal to a wide pool for personnel, it's important to know how to construct your ad.

HOW TO LURE THE CREAM OF THE CROP

• **Determine your best "key word."** Most newspapers run the employment ads alphabetically according to the first word in the ad. But not all sales-related positions, for example, should begin with the word "sales." Connie Gillan, senior division manager for the *Los Angeles Times* employment division telephone sales, says your first word really depends on whom you're looking to hire. "If you're really looking for a technical person to train as a sales representative," she says, "you might want to key the ad 'engineer' or 'chemist,' for example."

Marilyn Evans, telemarketing manager for the *Roanoke Times & World News*, agrees. However, she says her company's research has shown that individuals who are seeking a selling position will look under "sales" first and then under the areas of expertise. Running two ads, with one of them a cross-reference ("See our ad under Chemist") might be useful in some cases.

• **Run your ad for several consecutive days.** Four to seven are generally recommended. The more experience or expertise you're after, the longer you'll need to run the ad. If your company keeps its name before the public with ads in trade journals (or possibly in college newspapers), Ms. Evans says, you'll have the advantage of being a known quantity.

• **Sell the right candidates on your job.** The more information you include in your ad, the less time you'll have to spend fielding inquiries, and the more serious and qualified your applicants are likely to be. Include such basics as what work the recruit will be doing, type and amount of experience desired, salary/compensation plan, work hours, amount of travel required, and some reference to benefits (if applicable).

"I advise advertisers to write a 'product ad'," says Ms. Gillan. "Don't just say 'I've got a job.' Point out why someone would want it." She also suggests that you track your ads to see what works best for you.

• **Tell applicants what action to take if they want to respond.** You may or may not want to include your company name or the name and number of an individual to contact. Ms. Evans feels that the reputation of the company can be a definite asset in

recruitment. But Ms. Gillan points out that higher-salaried jobs are frequently listed through a box number. "This cuts the response rate about 40 percent," she says, "but applicants are usually of high caliber."

• **Don't be concerned about the ad's size or the day of the week it runs.** Neither of these factors has much bearing on response. "I've seen three-line ads succeed and full-page ads fail," says Ms. Evans. "The content is what's really important." While it's true that Sunday ads usually get the most exposure, the applicant you're seeking could be looking for a job any day of the week.

RECOMMENDATION:
Consider making newspaper advertising representatives a part of your recruitment effort. They are trained to help you create ads that sell. They can also help you get the most advertising for your dollar from among all pricing structures the paper makes available.

USE TV TO RECRUIT EXECUTIVE TALENT

A growing number of employers are putting their recruitment messages into TV commercials, reaching out to qualified technical or executive candidates who may not even be looking for a job actively. The tactic is aggressive, highly visible and surprisingly cost effective.

Because TV lets you combine recruiting messages with visuals, it allows you to show off company facilities, top executives and the people with whom a potential new hire might be working.

WHERE TO SHOW

The *CareerLine* show, a regular half-hour feature of the business-oriented Financial News Network (FNN), is the prime carrier of televised recruitment ads. The half-hour, cable-TV show includes 90-second to five-minute interviews with representatives from a variety of companies seeking prime executive talent. Each show is built around an abundance of career-oriented information designed to attract highly motivated viewers who are serious about advancing their careers.

Because the show is broadcast nationwide, it is a suitable recruitment vehicle for any company that seeks to cast a wide net rather than attract strictly local talent. Each broadcast reaches an average of 32,000 serious, upscale business people, according to Al Parinello, executive vice president for CAV Communications Corp., the show's producer.

• *Viewing times. CareerLine* is run sporadically throughout the year when there is enough interest from the marketplace for such a program.

The recruitment commercials are in the form of interviews with executives representing the employer.

▲ C O S T S :

From $3,500 to $14,000, depending on length, the amount of visual information a company wants to show and the amount of production help required. CAV will write the interview script if desired, or provide suggestions to the sponsoring employer on what to cover in the commercial. Interviews are videotaped at CAV's production facilities in New York City.

• *Some typical jobs advertised.* Mid-to-upper management positions paying at least $35,000 are the most usual. However, positions in sales, engineering and data processing have also been aired.

Programs use a toll-free telephone number to spark fast responses from interested candidates. They have generated as many as 150 replies for participating employers, according to CAV.

FOR MORE INFORMATION:

Contact Al Parinello, CAV Communications Corp., P.O. Box 279, Norwood, NJ 07648; 201-784-0059.

R E C O M M E N D A T I O N :

The point of video is its unique visual power. Use it to your advantage by showing employees in interesting work situations and displaying attractive aspects of the work, such as modern equipment, varied responsibilities, or appealing recreational and housing areas located near company facilities.

USE DIRECT MAIL ADVERTISING TO RECRUIT EMPLOYEES
■ ■ ■ ■ ■

Direct mail is a new trend in recruiting executives, professionals and technical employees. A mail program allows a company to hit its targeted audience precisely, and without competition from the jumble of jobs that appears in newspapers' classified ad sections. It also lets you reach a large number of prospective candidates without alerting rival companies that you're shopping for employees.

Experts say that direct mail has been used successfully to enlist managers, professionals and technical types for jobs ranging in salary from $25,000 to $150,000.

WHAT GOES INTO THE PACKAGE

A typical mailing package includes a brochure describing the company, selling the benefits of working there, and listing the specifications and qualifications for the types of jobs available. Also included is a return post card on which candidates can outline their interests, background and credentials. Company recruiters then call promising prospects to get additional information, constructing a résumé that can be reviewed by company managers and followed up as needed.

FINDING NAMES OF POTENTIAL CANDIDATES

• **Mailing-list houses** can break out names by industry, job classification, geographic area and other specifics.

• **Schools.** You can develop your own lists by contacting colleges to get the names of recent graduates. "Some of the finest schools, including Harvard's Business School, will sell you alumni rosters directly," notes a recruiting executive.

• **Professional contacts.** Many business, professional and technical associations can provide directories of their members. A source identifying many of these listings is the *Directories in Print*, a two-volume compendium available for $205 from Gale Research Inc., 835 Penobscot Building, Detroit, MI 48226. You can also add to your list by asking your employees who attend conferences and seminars to give your personnel office a list of others who attended. Seminar sponsors often provide these names at no charge to participants.

• **Job-fair services.** A number of recruiting firms operate job fairs, in which employers meet experienced job candidates from specific fields, such as nursing, data processing or engineering. Job-fair sponsors compile lists of thousands of potential candidates who have attended fairs all over the country and often sell these names.

> **EXAMPLE:**
>
> Business People Inc. (BPI) recently introduced a complete direct-mail recruitment service. The service uses a database of over 250,000 computer and engineering professionals who have attended BPI's "Tech Fair," which tours 15 to 20 major technical job markets each year.

BPI will develop a mailing to fit a wide variety of candidate profiles, based on education, specialty, industry and other specifics. It sends out these computerized mailings with a personalized cover letter on the employer's own letterhead, even duplicating an executive's signature through a digitized printing process. The cost of the service depends on volume but typically runs less than $3,000 for a mailing to over 4,000 people.

FOR MORE INFORMATION:

Contact Mike Hall, Business People Inc., 2985 Multifoods Tower, 33 S. 6th St., Minneapolis, MN 55402; 1-800-328-4032.

• **Cooperative mailings.** Your company may be already using this collective approach to direct mail, in which a dozen or more advertisers participate in sending out a stack of business-reply cards, each containing a brief advertising message and an offer to send more information. Although usually used to help sell business products or services, these card decks are increasingly including job offers from potential employers, experts say.

Many business and professional publications and other sources offer these cooperative direct mail programs. A directory of card-deck vendors is available from Standard Rate & Data Service ($99 for two issues a year), Wilmette, IL; 1-800-323-4588.

In many cases, sources of candidates' names can provide home addresses. Often, however, companies send discreet recruitment messages to prospects at their place of work. Instead of making a direct job offer, they describe available positions and say something like, "If you know any people who might be interested, please write their names and addresses on the enclosed reply card." This approach lets a company on the hunt for talent avoid being accused of "raiding" other employers.

EMPLOYEES CAN HELP RECRUIT JOB APPLICANTS

■ ■ ■ ■ ■

Most companies that who rely on in-house referrals express great satisfaction with the results. In a survey by the Bureau of National Affairs, Washington, DC, one-fourth of all responding companies said they reward employees who provide successful referrals of job candidates, and 87% of these provide cash rewards.

On the downside is the possibility that an employee referral program could violate federal equal-employment regulations. In some cases, federal courts have overturned referral programs as discriminatory because the job candidates recruited through this means were all white or all male.

HOW TO AVOID PROBLEMS WITH IN-HOUSE REFERRALS

• **Look at the makeup of your work force.** If your existing labor pool consists of mostly male or white employees, it's likely that people they refer to you will also be mostly male or white. In this case, it's wise to avoid relying exclusively on referrals for recruiting job candidates.

• **Don't automatically give preference to referred candidates.** Hiring should be based on objective criteria that enable you to support your hiring decisions with legitimate business reasons.

• **Don't ask applicants how they learned about the job.** If you do, minority applicants who don't have the benefit of a referral could accuse you of intentional discrimination if they're turned down for a job.

With these precautions in mind, however, an employee referral program can be an effective recruiting tool.

SETTING UP A PROGRAM

• **Don't overlook departing employees as a source.** If the employee has been a valuable worker, ask him or her for the names of one or more potential candidates.

• **Ask for résumés.** If you do provide rewards for referrals, ask employees to obtain a written description of experience from each candidate, to help you evaluate whether or not you want to follow up.

• **Give employees recruiting ammunition.** When they approach friends about the possibility of working for you, be sure they have printed material about your company, selling the benefits you offer.

• **Keep employees informed about progress.** To encourage their continued help in recruiting new employees, acknowledge their referrals and let them know when you have arranged for an interview. When you notify candidates of your employment decision, be sure to notify referring employees as well.

O B S E R V A T I O N :

Rewards for referrals range from $25 to $2,500, depending on the position to be filled. But many companies give relatively simple rewards, such as tickets to a show, gift certificates or dinner for two.

Cash awards are generally distributed only after candidates have successfully completed a probationary period—usually three to six months.

SIZING UP
JOB APPLICANTS
▪ ▪ ▪ ▪ ▪

• **Use résumés data only as a guide.** Thanks to résumé-writing services, headhunters and manuals, anybody can be made to look good on paper. It's common to find exaggerated job accomplishments.

▲ C O M M E N T :

Self-effacing candidates can understate their strengths and screen themselves out of jobs in which they might have done very well.

Use a résumé as a departure point for inquiries. Be sure to substantiate all claims made on any résumé—employment dates, degrees awarded, work accomplishments. If you discover disparities between what a person is implying in a résumé and what he or she actually accomplished, beware.

• **Don't hire based on one interview.** Studies have shown that most sessions reveal only about 12% of the information needed to hire intelligently. The reasons are that interviewers: talk more than they listen; trust gut reactions without validating them; or hire weaker candidates who seem able to fit into the organizational bureaucracy.

A BETTER WAY

This structured system has been developed by clinical psychologist Dr. William Knaus in over 15 years of helping his industrial and corporate clients evaluate job applicants:

• **Conduct pattern interviews.** Develop specific job-related questions and ask them of every candidate you interview.

E X A M P L E :

Ask candidates to explain the five most important duties they performed in their last jobs. Then ask how they performed those functions. This reveals their grasp of both function and process. If they claim to have performed some duty and can't convincingly explain how they did it, they're exaggerating their experience.

Also, ask questions regarding how candidates would react should a critical incident occur in the workplace.

EXAMPLE:

What would they do if they walked out onto the floor of the company's warehouse and found a forklift operator drunk. This focuses on the candidates' practical judgment.

• **Have candidates write biographical inventories.** Determine beforehand what experience and qualifications you want in a candidate. Construct questions that will reveal what you're looking for, and have candidates respond to your inquiries in writing.

EXAMPLE:

To rate maturity and interpersonal skills, have candidates explain the strengths and weaknesses of their past supervisors.

• **Give in-basket tests.** Present candidates with an in-basket full of simulated problems that they must prioritize and then solve.

▲ IMPORTANT:

Throw in a few irrelevant situations and questions. If a candidate gets stuck trying to respond to these hypothetical situations, he or she doesn't have a good sense of priorities.

Also, throw in more critical incidents—irate letters from suppliers and clients, or a letter from OSHA citing your firm for safety violations.

• **Simulate work situations.** Assign a short-term project that demands the skills required in the job you are trying to fill. Have other members of your staff join in the process. Do some role playing, and act

through simulations of actual job activities to see how the project is completed.

Throw in a few critical incidents again—have a member of your staff threaten another one, or call in claiming to be a customer about to cancel an account because of late deliveries.

THE EVALUATION PROCESS

Cross-reference the results of all the evaluation stages and look for consistencies and inconsistencies.

One example might involve Susan, a candidate who claimed in her pattern interview to have supervised a staff of ten field representatives on her previous job. Yet, she was unable to make sense of an expense report in the in-basket test and also lacked the needed assertiveness in the simulated work situation.

In conclusion, she's either exaggerating her experience or is not an effective manager. John, another candidate, stated that his greatest strength was the ability to perform well under pressure. Yet, when a plant emergency arose during the work simulation, he became angry—perhaps with the simulation itself—and wasn't able to apply an orderly thought process to solving the problem.

● BOTTOM LINE:

Applicants who are consistent in what they say, what they write and what they do have a higher level of competence.

RECOMMENDATION:

As a final safeguard, talk with your colleagues to see whether their views of the candidates match yours. Is the candidate really as good—or as bad—as you thought?

HOW TO FIND OUT WHAT YOU NEED TO KNOW

· · · · ·

Interviews and other aspects of the hiring process have come under close scrutiny since the passages of equal employment opportunity and protection of privacy legislation. While an interview remains an essential tool in assessing a person's job qualifications, it does carry the risk of violating a candidate's "protected" rights.

Many of these "protected" rights are contained in Title VII of the Civil Rights Act of 1964, which you should get to know. This act prohibits employers from discriminating against applicants on the basis of sex, religion, national origin, race or color, unless based on a bona fide occupational qualification.

WHAT YOU CAN AND CAN'T ASK

• You obviously need to know a person's name, but don't ask her to choose a prefix—Mrs., Miss or Ms.—since marital status is rarely a bona fide job qualification. Questions about child-bearing plans or number of children have been used more often against women than men, so don't ask them.

• Don't ask for a person's age, but inform the applicant that proof of the minimum age is a state requirement once he or she is hired.

• Asking for an address is acceptable, but don't ask whether the housing is rented or owned. This may indicate economic status and inadvertently discriminate against minorities.

• Avoid queries about height or weight, physical condition or handicaps, foreign language ability, arrest records or personal finance, unless they're needed to determine job qualifications. But keep in mind that under the recent Immigration Control Act, you must make a prospective employee document his or her citizenship.

Other sensitive areas include random drug, polygraph and AIDS testing, the right to confidentiality of medical records and the monitoring of a candidate's social life. There's a federal law that bars using lie detector tests for prescreening employees, except in the case of a few industries, such as those in the security field. Some 31 states have similar laws.

OTHER RESTRICTIONS

Seven states restrict random drug tests, and the Supreme Court is examining whether testing government employees violates the Fourth Amendment. Federal and state restraints on computer surveillance, which companies give access to vast amounts of personal information, is also under discussion.

"From a legal point of view, privacy is a very nebulous area," says David Twomey, a Massachusetts labor arbitrator. "Basically it's a matter of good judgment."

Twomey suggests that the interviewer bring up sensitive concerns in a conversational way—"Tell me about yourself." A good rule of thumb is to concern yourself with employees' off-the-job behavior only when it reduces their ability to perform regular job assignments.

GETTING THE INFORMATION YOU NEED TO CHOOSE

• Clearly define all the specifics of the job and the qualifications necessary to perform successfully, and ask questions pertaining to objective job-related criteria.

• Plan the interview to avoid asking questions that can be misconstrued later. Using résumés and application letters as a starting point, determine which key facts are missing, and target your questions to those areas. Ask questions that can't be answered with "yes" or "no."

• Question previous employers to learn why the person left his or her former job.

• Consider training your interviewers, through outside courses or in-house seminars, to sensitize them to unconscious pitfalls like stereotyping or making premature evaluations, and to further their understanding of the fair employment regulations.

INTERVIEWING TECHNIQUES

. . . . .

Knowing *how* to ask questions when interviewing candidates for a job opening is just as important as *which* questions you ask. To get more out of interviews:

• *Phrase your questions offhandedly.* For instance, "What would you say your greatest strengths are?" is less threatening than a flat "What are your strengths?"

• *Don't rush to break a silence.* Give the candidate plenty of time to respond to each question, and pause for a few seconds after he or she has stopped speaking. As you think about his or her response, your interviewee may add comments that give you further insights.

• *Try to link new questions with prior answers.* This type of bridge adds a relaxed, conversational tone to the interview and helps put the candidate at ease.

> EXAMPLE:
> "So you enjoy taking on responsibility. Now let's talk a little about how you like to supervise."

• *Probe in a nonthreatening manner.* Avoid putting the candidate on the defensive. A comment like "That's interesting—could you tell me more?" is better than using statements like "Why?" or "What do you mean by that?"

• *Mix harmless questions with pointed ones.* Focusing on too many critical issues early in the interview can sound like a grilling and unnerve the candidate. If an interviewee seems to be trying to dodge an issue, drop it; or if it's critical to the job, come back to it later.

WHEN AGE AFFECTS HIRING DECISIONS

. . . . .

Age can be a legitimate hiring factor for a job that's a stepping stone to the top office. In one instance, a company refused to hire a 55-year-old former executive as marketing director because he could not replace the company president in two-to-four years. The company subsequently hired a 41-year-old and extended the time period to fill the job. The older executive sued.

▲ DECISION:

The Third Circuit Court of Appeals upheld the company's refusal to hire the older candidate, holding that the eventual presidency was a legitimate job requirement and that relaxation of the time period was due to the difficulty in filling the job. Relaxing the time period did not alter that fact, the court said.

EMPLOYMENT TESTS THAT MEET NON-BIAS CRITERIA

· · · · ·

The use of pencil-and-paper hiring tests as a means of identifying reliable workers has been growing, thanks in large part to a 1989 U.S. Supreme Court decision. The court held (in Watson vs. Fort Worth Bank & Trust) that subjective criteria, such as managers' opinions, can unintentionally discriminate against minorities in hiring or promotion.

Written tests can circumvent those problems by scoring workers objectively on their honesty and positive attitude toward work. To meet equal employment opportunity requirements, however, you must be sure the tests are validated by research that shows they do not have a disparate impact on minorities. For instance, one criterion set forth by the Equal Employment Opportunity Commission (EEOC) is that the passing rate of women and protected minorities who take an employment test must be at least 80% of the passing rate of white males.

TYPES OF TESTS AVAILABLE

■ **Personality or psychological tests.** Marketers of these tests point out that their instruments measure a variety of job attitudes and behaviors that contribute to overall productivity, not just the job candidate's trustworthiness.

• One widely used instrument, from Personnel Decisions, Inc. (PDI), is the Employment Inventory, a test of approximately 20 minutes' length. It has been described as a "covert" honesty test because it does not question a job candidate's integrity directly. Instead, it asks the candidate to answer "true" or "false" to such statements as, "Most people get fair pay for the work they do," and "Everyone at some time in his or her adult life has stolen something."

George Paajanen, designer of the Employment Inventory, calls it a "test of productive vs. counterproductive behavior." In addition to testing for honesty, it asks multiple-choice questions designed to uncover the individual's likelihood of showing initiative, working extra hard, following rules and so on. It also tends to screen out individuals who are prone to unproductive conduct, such as quitting in less than six months, filing exaggerated workers compensation claims, abusing drugs or alcohol or being disciplined for rule infractions.

PDI's analysis of the test results shows, for instance, that 75% who score high on the test stay on the job for at least six months, compared to only 8% of those who score low. There's also a strong link between high scores and outstanding evaluations of employees by supervisors, according to Paajanen.

The test is administered and graded by the employer's own personnel department, using IBM-compatible software available from PDI. If desired, the company will also provide a small laptop computer dedicated to scoring and evaluating test results, along with training on how to administer the test. The cost ranges from about $4 to $13 per applicant, depending on volume, and large employers can also buy the test under a licensing arrangement.

The system is sold by a number of employee-testing firms, such as Humetrics, Inc., Houston, TX 77074; 713-771-4401. Or it can be purchased directly from PDI at 2000 Plaza VII Tower, 45 S. 7th St., Minneapolis, MN 55402; 612-339-0927.

■ **Honesty tests focus on establishing an employee's trustworthiness.** Most, however, measure other character traits as well, and proponents of these tests say they can be good indicators of a job applicant's likelihood of being on time, reliable and hard working.

Widely used tests are available from Reid Psychological Systems, 200 S. Michigan Ave., Suite 900, Chicago, IL 60604, 312-938-9200; London House, 1550 Northwest Hwy., Park Ridge, IL 60068, 708-298-7311; and Personnel Profiles, 8044 Montgomery Road, Suite 700, Cincinnati, OH 45236; 513-792-2266. Costs range from about $6 to $16 per applicant, and tests can be self-administered by the employer.

A FOREIGN ACCENT CAN BE A HIRING BAR

■ ■ ■ ■ ■

Some jobs are immune from federal anti-bias laws, provided they fall under the "bona fide occupational qualification" rules set forth in Title VII on the 1964 Civil Rights Act.

> **EXAMPLE:**
> Airlines are not subject to Age Discrimination in Employment Act penalties when they refuse to hire pilots 60 years old or older—the government has set an age 60 ceiling for pilots.

The Ninth Circuit Court of Appeals has now expanded bona fide rule protection against charges of national origin discrimination. The case was brought by an unsuccessful job candidate in Honolulu who had EEOC support.

The city had refused to hire him for a clerk's position that required constant contact with the public because of his "heavy Filipino accent." He claimed he was rejected because of his national origin, and pointed to his high score in written language tests.

Consequently, the court turned him down, ruling that his accent affected his ability to do the job, which required dealing with 200 to 300 people a day. Communicating effectively in English was a prerequisite for the clerk's position. The ruling also went against the position of the EEOC that a person discriminated against solely because of his accent is a prima facie case of national origin discrimination. (*Fragante v. City and County of Honolulu*, No. 87-2921)

OBSERVATION:
This case shows that you should stand your ground in choosing a job applicant where you can demonstrate that an occupation has special job requirements.

OFF-LIMITS INTERVIEW QUESTIONS

■ ■ ■ ■ ■

Ask job candidates questions prohibited by federal law and you could find yourself at the wrong end of a lawsuit. You can't ask women applicants anything you wouldn't routinely ask their male counterparts. And you can't ask *any* applicant a question that is not clearly job-related or that might indicate bias on your part. Examples follow.

WHAT YOU CAN'T ASK WOMEN

- What are your plans for marriage?
- What are your childbearing plans?
- What arrangements can you make for your children during working hours?
- Would you be inconvenienced by travel?
- Would you be inconvenienced by night work?
- How would you feel about supervising men?
- Is your husband likely to be transferred to another location within his company?
- What would you do if your husband were transferred?
- Do you think you can leave your family problems at home and concentrate on the job?
- Can you sell as aggressively as a man?

WHAT YOU CAN'T ASK ANYONE

- Do you live alone or with someone? (This could be considered an invasion of privacy.)
- Do you go to church regularly? (This could be viewed as religious discrimination.)
- Are you a Republican or a Democrat? (This could be an invasion of privacy.)
- Were you ever arrested? (Most states prohibit this question. But they usually permit the interviewer to ask if the applicant was ever convicted of a crime—especially if the job involves security or confidentiality You may also ask if the person can be bonded; convicted felons can't.)

- What type of military discharge did you receive? (This could be discriminatory because minorities have a disproportionately higher percentage of dishonorable discharges than whites.)
- Do you have any physical disabilities or handicaps? (The interviewer may only ask if the applicant has any disability that would interfere with his or her performance on the job.)

HOW TO EVALUATE YOUR HIRING TESTS
· · · · ·

If you're using written hiring tests, it's in your best interest to make sure that the tests are valid. You want to screen out only those job candidates who are *most* likely to be unsatisfactory. The reason? To protect your company and yourself from charges of discrimination against minorities.

WHAT TO LOOK FOR

- Ask how the test was designed. If the examination is intended for a particular type of job, find out if the test maker consulted actual workers on the tasks and skills required to do the job. Ask, too, about the qualifications of other experts who helped pick the test questions related to job aptitude and knowledge.
- Ask for evidence that the test itself was tested on actual workers before being put into use, to ensure that the questions are relevant and valid.

OBSERVATION:
You can get a good indication of this by looking at the results of individuals who

scored high on the test. Did the test maker examine this group to make sure that they generally answered each of the questions correctly?

• Find out how often the test was revised before being introduced. Most experts agree that at least three revisions are usually needed before a test can achieve the level of clarity and suitability needed.

• Check on validity. To be valid, a test should predict actual performance on the job in terms of productivity, positive supervisor evaluations or other criteria, with reasonable accuracy.

A BENCHMARK

One benchmark that experts use is a figure called the validity coefficient, which relates workers' job performance to their test results. A coefficient of zero means that the test is no better than, say, picking a name out of a hat, as a means of choosing the right person for a job. A coefficient of 1 would mean that all of the workers hired through the test results proved to be suitable. It's more realistic, however, to expect a test to achieve a coefficient of .4 (40% better than chance) or higher.

DO YOUR OWN VALIDITY STUDY

Any valid test you use should increase the likelihood of your choosing capable people. Compare your success rate—in terms of new employees receiving satisfactory job ratings within a year of hiring, for instance—with the same rate of success you had before you began using the test.

Then take that a step further and translate the rate of success into actual cost savings for your firm.

> **EXAMPLE:**
> If you find that you are enjoying a 20% higher hiring success rate with the use of a test, multiply the number of people hired in a year by that figure then multiply that result by the average salaries of those hired. Using that formula, 10 people hired in the course of a year at an average of $18,000, for example, yields $36,000 in savings. Subtract the cost of the testing from that figure and the result is your net savings.

PUBLIC RECORDS AID IN BACKGROUND CHECKS

■ ■ ■ ■ ■

Looking through public records takes time and effort. But when you think of the trouble you could be caused by hiring and training a dishonest or unsatisfactory worker, it is time well spent.

WHERE TO LOOK

• **Criminal records.** Even though you may not automatically exclude every applicant with a record of misdemeanors, it's good to know when applicants have concealed this information. Almost all counties in the U.S. will search for criminal records on request, either free of charge or for a nominal fee. In many cases, they'll report back to you by phone.

• **Driving records.** Even when they're hiring someone to drive company vehicles, employers often overlook this important check. Yet driving records are an excellent source of information for any applicant. For instance, a history of drunken driving or speeding tickets or violations for traffic safety could shed light on potential problems with applicants for certain sensitive jobs. State motor vehicle departments will provide this information by mail for a few dollars.

• **Workers' compensation claims.** If you want to keep your own workers' comp costs down, this check is highly recommended when hiring for physically demanding jobs. You can uncover a history of previous mishaps that indicate an individual may be prone to injury. Most states supply this information readily at little or no charge, often over the phone.

• **Educational institutions.** Falsification is common here. Yet few employers bother to check whether an individual ever attended a school claimed on his or her application, much less whether the applicant actually graduated or received the stated degree. If you want to find out if an applicant is reasonably honest, this is the information you should verify and it's easy to get.

▲ I M P O R T A N T :

For key managerial jobs, you'd be well advised to go beyond merely checking that an applicant completed the education claimed. Examining grades and subjects taken can tell you about the individual's motivation, ambition and credentials. You can go even further by talking to one or two of the applicant's former professors—finding out, for example, about special achievements or evidence of leadership.

R E C O M M E N D A T I O N :
The Guide to Background Investigations

(National Employment Screening Services, 4110 South 100th East Ave., Tulsa, OK 74146; 1-800-247-8713) is a worthwhile reference on sources for employers wishing to undertake background checks. The guide costs $95 per copy.

REFERENCE CHECKS: GETTING PAST THE LEGAL BARRIERS
 ▪ ▪ ▪ ▪ ▪

Fearful of the growing number of lawsuits, many companies no longer give out information on an ex-employee's job performance or on the person's reasons for leaving their employ. This stonewalling from former employers can make hiring decisions difficult.

ADVICE FROM HEADHUNTERS

• **Don't concentrate initially on a candidate's job references.** Pointed discussions with potential hires regarding their past experience and any problems they had with former bosses will generally set off "warning lights" of past problems.

John Semyan, managing director for Heidrick & Struggles' Washington office, says, "References are only part of the mosaic of choosing the best candidate for a particular position. Up front, we ask job candidates if there are any problems in their past that they want to talk about now. We emphasize that openness about their past job experiences is key to being considered for the position."

• **Analyze the résumé closely.** This will generally "red flag" problem areas in a person's past. Pay particular attention to short tenures at previous firms—anything less than 18 months—and gaps in employment history.

• **Warn job candidates that you'll be checking facts.** Right at the start of the interview, emphasize that negative information uncovered later will only hurt the person's hiring prospects.

• **Don't ask for a waiver unless you spot warning signs.** Despite the legal questions about asking a job candidate to sign a waiver allowing you to speak to former supervisors, most search firms concede that refusal to sign a waiver, if one is requested, will instantly eliminate that person from serious consideration for the job.

If there are indications of potential trouble during the course of the interview, ask for a waiver to speak to former bosses. Few candidates will object.

• **Ask about the candidate's approach to the job.** How does he or she get along with people? What motivates the person—financial compensation or psychological rewards? Pose hypothetical questions about problem solving specifically related to the job that's under consideration. A candidate's character flaws will often reveal themselves under probing questions.

• **Ask for at least six to eight references,** including former supervisors and subordinates. Assure the candidate of confidentiality and agree not to contact the current employer.

• **Contact individuals who have worked directly with the candidate.** When you call the person's former firm for references, don't expect much help from the personnel director, who will probably only confirm the dates of employment.

• **Do your own checking.** If you are in a closely knit industry, you may be able to find out much from your business contacts. But be discreet. For instance, call a competitor and ask for the names of the five best marketing people in the industry, if that's the position you're hiring for. Or name five people, including the one you're interviewing, and ask about their reputations.

• **Make sure to verify educational background.** If a candidate is hiding something in this area, misstatements will often show up here.

GUARD AGAINST HIRING TRADE SECRETS
· ■ ■ ■ ■

Employers often don't foresee the potential for a lawsuit when they hire a competitor's employee, but it's always there. So when you hire from a competitor, consider the following:

• Never assume that a lawsuit is unlikely. On the contrary, assume that it's likely and behave accordingly.

• If the new employee says he or she is not bound by a secrecy agreement, or the former employer never enforces the agreement, assume the worst: There is a contract—and the ex-employer intends to sue under it.

• Take a hard look at the former employer's trade secret claims. They may be so much air.

• Look at matters extraneous to the suit itself for negatives. Consider the morale of other employees, the possibility of disclosing trade secrets in the discovery process, and the time and money necessary to prosecute or defend a trade secret case.

• Consider carefully whether hiring a

competitor's employee may lay you open to counter-recruitment—and whether you're vulnerable.

• Watch out if the new hire was a director or officer of his former company. Courts demand a higher degree of loyalty from officers than they do from ordinary employees.

• Don't be too quick to entrust your new employee with the company's most sensitive information. After all, he might be a "Trojan horse" planted by your competitor.

Chapter 5

SALES MANAGEMENT

GETTING THE RIGHT INFO FROM REPS

• • • • •

You want to get all the business you can and make it profitable. Information is the key, and the most reliable carriers are your salespeople.

HOW TO GET WHAT YOU NEED

• **Be very specific about what you want.** An instruction like, "Keep me apprised of what's happening in your territory," will bring you some valuable information from some representatives—along with a lot of dross. From others, you'll get very little in either category.

"My salespeople," says David J. Oldroyd, sales manager for Metal Supply Company, Philadelphia, "are required to get back to me after every single quotation they make. I want to know whether there's going to be an order, whether they think our price is good or we're high. If we're too high, by what percentage and exactly where? Are we high on the material or on the cutting we're going to do? All that tells me what it will take to get the order." You can't get much more specific than that.

• **Have a plan to use what you get.** In addition to the field force, there is an inside telephone group at Metal Supply Company that sets up appointments and digs for information from customers. Often, an inside person will pick up something about a competitor's offer to an account that the field representative hasn't yet uncovered. The inside rep passes it on to the field rep and to Oldroyd. He puts it all together and decides "whether we can come in under the competition and still make money."

• **Make it easy to report.** When salespeople know precisely what intelligence they are after at any given time, there's little reason to load them down with reporting forms—and the fewer the forms, the better the chances of your getting what you want in a timely manner.

At Appleton Papers, says Jim McDermott, its regional sales manager in King of Prussia, PA, "Our salespeople are kept fully up to date on our overall marketing plan. They're encouraged to report directly to our market research people back in Appleton, WI anything they pick up that's pertinent to the plan." Reps who spot something relevant in a trade journal or a local printing publication just phone it in to the home office. If the intelligence applies to their immediate sales situation, any required management reaction comes fast.

• **Give your people a reason to believe.** At Appleton Papers, information is fed back to the field with recommendations on how to use it. In addition, the regions exchange information regularly—multiplying the value of the data. "The best reinforcement for continued information gathering is giving the salesperson something back that leads him to some business," says McDermott. At Appleton, the process is an unbroken loop.

MAKING SALES CONTESTS WORK

· · · · ·

Defeating the competition is important, but fostering a cutthroat environment for your internal sales competitions can be self-defeating.

NO LOSERS

• **Structure contests so that every salesperson has the potential to win.** Or at least temper the internal competition. Your goal: to win more—and long-term—by nurturing all your people as carefully as gardeners nurture their bonsai trees.

• **Target a real "enemy."** When you select a contest focus, make it something like increasing market share, either overall or by a certain percentage for each salesperson. That leaves no doubt as to who your people's opponents are: your competitors. If you feel internal contests are helpful, let them be for the greatest increase in the average sale or for the lowest bad pay or return rate. "No losers" then becomes your only game.

• **Praise winners without putting down losers.** Part of the prize your winners earn is fulsome, public praise from you and upper management. Give it to them in spades. But avoid comments like, "Losers who would like to shake that tag next time around. . ." Instead, thank the nonwinners for their "contributions to a contest that made us all winners." You don't want them feeling inadequate—or, more likely, negative toward you or the company.

• **Give more than lip service to the "learning experience."** The drumrolls, applause and cheers of your awards meeting should be followed by a working session. The goal is an exchange of information among the various contestants. The winners pass on their "secrets" of technique, prospecting, promotion—whatever. The rest not only learn, but should be encouraged to offer their own most successful methods for discussion. They are not "losers," and no doubt have worthwhile ideas to add.

● **BOTTOM LINE:**
Teamwork wins more for all of you than do cutthroat games that pit your people against one another.

RECOMMENDATION:
Cultivate the same "all for one, one for all" point of view toward your credit people, advertising think tankers, those who allocate your budgeted funds and so on. It will help you build a healthy corporate climate that's supportive of the field sales effort.

HOW TO GET NEW MANAGERS OFF TO A RUNNING START
■ ■ ■ ■ ■

● **Spotlight the first entrance.**
Whether the new manager comes from within the sales ranks or from outside your company, there will be some "show me" feelings present among your sales representatives. "Our salespeople don't take too readily to change for fear of its impact on their pocketbooks," says Charles Buckley, marketing director for Intercim Corp., Minneapolis. "So a senior member of management takes the new manager out to the field and introduces the person to the salespeople on a one-to-one basis. The goal is to make them feel comfortable that the new rep can be of benefit to them."

● **Go to the firing line without delay.**
It's important to establish early on the manager's authority and ability to sell. Async, a voice messaging service in Atlanta, promotes only from within, and only top salespeople get management jobs. Thus, the new manager already has established his

or her selling credentials. But because of salespeople's almost reflexive skepticism, "We get the new person out joint-calling very early," says Bryan Morgan, director of marketing and sales development. "We want to remind the reps how good the new manager is at what they do."

● **"But he doesn't know the territory,"** the uneasy traveling salesmen in Meredith Wilson's *The Music Man* chorused of newcomer Professor Harold Hill. That's a built-in deficiency that most new managers have to overcome quickly to earn the team's confidence. A new person has to be taught by each salesperson—and sometimes by senior management, as well—who the important accounts are in the territory, what's going on with them, the prospects of future sales at each, and how much and when. "Also, the new guy on the block must establish credibility with the customers, in terms of both his knowledge of our technology and as a service-oriented supplier," says Buckley.

● **The new manager is both courier and planner.** As a courier, the new person brings to the sales reps the company's short- and long-range goals. As a planner, he works with each rep to break down those objectives into individual goals. In the process, he underlines his leadership role.

RECOMMENDATION:
Caution new managers to respect the reps' selling time during the get-acquainted period. Async takes it to the nth degree. It has a firm rule that goal-setting discussions never take place between 8:30 a.m. and 5:30 p.m. as a way of showing its salespeople that their selling time is as precious to Async as it is to them. This consideration may even lead to a fatter bottom line.

OBSERVATION:
A break-in period that is carefully planned and carried out will not have a defined end. Eventually, both reps and manager will realize that for some time now they've been on the same wavelength—with shared goals that are also company goals.

TAKE CARE WHEN TAKING TERRITORY AWAY
■ ■ ■ ■ ■

Every time you add a person to an existing territory, you're invading the incumbent's turf. Getting that person to accept the change is a delicate matter.

HOW TO GO ABOUT IT

■ **Avoid dropping bombs.** Sudden announcements of a general realignment of territories, or even a single one, will upset salespeople no matter how logical the explanation. To avoid major shocks, Ronald H. Schmoll, eastern regional manager for Schlage Electronics in Annapolis, MD, says his company gives its people time to adjust to the idea. "From the time such a change is first talked about until its implementation could take six months," he says.

■ **Make the reasons very clear and don't leave any out.** The more detailed the case you present to the affected salespeople, the more their acceptance index will rise. Open with as much documentation as you can assemble. "You can generally sit down and show them statistics that document many prospects and areas still untouched," says James E. Waldron, regional sales manager in Dallas, TX for Medical Systems Support. "In our business, I can also remind them that mostly they've just been responding to phone calls or other quick leads."

■ **Underline the common interest.** "Salespeople have no difficulty understanding that a significant growth in production in the territory earns money for salesperson and company both," says Schmoll. "And it's that much tougher for the competition."

■ **Other advantages** you can include:

• In a smaller, denser market, there is more time for in-depth selling, which improves closing ratios as well as volume. It also improves the salesperson's technique—and earnings.

• In a very large territory, potential customers who are located long distances from the salesperson's base or the company's office may find that, in itself, a strong deterrent to buying.

• Covering less geography—and consequently reducing travel time—reduces the wear and tear on body and psyche.

■ **Listen and respond to objections.** Negative input from the salesperson whose territory is affected needs to be given some weight. Generally, he or she is the person who knows best what goes on there. "In our company, the impetus for adding a salesperson often comes from the territory manager himself," says Schmoll. "If the salesperson in the territory considered a split a poor move, we'd probably cancel the plan."

■ **Provide a financial bridge.** A salesperson whose territory is cut at Medical Systems Support is usually given 60 days to close anything he's been working on in the territory being reassigned. The new rep is given 30 days to identify any shaky sales, so that should they cancel, the cancellation isn't charged to him.

FIRING A REP
· · · · ·

• **Break the news face-to-face.** However crowded your calendar, that isn't enough reason to avoid looking the person in the eye. The representative deserves to hear it in person. If you must, postpone the chore until you are free.

• **Give the process time.** If the person thinks you're coming on just another field trip, don't add to that illusion by making joint calls, even as a way of further documenting your case. The decision is made, and your trip has no other purpose.

• **Avoid procrastination.** Just from your demeanor, the representative will know something is up. As soon as you've said hello and put your briefcase down, say it. "Listen, Bob, I bring you bad news. You're not making it; so I have to let you go."

• **It's time for silence.** Add nothing at all to what you've said until after the salesperson speaks. Whether you're uncomfortable or not, treat the situation as a silent close. The person needs time to absorb the blow, and consoling words from you will not console right now.

• **If there's a storm, don't close your shutters.** Whatever comes from the person—anger, confusion, sadness, blame for a galaxy of people—let it roll. Don't argue, defend, explain or turn away until the initial reaction is spent. Then talk for as long as the person seems to need it. One point to make is that he or she is probably better off shedding the tension of a job that the person simply isn't getting done.

• **Stick to your guns.** The salesperson may maintain that given one more chance, he or she will make it. As soon as that theme becomes clear to you, tell the person that while you're willing to listen, nothing is going to change the decision. Avoid wavering, because "sympathy time" is past.

• **Come knowing company procedures.** Be sure that you can fill the person in on termination pay, the time left on life and health insurance coverage and so on.

• **Go over account information.** Review the person's customer records in as much detail as possible. But wait until after the person has had a chance to voice his or her opinion fully, calm down and ask you any questions he or she may have.

RECOMMENDATION:
Tell the representative exactly what you will say to prospective employers, so that you both will be telling the same story.

REDUCE SALES FORCE TURNOVER
· · · · ·

With the high cost of replacing salespeople who resign or are terminated—the average cost of hiring a new salesperson is $20,000—efforts to reduce turnover in the sales force can mean big savings in recruitment and training—not to mention the reduction of lost sales volume.

A recent survey by Learning International, Stamford, CT, found that the top three reasons for leaving were inadequate pay, the lack of room for advancement and personality conflicts with the boss.

HOW TO HOLD DOWN DEPARTURES

• **Find out what motivates your heavy hitters.** Your biggest concern should be the attitude of your most productive salespeople. Get a group of them together for a gripe session with top management to find out what aspects of company policy and procedures they would improve. When strong salespeople leave, use exit interviews to dig out the reasons for their dissatisfaction, so that you can develop new programs to retain remaining salespeople.

• **Look at your hiring process.** If involuntary terminations are a problem, your hiring procedures may need revision. Identify the characteristics of your best salespeople to help you specify more precise hiring requirements in terms of experience, character and willingness to work. And stick to those criteria; don't let yourself be rushed into hiring replacements to fill critical gaps in sales coverage. To avoid emergency hiring, keep an active file of promising candidates whom you can identify through referrals from your salespeople, local job fairs, responses to past employment ads and unsolicited job applications.

• **Beef up training.** Learning International's study found that turnover was much lower in companies that had sales training programs than in those that offered no training—18% vs. 34%. The probable reason: Salespeople who are fortified with adequate product knowledge and sales skills do better than those who are sent into the field without such a foundation.

Provide ample initial and refresher training in how your products work, what applications they are suitable and unsuitable for, and how they are made—along with such skills as prospecting, planning for sales calls, identifying customer needs and handling the most frequent objections.

• **Reevaluate your sales tools.** Salespeople's complaints about inadequate pay and personality conflicts are often caused by unhappiness with support from management. Compared to the cost of hiring and training a new salesperson, a small investment in additional sales tools can pay off handsomely.

SOME MOVES YOU CAN MAKE

• **Set up a task force of salespeople and sales managers** to revamp brochures, visual aids and other promotional vehicles; increase your advertising and promotional spending to generate more sales leads; and revamp your lead-handling system to better identify the best leads and hustle them out to the field while they're still "hot."

• **Compare your compensation to what similar companies offer.** Even if your pay and incentives are comparable to the rest of the industry, you might want to look for ways to increase the income of your superior salespeople. For instance, additional sales support will help them land more and bigger sales. You might also consider increasing the size of their territories.

• **Increase the opportunities for advancement.** Although many excellent salespeople have little interest in being promoted to management, the findings of the survey suggest wide dissatisfaction among sales reps with promotion chances. In addition to broadening opportunities in sales management, you might also consider salespeople for other jobs for which their sales experience makes them uniquely well qualified—including executive positions in product management, marketing planning, market research, customer relations and sales training.

O B S E R V A T I O N :
Almost three quarters (72%) of the sales managers surveyed by Learning Interna-

tional said that turnover hurt sales by disrupting relationships with customers and reducing sales force morale.

REPS' COMPLAINTS MAY BE A WARNING SIGN
. . . . .

Brushing off salespeople's complaints unexplored could be perilous to your business. You must be able to determine what's valuable and what isn't. Consider these pointers:

• *Salespeople are an early warning system.* Competitors can take you by surprise with a promotion. Or your market may not respond to the value-added features built into your price. Or a competitor's newly expanded product line may be looking better than yours to customers. Or your advertising and promotion campaign may be falling flat. Any danger to your market share is encountered first by your salespeople. While you may have to dig to sort out legitimate complaints from mere gripes, that kind of digging is essential to your ongoing success.

• *See for yourself.* "Salespeople's complaints may be overstated, but there is usually a valid reason behind them," says Walter Podkul, national sales manager for Savage Laboratories, Melville, NY. He recalls a lot of sales rep unhappiness over the company's former promotional materials. The salespeople said that they simply were not doing the job. The response of the promotion writers was, not surprisingly, "those people are just complaining" (a common reaction from support people, who often wonder why salespeople

get so much attention).

Podkul got out into the field to see for himself. He agreed very quickly that "the material needed a lot of sharpening," which it got. That undoubtedly saved a lot of sales and, perhaps, some salespeople as well.

• *Unverifiable complaints may also have a message.* Complaint calls that turn out to be unfounded can be characterized as a way for the rep to kill a Friday afternoon. However, it's frequently just a salesperson wanting contact with the boss. Affirming the representative's "Things are rough out here, you know" will often make the complaint disappear.

• *Watch the numbers.* Pay close attention when you're getting the same complaints from a number of salespeople. Also, check the source. If the alarms are coming from a major segment of your market, immediate action may be necessary.

OBSERVATION:
While it's natural to want to ignore comments that suggest that management's assessment of the market environment is not matched by the facts, letting your ego shape your response to a salesperson's complaint isn't prudent. No matter how garbled or unflattering your salespeople's messages, they're worth clearing up and evaluating.

BEWARE OF SALES STAFF OVERLOAD
. . . . .

Sometimes so many extra jobs have sneaked up on your sales staff that they may be diverted from the main task—bringing it all home. Here's a list of extras that salespeople often shoulder. If yours perform any of them that you could get done some other way—even if only in part—reassigning the responsibility would create more sales time. That could only be a plus for your people, your company—and you.

- *Service person.* The potential time cost here is almost unlimited.
- *Collector of slow pays.* A good way to get the money—but is there a better one?
- *PR person.* Might it cost less were a member of management to substitute?
- *Stock filler.* Consider training others to do this full-time, leaving salespeople to sell.
- *Inventory checker.* Often coupled with stock filler. Get the same "others" to take over here, too.
- *Trainer of new sales representatives.* Good choice—but too much of this good thing can cost sales.
- *Market researcher.* Do you still need all the data that they're spending their time acquiring?
- *Appointment maker.* Could your business support the use of full-time telereps as substitutes?
- *Sales forecaster.* Indispensable—but could a software program lighten the burden of the workload?

- *Special deliverer.* Builds goodwill—but so does overnight commercial delivery.
- *Reporter* of personal on-the-job development, calls, etc. All needed?
- *Entertainer* of customers. Traditional in your business. Still paying back?
- *Financial analyst.* If that's what your representatives must be to fill out an expense report or to figure their commissions or bonuses, can the form or the plan be simplified in some way?
- *Fixer* of customer's problems with the home office. Would customer service reps pay off?
- *Order chaser.* Where is it in the cycle? Could a software program find out?
- *Point-of-purchase display arranger.* A task that cries out for an outside service.
- *Meeting attender.* Could some be optional based on the salesperson's assessments of needs?

OBSERVATION:

It could take a lot of your time to thoroughly analyze the possibility of relieving your salespeople of some of these responsibilities. But if you suspect a payoff hiding in there somewhere, make an effort to find that time.

MANAGING
your
BUSINESS

Chapter 1

BUSINESS
STRATEGIES/TACTICS

PUT ALTERNATIVE PLANS TO FINANCIAL ANALYSIS

· · · · ·

Computer spreadsheet programs may be used to explore alternative strategies, but their capabilities are limited. You can find the better of two alternatives, but you need extra power if you want to find the best among dozens or even hundreds. Here are some powerful programs now available for PCs:

CFO Advisor lets you perform "what-if" evaluations to determine your most profitable, least expensive, or least problematic courses of action. You enter data by keyboard or by importing it from your spreadsheet or general ledger system. Then you direct *CFO Advisor* to figure out your current financial position and estimate the financial results of the alternative courses of action you are considering.

Unlike standard spreadsheet and accounting software, *CFO Advisor* will also perform such advanced spreadsheet functions as ratio analysis, cost of sales control, work-in-progress inquiry, fixed assets inquiry, raw material estimation and operating expense control.

▲ COST:

Price is $995, from Financial Feasibilities, Inc., Beverly Hills, CA; 213-278-8000 or 1-800-247-4452 in California.

MindSight, offering similar capabilities, is a less expensive package for Apple Macintosh users. The $249 program translates problem statements and data into spreadsheets, reports and graphs. From Execucom Systems Corp., Austin, TX; 1-800-531-5038 or 512-346-4980.

If you have an IBM-compatible PC and want to work with data from your company's mini- or mainframe computer, Execucom's *IFPS/Personal*, $595, may be just what you need. Like *MindSight* and *CFO Advisor*, this program offers sophisticated decision support functions that help you to analyze financial alternatives.

FRANCHISING AS A GROWTH STRATEGY

■   ■   ■   ■   ■

If your company is poised for growth, hiring people and expanding your facilities is one option. Contracting to have work done outside is another. A third option— one that combines some of the best features of both the others—is franchising.

AN INCREASINGLY POPULAR OPTION

More and more companies are going the franchise route. According to the Commerce Department:

• Franchised sales exceeded $590 billion in 1987, up 77% from 1980 sales.

• 34% of all retail sales are through franchised establishments.

• One out of seven employed people, or over 7 million, work in or own a franchise.

• There are about 500,000 franchised establishments so far.

NOT JUST FOR BIG CONSUMER-ORIENTED OPERATIONS

According to the Commerce Dept., most franchise companies are small. Two-thirds consist of 50 or fewer operating units. And business-to-business firms are very much a part of the phenomenon.

"Over 70 industries, many with no retail stores at all, are now franchising," says Philadelphia attorney Steven S. Raab, who specializes in franchise law and development. The businesses include air freight forwarding, office equipment, barter exchange, corporate investment, medical office billing, business interior design, offset printing, photographic development and employee recognition products.

IS FRANCHISING AN OPTION FOR YOU?

Manufacturers may be better off growing through manufacturers' reps than via franchising, says Raab. "People in any other type of business should consider it." Raab points to three key advantages:

• *Rapid growth.* It takes time to find new business locations, provide new equipment and facilities, hire and train people, and develop a marketing program for each new location. With franchising, you need create only one functioning operation; your franchisees take over from there.

However, the number of franchises you can expect to sell early on depends on how you go about it. Franchisors who try to get others to invest in an unproven idea may have a tough time getting any takers at all. Those who demonstrate the profitability of an operation in one or more pilot locations may have little trouble selling several within the first 12 months. The number depends, too, on whether your market is national or regional and the size of the initial investment required.

• *Relatively small capital investment.* You can franchise a company for $40,000 to $250,000, experts say. If you wanted to open up 100 locations costing $120,000 each, you'd need $12 million. But you could franchise that kind of expansion with perhaps an initial investment of $100,000, plus $60,000 for training and servicing. Your franchisees would put up the rest.

• *Limited risk of loss.* You could lose your initial investment of $160,000, but not millions. When a local unit fails, it's the franchisee who loses his or her investment, not you.

COULD CREDIT CARDS HELP YOUR FIRM SPEED COLLECTIONS?

■   ■   ■   ■   ■

Offering business customers the option of paying by credit card might help you expand your sales base by giving prospects a convenient way to pay. As a credit-card merchant, moreover, you'd get your money right away instead of having to wait 30 days or longer, as you may often do now.

GROWING USE OF CARDS BY BUSINESSES

While most buyers of business products still prefer to submit purchase orders and pay by check, a growing number readily buy a wide variety of items via credit card.

• *Not just for small-ticket items.* In recent years, banks have been extending credit limits on card accounts, especially corporate accounts; so cards are often used to finance sizable purchases. A small outfit in particular may use a charge card to buy from a larger company.

• *Drawbacks to accepting cards.* You must pay fees of 2% to 6% or more, depending on the institution and your average sale price. While you receive an immediate transfer of funds, once you submit sales records, if a card holder disputes a sale, the merchant bank is obliged by federal regulations to charge back the amount to the merchant's account.

"If it's a phone order, the customer can say he didn't place the order," says a banker. "We have no choice but to debit the merchant, and the dispute is then between the customer and the merchant." You could end up with both no money and the problem of retrieving shipped merchandise.

OBSERVATION: Chargebacks need not be a serious problem if you screen buyers before accepting orders to make sure that they are legitimate.

• *Do pluses outweigh minuses?* If the fees are greater than your billing plus collection costs (including bad debt), think twice about accepting cards. If not, they could save you money.

To gain merchant status with American Express, just inquire at its nearest office. Check with your merchant bank about handling VISA or MasterCard.

OVERCOME ROADBLOCKS TO CREDIT-CARD SELLING

Although it is fairly easy to become, say, an American Express merchant, you may encounter problems when applying for

MasterCard or VISA merchant status. Here are the key roadblocks and suggestions for overcoming them:

• *Your sales volume is too low.* Larger banks require a minimum projected credit-card sales volume of $100,000 to $500,000 per year to take you on. If you project you'll fall short of that, convince them you're growing. Or apply to a smaller bank.

• *You sell consumer goods by mail or telephone.* If the bulk of your sales are trans-acted at a location where you deal in person with buyers, you should have little problem convincing a bank to accept you as a credit-card merchant. Banks are used to dealing with storefront operations where credit cards may be inserted into processing machines. They worry, however, about fraud and clerical error when a credit card number is simply written on an order card or spoken over the phone. They also worry about excessive chargebacks, since customers who buy by mail and phone often change their minds.

Counter the bank's objections by giving them your history of bad orders and order cancellations. If the rate is low, the banker's fears may be eased. Also, if you sell primarily to businesses, say so. Banks expect problems primarily from consumer tele-marketing and mail-order operations.

• *Your company is too young.* Most banks will not take you on unless you've been in business, or had an account with them, for a specified period.

If your company is new, you can overcome the time-in-business obstacle by applying to a bank with which a key principal has a long-standing business relationship. Or turn to a smaller bank. Many require no prehistory as a bank customer. You must simply establish a merchant account before being cleared as a credit-card merchant.

IF NO BANK WILL TAKE YOU ON

All is not lost. New financial organizations are springing up specifically to handle small-volume credit-card business and mail and telephone orders. Such organizations do "back order processing" for agent banks, in effect, packaging small accounts into chunks of business that are large enough to interest the banks. So if local banks turn you down, ask them about such organizations in your area.

IS TELECOMMUTING RIGHT FOR YOUR FIRM?

■ ■ ■ ■ ■

Critical technologies that permit fast, worldwide transfer of documents and decisions are tested and working well. They include overnight air delivery, electronic data transmission, improving global telephone service, and such devices as facsimile machines, modem-equipped personal computers and cellular telephones.

Major firms such as Boeing, McGraw-Hill, Travelers Corp., and Bechtel are already exporting some of their office work. Other large firms, as well as many mid-sized and smaller companies, are expected to join the trend.

THE CRITICAL FACTORS

When considering changes involving your own office work, ask yourself the following questions:

• *Does it have to be done by our people?* Manufacturers have discovered that many components could be made more economically by subcontractors. Similarly, ask yourself which "components" of your office operations could profitably be contracted out. Your accounting? Order processing? Internal printing?

- ***Does all office work have to be done at the same location?*** Many large firms have established multiple decentralized centers for their sales, distribution, administration and back-office data processing. You can do the same.

◆ REMEMBER:

With today's communications technology, distance doesn't matter much anymore.

- ***Where can I get it done best and cheapest?*** With the new technology, you are no longer limited to your neighborhood. Your labor pool has widened to include your region, the nation and the world. Shop around for the best source at the best price, whether in Peoria or Panama.

CONSIDER NETWORKING WITH YOUR COMPETITORS
■ ■ ■ ■ ■

- Automotive parts manufacturers in Flint, MI share manufacturing and brain power in the search for new markets and customers.
- Tooling companies in Meadville, PA have set up a shared teaching factory with state-of-the-art computerized equipment used by a number of firms.
- Marketers of credit-card imprinting machines in Ohio share marketing ideas.

Such cooperative approaches reflect a trend in the U.S., one that is gaining mo-

mentum on the heels of more advanced intra-industry sharing overseas. Most often dubbed "networking," these approaches are the company equivalent of individual career networking. They include a wide range of collaboration among competitors.

COMPANY NETWORKING IN OTHER COUNTRIES

Industry cooperatives and flexible manufacturing networks are well entrenched in Germany, Italy, Sweden, Japan, Denmark and other nations. In a variety of industries ranging from machine tools to furniture, competitors help one another to a degree unthinkable in U.S. industry—until now.

Companies pool their resources to acquire a higher level of expertise and strength. Network members share common sources of market research, technical training, and business loans. Companies also join together in purchasing consortiums, joint advertising ventures and public relations co-ops, and they share credit information. In addition, the networks provide for translation services, advice on exporting and political lobbying.

Foreign networking has helped to put many American industries on the defensive. Because of intra-industry cooperation, Japan already dominates in laser-optical memory, high-definition TV and VCRs. Japan's shared research in electronics has helped drive most American memory chip makers out of the business and is making the nation a major player in supercomputers and advanced knowledge-processing equipment. Networking was also a factor in strengthening foreign textile industries to the point where America has become merely a minor player.

CHANGING AMERICAN ATTITUDES TOWARD NETWORKING

In the U.S., company networking has been discouraged by competitive attitudes and government antitrust regulations. Both are changing, thanks to the pressure of foreign competition. A legislative proposal now making its way through Congress would allow businesses with 500 employees or fewer to establish informal partnerships for joint research, manufacturing and marketing by eliminating costly antitrust restrictions.

SIGNS OF INCREASED COOPERATION

New York state is providing funds to build industrial networks in the textile and auto-supply industries, offering belated help to depressed areas. Michigan now has an agency to build a variety of industry networks. One is the Flint River Project, which sparks collaboration among smaller firms that support the auto industry.

Some universities, such as Carnegie-Mellon and Stanford, are bringing together major corporations to sponsor joint research. Each sponsor enjoys the fruits of projects that few firms could fund alone. Many trade associations are also increasing their scope. In effect, they're acting as organizers of budding networks by adding services ranging from referral databases to discount purchasing.

YOU CAN BEGIN BENEFITING IMMEDIATELY

• Refer customers to competitors when you can't meet their needs. There's a lot to be gained from scratching one another's backs. Everyone benefits, and the customer is especially well served.

• Share ideas and knowledge more freely. Don't reveal trade secrets, of course, but do share marketing and operations techniques that have produced superior results or saved you money. If the exchange is equal, both parties will benefit. And you'll both fare better in an increasingly global marketplace.

RECOMMENDATION:

If it doesn't make sense to recommend competitors, at least consider the benefits of being on friendly terms with them. An excess of competitiveness tends to isolate and weaken a company.

CAUTION

Legislation continues to bar price fixing. To stay clear of trouble, avoid pricing discussions with competitors. Note, too, that the proposed Joint Manufacturing Opportunities Act would specifically bar small-business networks that absorb more than 20% of the relevant market.

YOUR PLACE OR MINE: WHERE TO NEGOTIATE

· · · · ·

Whether you're negotiating with customers, suppliers, labor unions, job candidates or anyone else, one way to gain the advantage is to know where you're going to talk terms—at your location, your opponent's or on neutral ground.

The following suggestions evaluate the pros and cons of each type of playing field, and include pointers on how to carry the home-field advantage wherever you go.

WHICH PLACE IS BEST

■ **Your location.** On home territory, you're the boss. You control the administrative details: seating arrangements, room temperature and interruptions.

▲ I M P O R T A N T :

You can marshal almost any resource you need to clarify a negotiating point. If, for example, your opponent questions your ability to ship an order within 48 hours, you can bring your production manager, complete with records, into the meeting. You also have time on your side. Your opponent may be quicker to make certain concessions just to be sure to catch a train or plane home.

■ **The other side's turf.** Even when your opponent enjoys all the home-field advantages, you can still turn the tables in your favor:

• *Be the first to suggest meeting at your opponent's location.* The gesture can unnerve even the most unflappable adversary. To your opponent, there's only one logical reason you would relinquish the home-field advantage: You're confident about your ability to win.

• *Arrive the day before negotiations.* That will give you time to tour your opponent's facility and, if appropriate, treat the opposing team to dinner. You can then update your plan of attack, based on what you've learned about your opponent's company.

• *Blunt any delaying tactics.* If your opponent needs to "check on some facts," there's no need to halt the meeting for more than a few minutes so he or she can retrieve the information required.

• *But use the delaying tactic yourself, when necessary.* If you think you're losing ground,

you can always use the old excuse, "I'll have to check back with the office."

• *Escalate the level of the negotiation.* Ask to meet your opponent's boss if that will expedite bargaining.

• *Stay flexible on hotel and transportation arrangements.* That way, you won't be tempted to cave in just to make a flight.

■ **Neutral location.** On neutral ground, neither side has an advantage: no home-turf edge and no on-call experts or easily accessible supporting data. In addition, because of travel costs and scheduling problems, the size of both negotiating teams will be limited.

There's still a way to take a lead in the session, however. Handle the administrative details, such as location, accommodations, room setup, breaks and meals.

When the opposing team arrives, review the schedule carefully with them. Point out that you've arranged for meals to be delivered throughout the day, and even provided for a midnight snack, "just in case."

▲ I M P O R T A N T :

You're prepared to negotiate seriously, and for as long as it takes.

CAUTION

If you're making arrangements, don't resort to the old dirty trick of placing the opposing team in an uncomfortable location, such as facing the sunlight or next to heating vents. That obvious tactic will be viewed as unprofessional.

Knowing when to negotiate is as important as knowing where. If you're at your best in the morning, arrange for an early start, so you can all take a break after lunch, when most people are least productive. The day of the week can also matter. If you're meeting with out-of-towners at your location, for instance, you're more likely to reach a speedier settlement with a Friday session. It's often tougher to reschedule Friday-night flights, and few people want a weekend layover—a point to keep in mind if you agree to negotiate on your opponent's turf.

On the other hand, if you're negotiating off-site, it's best to do so on a Tuesday or Wednesday, giving you the flexibility of staying late or overnight, if necessary. The trick is to draw the session out if you know that your opponent will get antsy about catching a train or car home. You may make a bigger win than you expected.

ZERO-BASED BUDGETS: ARE THEY FOR YOU?

∎ ∎ ∎ ∎ ∎

The idea of tracing dollars spent vs. dollars produced by each discrete group in a business has indispensable merit. Zero-based budgeting (ZBB) refines it further by asking: (1) What would happen if this unit were eliminated altogether, thus reducing its budget to zero (hence the name), and also eliminating its contribution? and (2) How can the unit's task be met most cost effectively?

There is no assumption that every component of a company has some essential role to play. The process may uncover the uncomfortable fact that some units make no contribution at all, or none that is significant.

HOW IT WORKS

Every unit head must ask and answer these two questions about his or her own operation:

1. What is the result of eliminating my unit, market research, for example?

• *A possible answer:* A savings on salary and overhead of $200,000 annually, but potential losses on the failure to research planned new products of $1.5 million.

2. How will the unit's task be met in the most cost-effective way?

• *The manager's response begins with a mission statement,* for example, to research—at the lowest cost—the probabilities of success of each of the three new products planned for this year.

• *This is followed* by the manager's recommended action to implement the mission.

• *The manager also presents at least two alternate plans,* one at a higher budget and one at a lower outlay. The higher-cost plan might recommend adding four people instead of two, with a parallel net-return forecast. The downside alternative might be to contract the job to an outside firm, thus reducing overhead—and probably net income as well.

Each of the alternate plans is compared to the recommended action in the manager's presentation. The presentation as a whole is called a "decision package."

A manager whose domain includes several entities would go through the process for each one. Then, he or she would rank the decision packages in the order of their importance to the overall goal.

● M A J O R A D V A N T A G E :

It enables top management to get a better look at what staff functions are contributing, often a mystery. It also becomes possible to consider, say, the market research department's projected contribution of $3 million at an added cost of $100,000 against, say, the advertising department's $2 million contribution at an added outlay of $500,000.

Once all the decision packages have been completed, they are distributed to a ZBB committee, which is made up of all the unit managers and top management. The committee discusses the numbers in question. Top management's presence tends to keep things honest.

OBSERVATION:

The process makes it possible for you to find fat that may have been hidden and use the newly available dollars for a better return.

To find out more about zero-based budgets, you might want to touch base with your personal accountant. Any accountant who is a member of the National Association of Accounting (10 Paragon Drive, Montvale, NJ 07645; 201-573-9000) can get answers to questions about the ZBB process from the association.

TEAM WITH OTHER FIRMS FOR BUYING, INFO

• • • • •

By joining with six or 10 other firms, you might be able to negotiate substantial discounts on such items as fuel oil, company vehicles, stationery supplies, accounting and market research. But most companies go it alone when it comes to purchasing because they fear that participation in cooperative purchasing groups would get them in trouble with the antitrust laws.

Even though co-op purchasing is not banned, they fear that they might be suspected of exchanging information with a competitor and fixing prices.

TWO GOOD APPROACHES

• **Independent associations.** If competitors belong to an independent buying association, price-fixing and monopoly suspicions are held at bay. Examples of industry buying associations include the Independent Grocers Association, as well as hospital buying groups such as Arizona's Hospital Purchasing Council.
• **Getting together with noncompetitors.** Nothing in the antitrust legislation says you can't rub shoulders with representatives of other industries. You can check with your trade association to see if a buying co-op already exists for your industry. If not, investigate the interest in starting one under the association's umbrella.

FIND BID REQUESTS ONLINE

• • • • •

If you make it an everyday habit to check trade journals and the business press regularly for Requests for Proposals and Requests for Quotations (RFPs and RFQs), now there's a faster way to search. NewsNet—the Bryn Mawr, PA online service, 1-800-345-1301 or 215-527-8030—offers a method of locating them automatically. The service scans for any bid requests in the electronic editions of dozens of trade newsletters, including *Federal Grants and Contracts Weekly, American Marketplace, The Federal/Industry Watchdog, Defense Industry*

Report, Opportunities for Export, and *Communications Daily*.

● ADVANTAGES:

You save time because you no longer have to waste time by perusing each individual page, looking for any articles that might mention bid requests. You're also likely to turn up many more opportunities because you can have NewsNet scan more than 100 publications.

How the search method works: You dial up NewsNet from your modem-equipped PC and enter in a keyword search phrase. If constructed properly, the phrase will turn up only articles mentioning bid requests that relate to your industry, product or service. A firm that sells pushbrooms might enter either RFP (or RFQ) and BROOMS or—since not every article specifically mentions RFP or RFQ—CONTRACT and BROOMS.

Constructing the right phrase (neither overly general nor overly narrow) requires some experimentation. NewsNet sends an instruction booklet that gives helpful tips to its subscribers.

The cost varies according to search time. The minimum monthly charge is $15. For that, you could regularly scan a handful of publications.

OBSERVATION:

NewsNet also offers a special NewsFlash service. It is like the regular search service, except that the main difference is that you don't have to initiate each search. News-Net automatically scans new editions of publications as they become available to the service and delivers the "hits" to you when you dial up.

A COMPUTER CAN HELP YOU VALUE YOUR BUSINESS

■ ■ ■ ■ ■

Few business owners or executives know much about business valuation. Consequently, when selling, they may spoil the deal by settling for too little or asking too much. When buying, they may spend more than they can hope to recover in revenue, or they may pass up a golden opportunity because they fail to appreciate key points of value. In both cases they will need help.

DealMaker, a software program for IBM and compatible PCs and the Apple Macintosh, is an estimating tool that assists in the formatting, calculation and reporting involved in valuing any business, be it a small delicatessen or a multi-million-dollar manufacturing company.

While the software program is used mostly by professionals—CPAs, lawyers, bankers and business appraisers—it's not so complicated that business owners or potential owners who know nothing about appraising couldn't use it.

HOW TO USE IT

● You can do the preliminary valuation work, after which you can consult a professional. "It can save you a large sum of money versus paying a consultant or lawyer to teach you the basics," says Debbie Barrett, vice-president of JIAN, a California firm that distributes *DealMaker*.

If you hire someone—a CPA, a lawyer, or a business appraiser—you will nevertheless have to do a lot of the preliminary work yourself, such as digging up historical financial statements, developing figures for long-term debt and forecasting post-purchase sales. If you let *DealMaker*, rather than a human professional, "hold your hand" in the early stages, you should be able to save many hours of professional time—at $100 or more per hour.

• Do a complete appraisal yourself. This method is not normally recommended. In fact, the software's marketers explicitly suggest that its users consult a lawyer before sewing up any kind of deal. However, when the deal in question was small, many individuals have relied solely on *DealMaker* to do the job. The program offers better guidance than "guestimating" or negotiating casually over lunch.

▲ N O T E :

Professionals charge from $1,000 to hundreds of thousands of dollars for an appraisal, depending on the company's complexity and size.

HOW IT WORKS

You input financial information, such as the figures from your profit and loss statements and the values of your tangible and intangible assets. *DealMaker*, crunching the numbers, comes up with the following appraisal information:

• Asset value, including book, adjusted book and liquidation values.

• Income, including price/earnings ratio, capitalization of excess earnings and discounted future earnings.

• Market data, including the prices of recent sales of similar companies.

• Cost, including the estimated cost of replacement with appropriate adjustments made for depreciation.

Using all of these ingredients, the pro-

gram can generate an overall average value, if desired.

You can also isolate the financial impact of key negotiating points, and *DealMaker* will manage the thousands of calculations to yield an alternative bottom-line figure. The final valuation, of course, depends on the human participants; the program merely brings key considerations into play and performs the requisite calculations.

Once you are satisfied with the valuation as performed by *DealMaker*, you instruct the program to put the deal together in the form of a written prospectus. This is done automatically, in plain English, with spreadsheet printouts interspersed for support.

The developer of *DealMaker* is ValuSource, San Diego, CA; 619-483-1172.

▲ C O S T :

$590. A key distributor of the program, which offers other business planning software as well, is JIAN, Los Altos, CA; call 1-800-442-7373.

SOFTWARE CAN SPEED BUSINESS-PLAN PREP
■   ■   ■   ■   ■

Putting together a business plan can take days of research and writing. A new software package, *Business Plan Toolkit*, can cut that time significantly. Supplemented by a loose-leaf guide, it provides an organized, smooth procedure for developing a business plan along accepted lines.

HOW IT WORKS

Using questions, sample documents and electronic fill-in forms, it helps you:

- Fine-tune your goals.
- Define your market.
- Say exactly what you plan to sell.
- Explain why people will buy it.
- Include the data that financial people like to see in narrative portions of plans.
- Complete the necessary financial documents you need, including cash flow projections, financial statements and ratio analyses, sales forecasts and break-even analyses.
- Create a realistic schedule for implementing the plan.

Spreadsheet templates are included, so all you need do is key your numbers into the forms. Once you've finished, you'll be able to print out a report plus tables and graphs.

The software is compatible with most of the spreadsheet and word processing programs available on the market.

▲ C O S T :

$99.95, from Palo Alto Software, Palo Alto, CA; 1-800-336-5544; in California, 415-325-3190. It works on both Apple Macintosh and IBM-compatible PCs.

Chapter 2

BENEFIT PLANS

DEFERRED PAY PLANS GROW

· · · · ·

To avoid the complexities of federal benefits laws, companies are increasingly setting up deferred compensation plans as a way of providing for their key employees.

MANY TYPES OF PLANS

The arrangements can cover a wide variety of situations, as illustrated by some that have just been approved by the IRS in recent months:

• *Retainer into trust.* Part of the key employee's monthly retainer will be paid into a trust. He will not be taxed on the income, and the company cannot deduct the money until it is paid out when the employee leaves the company, dies or becomes disabled.

• *Pay for 18 years.* Participants who retire will receive their annual pay for 18 years. If they die, their beneficiaries will be entitled to the deferred pay.

The form, timing and contributions of the payments into a trust will be determined by the board of directors, who can also amend the trust agreement. The participants won't be taxed on the money, and the company can't take the deductions until the money comes out of the trust.

OBSERVATION:

In these and similar arrangements, there's one drawback for the participants. If the company goes bankrupt, the principal and interest in the trusts are subject to the claims of the company's general creditors.

• *A president's deferral.* A plan involving a company president would defer part of his pay until retirement or death. The money would be put into a trust that's subject to any claims of the company's general creditors.

Because creditors could take some or all of the money if the company went bankrupt, the IRS says it's not income until the president actually takes the money out.

OBSERVATION:

That's a key feature of such arrangements, which are sometimes called "rabbi trusts" because the first one was set up for a rabbi. The company can't take a deduction for contributions to the trust until the money is paid out.

The company will keep control of the money and can terminate the trust at any time. But if it does, it must pay the accrued benefits to the president.

• *Supplemental retirement plan.* A company sets up a supplemental retirement plan for employees. Using "rabbi trust" techniques, the company contracted with a bank to hold the assets and pay out the benefits under the plan.

The IRS said that transferring the money to the bank wouldn't be regarded as income to the covered employees. Again, the company can't deduct its contributions until the bank pays the beneficiaries.

YOU CAN ALSO USE SARs

A plan to use stock appreciation rights (SARs) as tax-deferred compensation has won the approval of the IRS. The SARs are based on a multiplier of the annual growth in the book value of a share of the company's stock.

Any increase is credited to employees' deferred compensation accounts and is a bookkeeping entry under the plan.

Money that's credited to the accounts is payable on an employee's retirement, death or termination of employment.

The accounts can't be transferred or assigned to other persons and, unlike "rabbi trusts," aren't subject to claims by the company's creditors.

Taxes will come due on the accounts only when the money is actually paid to participants. But if the stock rights are converted to stock at any time, the conversion will be taxable at that time.

A WAY TO DEFER TAX ON BONUSES
• • • • •

Here's an IRS-approved way for key employees to defer paying taxes on incentive bonuses:

The company pays the amount of the bonus the employees want to defer into a trust. As the employees become vested, the company credits the money to them, along with any accrued interest.

Employees can choose from a variety of investment options, but they can't take the money out until they leave the company.

The IRS says that such a trust qualifies as a grantor trust, which some people call a "rabbi trust," because:

• The assets of the trust are subject to the claims of creditors if the company becomes insolvent or goes bankrupt.

• Vesting in the money doesn't result in any "constructive receipt or economic benefit" to any of the employees.

• The money in the trust can't be deducted by the company until it is actually paid to the recipients.

■ R E S U L T :

The IRS says the employees generally don't have to declare any of that money as income until they take it out.

INCREASE HEALTH & LIFE BENEFITS TAX FREE
■ ■ ■ ■ ■

A little-known provision of the Tax Code allows employees, and even the boss, to sweeten health and life insurance benefits without adding anything to taxable income.

The device is called a voluntary employees' beneficiary association or VEBA.

E X A M P L E :

A company has a basic group term-life insurance plan. In addition, the workers' VEBA provides supplemental group coverage, paid for by the employees. The company and the VEBA want to set up separate group contracts with the same insurance carrier, to save on premiums.

THE IRS SAYS OK

The IRS said this was all right, since:
• The company's not paying for any of the VEBA's coverage.
• The insurer will set a separate rate for each contract.
• There's no cross-subsidy of premiums between basic and supplemental policies.

Assuming that the employer chooses to treat the insurance coverage as separate policies, there's no income attributable to the employees, the agency concluded.

HOW TO QUALIFY

To qualify as a VEBA and gain the complete tax exemption under Sec. 501 of the Tax Code, it must meet four standards:
• It must be an employees' organization.
• Membership must be voluntary.
• The organization must provide benefits to cover sickness, accidents, loss of life, or the like, and substantially all of its activity must be aimed at providing such benefits.
• None of the organization's earnings may go to any individual, except for the benefits paid under the plan.

The VEBA must also be controlled by its members, by trustees designated by the members or by an independent trustee, such as a bank.

'COMMON INTEREST' ALSO REQUIRED

Though VEBAs are frequently comprised of union members, that's not a specific requirement. All that's really necessary is that the members have some employment-related common interest, such as working for the same company. People working for different companies in the same line of business also share the required common bond.

Even the proprietor of a business whose employees form a VEBA can join, according to IRS regulations—so long as 90% of the VEBA's members are employees. Moreover, if the boss is an employee for employment tax purposes, he or she is also an employee for VEBA purposes.

BUILD WEALTH WITH A TARGET BENEFIT PLAN

. . . . .

A little-known pension plan that blends some of the best features of more widely used benefit plans can be a boon to owners of small businesses.

The arrangement, known as a target benefit plan, favors those who are age 45 or older, because it takes years of service into account, as well as salary level.

As in a defined benefit plan, an actuarial formula determines the annual contribution needed for each employee to reach the target retirement benefit, based on age, years to retirement and salary.

As in a defined contribution plan, the actual retirement payout may be higher or lower than the target, depending on the fund's investment performance during the period contributions are being made.

Contributions are limited to 25% of compensation, with a maximum of $30,000 per year, as in a defined contribution plan.

CONTRIBUTIONS VARY WITH AGE

The contributions will vary with age for the same pension target. That means you can credit more to an older employee's account than to a younger one's, because the older employee has less time for meeting the target.

OBSERVATION:

Given the fact that target benefit plans are intended to favor older, higher-paid employees, they will almost always be "top-heavy" under tax law.

This isn't necessarily fatal, though, since the nondiscrimination provisions of the tax law aren't all that hard to meet.

Because target benefit plans are hybrids, they have to meet the criteria for both defined benefit plans and defined contribution plans.

For a defined benefit plan, each employee has to accrue a benefit equal to at least 2% of his or her current salary for each year of service. The minimum contribution to a defined contribution plan is 3% of annual compensation.

For funding purposes, the IRS treats target benefit plans as defined contribution plans. As a practical matter, that means you have to make a contribution of at least 3% of compensation yearly, but you can set up the plan by defining the desired benefit and working backward.

PROS AND CONS

The principal advantage of these plans to the business owner is that he or she can finance the plan with a lower annual outlay and shift a higher percentage of benefits to high-paid employees than is possible with either a defined benefit plan or a defined contribution plan.

♦ DRAWBACKS:

There's a selling effort needed with employees, who may not see why the amount set aside for one employee can differ from that set aside for another, even though they're earning the same salary. Also, plan maintenance can be a significant cost, especially as the number of participants goes up.

You don't need to consult an enrolled actuary to set up a target benefit plan, as is required for a defined benefit plan. But it's wise to have one make the periodic adjustments to contribution levels needed to ensure that the target will be reached.

SPLIT-DOLLAR INSURANCE PLANS HOLD MANY BENEFITS

■ ■ ■ ■ ■

Take a new look at split-dollar life insurance plans. Amid their myriad variations there are solid benefits for both companies and key employees.

The term "split-dollar" simply means that an employer and employee split the premium on a life insurance policy. Basically, the employer pays the part that funds the investment portion, and the employee pays for the insurance protection.

Typically, the company is the beneficiary up to the amount of the money it has put into the policy, while the employee's family gets the balance.

HOW BOTH PARTIES BENEFIT

■ The company:
• Can offer the plan to a few employees and leave out others, with no IRS concerns over "discrimination."
• Eventually gets back all its money, not just a tax deduction. And usually gets back more than it put in, so the plan can be considered an investment.
• Can borrow against the growing cash values.
• Sets up the benefit easily and inexpensively—without IRS approval.
• Has a golden handcuff that binds the worker to the company.

■ The employee:
• Gets cheap maximum life protection.
• Uses corporate dollars, not all his own money.
• Can make the plan self-completing in case of disability.
• Gets death benefits that can be used to provide estate liquidity or income for the surviving family.

TAX CONSIDERATIONS

The employee must report and pay tax on the value of the insurance protection, less the premiums he or she contributed.

At his or her death, the family's portion of the insurance proceeds is income tax free. The company can't take a tax deduction on its share of the premiums, since it has a share in the cash value of the policy. But the company has no tax liability when it recovers its equity.

SOME VARIATIONS

Ask your insurance agent about some of the following variations, which can add attractive features:
• A split-dollar retirement plan, which puts living benefits into the worker's hands at retirement time.
• A rollout split-dollar, whereby a later agreement enables the company to take back its cash investment and the employee to own the plan with no further premiums.
• A double-bonus split-dollar, with the company putting in more and the employee paying little out of pocket.

OBSERVATION:

In many cases, the features don't seem very important in the first few years, but build up to very large amounts later on.

EXAMPLE:

A corporation agrees to lay out $20,000 annually for 10 years on a combined life insurance and retirement plan for a 35-year-old executive. If he dies 20 years later, his family receives a death benefit of $1,385,000. The corporation, having made a cumulative outlay of $200,000, receives a cash value of $730,500. But if the executive lives to be 75, he will receive a retirement income of $1,000,000, and the death benefit will amount to $3,845,000—as against his own cumulative outlay of only $21,775.

PRERETIREMENT PLANNING

■ ■ ■ ■ ■

Preretirement planning has become more than just a case of personally counseling retiring employees on a one-to-one basis. It's a benefit that's growing in popularity among employers of all sizes.

A basic preretirement program includes information on the employer's pension plan, health and life insurance coverage, other postretirement benefits, Social Security and Medicare payments, according to Buck Consultants, a New York City-based firm of actuaries and consultants that conducts surveys on the subject. Plans with more frills add information on savings and investment strategies, income taxes, projecting retirement income and expenses, adjusting for the impact of inflation, postretirement employment, estate planning, using professional financial advisors

and related economic matters, Buck finds.

In a survey in the summer of 1989, the consultants' firm found that although such programs were offered mostly by larger employers, a number of small businesses also offered them. "A number of the small employers that were not offering a pre-retirement planning program at the time of the survey planned to offer one in the future," Buck points out.

The programs are offered mainly to bolster employee goodwill, but they also help workers manage their benefits both before and after retirement, especially where defined contribution plans and restructured retiree health plans shift greater responsibility for financing retirement onto employees' shoulders.

Based on their survey results, Buck Consultants offer these suggestions for starting and operating a preretirement program:

■ **Make sure participants understand their employer-provided benefits,** along with Social Security benefits and the financial planning process.

■ **Transmit information and answer questions about the program via group meetings,** workshops or seminars, rather than memos or reports. Direct transmission avoids confusion and tends to build goodwill among participants. Many firms employ workbooks in conjunction with their seminars. They also include projections of benefits, taxes and savings.

OBSERVATION:

As for who should be included, four out of five of Buck's survey respondents indicated that they limit participation. For example, about 40% require a minimum age for participants of between 50 and 54 years old; another 40% had a minimum age of between 55 and 59.

Chapter 3

COST CONTROL

SPEND YOUR WAY TO COST CONTROL

■ ■ ■ ■ ■

Don't make the mistake of thinking that purchasing decisions should be left entirely in the hands of purchasing agents, production managers or financial people. You can and should have a strong influence.

TIPS FROM PURCHASING PROS

• **Frequently reconsider make-or-buy options.** Organizations get stuck in a rut. They continue making an item themselves because they've always made it. Or they continue buying it because they've always bought it. But times and economics change the bottom-line benefits.

EXAMPLE:
It used to be that ordering forms from a supplier was the only way to go. Now, with desktop publishing it may be cheaper to produce your own forms. On the other hand, with the proliferation of good, affordable research services, it often costs less to buy "take-out" research than to build your own research staff.

• **Trim costs in advance by impacting design decisions.** Your marketing people know what features your target market wants. Don't settle for the mere appearance of those features in the finished product or service. Keep close tabs on the design process to be sure unnecessary embellishments are not included—at a cost that may far outweigh their value to the customer.

"Team designing," which includes strong input from marketing, is becoming standard procedure at large organizations such as Ford and Boeing. In one instance, input from marketing and finance stopped engineers from overdesigning a cargo-handling system for a jumbo jet. The saving in purchased metal alone was $3 million on the first production run.

• **Negotiate on price.** People often hesitate to do this, but it can reduce prices by 10% or more on some items. Top purchasing agents recommend:

1. Requiring salespeople to quote price in person, since you can't talk back to a paper quote.

2. "Double-flinching"—saying "ouch" at the price and, when applicable, having your partner or boss say "ouch" too.

3. Asking for a much lower price than you expect to get, to encourage a greater concession than you might otherwise expect to be able to negotiate.

CAUTION

You are after overall value, not just the lowest price. Negotiate also on quality, delivery, service and other elements of the total package.

• **Investigate multiple suppliers as well as sole sources.** In general, competitive bids reduce costs. Quotes for products ranging from plastic components to printing services often vary by 30% or more within the same quality range — a fact well-known to marketers but often overlooked by those who get comfortable with favored sources.

It's not always best to go the multiple-source route, however. Sole sourcing can be economical if you keep your fingers on the price pulse and monitor the supplier. A sole supplier may be able to shave prices in return for your quantity order. A sole supplier also has the incentive to introduce long-term efficiencies in other areas—by investing, say, in new equipment—because it knows it can count on your business so long as it continues to meet your needs cost effectively.

OBSERVATION:

In contrast to other methods of cost control and profit enhancement, wise purchasing is cheap and risk free. With staff reductions, you cause human suffering; with price increases, you jeopardize market share; with special promotions, you incur hefty sales expenses. Wise purchasing alienates no one except poor suppliers, and it only costs good sense.

HEALTH-CARE AUDITS KEEP COSTS DOWN
· · · · · ·

With health-care costs rising between 20% and 30% annually for many employers, an audit of medical plan expenditures can be a rewarding first step in getting those costs under control. Many health-care insurers offer auditing services, as do a number of consulting firms such as Coopers & Lybrand and Tower Perrin Foster & Crosby. In addition, there are companies specializing in medical-bill audits, such as Equifax, Atlanta, GA.

ASTOUNDING ERRORS

In some cases, audits have turned up astonishing errors. In examining hospital bills for one patient, for instance, auditors found $6,000 in overcharges on a bill totaling $14,000. Another patient was billed $28,000 for services ordered but never provided, plus $26,000 for services that were not even ordered.

More often, audits turn up less dramatic mistakes that, taken together, can still add up to substantial savings.

OBSERVATION:

Auditing is most likely to pay off in situations where hospital bills are *over $3,000*, and in big cities. Mistakes are more likely to occur in urban hospitals than in suburban and rural institutions.

COMMON MISTAKES

Some of the common mistakes auditors find in medical claims:

• *Duplicate payments.* One big company was found to have 1,500 duplicate claims in a year, totaling $250,000 in overpayments.

• *Invalid bills.* Auditing will ensure that patients aren't being reimbursed for procedures specifically excluded in your insurance policy, or for inpatient operations that are supposed to be performed on an outpatient basis.

• *Uncoordinated benefits.* Auditing will check on whether other coverage is available to the employee through a spouse, and whether payments with the other carrier were coordinated correctly.

If your audit finds mistakes, you'll get the immediate benefit of recovering the overcharges. But there are other ways to gain from an audit:

• You may identify local hospitals and physicians whose charges are excessive or ones that confine patients longer than is the norm. This will tip you off to the need to educate employees on their right to question charges and to seek a second medical opinion.

• The audit may uncover recurring problems where you will be able to better realize your long-term savings by instituting better controls and procedures. For instance, several companies have instituted a policy of sharing savings with employees who catch mistakes on their hospital bills, resulting in thousands of dollars of savings annually.

RECOMMENDATION:

If you choose to go with an outside firm to audit your medical bills, you'll want to make sure that the savings are worth the expense. Ask the firm to perform a preliminary screening of hospital charges incurred over the past six to 12 months, to search for obvious mistakes. If this scrutiny uncovers significant overcharging, you can then proceed with a more in-depth audit.

SNOOP OUT HIDDEN WASTE

■   ■   ■   ■   ■

Unproductive office routines put extra demands on people, equipment, supplies and time. You can drastically cut costs and boost overall results by exposing these often-hidden practices:

• *Identify the unessential.* Look for the value that each task adds to the prime work of the office; you may discover that some may be needless. One manager, for instance, found that employees who worked late had to fill out time-consuming expense reports every time they bought themselves dinner. She got top management to agree to pay expenses under $50 out of petty cash, thereby reducing expense-voucher volume by 14%.

• *Streamline.* Break major work processes into steps and diagram their work-flow pattern. Then look for ways to simplify. At one company, managers found 198 steps in the monthly billing routine. After diagramming, they boiled these down to 14.

• *Eliminate "assembly-line" tasks.* In one insurance office, every customer problem was handled by three or four people. When the manager let representatives handle problems from start to finish, productivity soared.

• *Look for uneven workloads.* Often, employees who complain the least get the most work. Instead of bogging down your best workers, keep a log of assignments, showing who has been given what jobs and when the work was started and completed.

• *Put deadlines on everything.* Get into the habit of setting a completion time for each assignment you hand out. Otherwise, the old axiom known as Parkinson's Law sets in: "Work expands to fill the time available for it."

• *Watch for false thrift.* One research manager prided himself on keeping the department's support staff as thin as possible. But the lack of clerical help forced technicians to type their own reports. He overlooked the cost of highly paid "typists" doing routine work.

OBSERVATION:

If your office is typical, 20%–30% of the tasks handled by senior workers could be done by less experienced, less highly paid employees.

AUDIT YOUR ACCOUNTS PAYABLE
· · · · ·

Vendor mistakes—honest or otherwise—are inevitable. So if your accountants or purchasing people aren't looking for them diligently, the savings you've negotiated with vendors up front may be lost at the back end.

Scrutinizing all your bills would probably be too costly or impractical. But you can have your staff or an outside accounting firm do this on an occasional basis. They don't have to look at every invoice in detail; they can simply sample a small portion and, if they find significant errors in, say, 15% of them, that's a clue that a more complete inspection is required.

COMMON GROUNDS FOR ERROR

There are a number of various billing mistakes that seem to crop up again and again, no matter how hard the vendors try to eliminate them. Have your accountants look carefully at all invoices involving the following:

• *Service contracts.* Whether you're using legal or janitorial services, make sure that your bills accurately reflect the correct hourly rates, whether the work described was actually done and whether the service's people worked the amount of time reported. Verify, too, that the work done was authorized by responsible employees on your staff.

• *Cost-plus contracts.* Include in your contracts the right to audit charges for labor, etc. Exercise that right annually.

• *Automatic payments.* If you've arranged with certain vendors to send monthly bills directly to your bank for immediate payment, this can be a money-saving arrangement for both buyer and seller. Just make sure that your accounting or purchasing staff sees a copy of the bill your bank receives, and that it doesn't include excessive charges or double billing.

• *Blanket orders.* Establishing an open order for certain recurring supplies is a good way to save money. Where you have this arrangement already in operation, however, be sure that you're being charged for the correct items at the right price. Check vendors' price sheets or catalogs regularly to verify prices.

• *Data processing.* If you're using outside computer bureaus to service branch offices, don't assume that charges are correct. If a service bureau contracts to supply your company's remote offices with sales leads, for example, send each branch manager a copy of the invoice. Ask him or her to check that the manager is getting what you're paying for.

• *Shipping and receiving.* Some trucking firms bill both the shipper *and* the receiving firm. Check with your customers and suppliers to make sure that you're not being double billed for the same services. In addition, call truckers to verify rates, and be sure that weights and other particulars on your bills are correct.

RECOMMENDATION:

Although the buyer is normally responsible for auditing bills, there's a way to cut down on errors by reversing the charges for audits. Before signing a contract, get each vendor to agree to pay for a complete audit if your spot-check of the vendor's bills finds that 10%–15% are in error.

NEGOTIATE FOR PROVISIONS TO REDUCE COSTS
■ ■ ■ ■ ■

When you're looking for ways to reduce the costs of equipment and supplies used by your business, don't concentrate solely on finding the best price—you can often bargain for other concessions that reduce your overall expense for holding these goods. Even when price reductions are hard to get, sellers may agree to other money-saving terms.

NEGOTIATING WITH YOUR VENDORS

■ **Can they help cut paperwork?** Vendors can let you order by phone, facsimile machine or computer—reducing the requirement of making out multiple order forms for each shipment. They might also agree to bill you monthly, instead of with each delivery, to further simplify your accounting routine.

• Another way to save your accounting department some time: Get vendors to adopt simplified invoices. A number of buying companies, tired of trying to figure out mysterious billing codes, are demanding invoices that are easier to read. This enables accounting staff to verify quantity and price easily and to reconcile information with shipping documents.

• To cut down on vendors' mistakes in billing, some companies negotiate agreements whereby vendors agree to pay the buyers' costs of auditing bills, if the buyer is erroneously charged more than 10% of the invoice's dollar value. At the very least, any vendor should agree in writing to make prompt reimbursement when you find an error in billing.

■ **Can they reduce your holding costs?** Once you receive the goods, you begin to run up expenses for storing, moving, securing and insuring them. Ask vendors to help you cut these costs by:

• Holding the inventory for you in warehouses until needed.

• Making packaging easier to handle or to open. For instance, if you routinely break a bulk shipment down into drums or other packages, a vendor might agree to start shipping them in more convenient containers, saving you labor costs.

• Delivering materials close to where they're actually needed—supply areas or assembly lines—rather than leaving them at your receiving dock.

• Disposing of empty shipping containers. See if the vendor will pick up and recycle its packaging.

• Accepting trade-ins on your used equipment.

■ **Can they improve technical support?** For instance, some vendors will furnish customers with special equipment essential for handling or testing their products. And if asked, they'll often provide free or low-cost training to your employees in correctly using the product so as to reduce waste and repairs, improve product quality and so on.

In addition, look into each vendor's ability to provide you with useful reports on product usage. Chances are, you are paying your own employees to count and record each vendor's materials and supplies. The vendor's employees can compile regular reports on back orders, inventory counts and so on, relieving your staff of this time-consuming work.

SAVE ON ENERGY COSTS
■ ■ ■ ■ ■

Although energy conservation is no longer the concern it was a decade ago, it can still represent an opportunity for cost reduction, precisely because companies seldom look for savings in this area.

STEPS TO TAKE

Even if your business is not energy intensive, these moves may be worthwhile:

• *Authorize an energy audit.* Have an industrial engineer or energy consultant identify and measure energy consumption for each key operation: office, plant, processes, equipment and so on. This helps you to focus conservation efforts on areas where potential savings are greatest.

• *Look at the ROI.* Before investing capital in a proposed energy-savings project, evaluate the potential return on your investment (ROI). Compare the cost of funding the project to the potential payback of other possible undertakings, which the company may need to engage in to stay competitive.

• *Shoot for double benefits.* Some energy-reducing moves may not pay back their cost for five years or more—and are hardly worth the money or trouble. But when comparing different energy-saving proposals, don't overlook advantages, other than cost, that can swing your decision in favor of a scheme.

There may be *safety* improvements, for instance, in replacing older machinery with equipment requiring less energy. Or the replacements may be justifiable because of reduced downtime or other improvements in efficiency.

DON'T OVERLOOK THE OBVIOUS

Even if your company has made significant strides in reducing energy consumption, there are probably still some moves open to you that would require little time to implement and give you a relatively high payback on a small investment. The following provide some examples:

• Painting walls a lighter color to reduce lighting requirements.

• Fixing any leaks in your steam and water systems.

• Installing time clocks on water heaters, outdoor lighting and other fixtures.

• Monitoring the fuel use in company vehicles.

• Cleaning dirty walls, ceilings and other reflective surfaces.

• Installing solar-window film on south and west windows.

• Ordering the inspection and repair of broken windows—and weatherstripping and insulation for water heaters, boilers, pipes and air ducts.

A CHECKLIST TO TRACK QUALITY COSTS

▪   ▪   ▪   ▪   ▪

If you find that you've been falling short of your company's goal to improve its products, here's a possible cure: a checklist of all the costs of making—and trying to avoid making—faulty products. To give the checklist real punch, have your cost accountants compute all these outlays as closely as they can. Then post the list where everyone can see it. It could open a lot of eyes, including yours.

PREVENTION COSTS

These are largely unavoidable, but they reduce most other quality-control costs. They include:

• Administration of quality control.

• Product-design review.

• Quality engineering.

• Production or process controls.

• Supplier education and evaluation.

• Employee training.

• Equipment, personnel and space for testing products.

• Preventive maintenance of production equipment.

• Review and improvement of all specifications.

APPRAISAL COSTS

You may want to send this part of your list to all of your firm's suppliers, because their inconsistency in providing perfect goods creates a number of your product-appraisal costs, including:

• Testing incoming shipments, which covers equipment, supplies and plant space used, as well as products damaged during testing.

• Outside testing.

• Visiting or meeting with suppliers.

• In-production inspection of outside components and parts.

• Record keeping of all of your supplier's performance.

• Evaluation of new production materials or components.

• Machine operators' self-inspection routines.

• Packing and shipping defective parts back to the supplier.

• Safety stock carried in anticipation of defects.

• Production delays because of bad parts or materials.

FAILURE COSTS

These expenses can occur before or after shipment:
• Product value lost through scrap, rework or repair.
• The reduced value of defective products sold "as is."
• Taking back defective shipments.
• Replacing defective shipments.
• Field repairs under warranty.
• Overhead costs for field maintenance operation.
• Complaint processing.
• Product liability insurance.
• Efforts by salespeople or others to restore goodwill with dissatisfied customers.
• Sales lost due to defective or malfunctioning products.

OBSERVATION:

Although the cost of lost sales can be tough to judge, surveys of customers and former customers can give you a handle on this. This cost alone can equal or exceed all other quality costs. It is one reason why many manufacturers are keeping their defective shipments as close to zero as possible.

RECOMMENDATION:

Reward those suppliers who help keep your quality costs low by giving them exclusive contracts or vendor-of-the-year awards. Be sure to enforce your standards by charging all vendors for shipping and handling for returns, billing them for scrap or rework caused by their defects—and by complaining as often as necessary to prevent any further problems.

GET THE RIGHT COPIER FOR YOUR BUSINESS

If your company is looking for a new copying machine, it has a lot of options to choose from these days. Knowing what the choices are and which ones are right for your business will help you get the best buy and produce the best results.

WHAT TO CONSIDER BEFORE BUYING

■ **Evaluate your future needs.** Even if you're leasing copying equipment, make sure your machine will fit your requirements for a while, so you won't have to make the purchasing decision all over again a year down the road. If you're buying rather than leasing the equipment, project your requirements for up to three years, which is the average lifetime of a copying machine when put through heavy use. Start by having your current rate of use calculated, which can be obtained simply by noting the copier's counter reading at the beginning and end of each month.

■ **Identify any special requirements.** Today's copiers have a variety of capabilities, and the options you choose will have an impact on your cost. The following are a sample of what's currently available in the market:
• Machines in the $2,000 range generally produce about a dozen copies per minute. A few have more than basic features, although some offer color highlighting (enabling you to add one color to a document) and sheet bypass (allowing users to hand-feed paper).

• For about $5,000 to $7,000, you can get 30–50 copies per minute. Some machines in this range offer editing (enabling you to mask or move elements on a page), automatic duplexing (copying on both sides of a sheet), collating, automatic feeding and the ability to erase punch-hole images, plus other convenient features.

• For $15,000 and up, you can get machines that produce one copy per second, or even faster, along with high uptime (the time that the machine is in condition to be used), excellent resolution, diagnostics (alerting operators to specific malfunctions), automatic insertion of preprinted cover sheets, automatic selection of correct paper size and other fancy features to improve the quality of your work output.

■ **Ask individual departments in your company what features they would need in a copier,** such as high-quality reproduction for artwork, color, reduction or enlargement capability, the ability to use special stock and so on. Get estimates of the frequency or volume of these requirements, so you can determine whether you'll want to acquire a copier with these capabilities, or simply send the occasional special job out to a copying service center.

■ **Calculate total costs.** Ask around at different dealers for the average cost of maintenance, supplies (paper, toner, drums, developer, rollers and so on) and service. As a rule of thumb, these generally add up to between 60% to 70% of the copier's cost annually. Factor in any financing charges you think will be needed; then total up all projected costs and divide the total by your expected annual volume, to get your estimated total cost per copy. Use this data to help you shop for machines in your price range, being sure to compare machines with similar features.

OLDER COMPUTERS STILL HAVE VALUE
· · · · ·

As long as they still run reliably and are compatible with your newer equipment, older computers can still have considerable utility value. In fact, many companies have gained a faster payback on costly high-tech computers by using older machines to serve as a temporary backup.

RECOMMENDATION:
If you are introducing a whole new computer system, hedge your bets by using the old machines during the break-in period. New systems are often troubled with bugs that prevent them from becoming fully operational for months. Having the old machines as backup can be a lifesaver if, for example, your first attempt to run a billing program on the new system bogs down.

HOW TO USE OLDER EQUIPMENT

Relatively slow machines can still perform serviceable functions. Some businesses operate them after regular work hours to compile management reports, do payroll or run off mailing labels. By taking over duties that don't have to be done rapidly, they allow you to reserve the capacity of new machines for rapid processing of more vital information.

• *Assign them utility functions.* To save money when buying a new system, ask your computer experts to integrate old machines into the new as much as is practical. It's possible to assign useful duties to otherwise obsolete machines, such as running printers or providing additional file storage. This can eliminate the need to buy a disk drive for each new computer and gives computer work stations a greater memory capability.

• *Open up computer access throughout the organization.* You can give a morale boost to secretaries or clerical workers who have not had access to computers by passing along your old machines to them for word-processing duties. Or send the machines to field offices to make them available for salespeople for paperwork or to give them access to the company's customer database.

• *Reserve them for infrequent applications.* Rather than tie up computer memory with special programs that are needed only occasionally, such as graphics software for slide presentations, install the software on old machines so that managers can use it as needed.

• *Sell or give them to employees.* If the trade-in value of your old system is low, it may still be seen as highly valuable in the eyes of employees. You're likely to find that some advanced computer users want a second machine for home use, while employees who are parents would jump eagerly at a chance to give their children access to a machine they could afford.

• *Give them to charity.* Rather than having to search for a buyer for outmoded equipment, this approach gives you the satisfaction of knowing that the machines are being put to good use. And you can get a modest tax write-off for what you give away, if it still has residual value. Check with your local unit of the United Way or the Better Business Bureau for help in finding organizations that can take the machines off your hands.

RECOMMENDATION:
When you pass on older equipment to other departments, some employees may complain about their hand-me-down status. You can avoid this problem by increasing the capacity of older machines with expanded memory cards or hard-disk drives.

HEDGE TO BEAT RISING PRICES
• • • • •

Want to ensure today's prices for tomorrow's key materials? Try hedging.

Hedging is a common practice in the baking industry, where it can be difficult to predict the future prices of wheat. Because they may contract months ahead of time to deliver bread and other goods at a set price, many bakeries buy wheat futures on the commodity markets. Thus, if wheat prices go up three months from now, the wheat contract they've purchased today prevents them from losing a lot of dough three months from now.

Even though your business may not purchase commodities, there may be ways to apply the hedging tactic to your purchasing decisions, to dodge fast-rising prices.

CONSIDER THE TACTIC WHEN. . .

• You anticipate increasing prices due to expected shortages caused by supplier labor difficulties, unreliable foreign sources or other problems.

• You often purchase goods that have recently shown a good deal of price volatility.

• The economy undergoes a period of high inflation, as it did in the late 1970s.

HOW-TOS

Strategic use of hedging can give your company an important cost edge over competitors if prices for major supplies start climbing quickly.

• *Build up inventories.* Although this advice goes against the grain of today's trend to keep inventories slim, don't hesitate to stockpile key supplies where you expect price increases of *10% or more within a year.*

OBSERVATION:

When you consider stockpiling, evaluate all the perils involved, including the costs of financing, handling and holding the inventory; the possibility of loss through theft or damage; and the possibility that the goods will become obsolete.

• *Have the supplier hold the inventory for you.* You can do this by placing a deposit on the goods to contract for future delivery at today's price. Make as small a deposit as you can, in case you can't use all the goods.

• *Stockpile the raw materials yourself.* This can be a useful tactic when you depend on small suppliers that can't easily squirrel away large quantities of supplies because of their limited financial resources. If you have surplus cash, you might accumulate the materials against future price increases, reserving them for your own use.

EXAMPLE:

If you expect a big surge in the cost of the paper that a local printer uses to produce your company's catalogs, you might stockpile several months' supply of the paper. Later, when prices surge, you can sell it to the printer at cost, preserving the price you pay for the catalogs.

• *Buy the company.* Acquiring the vendor company can be a sound tactic for materials and products that you depend on. If you're in the market for an acquisition, this is an option to consider. You have to decide, however, whether you want to get into another line of business. If so, ask your purchasing manager to nominate some likely acquisition targets among the suppliers he or she deals with.

SMART BUSINESS TRAVELERS SAVE COMPANIES MONEY

■ ■ ■ ■ ■

Are your employees smart business travelers? There's one way to find out. Have them answer a sampling of the 24 questions that 1,000 other Americans responded to in a survey sponsored by Omni Hotels:

	True	False
1. Travel agents charge consumers for booking reservations for them.	☐	☐
2. On weekends, hotels offer the same rooms at much lower rates.	☐	☐
3. A "direct" airline flight is the same as a "nonstop" flight.	☐	☐
4. The per-mile cost of driving is cheaper than flying.	☐	☐
5. A hotel can charge guests for their rooms if they fail to call and cancel their reservations.	☐	☐
6. The term "European plan" means meals are included in the hotel-room rate.	☐	☐

The answers to the questions are: 1. False; 2. True; 3. False; 4. False; 5. True; and 6. False

HOW DID YOUR PEOPLE DO?

If the answer is poorly, don't feel bad. In terms of the overall test, six out of 10 of the original respondents answered fewer than half the questions correctly.

COST-SAVING TIPS

Here are some cost-saver tips to share with your people:

• Most hotels offer the same rooms at lower prices on the weekends due to lack of occupancy. If an early morning meeting at the destination location with a stay-over the night before is the plan, scheduling it for Monday morning would allow your company to take advantage of the hotel's lower Sunday-night rate.

• A "direct" flight is cheaper than a "nonstop," but it makes stops en route. To get the best value, you'll have to weigh cost, time en route and possible sleep disruptions when early and late-night flights are part of the package, against the time and energy available for productive work.

• For those who think driving is cheaper than flying, think again. It costs about 23 cents per mile to drive, compared with 11 cents per mile to fly.

• Despite the fact that eight out of 10 polled thought the European Plan included meals in the room rate, the American Plan is the one you should choose to get meals included in the room rate.

Chapter 4

CREDIT & COLLECTIONS

TIPS FOR IMPROVING CASH FLOW

. . . . .

Don't let banks and customers sit on cash your firm could put to good use. The time to free up cash is when you have ample time to look for pockets of idle money, not when creditors are pushing you to pay bills and customers are slowing down their payments to you.

SEARCH FOR IDLE INTERNAL FUNDS

• Look into the use of multiple lockbox locations to speed up the receipt of funds. One recent development: lockbox networks, through which one bank offers several cities for collecting large payments.

• If your business has expanded or grown substantially in recent years, consider putting your banking business out for bids again, renegotiating fees and services received in return for consolidating your accounts in a few banks.

• If you are keeping a high compensating balance to pay for bank services, such as lockboxes, find out if you can pay the bank for its services by flat fees instead. This can save you money by allowing you to reinvest the freed funds in other vehicles.

• If you normally transfer excess funds from financial institution accounts to money-market accounts, ask your bank whether it can do this for you automatically.

• Look for a lockbox bank that can communicate computer-to-computer overnight, so you have up-to-date accounts receivable information each morning.

• Don't use modern electronic systems, such as wire transfers, to pay vendors.

Paying by mail gives you better floats.

• Offer direct deposit for your employees' payroll checks. This will save you administrative costs, even if it doesn't increase your float on these funds.

• Mail payments to vendors at the end of each work week, rather than on a daily basis, to gain additional float.

TIGHTEN UP

• Stop providing cash advances; give credit cards to traveling employees.

• Make sure your customer-credit terms are no more generous than necessary. If competitors are charging interest on overdue balances, for instance, there's no reason you shouldn't (although you may well find that you can't enforce payment).

• Get your invoices out faster. Set up your billing system so invoices are sent on the same day as shipment of goods or delivery of services.

• Stick to your credit terms. If, for instance, you have customers taking unearned discounts, start to bill them.

• Slash inventories by removing or reducing the number of low-profit or slow-moving items.

• Start turning overdue accounts over to your collection agency sooner. If you normally wait 90 days or more, for instance, cut this to 60.

TAKE A GOOD LOOK AT YOUR RECEIVABLES

· · · · ·

Whether your business is slowing or improving, a spot-check of credit limits and billing procedures may cut payment delays and free up some needed capital.

STEPS TO CONSIDER

• **Bring credit limits up to date.** Have credit and sales managers review customer account balances to see which might be good for higher credit margins. Then identify these good customers for salespeople, so that they can pursue more business from them.

• **Prune marginal accounts.** Whether business is improving or slumping, it's probably time to prune accounts with slim profit margins that you've been carrying too long. Chronic slow payers and small-order buyers add carrying and collections costs you don't need.

• **Accelerate billing.** Errors by your shipping and billing departments will slow down receipt of payments. Your invoicing routine may be able to improve its use of computers or to modify clerical procedures—by double-checking paperwork, for instance—to boost cash flow.

• **Improve information on collections.** Monthly aging reports, which give you a reading on outstanding receivables, may be refined for faster credit and collections decisions. For instance, most aging reports lump unpaid accounts under "0–30 days," "31–60 days," and so on. Instead, have reports issued every 14 days, and modify them to include a column reporting receivables that are unpaid only two weeks after billing.

This will let accounts receivable personnel monitor early increases or decreases in the number of unpaid accounts. Adverse changes can alert them to a need to follow up sooner and identify internal problems, such as shipping delays, that may be contributing to payment slowdowns.

• **Check major accounts frequently.** Get timely warnings of possible impending problems with your largest accounts by reviewing their credit ratings at least quarterly. These customers are important, but are also where your most serious bad-debt losses may occur. If you think you need to double-check normal credit sources, ask your banker to verify a customer's credit standing with the financial institution handling the customer's account.

• **Ask accounting and sales to be alert for problems.** Accounting should monitor all accounts closely for any signs of adverse changes, including customers who suddenly stop taking advantages of discounts for early payment or who have slowed payments over a long period.

Sales reps and managers can spot major signals of financial weakness, such as frequent turnover among financial people; increased requests for delays of shipments; excessive complaints (possibly an excuse to delay payments or frequent returns of goods); or frequent switching among different suppliers.

COUNTER DELAYING TACTICS

■ ■ ■ ■ ■

Here are some customer tactics for slowing down payments, along with ways to parry them:

DRAWING CHECKS ON REMOTE BANKS

To maximize the bank and mail "float" on checks made out to your firm, some customers may set up accounts in several widely scattered banks—often where there's no Federal Reserve Bank or process-

ing center. Then they'll disburse payments from the bank farthest from you.

◆ A D V I C E :

Reverse the tactics. Set up lock boxes in the same areas as remote customer banks. Have customers mail checks to the specified post offices for daily pickup by a local bank.

STAMPING POSTMARKS PREMATURELY

To delay payment and still qualify for cash discounts, some customers may run envelopes containing checks through their postage meters, then hold them up for a few days before mailing. If you object, they'll blame the post office.

◆ A D V I C E :

Tie discounts to the date you *receive* payment; if the customer protests, advise the account to talk with the post office.

QUESTIONING THE INVOICE

If a customer often waits until an invoice is due to claim it's been lost, to challenge charges or to ask for proof of delivery, it may be trying to drag out payments.

◆ A D V I C E :

If you suspect delaying tactics are making an account marginally profitable, it may be time to reduce its credit line or put it on a C.O.D. basis until matters improve.

R E C O M M E N D A T I O N :

The root of payment problems may not be under the control of your credit, collection or sales departments. If they stem from billing delays or customer complaints, for instance, the responsibility may lie with the production department, scheduling or shipping. Make sure that all departments understand that payment delays are their problem, not just accounting's. A payment holdup of even one day hurts your cash flow.

CHECK YOUR
CREDIT POLICIES
■ ■ ■ ■ ■

Adopt these basic standards:
• Do extensive credit reference checks before granting credit. This will help you to avoid losing money through scams, as well as to deadbeats.
• Whatever your terms for credit are, make them clear to the customer at the outset. If terms are net 30 days, calling on the thirty-first day makes it clear that you expect the terms of agreement to be kept.
• If bills are unpaid after 30 days, follow the tips on page 119. There should be no exceptions, including friends and relatives.

DANGER SIGNALS

In considering whether to grant credit, check these signals:
• A customer that has pledged its accounts receivables or other assets to a bank.
• A company that other suppliers have sued for collection or have payment claims against.
• Refusal by a potential customer to share its financial information—a possible sign that it has something to hide.
• A history of slow payments and a pat-tern of excuses, including the old standby, "The check is in the mail." You may find this out by talking to other firms with which the potential customer has done business.
• The downgrading of a firm's credit rating.
• A company that has gone through a frequent change of banks.

BE ALERT
TO POSSIBLE SCAMS

Here are some danger signs to watch for:
• Orders from new firms whose names are similar to those of reputable companies.
• Trade show orders when credit checks may be rushed or difficult to carry out.
• Rush orders from new customers.
• Unsolicited orders, especially from parties that seem unrelated to your business. Scams involving unsolicited orders generally involve a party reselling your product after neglecting to pay you.

BOOST CASH FLOW
WITHOUT A
COLLECTION AGENCY
■ ■ ■ ■ ■

There's more pressure than in the past on credit managers to keep delinquent accounts to a minimum and to classify them as delinquent after 60 days, rather than the traditional 90 days. Some firms now list accounts as delinquent after only 30 days to keep their cash flow strong.

LOOK INSIDE FIRST

Failure to identify early legitimate customer billing disputes account for a large number of uncollected debts. Often, the customer has been wrongfully billed and the company is at fault.

■ RESULT:

You lose the customer and the money that is owed to you.

• *Send monthly billing statements to customers.* Many small firms have no formal collection policy. Some fail to bill customers until they are 90 days in arrears.

• *Call before an account is 60 days overdue and ask for payment.* Be sure that your credit department staff is trained in correct telephone etiquette. You want your rep to present a friendly, low-key persona when calling customers.

WHEN THE CUSTOMER DOESN'T RESPOND

• **Follow phone calls with letters.** If the account is 60 days overdue and you've made several phone calls, send out a series of three dunning letters. The first letter should read: "We know you must have overlooked the bill, but we would appreciate your taking care of this at your earliest convenience." The second letter: "You are placing your credit in jeopardy by ignoring our requests to you." The third letter: "You must pay within the next seven days or we will regretfully be forced to turn your account over to an outside collection agency, which could result in costly legal fees and a mark against your credit."

SET A 90-DAY LIMIT

Don't wait any longer than 90 days to turn over your delinquent accounts to an outside collection agency. The "hit" rate, or the rate of successful collection of debt payment, is 80%–90%, if accounts are turned over to commercial collection agencies within those 90 days.

HOW TO DEAL WITH A TROUBLED FIRM
■ ■ ■ ■ ■

It is possible that one or more of the vendors, suppliers or customers on which your growing business depends may file for bankruptcy protection someday. Although many businesses that file are hopelessly insolvent and cannot continue to operate under the weight of staggering debt, a company need not be insolvent to file for bankruptcy. For example, a company faced with many ongoing lawsuits and a chance of significant future liability might file for bankruptcy to cut its legal bills and force the consolidation of thousands of lawsuits into one court.

TWO TYPES OF BANKRUPTCY

If you're forced to deal with a bankrupt firm, chances are it will involve either Chapters 7 or 11 of the Bankruptcy Code.

In a Chapter 7 bankruptcy, the business debtor goes out of business and a Chapter 7 trustee is appointed to liquidate the business by collecting and selling the debtor's assets and distributing the sales proceeds to the creditors.

In a Chapter 11 bankruptcy, the debtor usually continues to operate its business under Bankruptcy Court supervision while it attempts to negotiate a plan of reorganization with its creditors.

WHAT YOU CAN DO

Follow these tips when dealing with a bankrupt firm:

• *Don't violate the automatic stay.* Immediately upon the filing of the bankruptcy, an automatic stay goes into effect. This is equivalent to a court order and prohibits all acts to enforce or collect debts owed by the debtor. As a result of the stay, you, as a creditor, may not call the debtor and harass the troubled firm for payment.

OBSERVATION:

A Bankruptcy Court may impose severe penalties against a creditor for violation of the automatic stay, including damages, attorneys' fees and, in the case of willful violation, punitive sanctions.

• *Become a secured creditor.* You'll be at the top of the bankruptcy pecking order. Secured creditors are paid before general unsecured creditors, unsecured priority claimants, unsecured taxing authorities and even the debtor's bankruptcy attorneys.

Any company that sells goods to others can usually take a security interest in the goods sold by including security agreement language in its sales contract. You should make sure that you have this security interest arrangement upon the very first news that a company you are dealing with is experiencing financial trouble.

• *Exercise your right to reclaim property.* If your company sells goods to others, you should be aware of the right to reclaim or repossess goods sold on credit.

To reclaim goods successfully, you must be extremely fast. The Uniform Commercial Code provides that a seller can reclaim goods from an insolvent buyer if the seller demands that the goods be returned within 10 days after the buyer receives them. The Bankruptcy Code generally recognizes this right to reclaim goods even after the filing of the bankruptcy case. But it permits the Bankruptcy Court to deny reclamation under certain circumstances.

• *Put troubled companies on cash-on-delivery terms.* When your company recognizes that a customer is having trouble making payments, it is often wise to place the customer on C.O.D. terms, rather than allow accounts receivable to accumulate.

A less dramatic step might be to require either a substantial partial payment upon delivery or a substantial up-front deposit.

• *File a proof of claim.* If all else fails and your company finds itself holding a claim against another company in bankruptcy, your company must file a proof of claim in order to be assured of any chance of payment. The proof of claim is a relatively straightforward, one-page form available from your attorney or from the Bankruptcy Court. You must fill out the claim completely and attach copies of all supporting documents. The most important step is to file it promptly.

WATCH YOUR TIMING

In Chapter 11 reorganization cases, there is no general deadline for filing proofs of claim; Bankruptcy Court establishes the date. In Chapter 7 liquidation cases, however, all proofs of claim must be filed within 90 days after the date first set for the general meeting of creditors.

CAUTION

Failure to submit a proof of claim on time may prevent your company from being allowed to vote on a plan of reorganization. It could even keep your company from receiving any payment on it.

• *Keep in mind that bankruptcy no longer means losing the right to use technology.* In general, most technology licenses are treated as executory contracts under the Bankruptcy Code. Executory contracts are agreements in which both sides have significant ongoing obligations, such as obligations to pay royalties or obligations to provide updates for consultant services.

Under the current Bankruptcy Code, if your company uses technology licensed under an executory license from a company that files for bankruptcy, it retains its right to use the license technology.

USE CREDIT INSTEAD OF CASH TO FINANCE YOUR BUSINESS

▪ ▪ ▪ ▪ ▪

Traditional wisdom contends that (1) a healthy business ought to have a certain amount of cash assets available in reserve, and (2) when borrowing money, borrow at the lowest possible interest rates.

"Ostensibly, that's like good business," says Steven D. Ettridge, CEO of Temps & Co., a temporary staffing service in the Washington, DC area. "But that isn't a complete picture. Take a closer look, and you might find a less expensive way to finance your business."

On a day-to-day basis, there are few differences between having "real" cash in the bank and having an available line of credit tied to a checking Zero Balance Account (ZBA), in which you make deposits to pay down the line of credit. A check drawn on a line of credit pays the bill every bit as well as one that's drawn on cash. Your vendors or employees don't know or care about the source of your money, says Ettridge.

"Cash is only a concept," he adds. "Real cash is no different from the right line of credit."

THE FIRST STEP TO TAKE

Before you borrow, decide how much money you need to run the company. For the sake of example, Ettridge has determined that he needs $2 million to run his company. Since you're planning for future emergencies, keep in mind that you probably won't use the total sum; part of it will be held in reserve for unforeseen business circumstances.

Once you've determined the amount you need, should you obtain a loan or a line of credit? "Traditional wisdom says it's best to borrow at the lowest interest rate," says Ettridge. "Counterintuitive thinking says that it's better to have a ZBA with a line of credit that costs a point or two over the prime rate than it is to have a large-term loan at the prime rate."

THINK DOLLARS, NOT INTEREST RATES

People commonly make the mistake of thinking in terms of interest rates instead of absolute dollars, Ettridge says. Say you borrow a fixed sum of $2 million at 10% interest. It will cost you $200,000 a year in interest—whether you need the money or not. And since your financial needs fluctuate, you won't need the full $2 million most of the time.

The alternative to a fixed loan is a ZBA tied to a $2 million line of credit. Instead of paying 10%, you will have to pay a point or two extra, say 12%. At a glance, it will look as though you're paying *more* than with a fixed term rate, Ettridge says. But a closer look reveals that you're not, because with a ZBA you only pay interest on the credit you actually use.

> **EXAMPLE:**
>
> If your cash/credit needs fluctuate between $500,000 and $2 million from week to week and month to month, your average daily borrowing over the course of the year may be only $900,000. Thus, the line of credit would cost you $108,000 ($900,000 × 12%) for the year, a savings of $92,000 over the $200,000 in interest on a fixed loan.

ADDED ADVANTAGES

If you do elect the fixed loan route, you undoubtedly are going to invest that portion of the $2 million you're not using to recoup some of your interest costs. If you need to keep the money flexible, you're going to have to put it in overnight accounts. That means you may have to pay somebody to manage the money, thus adding to the expense of the term loan.

"With a line of credit tied to a ZBA, you make deposits to pay down the line," says Ettridge. "The bank manages your money—no hassle, no extra charge."

Another liability of a term loan is that once you pay it down, it's not as easy or inexpensive to borrow it back again. You have to apply again and go before a loan committee. You also have the cost of your time in filling out forms, going to the bank and contacting references. It may take two or three weeks to process, and by the time you get that second loan, it could be too late.

"And that's *if* you get it," Ettridge adds. "As we all know, the one time a bank usually doesn't want to lend you money is when you need it."

> **OBSERVATION:**
>
> That could actually turn out to be the greatest cost of a term loan, because if you can't get additional money when you need it, it could end up costing you your whole business.

Chapter 5

CUSTOMER RELATIONS

WHAT DO CUSTOMERS SEE, HEAR & THINK ABOUT YOU?

■ ■ ■ ■ ■

We are told many times throughout our lives that a chain is no stronger than its weakest link.

As an executive, you are in the position where you run a chain with links galore—from salespeople to service people to production to support services—and many points in between. Each is a market link, and each has the power to define you to your customers.

Use this quiz to check on how well your links are withstanding the stresses of the marketplace.

■ **Your salespeople:**

1. Keep their promises.

☐ Yes   ☐ No

2. Maintain solid product knowledge.

☐ Yes   ☐ No

3. Deliver lively presentations.

☐ Yes   ☐ No

4. Deliver appropriate service.

☐ Yes   ☐ No

5. Respond to complaints.

☐ Yes   ☐ No

6. Are knowledgeable and professional about the competition.   ☐ Yes   ☐ No

■ **Inside personnel:**

1. Answer phone calls quickly, courteously, smilingly and intelligently.

☐ Yes   ☐ No

2. Use callers' names when they give them.   ☐ Yes   ☐ No

3. Keep callers on "hold" no more than 60 seconds, after which a return call is arranged if required.   ☐ Yes   ☐ No

4. Your people are scrupulously careful to be totally accurate and on target in their responses. ☐ Yes ☐ No

5. Return calls are made as promised. ☐ Yes ☐ No

■ **Packaging:**

1. Your package and logo/trademark look contemporary. ☐ Yes ☐ No

2. If your product name has become better known than your company name, your package reflects it. ☐ Yes ☐ No

3. Your package is biodegradable. ☐ Yes ☐ No

If yes, the package—and your advertising—shout the fact. ☐ Yes ☐ No

■ **Advertising/Promotion:**

1. The message you want to deliver—high quality, low price, top service, etc.—is still being delivered. ☐ Yes ☐ No

2. The message is being delivered in up-to-date language. ☐ Yes ☐ No

3. When people see it, hear it or read it, their experience confirms it. ☐ Yes ☐ No

■ **Sales literature:**

1. Looks up to date. ☐ Yes ☐ No

2. Incorporates all the benefits you offer in today's language. ☐ Yes ☐ No

3. Even though the answer to one of the above is no, you avoid discarding the literature because you think that would be a waste of money. ☐ Yes ☐ No

If yes, is that prudent? ☐ Yes ☐ No

■ **Sales Presentations/Visuals:**

1. Sound and look up to date. ☐ Yes ☐ No

2. Visuals are accurate. ☐ Yes ☐ No

3. You have traveled in the field recently to observe how customers are responding to the show-and-tell your salespeople offer them. ☐ Yes ☐ No

OBSERVATION:

If all your links seem secure, double-check with your customers. A customer survey and/or some travel in the field is the acid test of what customers think of your people and your company.

MONITOR YOUR SERVICE TO GET & KEEP CUSTOMERS
■ ■ ■ ■ ■

If your customers can't count on you, there's no reason to stay with you. To seal both established and new accounts:

ASK YOUR CUSTOMERS WHERE YOU STAND

Companies from banks to foundries now call on every single customer at least twice a year to ask for evaluations. Many use their field managers to perform the job. Is the product quality satisfactory? Is the price-value equation balanced? Is the sales rep alert to their problems? How do we compare to competing vendors in quality, price, service?

This often creates a serendipitous wedge. So does probing for what various ancillary services or products customers would buy. Just your asking for the evaluation impresses customers favorably. And if there's a leak in your dike, you can fix it before it becomes a flood.

OBSERVATION:

If you have too many customers for this situation to work, you can accomplish much of the same thing by using a mail survey. Or use your own trained telemarketers—or those available from an outside service.

CALL DORMANT ACCOUNTS BEFORE THEY DIE

"Dead" accounts are always a source of business, but it's harder to bring back the dead than to wake the sleeping. As business drops off from accounts, a caution light should start to blink and a telemarketer should make a call. If someone goofed, maybe you can fix it. If you don't ask, only the competitor who takes the account away will know why.

GET YOUR OWN PEOPLE MORE INVOLVED

■ **Use off-site service people as intelligence operatives.** People who work on your customers' premises can learn a lot about how you are perceived. Did the sales representative promise more than you can deliver? Has the customer been overloaded with inventory? How was the service phone call handled? Did your service person arrive on time and give satisfaction?

Give off-site service personnel an understanding of how acquiring this type of intelligence relates to their own jobs.

■ **Teach customer service people to live the name.** Is every phone call answered within five rings? Is the representative's response unfailingly courteous and polite? It takes more than just picking up the phone and using the proper words in a conversation. Saying, "Thank you for call-

ing Ajax," in a voice that comes across as bored, runs too fast or has no life will turn off any caller.

• *Are computerized customer records instantly available?* If service reps must do lookup, do they promise to call back promptly—and do so? Do they have the discretion to make adjustments on the spot? Companies that allow their representatives such latitude find that trained employees make intelligent decisions.

• *Are people who demand a "supervisor," or threaten legal action, turned over to a manager?* Do representatives let angry customers unload their anger while retaining their own composure? The above situations call for nothing less than common sense. But unless it's someone's job to monitor it all, you don't know whether guidelines are followed.

OBSERVATION:

A team of employees who know they are all customer service people—because management never lets them forget it— will go a long way toward keeping you on track and in business.

A MODEL CUSTOMER SURVEY

· · · · ·

Here's a survey to use when you want to find out what your customers are thinking about you. Send them this, along with a cover letter from you, your top executive or the marketing VP. Be sure that your letter looks as though it was individually typed on quality paper. Promise to report on the results in general, and to investigate and respond to any common complaints—or to specific problems from those respondents who care to identify themselves. Enclose a stamped return envelope that has been coded to reach either you or whoever is the appropriate person.

PLEASE RATE US ON HOW WE SERVE YOU

1. Our rep calls
   ☐ Often ☐ Seldom

2. Our rep's service is
   ☐ Good ☐ Not too good

3. Our product (service) is
   ☐ Good ☐ Adequate

4. Our billing/credit practices are
   ☐ OK ☐ Annoying

5. Our delivery schedule is
   ☐ Reliable ☐ Erratic

6. We respond to complaints
   ☐ Promptly ☐ Slowly

7. Overall, we do the job
   ☐ Well ☐ Adequately

8. You are a customer who is
   ☐ Satisfied ☐ Dissatisfied

9. You would recommend us
   ☐ Highly ☐ As not bad

10. Please tell us, in the space below, anything you think we need to know to do a better job for you.

_____

_____

_____

Be sure to report the overall results to your customers as soon as they are tabulated. It would be ironic to get generally good ratings in the survey and then prove yourself unreliable by not keeping your promise to report. People who respond want to know the results.

STAFFING A CALL CENTER? COST OUT SERVICE LEVELS

■ ■ ■ ■ ■

If the comptroller of your company were to ask your customer service manager the cost differential between answering 80% of all incoming customer calls within 20 seconds and answering 95% of them within 15 seconds, could he or she give the comptroller an accurate answer?

THE USUAL, BUT INACCURATE, FORMULA

In response to questions of this nature, many managers make the mistake of multiplying the number of calls they get in a half-hour by the average number of seconds their telephone service representatives (TSRs) spend on each call, including actual phone time and post-call paperwork.

They divide the answer by 1,800 (the number of seconds in a half-hour) to arrive at what they think is the correct number of representatives needed at each of the customer service levels under consideration.

That approach is misleading because calls tend to bunch up. In order to answer a call within a firm's prescribed time guidelines—say, 20 seconds—you have to have a TSR who is free to pick up, not on the phone with another customer.

A MUCH BETTER AND MORE EXACT METHOD

Link your resources—your TSRs and trunk lines—to the service levels under discussion. In this case, 80% of calls in 20 seconds and 95% in 15 seconds. Then you do some calculations using the Erlang tables, the queuing formulas most commonly used in telecommunications. (The tables are available in *Tables for Traffic Management and Design Book 1-Trunking*, by T. Frankel; ABC TeleTraining, Inc.; 708-879-9000; $14.95.) You use Erlang C for TSRs and Erlang B for trunk lines. Each calculation will take you about 15 minutes.

To calculate the number of TSRs needed to answer 95% of calls in 15 seconds, you input your telephone representatives' average talk time, average postcall time, and the number of phone calls you expect to receive in a given half-hour period.

To calculate the number of trunks needed, you input the percentage of calls to be carried by each of your trunk groups and the percentage of allowable busy signals.

If you find, for example, that you need five TSRs and three trunks, you can determine from your budget what your costs per TSR and trunk are. Then multiply the TSR cost by the five TSRs you need and the trunk cost by the three trunks you need. Add the results together to arrive at your total cost.

CAUTION

The Erlang tables have a shortcoming. They assume that all calls will be answered, and thus do not factor in for lost or abandoned calls. This deficiency will throw off your results a bit, but it should not make a major difference.

If you have *Lotus 1-2-3*, Erlang software offers several programs that are available to the public to do the calculations for you. Pacecom Technologies (206-641-8217) has one for $395. MTC Systems (416-449-7620)

offers a system that will calculate your staff and trunk needs as well as do such things as monitor your toll-free line. Cost ranges from $9,800–$30,000.

FOSTER CUSTOMER 'OWNERSHIP'

Customers who become involved in what you do, make or sell are customers who will stick. There are various ways to achieve that involvement. As long as you and your people use them to bring your customers genuine benefits, your accounts' loyalty will be genuine, too.

LISTEN TO WAYS

• **Make customers technical consultants.** In the production of software, for example, customer involvement is critical, because whether a new program will impress the intended users is always an unknown. A software company, for example, does the initial testing in-house. Then it sends the new software out to a few accounts that are willing to test it on their own computers. This cannot help but establish a strong bond with those customer-testers. They become an integral part of the product development process.

• **Bring customers on board your ship.** For example, when the software company installs customers' newly purchased software, it has people from both companies working on each others' premises. First, its people spend time at the customer's installation familiarizing themselves with the data that are to be incorporated into the new product. Then, they return home and build the data into the new system. Finally, the customer's people come to the manufacturer's premises and run the system there until they're completely satisfied and at home with it.

This exchange of home bases creates a kind of camaraderie that is rare in business. It builds a bond that's very hard for any eager competitor to break.

GET THE SALES FORCE INVOLVED TOO

• **Keep salespeople in the act** when the customer asks for help. No customer is going to be happy if he or she asks for help and hears, "Call Tom Brown in our Packaging Group." It may be that Tom Brown is great at handling that particular problem. But that's not what the person wants to hear. It's much better for the salesperson to make that call right from the customer's premises, explain the problem and introduce the customer to Tom Brown on the phone. Then, the customer's stress index doesn't rise when she has a similar problem. She's at home with the help line—and pretty happy with the vendor.

• **Ask customers how they want to be sold.** Survey your customers periodically, or meet with them in person. More and more vendor companies are arranging monthly meetings between a few invited buyers and their own salespeople. The purpose of the meeting—a seminar, really—is to let the buyers talk about what they like and don't like in the performance of the representatives who call on them. That information can be priceless. Implementing what you hear—in all your territories—may enhance or even save some of your accounts' business.

RESPOND TO SPECIAL NEEDS

You may find a treasure trove as your reward. For example, modifying a service or product to fit a certain customer's needs may uncover a new niche for you.

Chapter 6

FINANCING METHODS

THE ABCs OF BANK BORROWING

· · · · ·

If you're a small company, you probably do nearly all your financing through bank loans, which means that you'll be taking on debt. There are sound reasons for financing the growth of your company by using debt rather than the other principal form of financing—selling shares in the company.

Debt-service payments are a deductible business expense; dividend payments are not. When you issue new debt, you leverage your company to increase earnings potential. Issuing new common stock dilutes your earnings. Most important, new debt does not weaken control of the company, as would an equity financing.

SHOP AROUND

If it's a bank you need, be sure to shop around and know what to look for. It's important, for instance, to find out which banks are in the best position to lend money—and may even be under pressure to make loans.

A key number to know is the bank's loan-to-deposit ratio. This will tell you what percentage of a bank's deposits is tied up in loans. Historically, the loan-to-deposit ratio was around 60%. Today, it's more like 73%–75%. This loan and deposit information is easily obtained through your state superintendent of banking.

DEVELOP A SOLID RELATIONSHIP

Even though banks supply well over 90% of the capital needs of small and midsize firms, few businesspeople take the trouble to develop a solid relationship with their bankers.

The best time to get to know your banker is when you don't need a loan. If you are in a position within your company to get to know the company's banker, take full advantage of that opportunity.

It's a good idea to invite your banker on a tour of your facilities. Also, keep him or her informed of your company's progress by sending quarterly statements with appropriate comments to his or her office.

OBSERVATION:

Even if you don't intend to borrow from your bank in the foreseeable future, a good banking relationship can help you in other ways. For one thing, a banker makes an excellent character reference. As such, his or her endorsement might help in obtaining better terms from suppliers, equipment manufacturers and the like.

PRESENTING YOUR CASE

The most frequent mistake that managers make in applying for a bank loan is submitting a late request for funds. To a banker, an emergency loan is anathema. It is an obvious sign of poor planning. No competent manager should ever allow a need that should have been anticipated to turn into a financial crisis.

Thus, if you expect to have any chance of getting a bank loan approved, you must anticipate your cash needs well in advance, providing enough time for the bank to process your application. It takes at least three weeks, and sometimes more, to process a loan.

■ **Provide the proper information.** This is similar to the ingredients found in your business plan. These include:

• *Financial statements.* Three years back is the norm, but some institutions prefer five years.

• *Personal statements.* These should describe the experience and capabilities of top management.

• *Statement of purpose.* This statement should describe how the funds will be used, and how they will be repaid. A cash-flow budget covering the length of the loan, although not always required, is helpful.

THE LOAN INTERVIEW

If you've done your homework properly, the battle will nearly be won by the time you appear for your loan interview. In many respects, your business plan or your supporting documents will do your talking for you. Nevertheless, you should take this interview seriously and be prepared to answer the banker's questions, which will be similar to these:

• *How much?* Tell your banker exactly how much money you need. Don't be vague.

• *How long?* Indicate how long the funds will be needed.

• *What purpose?* Be specific about how you will use the money. "General corporate purpose" is no answer.

• *How will you repay?* Again, be specific. If it's from cash flow, be prepared with a cash-flow projection for the duration of the loan.

• *What if something goes wrong?* Prepare your ace in the hole: an emergency plan to be used if the loan doesn't work out. You could plan to sell an asset, borrow elsewhere, or have a new investor on tap. A sound emergency strategy can be most convincing to a banker.

PREPARING YOUR FINANCIAL PROPOSAL

■ ■ ■ ■ ■

No sensible businessperson merely goes, hat in hand, to his or her local bank or other potential sources of capital when new funds are needed. To get an idea of what's required, just recall what you went through to get a home mortgage.

If you are to be taken seriously at any of the traditional capital sources, you will need a properly prepared financing proposal.

Financing proposals come in all shapes and sizes, and the final form of your particular proposal will probably depend largely upon the requirements of the capital source that you intend to approach.

O B S E R V A T I O N :

Even though banks and other lenders do not usually require a business plan (except for long-term loan applications), a well-structured plan can materially improve your chances of getting a loan.

THE CONTENTS OF A BUSINESS PLAN

A typical business plan consists of three main sections, with each section containing specific information about your company's current business and financial position. Here is a brief rundown on each element of a business plan:

■ **The introductory section:** Usually running only three to four pages, the first section is intended to give the reader a brief overview of the proposal. It should consist of the following:

• *A title page* identifying the company and its principal officers, with names, addresses and telephone numbers.

• *A table of contents,* listing the three principal sections and all major headings.

• *A brief statement of purpose* (approximately one-half page) summarizing the proposal, spelling out how much money is involved, how the funds are to be used, how the firm will benefit and how the funds will be repaid (in the case of a loan).

■ **The descriptive section:** The comments in this section should spell out your company's current business position and its plans for the future. Be certain to address at least these five areas in your comments:

• *Describe your business as succinctly as possible.* Tell what your business is, how you run it and why you are successful.

• *Describe your market and your company's market niche.* Give some idea of your market's size and potential, and your marketing strategy.

• *Describe your competition* and give some idea of how you handle it. Mince no words. If competition is severe, say so.

• *Describe your management team,* emphasizing the business background and experience of each member of the team. Some personal data, such as age, special interests and place of residence, should be included.

• *Describe how the new capital will be applied.* Spell out what projects the funds will be used for. You should be as specific as possible, which means that you will have to reach some hard decisions *before* seeking the new capital.

■ **The financial section:** Your "financials," as they are commonly tagged by lenders and other providers of capital, should be aimed at providing support for the statements made in the descriptive section. You will need both historical data and projections for the future.

Start off with a Source and Application of Funding statement, which shows in detail how the proceeds of the financing will be used (e.g., percentages allocated to equipment, advertising, product distribution). You can then move on to the more traditional financial statements:

• *Historical statements* should go back about five years in most cases. However, if your business is cyclical in nature, you should cover a complete business cycle, even if it means digging further than five years into the past. The reports should include balance sheets, income statements and cash-flow statements.

• *Projections* should also include pro-forma balance sheets, income statements and cash-flow statements. Summary reports are acceptable in most cases. Make sure that you include projections for at least the entire period during which the funds will be used and repaid.

WHEN A SHORTER PROPOSAL WILL DO

Even though you will usually need a full-blown business plan, running about 12 pages, to ensure proper treatment on most financing expeditions, there are times when a less thorough treatment will suffice.

EXAMPLE
You may already have established a close relationship with your bank and merely need to present a documented proposal to the loan committee. Or, you may be attempting to arrange new financing from a private investor who is already familiar with your company's operation. In such cases, a summary financing proposal can usually be substituted for a formal business plan.

A summary financing proposal is a "mini" business plan consisting of no more than six or seven pages:

• *The first page* contains the proposal itself, detailing the amount of cash needed, repayment schedule, collateral and any other pertinent details.

• *The second page* summarizes how the funds will be used and how your firm will benefit. In brief, this section sets forth your arguments on why the proposal will be a good loan or investment.

• *The following two to three pages* outline your company's history, its product and marketing position, its management team, and provide a summary of its prospects for the future. In short, this is a capsule version of the descriptive section of a formal business plan.

• *The final page(s)* should include a condensed balance sheet and income statement, plus a year or two of projections. Cash-flow statements would give a substantial boost to your argument here.

ASK FOR THE RIGHT TYPE OF LOAN

· · · · ·

One way to impress your banker is to speak his or her language—to structure your loan proposal so that it fits neatly into one of the many loan categories that the bank uses. There is plenty of room for maneuvering within these categories, but to keep the bank comfortable, your loan request should fit into one of the following groups.

Most term loans are written to cover the life of an asset, or for a five-year period with a refinancing clause. They are written for 80%–90% of the total cost of an asset. Payments are made quarterly, consisting of equal amounts of principal with interest computed on the outstanding loan balance.

Since small companies often find quarterly payments burdensome, many banks will work out a schedule of monthly payments. Most banks will also tailor payments to meet the company's needs, such as accepting lower payments in the early years of the loan and higher payments later.

SHORT-TERM LOANS

Short-term credit is the backbone of commerce. Businesspeople use short-term loans (defined as loans reaching maturity in one year or less) to finance everything from inventory to emergencies. The following are a few of the most common short-term loan classifications:

• *Time loans.* For companies with good credit ratings, the time or commercial loan is the chief source of financing. It keeps bookkeeping to a minimum and can be used for any purpose, including inventory and accounts receivable. Time loans usually mature in three to six months, but can be refinanced for longer maturities.

• *Accounts receivable.* In this type of loan, the bank lends you 70%–80% of the value of eligible receivables. As checks in payment for receivables come in, you forward them to the bank, which deducts its portion and deposits the rest in your account. Interest is paid only on the amount of the loan outstanding. To be eligible for financing, receivables must usually be less than 60 days old, and your customers must be creditworthy.

• *Line of credit.* A line of credit is by far the simplest and most flexible short-term financing available for a business, especially a small one. There's a catch, though: Credit

lines are usually granted only to the most creditworthy customers.

MEDIUM-TERM LOANS

The principal difference between a short-term and medium-term loan is the importance of collateral. Medium-term loans are for up to five years. Normally, they are used to finance equipment purchases or plant expansion. In granting such loans, the bank will usually expect you to pledge an asset that will generate the revenues needed to repay the loan.

■ **Collateral.** A banker regards collateral as a safety valve. While your ability to repay the loan out of your cash flow is the key factor in getting the loan approved, your bank will also request that the loan be supported by collateral, just in case something goes wrong. Here is a rundown on some of the most common asset types and how your bank is likely to regard them as collateral:

• *Liquid assets.* Money market accounts, savings deposits and bank certificates of deposit (CDs) can be taken at face value, as can short-term U.S. government securities, such as Treasury bills. However, longer-term Treasury or municipal bonds are taken at market value. Listed stocks and bonds are usually discounted from market value, with the discount running as much as 25% of the face value.

• *Accounts receivable* can bring as much as 60%–80% of face value, provided they are "eligible." This means weeding out older accounts, doubtful accounts and slow payers.

• *Inventories* are less valuable as collateral, primarily because they are more difficult to sell. Figure on an average of approximately 30% of the cost of raw materials and finished goods.

• *Machinery and equipment* is measured by its auction value. You can usually use 50%–70% of the auction value of machinery and equipment as collateral.

LONG-TERM LOANS

Long-term loans (over five years) have been virtually nonexistent for the past several years. From a businessperson's point of view, the interest rate is too high, and the bank is hesitant to commit its capital for a long term when the value of the asset to be financed might be eroded by inflation. When long-term loans are used, they almost always involve real property.

• *Business property mortgages.* In more stable times, commercial and industrial mortgages were not unlike residential mortgages. They ran for as long as 25 years and were paid off in monthly installments.

Nowadays, you may not be able to get a commercial mortgage for more than five to 10 years. These mortgages usually involve equal monthly installments, with a balloon payment at the end.

Only rarely is refinancing guaranteed, although most companies are able to negotiate a new deal when the balloon payment is due.

• *Real estate loans.* If you have substantial equity in your building, it may still be possible to arrange a second mortgage. However, interest costs could be very high in some areas.

A whole new refinancing package might also satisfy your cash needs, but you'll probably be swapping a low-cost mortgage for a high-cost one.

In short, unless you are certain that the return on your proposed new investment will be very high, you would be better off leaving the equity in your plant untapped.

WHAT TO DO IF YOUR BANKER TURNS YOU DOWN

■ ■ ■ ■ ■

Most businesspeople have been turned down for a business loan at least once in their careers.

If your loan request is refused, don't panic. Your company will probably prosper, even without the extra cash. However, you have some work to do:

FIND OUT WHY YOU WERE TURNED DOWN

Ask your banker directly, and ask him or her to be specific. Don't settle for a vague answer, such as "undercapitalization." You can't correct the situation unless you know what is wrong.

Most loan requests are turned down for one of the following five reasons:

• *Poor communication.* If you and the banker don't hit it off, the chances for your loan drop precipitously.

■ SOLUTION:

Ask to be serviced by another loan officer. You have a right to expect that the person serving you will have empathy for your problems.

• *Uncontrolled expansion.* Banks shy away from a company with a revenue growth rate that surpasses its ability to finance necessary expansion.

■ SOLUTION:

If you wish to finance an expansion program, make certain that your business plan includes a full explanation of how your company expects to keep pace with sales growth.

• *Overly optimistic business plan.* Your bank will check your sales and earnings forecasts against industrywide forecasts. It may also match your projections against those of a company in a similar business. If your forecasts appear too optimistic, your loan will probably be turned down.

■ SOLUTION:

Keep forecasts realistic. If anything, be conservative.

• *Past misuse of loan funds.* If you use funds for a project that is not in your statement of purpose and the bank finds out, your chances of receiving another loan from that bank are slim.

■ SOLUTION:

If circumstances beyond your control intervene to make it impossible to fulfill the loan conditions, inform your bank at once.

• *Rapid inventory buildup.* To a bank, a sudden surge in inventories means one of two things: poor planning or an unanticipated drop in sales. In either case, there is reason to hold off new credit.

■ SOLUTION:

Make sure your inventories are in reasonable shape before you apply for a loan. Don't expect the bank to finance inventories above the range you normally carry.

ASK FOR SUGGESTIONS

No bank enjoys turning down a loan request. Quite apart from the fact that the bank makes money by lending funds, the bank understandably wants to be viewed favorably by its customers and prospective customers. Therefore, if you are turned down by a bank, you probably have the full sympathy of your banker at that moment. You might be able to use that sympathy as a bridge to your next move, by asking for your banker's help with such questions as: "What would you do if you were me?" or "What source should I try now?"

WHAT TO NEGOTIATE WITH A VENTURE CAPITALIST

■ ■ ■ ■ ■

These five key questions should be answered to your satisfaction before any deal is "done":

• *When do you get the money?* You'll want to clarify whether the whole amount comes to you up front or in a series of "takedowns" or installments. If you choose the takedowns, make sure that the money will be there when you need it.

• *How much equity do you wind up with, and what type will it be?* Here, you'll want to make certain that you will have all of the rights that you anticipated when negotiations began.

• *Are the employment contracts satisfactory?* You'll also want to make certain that you and your key personnel are given enough time to do the job required.

• *Are you safe from further dilution?* You don't want your already-depleted interest diluted further by the issuance of new stock, at least not until you're ready. Insist on a tough anti-dilution clause.

• *Is your position on the board tenable?* Be certain that, under the board structure, you still wield enough clout to run the firm effectively. Even well-intentioned interference could hurt the company's prospects.

HOW TO JUDGE A POTENTIAL JOINT-VENTURE PARTNER

. . . . .

If you're seeking to accelerate your company's growth with the least possible financial risk, a joint-venture agreement with another firm can be an excellent route.

TIPS FOR SUCCESS

Because a joint venture is a separate business enterprise over which you have to share control with others, it is not without its own dangers. Here's what you need to do to make a cooperative enterprise successful for you—and your partner.

• *Evaluate your firm's contribution to the partnership.* Analyze what your company would bring to an alliance in the form of management expertise, marketing and sales experience, equipment, capital, market contacts, familiarity with technology and other resources. This will help you not only in identifying potential partners with complementary strengths, but also in convincing such a partner that your company would bring important depth to an alliance.

• *Evaluate your partner's contribution.* Look at what the prospective partner has that you don't have at present (capital, patents, customers, suppliers, the ability to add economies of scale and so on). Declining firms that would depend on the new alliance for their survival are seldom good candidates for joint ventures.

• *Come to an understanding of goals.* Compatibility with your prospective partner's goals, operations, culture and management styles is vital. A key point to discuss: How soon does your ally expect the venture to turn an acceptable profit?

If the company is bigger than yours, it may have more time to invest than you'd be willing to wait before the venture provides a satisfying return on investment. On the other hand, a company that is seeking a fast return on investment may not be a suitable partner, since it may be unwilling to commit its resources for the duration.

• *How fast can the partner make decisions?* Don't enter into deals where the person you'll be working with has limited decision-making authority. New ventures require fast action that is impossible with an executive who has to clear every agreement with a bureaucratic corporate hierarchy.

• *Don't lose sight of the risks.* A joint venture reduces the financial risk of expanding into a new line of business, but it doesn't eliminate it entirely. Don't invest time and money where you perceive the chance of success to be less than 60% to 70%.

Part of your risk assessment should be to recognize and accept the disadvantages of a joint venture: incomplete control over operations and decisions, or the possibility that your management restructuring or other changes in your partner company may cause it to lose interest in the venture.

For assurance of satisfying results from entering a joint venture, look for potential partners with which you've had a history of satisfying working relationships. This can come from customers, vendors, distributors, companies with which you have entered into licensing or patent arrangements, or other firms that have collaborated with you.

Joint ventures are also getting a sympathetic hearing in Congress. The National Cooperative Production Amendments of 1990 (H.R. 4611), for example, would allow small businesses to establish informal partnerships without antitrust complications.

RAISING CAPITAL THROUGH A PRIVATE PLACEMENT

■ ■ ■ ■ ■

If you're one who has considered using private placement, you'd be interested in the views of the experts. Lance J. Strauss, a venture capitalist and president of Strauss Enterprises, Inc. in Carmel, CA, advises firms to begin by figuring out whether they are indeed candidates for private placement.

WHO USES PRIVATE PLACEMENT?

The average firm using this method to raise capital:
• Is a small, later-stage company with revenues under $10 million.
• Has a minimum of two years of profitability where profits equal 5% to 10% of revenues.
• Has stable management and contracts in place for top-level executives.
• Has an annual revenue growth rate of at least 5% for the past two years.
• Has short- or long term-debt that doesn't exceed total capitalization.
• Shows potential for increasing sales and market share.

In electing the private placement route, you should also have a need to raise short-term or bridge capital and know a small pool of interested potential investors. Your company, as well as your industry, should be in a strong growth mode.

HOW TO GO ABOUT IT

Once you've selected the private placement method of raising capital, proceed in the following manner:
• *One year prior to the offering,* develop a business plan, target your company's market with a major sales campaign and retain third party professionals, such as a certified public accountant, an attorney, a financial printer and an investment banker.
• *Six months prior to the offering,* conduct a complete legal review of your corporate charter, by-laws, stock options and employment contracts; compile audited financial statements covering company operations over the last three years, and develop and refine your list of potential investors, keeping in mind Securities and Exchange Commission (SEC) regulations and limitations.
• *Three months prior to the offering,* hold a planning session with your management and your advisors to prepare a private placement memorandum, and prepare an investment letter with disclosure information for every qualified purchaser.

CAUTION

In filing for the offering, you must carefully set forth the various SEC exemptions to fully registered initial public offerings (IPOs); you must be fully aware of Rule 144 stock resale restrictions, and be aware of "bad boy" provisions which prohibit certain types of misconduct in the offering process. Your advisors can counsel you on these factors.

THE PROS AND CONS

The advantages of private placements are that you avoid the time-consuming SEC registration/disclosure provisions of IPOs, they're quicker and cheaper than IPOs and more control is retained by company founders and owners.

Also, you'll pay slightly less for a private placement than a public offering. The costs can range from $20,000 to $500,000 depending on the extent of your legal, accounting, filing and printing needs.

There are, however, some disadvantages:

• Limitations are placed on the number and qualifications of private investors, as well as the amount of money that can be raised.

• Limitations are imposed on the resale of the stock, and there's no public market for it.

• As a private company, you don't achieve as much media and analyst attention as public companies. This makes it difficult to attract investors.

• Private companies cannot be listed on NASDAQ or major stock exchange listings where markets can be made for stock.

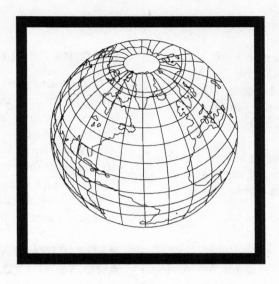

Chapter 7

IMPORT/EXPORT

SMOOTH IMPORT/EXPORT WITH 'MINI-CUSTOMS'

■ ■ ■ ■ ■

If you use air transport to ship your products abroad or to import foreign-made parts or products, it is no longer necessary to put up with the delays and other inconveniences of clearing them through customs at a major port of entry airport. A dozen smaller airports scattered across the U.S. are now set up to process cargo through "mini-customs" offices. They're not fields set up to handle jumbo jets, but smaller airports in places like Allegheny, PA and Fort Myers, FL.

Known as "user fee" customs offices, the facilities are funded by the companies or localities using them. For example, at Baer Field in Fort Wayne, IN, space and the salaries of two customs officers are provided by the primary user, Burlington Air Express, Irvine, CA. The facility was set up to spur local and regional business.

ADVANTAGES OF LOCAL CUSTOMS SERVICES

Time saving is the biggest plus. There's less traffic and a quicker turnaround, users agree. With paper processing, it can take a week or more to go through customs at a big airport, a fraction of a week at a smaller facility. Other advantages: lower transport costs to nearby facilities and the elimination of intermediate warehousing.

DISADVANTAGES

Officers may not be available when you want them. Big airports have 24-hour-a-day service. At small ones, customs officers are on call, or work only during the day. Also, a smaller facility may not be able to handle every type of product. For example, there may not be fish and wildlife, or food and drug people available.

Note, too, that the smaller offices do not handle passengers, although some are set up to process executives flying abroad in company jets.

THE COST

Customs-processing fees, set by local authorities, are nominal and may be less than those at major airports. Backers of facilities such as the Baer Field office keep fees low to spur local business participation.

SELL ABROAD WHILE STAYING AT HOME
· · · · ·

With the recent addition of Mexico as an international 800-service nation, it is possible for even very small U.S. companies to gain a local presence in 33 countries and territories—without incurring the expense of foreign offices. AT&T's international 800 service works exactly like its U.S. 800 service, except that the toll-free calls are routed over international boundaries.

International 800 service permits direct marketing around the globe. You simply advertise your product in Mexico or another foreign nation, and buyers dial the number. Unknown to them, no phone rings in their country; rather, the call is routed directly to your location here in the U.S., where an operator speaking the appropriate language picks it up.

WHO BENEFITS

• *Financial service firms* could make toll-free calling available to associated banks, investors and pension funds in foreign countries.

• *Some manufacturers* could take orders from customers or distributors without ever sending a sales rep out of the U.S.

• *Retailers* could expand their catalog businesses around the world.

PARTICIPATING COUNTRIES AND TERRITORIES

In addition to Mexico, locations that have international 800 service include Antigua, Aruba, Australia, the Bahamas, Barbados, Belgium, Bermuda, the British Virgin Islands, Canada, Cayman Islands, Denmark, the Dominican Republic, Finland, France, Hong Kong, Israel, Italy, Jamaica, Japan, the Netherlands, Norway, Panama, the Philippines, Singapore, South Korea, St. Kitts, Sweden, Switzerland, Trinidad and Tobago, Turks and Caicos Islands, the United Kingdom and West Germany.

The cost of international 800 service varies by location. For information, call AT&T at 1-800-222-0400. (For additional information on whether or not to use an 800 number, see "Don't Let An 800 Number Turn Your Customer Off," page 163.)

TAP OPIC TO FIND OVERSEAS PARTNER
· · · · ·

If your company is a smaller U.S. firm interested in undertaking a joint venture in an underdeveloped nation, the Overseas Private Investment Corp. (OPIC) is anxious to help. This federal agency is offering a database that can help you identify potential partners overseas. If you find such a partner—whether it be a local business or a foreign government agency—OPIC is also interested in helping you to finance your part in the venture.

• *Opportunity Bank.* OPIC's Opportunity Bank is a computerized system that matches a U.S. investor with specific business opportunities in more than 110 countries in the developing world. A U.S. firm can use the data bank to gain information on more than 2,000 such overseas opportunities already listed with the service. It can also list its requirements and wait until a suitable investment comes along.

• *OPIC's requirements.* The database is designed to assist a small business, which OPIC currently defines as either an industrial company with annual sales of less than $142 million, or a nonindustrial firm with stockholders' equity of less than $48 million. Larger firms, however, are also encouraged to register with the system.

THREE-STEP PROCESSING

To register in the bank and obtain information on existing overseas opportunities, a company follows a three-step procedure:

• *The company completes a profile form,* listing projects, products or services it is interested in and the countries in which it wants to do business.

• *It then receives from OPIC a summary of existing projects* that correspond to the company's interest areas.

• *If any projects spark the company's interest,* it can obtain further information by paying a $50 fee, which will cover up to 10 in-depth profiles of specific opportunities, describing the project and outlining its

status, local resources available, estimated cost and the name and address of the principal contact. Projects recently underwritten by OPIC include dairy farms in India and Pakistan, health-care products in Turkey, a computer venture in El Salvador and a spark-plug plant in Korea.

• *Limitations.* OPIC stresses that its databank and other assistance is not available to help U.S. firms that are looking for cheap foreign labor. It won't assist any venture that involves closing an existing U.S. facility and throwing American employees out of work. It also won't consider any venture that entails gambling or the manufacturing of alcoholic beverages.

FINANCIAL AID

If a venture does meet its requirements, OPIC can provide a variety of financial assistance, from direct loans ranging from $500,000 to $6 million to loan guaranties ranging from $2 million to $25 million or more. In 1989, OPIC made financial commitments of $198 million.

It also provides inexpensive political-risk insurance to protect the venture against government confiscation, war, civil strife and other adverse developments. For 1989, the insurance volume was $1.5 billion.

OBSERVATION:
OPIC lists 110 countries as "developing nations." In 1989, it supported 123 projects in 35 nations, representing a total investment of $3.3 billion. U.S small-business firms were involved in 30% of the ventures. For more information, write to Opportunity Bank, OPIC, Washington, DC 20527, or call 1-800-424-OPIC. (In the District of Columbia: 202-457-7010.)

MAKE YOURSELF AT HOME IN FOREIGN MARKETS

.   .   .   .   .

If you aren't already exporting, chances are it's time you got your feet wet. Keep one thing in mind: It's what you have to offer, not size, that determines a company's potential for a profitable export business.

A survey by Cognetics, Inc., Cambridge, MA found that more than 50% of all exporters have fewer than 100 employees. Firms with 20–49 employees account for 27.4% of U.S. exports; those with 500-plus workers account for only 16.7%. Most small firms export low-tech products, such as metal-working machinery.

How does Mr. Small find an international market? Use either an ETC or an EMC.

SELLING THROUGH ETCs

Export trading companies (ETCs) function much like domestic manufacturer's reps. They sell the products or services of several companies, so they can afford to make sales calls that an individual exporter would find unprofitable.

Unlike domestic manufacturer's reps, however, ETCs take title to the goods after they've sold them. Thus, they handle the logistics, shipping, financing and collections. That means that the manufacturer doesn't have to set up its own international department and doesn't have to become an expert in international law.

SELLING THROUGH EMCs

Export management companies (EMCs) can be a good choice for firms wanting to develop the expertise to go it on their own internationally in the future.

In theory, and often in practice, EMCs provide a wider range of services than ETCs and put the clients in closer touch with foreign markets. Such organizations act as a client's "international department," overseeing everything from advertising to licensing of technology. "We gain exposure in the foreign trade press [for the manufacturer], identify prospective markets and find specific customers," says one ETC firm's president.

■ **Specific services EMCs offer include the following:**

- Advising on local laws.
- Counseling on protection of patents and trademarks.
- Preparing foreign-language advertising and sales literature.
- Exhibiting products in international trade shows.
- Appointing distributors or commissioned representatives.
- Handling export declarations, insurance, banking transactions and other details of getting the goods to customers.
- Combining several manufacturers' goods to save on shipping.
- Costs. Some EMCs work on a fee basis, like consultants; others work on commission. Still others, like most ETCs, take title to your goods and collect the payment from foreign buyers.

OBSERVATION:

EMC and ETC services overlap. All ETCs also handle paperwork and combine manufacturers' goods to save on shipping. Many are involved in the preparation of foreign advertising and participate in foreign trade shows. ETCs also either appoint distributors or act as distributors themselves.

USE AN EMC OR AN ETC?

If you think your products have the potential for substantial sales abroad, an EMC may be a better choice for you than an ETC. You'll get more help with marketing, learn more about international trade, and gain the wherewithal to "do it yourself" in the future. Some EMCs, can also help clients set up their own international marketing departments when the parties involved decide the time is right.

HOW TO FIND
THE RIGHT MIDDLEMAN

Look in the *Yellow Pages* under "exporters," "export representatives" or "export management," or call a local office of the Commerce Dept.'s U.S. and Foreign Commercial Service. Look for a firm that handles your type of product or service and is comfortable with your company's size and its prior international marketing experience, if any.

For more on EMCs, you can also check the *U.S. Export Management Companies Directory*, produced by the International Trade Administration of the Commerce Department, and the *Foreign Trade Market Place*, published by Gale Research, Detroit, MI. Both are available in reference libraries.

O B S E R V A T I O N :

ETCs and EMCs do not accept all comers. Like good independent reps and consultants, export trading and management companies carefully pick the manufacturers they want to represent. Some will work with neophytes. Others welcome inquiries from companies that have already had a taste of international marketing.

CAUTION

Like manufacturer's representatives and consultants, ETCs and EMCs range from the highly reputable to the fly by night. Always ask for and check references.

INTERNATIONAL PROTOCOL
■ ■ ■ ■ ■

When American executives conduct business together, mutual trust is often nurtured by a down-to-earth atmosphere where straight talk and casual manners prevail.

◆ P R O B L E M :

This attitude seems disrespectful in most foreign countries, where business etiquette is more formal.

To transact business abroad more effectively, follow these guidelines:

■ **Never refuse food or drink.** It can be perceived as an unwillingness to do business or a rejection of hospitality.

■ **Never comment on government, culture or technology.** This holds true even if your host does so or invites your remarks. Don't even complain about the difficulty of placing a long-distance call.

■ **Don't give liquor as a house gift.** It's generally perceived as too informal. Flowers or chocolate would be better.

In addition to the general guidelines outlined above, review these specific rules for different countries:

• *The United Kingdom.* Business protocol is formal. Don't offer personal information about yourself or your family, or ask for such information from your business contacts.

• *France.* Always use titles, even when addressing an assistant, and remember to shake hands when you leave as well as when you arrive. When you make an appointment ahead of time, reconfirm it in writing.

• *Italy.* Use professional titles, such as *Dottore* (for physicians or others who have a university degree). Calling an *Architetto* (architect) or *Ingegnere* (engineer) simply *Signor* or *Signora* conveys disrespect.

• *Germany.* Germans value punctuality, and may hesitate to deal with foreign businesspeople who have not been introduced by a colleague. An invitation to dinner is considered purely social, and discussing business over a meal is considered a *faux pas*.

• *The U.S.S.R.* Don't comment on the government or social structures. Never call the Soviet Union "Russia," or its citizens "Russians."

• *The Orient.* Direct eye-to-eye contact offends people in most Asian cultures.

Casual chatting with a receptionist is just not done—sit silently and wait for your appointment. In Japan, you can break the no-liquor rule and give Scotch whisky as a house present.

● N O T E :

Women: Don't wear white (except a white business shirt) in Hong Kong—it signifies mourning.

• *Islamic countries.* Never smoke or drink in public, even if others do. To refuse food is considered a true insult. Remember that business is not conducted from Thursday evening through Friday evening, or during the spring holy month of Ramadan.

• *Latin America.* Dress is formal, and handshakes are hearty and frequent. Latin Americans are very hospitable and frequently invite foreign visitors into their homes. Be sure to compliment the home, the spouse and the children. And don't forget to bring a gift.

Chapter 8

LEGAL/REGULATORY ISSUES

WHAT YOU SHOULD KNOW ABOUT SHUT-DOWNS & LAYOFFS

· · · · · ·

The Worker Adjustment and Retraining Notification Act (WARN) requires an employer to give workers at least 60 days' notice of a planned plant closing or a mass layoff. You're subject to the act if you have 100 or more employees, excluding part-time employees, or 100 or more employees in your service, including part-time employees, who in aggregate work at least 4,000 hours per week, exclusive of any over-time hours.

DEFINITIONS

■ The Department of Labor (DOL) defines a "plant closing" as the shutdown of one or more facilities that results in the loss of jobs during any 30-day period for 50 or more employees, excluding any part-time employees.

■ The DOL defines a "mass layoff" as a reduction in force which, first, is not the result of a plant closing, and second, results in an employment loss during any 30-day period for:

• At least 33% of the active employees, excluding part-time employees, and

• At least 50 employees, excluding part-time employees.

Where 500 or more employees (excluding part-time employees) are affected, the 33% requirement doesn't apply, and notice is required if the other criteria are met.

EXCEPTIONS

WARN points out three situations in which notices may be given less than 60 days in advance of the event:

■ **If you can fulfill the criteria of a "faltering company,"** you're exempt from the 60-day plant closing notification only. To qualify for reduced notice under this exception:

• An employer must have been actively seeking capital or business at the time that the 60-day notice would have been required. That is, the employer must have been seeking financing or refinancing through the arrangement of loans, or the issuance of stocks, bonds, or other methods of internally generated financing; or the employer must have been seeking additional money, credit, or business through any other commercially reasonable method.

• There must have been a realistic opportunity to obtain the financing or business sought.

• The financing or business sought must have been sufficient, if obtained, to have enabled the employer to avoid or postpone the shutdown. You also have to demonstrate this.

• The employer, reasonably and in good faith, must have believed that giving the required notice would have precluded him or her from obtaining the needed capital or business.

■ **If you underwent "business circumstances"** that were not reasonably foreseeable at the time that the 60-day notice would have been required, you're exempted from the 60-day closing notice for both plant closings and mass layoffs. This unforeseeable circumstance may include an economic downturn or the sudden and unexpected termination of a major contract with your company.

■ **If your business is hit with a "natural disaster,"** such as a flood, an earthquake or a storm, you don't have to adhere to the 60-day notice for both plant closings and mass layoffs.

WHAT TO SAY IN THE NOTICE

In case of a planned plant closing or mass layoff, you should notify each affected employee in writing and in understandable language. The notice should contain the following:

• A statement as to whether the planned action is expected to be permanent or temporary and, if the entire plant is to be closed, a statement to that effect.

• The expected date when the plant closing or mass layoff will commence and the expected date when the individual employee will be separated from the firm.

• An indication of whether or not bumping rights exist.

• The name and telephone number of a company official who can be contacted for further information.

The notice may include additional information useful to the employees, such as information on available dislocated worker assistance.

OBSERVATION:
The 60-day advance notice is meant to provide workers and their families with some transition time to adjust to the prospective loss of employment, to seek and obtain alternative jobs and, if neces-

sary, to enter skills training or retraining that will allow these workers to successfully compete in the job market. Workers may also initiate civil action against violators of the act.

BORROWING FROM EMPLOYEE BENEFIT PLANS

■ ■ ■ ■ ■

If you have loan provisions in your employee benefit plan, make sure they jibe with the final regulation that the Department of Labor (DOL) put into effect in October, 1989. In brief, the rule clarifies and defines certain loan provision terms as they appear in the Employee Retirement Income Security Act of 1974 (ERISA).

RULES ON MAKING LOANS

There are four ingredients that a plan must contain to make loans to plan participants and beneficiaries:

■ **Loans must be available to all participants and beneficiaries on an equal basis.** In clarifying this particular provision, the DOL ruled that:

• *Fiduciaries who are plan participants* are permitted to receive loans. To guard against potential abuses, however, the DOL "will subject loans to fiduciaries to special scrutiny to assure that the conditions of the regulation are met."

• *In determining loan qualifications,* plan sponsors must use criteria that a normal commercial lender would employ. This means that a plan could consider financial need in determining loan worthiness.

• *As a further modification* of this

provision, the DOL said that participants and beneficiaries other than active employees may be offered loans on different terms, as long as they are based on factors that a commercial lender would legally consider.

• *To alleviate the administrative costs* of such loan programs, the DOL said plan sponsors could set minimum loan amounts up to $1,000 without violating ERISA.

■ **Equal availability required.** Plan loans cannot be made available to highly compensated employees, officers or shareholders in an amount greater than that made available to other employees. It's okay, however, for a plan to set a maximum dollar limitation on loans, or a maximum percentage of vested accrued benefit that no loan is to exceed.

■ **All loans must be made in accordance with specific written provisions.** They must also include:

• The identity of the person or position within the company authorized to administer the participant loan program.

• A procedure for applying for loans.

• The basis on which loans will either be approved or denied.

• The limitations (if any) on the types and amounts of loans offered.

• The procedure under the program for determining a reasonable rate of interest.

• The types of collateral that may secure a participant loan, and

• The events constituting default and the steps that will be taken to preserve plan assets in the event of such a default.

The DOL added that a company's summary plan description (SPD) would satisfy this written requirement as long as it contains the above provisions.

■ **Loans must generate a reasonable**

rate of return. The DOL ruled that a reasonable rate is one that "provides the plan with a return commensurate with the prevailing interest rate charged on similar commercial loans by persons in the business of lending money."

CAUTION

The DOL did have this warning in its final rule: "Because participant loans are plan investments, a participant loan program that limits its interest rate to a maximum state usury ceiling when higher yielding comparable investment opportunities exist may not meet the requirements of ERISA."

In a further clarification, the DOL said that with respect to geographical differences in the market rates, plans can adopt a national rate of interest that can be administered on a nationwide basis, thus easing administrative costs. Plans may also use regional market rates as benchmarks for their loan rates.

■ **Loans must be adequately secured.** It's permissible to use at least a portion of a participant's vested accrued benefit as a form of security.

Plans must follow a general requirement, however, that the security for all participant loans be such that the plan will suffer no loss of principal or income if a default occurs. To this end, the DOL's final regulation permits up to 50% of the present value of a participant's vested accrued benefit to be used as security for participant loans. A participant loan program can only exceed the 50% cap if it receives additional collateral that is equal to or greater than the amount exceeding the 50% cap.

EARLY RETIREMENT RIGHTS
· · · · ·

Robert Patterson, a 55-year-old tool designer at Xerox, was offered a chance to take part in a "voluntary" reduction in force if he signed a waiver of all claims against the company.

If he chose not to accept the agreement, which included an extra three months' severance, there was a 99% chance he'd be laid off. Patterson took the deal.

After he left Xerox, he found out that the company had hired three young contract draftsmen in his old department. He filed an age discrimination suit.

◆ PROBLEM:

The courts haven't made up their collective mind whether signing a waiver of the right to sue bars claims under the Age Discrimination in Employment Act (ADEA).

Legislation has been before Congress that would prevent older workers from signing waivers not supervised by the Equal Employment Opportunity Commission or the courts.

NEGOTIATING AN EMPLOYEE'S EARLY RETIREMENT

Explain the waiver and what it means in great detail. Encourage the potential retiree to get outside advice. Build a paper trail that documents your efforts. As long as Congress hasn't revised the law and the courts remain uncertain, a written record is your best defense.

WATCH YOUR BIDDING

· · · · ·

A company bidding on a big job may well, with no evil intent, simply make an error and thereby submit a bid that is a sure money-loser. What happens then?

It depends on the kind of business being bid on. Generally, the courts say that when a bid contains a factual mistake and the buyer wants to go ahead with the deal, no legal agreement has been reached.

◆ EXCEPTION:

The law treats government construction contracts differently, making it tougher for the bidder to back out of its quoted price.

The rule is that a bid becomes irrevocable as soon as it is opened—a rule that is meant to encourage accuracy and to reduce the possibilities of collusion. But the rule is not an absolute one.

Many states follow the formula laid down by the Illinois Supreme Court in 1977: A bidder can back out of an erroneous bid if he can show that the mistake was not due to negligence and if the public agency isn't harmed by withdrawing the bid.

▲ DECISION:

The Colorado Supreme Court set a standard even easier on the bidder: The company need not prove that it was not negligent, but merely that it made its bid in good faith.

The Colorado Court standard will apply only when the too-low bid resulted from an arithmetical or clerical error, not when it was caused by a technical miscalculation of the professional staff. (*Powder Horn Construction v. Florence*, No. 855C502)

OBSERVATION:
The newest ruling reemphasizes the importance of doing a recalculation shortly after the bustle surrounding a bid submission deadline. The right to withdraw applies only *before* a contract is actually awarded.

NEW PACKAGING LAWS

· · · · ·

Bill Armstrong, technical development manager of Sealed Air Corp., Danbury, CT, says the days are gone when packaging design was based solely on cost and performance. "Increasingly, states are enacting legislation regulating packaging materials—whether they're bans, higher taxes, or required recyclability or degradability," says Armstrong, who is also president of the Institute of Packaging Professionals, Reston, VA—previously called the Society of Packaging and Handling Engineers.

WHO IS AFFECTED

• Though the focus now is primarily on consumer packaging, especially plastics, he and others believe business-to-business packaging will soon feel secondary fallout. If bans on styrofoam cups become widespread, for example, businesses may soon thereafter be barred from using Styrofoam peanuts, boxes or wraps to protect the equipment they ship.

• Multi-material packaging—combinations of, say, paper and aluminum or various plastics—may also be in trouble. Environmental groups have worked in some states to impose extra taxes on multi-material packaging because it is so difficult to recycle. But according to Dan Toner, senior research fellow for Campbell Soup Co., "You might have to use four times the amount of a single plastic to match the properties you could achieve with a multi-material package. With multiple materials, you can put in more bounce to the ounce." Toner and other package designers, however, are attuned to the political realities. "A basic part of design now is how to dispose of the package," he says.

◆ PROBLEM:

One headache for manufacturers is that some states are following their own individual agendas without any real guidance from the United States Environmental Protection Agency. Some businesses dealing in consumer products are already experiencing nightmares when shipping containers across state lines—when a particular state suddenly decides it wants to collect a tax on a certain type of packaging or product without any prior warning.

WHAT TO DO

• **Have your marketing managers prepare environmental asset statements** if they haven't already done so. They should take each of your products and analyze the positives and negatives. Is it recyclable? Is it reusable? Can it be made degradable?

• **If it can be recycled, ask yourself how.** Through what recycling group? Can you mix plastic wraps with plastic milk cartons, and so on?

These are questions that Sealed Air Corp. is currently asking itself, according to Armstrong. "Are we using any packaging that is unnecessary? Could it be viewed as

such? Can we justify it in three words or less? That's the amount of time you get to explain it to a government subcommittee," he points out.

• **Do you ship overseas?** With the trend toward globalization, Armstrong says that it is wise for businesses to familiarize themselves with packaging regulations set forth by the European Economic Community and even the United Nations. "We are changing our standard practices to meet regulations that are developed primarily offshore," he says.

• **Consider reusable containers.** Alfred McKinlay, a Schenectady, NY packaging consultant, says there is a strong trend to reusing containers. "This got started in the automotive industry years ago, but now it's spreading to other industries, too," he notes. "Companies want to make both their containers and interior packaging returnable for a number of trips. There's less waste all around, and that way, the companies receiving the materials don't have an expensive disposal problem."

Of course, companies on the receiving end don't want to have a lot of boxes cluttering up their plants. So they often specify that the packaging must nest according to certain prestated standards for both storage and shipping.

• **Get the marketing edge.** You needn't wait for a customer's request. "Anytime there's a fair amount of traffic between two points, this (i.e., adopting reusable containers and packaging that nests) can give a supplier a marketing advantage," states McKinlay. It takes a fair amount of effort to set such a system up, however, so you'll want to plan carefully before you start one. "For instance," McKinlay says, "if you changed your product so that it didn't fit the package anymore, you'd have a lot of scrap material."

HIRE THE REAL THING: THE 'BETTE MIDLER' RULING

• • • • •

An advertising ploy that looks as though it can save money—hiring imitators to mimic famous voices rather than signing celebrities—may turn out to be costlier than the real thing.

The U.S. Court of Appeals in San Francisco has ruled that such commercials violate California tort law, even if the celebrities are never identified by name or shown in the campaign.

Ford Motor Co. was the defendant in the case, arising out of its television campaign to reach "yuppies" by running commercials built around songs popular in the 1970s, when the target customers were first driving on their own.

Ford's ad agency, Young & Rubicam, actually tried to hire the original stars to recreate the numbers, but a few said no. The agency then hired singers with similar voices, and told them to sound as much like the original singers as possible. One of those imitated, Bette Midler, objected to her version of "Do You Want to Dance?"

▲ D E C I S I O N :

Even though the commercial was made with a license from the owner of the song, it injured Midler to appropriate her distinctive voice without her permission, the judges said.

They built their ruling on a 1974 decision allowing an automobile race driver to sue for showing his car in a cigarette commercial. A voice is a more personal attribute than a car, Judge John T. Noonan noted. And when it is famous, it is a property right which can be protected like any other. (*Midler v. Ford Motor*, No. 87-6168)

NO OSHA FISHING EXPEDITIONS

• • • • •

OSHA inspectors need a warrant to obtain an employer's health and safety records, unless their release is needed for a specific enforcement act. Fishing expeditions are out. They violate the privacy provision of the Fourth Amendment.

An OSHA inspector showed up at an amusement park. Employees had complained that the fog used in a stage show caused irritation.

During the investigation the inspector asked for the employer's OSHA Form 200s to review the park's overall hygienic and environmental problems. He did not have a search warrant, but cited the "upon request" provision in the OSHA law. A court case resulted.

The case pivoted on a requirement in the OSHA law that employers keep records on occupational accidents and illnesses. Moreover, the Act requires that "each employer shall provide, upon request, records. . .for inspection and copying by a representative of the Secretary of Labor. . ."

The Secretary of Labor argued that the provision reduced an employer's expectations of privacy. Moreover, he said, obtaining subpoenas or warrants was too burdensome.

For a decision, the court didn't buy the argument, laying down these criteria for a warrantless search:

• Substantial government regulatory in-

151

terest in the appropriate material.
- Furthering OSHA regulations.
- A defined scope for the search.
- Employer notification.

The Labor Department failed to meet these guidelines, the court held, and therefore to attempt such a search violates the employer's Fourth Amendment rights. (*McLaughlin v. Kings Island*, No. 87-3457)

▲ COMMENT:

OSHA inspectors need a warrant if they want to obtain general information from an employer, the case makes clear. And they need clear-cut specifics to obtain data without one.

PERILS OF PICKING ON A COMPETITOR

· · · · ·

There are some important do's and don'ts for companies engaging in the practice of "comparative advertising." Lawsuits alleging misrepresentation in ads—where a company makes claims that reflect negatively on its competition—are on the rise. One reason for the spurt in legal action is a recent federal law that greatly expands the territory for filing damage claims.

GUIDELINES TO FOLLOW

Here are some do's and don'ts for comparative advertising, as spelled out by New York University marketing experts Bruce Buchanan and Doron Goldman in an issue of the Harvard Business Review:
- *Don't set out to make any false or misleading claims.*
- *Be able to verify a factual statement*, such

as a claim that your airline makes more flights to Chicago than your competitor does.
- *Be able to prove the truth of your product research claims* by showing that the researchers are qualified, that the conditions were unbiased, and that the ad reflected supporting data with fidelity.
- *Don't exaggerate by making claims* beyond what your product offers.
- *Don't stretch research results*, where the claim goes beyond the findings.
- *Don't overstep data*, with unqualified claims based on qualified results.
- *Don't pick and choose data*, leaving out the unfavorable and reporting only the favorable.

While the courts will enjoin advertising that misrepresents, the burden of proof lies with the plaintiff, who must prove the claim is false; the defendant need not prove the claim is true.

TWO ENJOINED ADS

The NYU experts give these examples of enjoined ads:
- A NOW cigarette ad claimed that its product had the lowest tar content of all cigarettes at two milligrams; Carlton 70, though shorter, had one milligram.
- In another case, the Quaker State Oil Company won an injunction against a claim by Castrol GTX that, unlike Quaker State, its oil did not lose viscosity. In issuing the injunction, the Court said that all oils lose some viscosity.

Most of the federal court suits seek prompt preliminary injunctions to bar the running of an ad. But claims may also be made for compensatory and punitive damages where a company can demonstrate direct harm to its own product from a competitor's misrepresentation.

OBSERVATION:

Bear in mind that some states also have laws prohibiting defamation and disparagement in comparative advertising cases, making it doubly important that you be able to back up any advertising claims about your product or that of your competitor.

STIFF PENALTIES FOR VIOLATING OSHA WORKPLACE RULES

· · · · ·

States now have the power to jail employers who violate federal safety and health rules in cases involving serious injury to, or death of, employees. In the past, lower courts have ruled that penalty regulations of the Occupational Safety and Health Administration (OSHA) preempt states from carrying out such strict state penalties.

However, the Supreme Court declined to hear an appeal against a state indictment of corporate officials for OSHA violations. In doing so, the high court, in effect, gave its tacit approval for the states to criminally prosecute companies for violations resulting in serious injury to, or death of, employees. In such cases, firms can now be hit with both state and OSHA penalties.

The seriousness of the matter is reflected in the fact that violations of workplace health and safety rules have generally led to fines by OSHA; now, the states can send violators, such as corporate officials, to prison.

OBSERVATION:

In the appeal the Supreme Court refused to hear, company officials for the Magnet Wire Corp. in Chicago were indicted for aggravated battery under Illinois state law for "wantonly and recklessly" allowing Magnet employees to be exposed to poisonous gases. In all, 42 workers suffered serious injuries.

WHY YOU NEED A SAFETY AUDIT

· · · · ·

To protect your company against potential product-liability lawsuits, you might want to have your products or manufacturing processes subjected to a professional safety audit. While the cost of an audit is sometimes expensive, it will pay for itself by reducing the likelihood of a lawsuit and, often, by shaving liability insurance premiums as well.

PRODUCT-RELATED ACCIDENTS

Even if you believe your product is safe, there may be unpleasant surprises in store for you down the road. Dr. Vassilis Morfopolous, technical director, American Standards Testing Bureau (ASTB), cites three sources of product-related accidents that supposedly weren't supposed to happen:

• *Misuses by customers*. Some equipment manufacturers, for example, have been held liable for injuries sustained by workers who had bypassed safety measures installed on the machines. Courts have ruled for the plaintiff in some cases because the manufacturer should have foreseen potentially dangerous user modifications to equipment.

• *Product aging*. Manufacturers don't always anticipate what will happen when their products reach the end of their useful lives. Dr. Morfopolous recalls the disastrous lawsuits that hit the laundry extractor industry some years ago. The machines, once widely used in laundromats to spin-dry wash, worked fine for up to 30 years. Then the braking mechanisms, designed to stop the machines before customers could open them, began to wear out. The results: numerous severe hand and arm injuries, and lawsuits that wiped out the industry.

• *Packaging problems.* A large rectifier machine was shipped out in good condition by a Philadelphia manufacturer to a user in Kentucky. It checked out O.K. upon arrival, but testing did not uncover the fact that electrical insulators had cracked while the equipment was en route to the customer, due to an inadequate shipping container. The resulting fire wiped out the customer's planning facility and the manufacturer was held liable.

TO PROTECT YOURSELF

• **Don't rely on customers' good sense** to use your product as it was designed. Be sure that your product is adequately labeled with hazard warnings and that complete instructions for its safe operation are included. If your product is installed by a dealer or other third party, send a salesperson or technician to check on proper installation and ensure that the seller provides adequate customer training.

• **Keep an eye on your product life cycle.** Be sure that users have adequate instructions and timetables for replacing critical parts that could pose safety hazards in the future. Keep track of where the machines are, and offer service contracts so you can stay on top of maintenance and repairs.

• **Provide users with adequate in-**

structions for testing, or conduct on-site tests yourself, to ensure quality standards aren't compromised after you've shipped the product.

OBSERVATION:
ASTB will do a product performance certification, which tests industrial or consumer products for compliance with standards, provides simulated testing and projects a product's useful life, along with any potential hazards that might occur as the product ages. These audits can take from one to 10 weeks to complete, at a cost generally ranging between $3,000 and $30,000.

FOR MORE INFORMATION:

Contact American Standards Testing Bureau, 40 Water Street, New York, NY 10004; 212-943-3156.

GROWING PROBLEMS WITH VDTs

Business should be alert to the potential problems arising from the use of video display terminals (VDTs). The problems aren't new, but they're becoming magnified by a sharp rise in repetitive-motion injuries from computer usage and heightened concern over low-frequency radiation and its effect on pregnant employees.

▲ FACT:
The Bureau of Labor Statistics (BLS) figures on worker injuries show a big rise in 1988, with repetitive-motion disorders accounting for the lion's share. There was

a total of 240,990 cases of on-the-job injuries reported, representing about a 25% increase over the 190,400 injuries reported in 1987. An overwhelming 80% of that increase stemmed from ailments arising from repeated motion, pressure or vibration, such as carpel tunnel syndrome, an affliction involving the carpus or wrist bone.

COMPUTERS AND HEALTH PROBLEMS

• The increased use of computers— some 40 million are currently employed in the workplace—accounted for a substantial portion of the repetitive-motion injuries on record, according to BLS officials. This represents a significant shift in a trend in which many of the repetitive-motion illnesses that were reported in the past occurred mostly in the meatpacking and poultry businesses, and in the automobile and other manufacturing industries.

• Concerning safety threats to the fetuses of pregnant employees, while one study did report an excess of miscarriages among VDT-operating pregnant women, several other major studies failed to find that such a link existed. Sponsors of these studies did theorize that the miscarriages may have stemmed from various ergonomic factors, such as uncomfortable VDT operating arrangements.

Even though there isn't conclusive proof that VDTs are a safety threat, this has become a workplace issue, generating growing safety consciousness among users and computer manufacturers. IBM, for example, has said that its future models will have increased radiation protection, a move meant to alleviate the concerns of pregnant workers.

RECOMMENDATION: With VDT usage becoming a growing safety issue, you'll want to take note of employee concerns. Make ergonomic adjustments, such as more comfortable VDT chairs and no-glare screens. Vary the time operators spend on the VDT. You might also consider shifting pregnant employees to non-VDT assignments to alleviate their concern.

AVOID PROBLEMS FROM INDOOR AIR POLLUTION
• • • • •

It might be wise for you to take the time to check out the air quality of your workplace, or you may find yourself on the wrong end of a "sick-building syndrome" suit involving your own employees. Lawyers and air quality experts say that the field of indoor air pollution litigation could rival those suits involving the presence of asbestos in buildings.

WHAT IT'S ALL ABOUT

The sick-building syndrome is an outgrowth of the energy crisis of the 1970s, when buildings were designed with sealed windows and heavily insulated walls to cut costs. Inadequate fresh air and poor ventilation systems have created a pollution build-up inside the buildings.

In a report, the Environmental Protection Agency (EPA) estimated that the economic cost of indoor air pollution could total billions of dollars in terms of lost productivity, direct medical care, lost earnings and employee sick days.

MORE WORKERS BRING SUIT

In the past, workers' compensation laws prohibited employees from suing their employers over most safety and health issues. But attorneys familiar with the new area of law say that workers are getting around that caveat in workers' compensation laws by contending that their employers knew about the health problem and failed to act in time.

OBSERVATION:

There has been enough heat from constituents to get Congress involved in the issue. There have been bills in the House of Representatives and the Senate that would authorize an expanded research effort on the dangers of indoor air pollution and the publication of health advisories for consumers.

Even the EPA employees picketed their Washington, DC headquarters to protest that agency's handling of complaints. Workers blamed respiratory and other illnesses on fumes from new carpets installed in a poorly ventilated area of the office. Now the EPA employees' union is pushing the agency to adopt uniform indoor air standards that manufacturers would have to comply with, as well as testing procedures for new carpets.

RECOMMENDATION:

Don't wait to be blind-sided by an employee suit. Order semiannual air quality tests in all of your firm's work areas. Be sure to let workers know you are sensitive to the issue of clean air in offices and plants, and announce the results of the tests. Ignorance is no excuse in case of a lawsuit.

MUST YOU SHOW UP IN COURT?

· · · · ·

In general, executives need not appear in court when their company is engaged in a lawsuit. But that practice does not confer the right to refuse to show up.

The Seventh Circuit made that point in upholding the action of a federal magistrate who had ordered a company engaged in litigation to send an executive with authority to settle the case to a pretrial conference.

The company refused on the grounds that it had already made clear it would not accept any settlement that involved monetary liability. That refusal cost the firm nearly $6,000 in sanctions.

In its appeal, the company argued that Federal Rule of Civil Procedure 16 barred the courts from requiring parties to attend. The rule allows courts to summon lawyers to pretrial meetings.

▲ DECISION:

The Seventh Circuit Court disagreed. Federal rules don't decide judicial authority to manage trials. Lack of specific language doesn't imply a ban on procedures.

For another, Rule 16 is designed to encourage active judicial management of dockets from the beginning. That includes ordering parties to appear, if needed.

Finally, the magistrate had not abused his discretion because he had only ordered the executive to discuss the case.

The courts can't coerce settlements, but they can require an officer who can consider the possibility of settlement to show up. (*G. Heileman Brewing Co. v. Joseph Oat Corp.*, No. 86-3118, March 27, 1989)

Chapter 9

MARKETING

CREATIVE ALTERNATIVES TO DISCOUNT PRICING

■ ■ ■ ■ ■

When you're tempted to cut prices or offer special discounts to stimulate sales, stop and think for a moment. The move may cost you more than margins. You could:

■ **Cripple your ability to meet your forecast.** Suppose your campaign works and customers load up. How much will you sell in the next period when their inventories are full? Also, prices, once officially cut or discounted for a long period of time, may be hard to raise again.

■ **Tarnish your image.** Special discounts and sales seem "low-class" to many buyers. If the product is top quality, why does the maker have to push price? Aren't enough people buying the product? Is it really second rate?

CREATIVE ALTERNATIVES

Instead of offering discount periods or cutting your prices, consider implementing less costly incentives—preferably ones that will enhance your image. Here are some examples:

• *Pick up* the "costs of changing."

• *Extend credit terms.* Also, consider offering a lease option, if appropriate for your product and industry.

• *Hold the line.* If you have a premium image you want to uphold, the best course may be to hold your price and say so.

• *Enhance value.* Increase the worth of your product or service rather than reducing its price.

EXAMPLE:
Offer a better warranty, user training or a free cost-effectiveness analysis.

• *Personalize discounts if you must discount.* Make your promotional pricing memorable in some way. In 1989, in college alumni magazines, the Hotel Sofitel, Redwood City, CA offered nightly rates based on the guest's year of graduation. Those graduating in 1989 paid $89 per night; members of the class of 1970 paid just $70; and so on. It was personal and memorable.

NEW PRODUCT IN WORKS? CHECK CATEGORY'S FUTURE
■ ■ ■ ■ ■

A key question to answer when reviewing potential new products and services is, "Is this a category we want to participate in?"

Given today's shortened product life cycles, the outlook for a product's category can be more important than the outlook for the product itself. So explore the growth potential of the product category early on. That can help you decide not only whether an entry is feasible, but also what strategy you should pursue.

• Individual products "peak" much more quickly than product categories and subcategories. According to The Futures Group (TFG), a Glastonbury, CT marketing consulting firm, a new product achieves 90% of its sustainable market share in one to three years. In contrast, a new category can take as long as a decade or more to realize its full potential.

• A number of studies have shown that profitability and sales growth come most rapidly for companies that recognize the importance of a category at the outset and add products sequentially "to satisfy first one segment, then another and another."

CAUTION

Monitor customer attitudes toward categories you are in or are considering entering at all stages of product R&D. Customers' wants and needs can change quickly.

OBSERVATION:
The homework you do to determine whether you want to participate in a given category can uncover many new product ideas and market segment opportunities. So even if you decide that the category's not for you, you won't have wasted your efforts.

SUPPOSE YOUR PRODUCT IS JUST TOO SUCCESSFUL?
■ ■ ■ ■ ■

A new product that doesn't take off is tough to take. But one that succeeds beyond your expectations or preparations can give you a different variety of headaches: You lose sales and face, and you may also give the competition an opportunity to copy what you've done, killing your "skim" period. It's prudent, therefore, to consider how you'll handle an unlooked-for sales explosion before you hand the ball to your sales force. Here are some guidelines:

PRODUCTION

Before you introduce the product to the sales force or begin shipping it into test markets, schedule a meeting with production management to coordinate your efforts and familiarize yourself with any potential problems that may arise.

• *Lead times.* With production, establish lead times from sale to delivery for specific levels of market demand over projection: 10%, 20%, 30%, etc. At which of these levels are specific contingency plans required? Will meeting any of these production levels result in extended lead times for other products?

• *Slowdowns.* If there is a need to slow the pace of production on other products, how will that affect your customers? How will you deal with any customer problems that may ensue in a way that avoids hurting present business?

• *Cost increases.* What kind of cost increases do production people see from going into overtime, adding shifts, and the like? Are you prepared to work these higher costs into appropriate price increases? Or would it be better to eat some or all of those costs to keep competition out?

• *Outside help.* Could your purchasing people find subcontractors to pick up any production slack?

• *Early warning.* Do you have a system in place that will give you sufficient warning when demand is going to significantly exceed your projections? If not, would arranging regular, frequent phone contacts with key customers or distributors give you that warning?

• *Pricing.* Would a price increase be in order in the event of runaway demand? Is there someone else with whom you should discuss and plan for that possibility?

THE SALES EFFORT

If a surge in demand causes a shift in your marketing plans, what medium will you use to get word to the field quickly?

• *Sales efforts.* Will you have the field reduce or temporarily halt its sales efforts? Or would it be better for your salespeople to write all the business they can get but warn customers of the delays in completely truthful terms?

• *Deliveries.* Would it be acceptable simply to deliver the product in the order that sales come in? Or would it be preferable to develop a written system of allocation?

• *Alternative shipping.* Would another acceptable alternative be to offer partial timely deliveries and back orders on the balance?

• *Customer follow-up.* How practical would it be for salespeople to call customers who have already ordered and ask them if partial deliveries would be acceptable until production catches up?

• *Advertising and promotion.* Would turning off any advertising or other ongoing promotional efforts be an acceptable way to stem the flood? Or would it be better to explain the situation in your ads, apologize, and include a date by which lead times will be back to normal?

SOFT SELL EFFECTIVELY WITH USER SEMINARS

· · · · ·

If the value of your service or product depends on how it is used, a seminar could help you sell it. That's the experience of companies ranging from the Fortune 500 to local distributorships and retailers.

One big, current advocate of seminar "selling," IBM, has been using the strategy since 1986. Yet, it already considers seminar selling "a prime tool in developing new accounts." The factors that IBM considers important to success are within the reach of nearly any marketer:

• *Sell solutions, not just a product.* A sales seminar should be educational, not a sales presentation in disguise. IBM's seminars do not feature its equipment directly. Instead, they are tailored to specific market niches. Topics include: "Apparel: Manufacturing and Distribution," "Benefit Funds Management," "Book Publishing" and "Property Management." Newspaper ads promote the tailoring, telling potential participants, "The seminar you attend will focus on computer solutions for your kind of business or profession." That builds credibility with prospects.

The seminar agendas help to drive that message home. An IBM representative leads the first 15 minutes of the seminar. For the next hour to hour and a quarter, an IBM "Partner" takes over. The Partner, a software developer or a remarketer of IBM equipment, is the key supplier of the seminar's application-specific intelligence.

• *Invite prospects who have a need to know.* Look for those who could benefit from learning what the particular seminar imparts. For example, IBM asks representatives of the "Partner" involved in its "Construction: Interior Renovators" seminar to invite people involved in design and renovation and to contribute their personal stories.

• *Make your commercial interest clear.* Prospective participants will be suspicious if you don't seem to be selling anything. They know there are no free lunches. While they don't want a hard sell, they are most comfortable if you make it plain that you hope they will consider your service or product once they get to know you or learn how to use it profitably. Right below their "Manage Your Business Better" headline, IBM's seminar ads clearly state, "Come to a free IBM seminar. You'll find out how an IBM computer can help you reduce paperwork and manage better."

• *Capture information for closing sales.* You may or may not find it practical to take orders at the seminar, but you should certainly glean qualifying data. When people first come in, IBM has them go through a little program on its PCs (scattered around the room) to tell about their business. There are also brief exit interviews, asking, "Is this solution right for you?" Depending on their answers, seminar participants are categorized A, B or C for high-, medium- and low-priority follow-up by IBM and its "Partner" representatives.

MAKE YOUR DIRECT MAIL MORE POWERFUL
· · · · ·

If you use direct mail—or are thinking of using it—to sell your product or develop leads, how can you get the greatest return for your money?

The following strategies could help you improve your direct-mail results:

• *Mail to the right title.* Ask yourself who the real buyer is. Address that person, not the president or CEO.

• *Tailor the mailing to the buyer.* Would you send the same letter to Lee Iacocca that you'd send to the manager of a local dry cleaning company? For senior executives, use a finer grade of paper and have the recipient's address printed or typed on the envelope instead of using address labels. Also, go easy on the sell.

The lower the rank of the recipient, the more appropriate hard-hitting copy is, experts say. Higher-ups, especially those with large companies, prefer a more relaxed approach. Also, slick sales pieces, such as flyers and catalogs, get the best reception from lower-level personnel in large firms and executives of smaller companies.

• *Tailor the offer to the buyer's needs.* When mailing to disparate companies or departments, change your offer to reflect the differences.

EXAMPLE:

In promoting the services of a computer leasing company, you'd send different letters to chief financial officers and data processing managers. To the former, you'd emphasize the tax benefits of leasing; to the latter, the budgetary benefits. One-size-fits-all promotions don't work well.

WHAT IT TAKES TO MAKE PRESS RELEASES SUCCESSFUL
■ ■ ■ ■ ■

Editors like to receive informative, concise press releases to find out what companies are doing. Here are some guidelines to help ensure that yours succeed:

• *Come straight to the point.* Begin with a caption or summary that clearly states your message. Editors don't have time to search through releases for buried news.

• *Identify your firm concisely.* If your letterhead doesn't explain your company, develop a simple, one-sentence statement such as, "Argus, the leading distributor of orange pipes. . ."

• *Be brief.* Most editors prefer one-page releases. Conserve space by eliminating information that is of little interest to the publication's readers. Editors will call if they want more in-depth information.

• *List a contact person,* and make sure he or she is available and knows the facts. Editors say that about one-third of the people named on the releases they get are either unavailable or don't know the topic.

• *Give all the relevant facts.* Often missing are: accurate price information, how long it will take before a new product is available for purchase or delivery and, on personnel releases, a complete capsule history that includes previous employment.

• *Identify the audience and send only to the appropriate media.* If yours is not a general-use product or service, tell for whom the announcement is useful.

• *Watch your appearance.* Blotchy type or bad photocopies present a negative company image. Bad grammar or slipshod punctuation also create a second-rate effect.

• *Identify photographs* and key them to the release. Photos are often separated from the text. Unidentified, they may be rendered useless.

• *Don't blow your own horn.* Editors are uniformly scathing about press releases full of self-praise instead of news.

• *Offer real news promptly.* This is especially important if you are going for the big time. A *Wall Street Journal* editor says that time-sensitive news should get in early in the day. If needed, use a messenger, overnight delivery or electronic transmission.

EASY, INEXPENSIVE NEWS RELEASE MAILINGS

· · · · ·

If you don't use a public relations firm to send out news about your firm, you probably employ the time-honored do-it-yourself approach: getting media names out of directories, putting the names and addresses on file cards, typing or photocopying labels each time you send out a release, photocopying your release or sending it to a printer, and finally, stuffing and mailing the releases.

If you send out only one or two releases a year to a very small list, that may be your best way of doing things. But if your list is long or your mailings are more frequent, there are better ways.

OPTION ONE

Send a single copy of your release to a media distribution service and let it handle everything.

• *Potential money savings.* Experts estimate that a company can save as much as 15% to 25% on its distribution costs by employing a distribution service.

Media Distribution Services (MDS), New York City, charges $94 to send out 100 copies of a two-page release. Included in the price are media selection, duplication of mailing labels, printing of the release, folding, inserting and mailing. (Postage is extra.) Bacon's Publicity Distribution, Chicago, offers the same services for $83.00. If you check your labor costs, you may find that you are paying your own people more and getting less for your outlay.

• *Get your news out faster.* A do-it-your-self PR mailing may take a couple of days to a week or more to get out; the services are set up for 24-hour turnaround. If you fax a release to a service Monday morning and specify "rush," it may be able to get it in the mail that afternoon.

• *Target the media better.* Peppering the land with releases is a waste. A media distribution service helps clients target the media most likely to use the release. The services also update their lists of editorial contacts frequently. Thus, they can direct the release to the appropriate editor (business, health, financial, etc.) by name. That improves the chances of its being used.

• *Send odd mailings without a hassle.* The services are set up to handle press kits, photographs and product samples as well as releases. Bacon's, for example, has mailed food products for Kraft and Uncle Ben's, as well as musical buttons and basketballs for sports teams.

• *No real drawbacks.* A service can do everything you can do more conveniently: print releases on your letterhead; select media by locale, industry or circulation size; and handpick publications. If you mail at least three times a year, it will maintain your private PR mailing list, including members of your own firm.

OPTION TWO

Get your news releases on a wire service. PR Newswire, New York, NY offers a low-cost electronic supplement, or replacement, for your present method of sending out news releases. The service operates much like AP and UPI—the leading newswire services—except that anyone can get a story on it by paying the going price. Over 17,500 companies, associations, and so on, including 85% of the Fortune 1,000, are already taking advantage of this option.

As with AP and UPI, stories are transmitted electronically and received on the subscribing news organizations' terminals or computers. More than 1,500 newspapers, magazines, trade journals, and radio and TV stations subscribe. The major news services, including AP and UPI, also subscribe, as do more than 20 leading databases. So there's a chance your story will get picked up for additional exposure in media that don't subscribe to Newswire.

• *Low cost.* Users pay a $75 annual fee plus service charges for each release they send. You can send a 400-word release (about two typed, double-spaced pages) to the nation's 950 leading newsrooms for $375. That's just slightly more than the cost of postage. There's no charge for printing, folding or inserting because it isn't necessary. It would cost $325 to $450 or more to send out an equal number of printed releases on your own or through one of the media distribution services.

• *Fast, reliable delivery.* Releases are put on the wire immediately, or at a time specified by you. They arrive at all newsrooms simultaneously, a big advantage over erratic mail delivery.

• *Targeted distribution.* PR Newswire has a number of services for organizations with specialized needs. They range from national to regional and local distribution. You can also target specialized audiences, such as the Hong Kong press (and no other groups) or aerospace trade journals, for double to triple the local rates.

• *Drawbacks.* Traditional media distribution services may offer a greater selection and greater selectivity of news organizations and editors. They can also send photos. In contrast, a PR Newswire "release" can only say that photos are available. If you want to send out a thick press kit, the electronic method isn't practical, and, of course, PR Newswire can't deliver any product samples.

It can be reached at 212-832-9400.

DON'T LET AN 800 NUMBER TURN YOUR CUSTOMER OFF

For most companies today, the question is not, "Should we have an 800 number?" but "How soon can we get one?"

That's not surprising: People who call in with inquiries are three times more likely to become customers than those who mail in inquiry cards. Studies show that a space advertisement with an 800 number will generate 20% more orders than the same ad without one.

Installing the 800 number is only the beginning, however. Here are some things to look for to make sure your new 800 number does the job:

• Can your callers get through?

• How many rings does it take before the call is answered?

• How often are people put on hold, and for how long?

• How many people give up?

• Are there peaks and valleys in call volume? Why?

• Are your phone hours convenient for your customers or only for you?

Know what your phone system can provide, including the reports it can generate; you'll need them to answer the above questions and make any desired adjustments. If you need more telephone representatives to handle the volume, hire them.

• What happens when the call is answered?

Implementing an 800 strategy requires careful planning.

• Has a process been designed to move your callers from suspect to prospect to satisfied customer?

• Has a system been implemented to facilitate that process?

• Do your phone reps know the system and understand the rationale behind it?

• Do they present themselves—and your company—professionally and courteously to customers?

A computerized or manual system for handling customers should be in place before the first call comes in. Hire phone representatives against stringent standards and provide the training they would need in order to present a professional image.

• What happens when the call is over?

• How long to fulfill the order?

• How long before an inquiry is converted into a sale?

• How efficient is follow-up?

• What new market opportunities exist in your growing file of demographic and market information?

THE RIGHT NUMBER OF REPS IN THE FIELD: A FORMULA

· · · · ·

If you know what it takes for your average representative to do the sales job and you have a fix on your customers, you can calculate the number of reps that you should have selling your service or products.

• *Assign values to your customers.* Rate every customer and targeted prospect in your area. Use "A," "B," "C" or any rating system you prefer.

• *Give each a call frequency value.* For example, an "A" is worth two calls a month, a "B" rates monthly calls, and so on.

• *Add them up.* Say you have 150 "A" accounts at 26 calls a year, 250 "B" accounts at 12 calls a year and 200 "C" accounts at 8. You require 8,500 [(150 × 26) + (250 × 12) + (200 × 8)] calls a year.

• *Decide on a daily call rate.* You probably already know from experience the average number of sales calls that your average rep can make daily. You have included in that calculation the time required for paperwork, prospecting, service calls and so on. For example, you may come up with four calls as the average daily figure.

• *Figure an average annual call rate.* With holidays, vacations, sick days, etc., considered, most estimates round out to about 180 working days a year. (If your average number is different, use it.)

Multiplying 180 × 4 (the average daily call rate), you get 720 calls a year per sales representative.

• *Divide the total number of calls you require by the average annual call rate;* 8,500 (from Step 3 above) ÷ 720 (from Step 6 above) = 11.8 sales reps required. With this kind of fractional result, you'd probably go with 12 representatives, not 11. (More often than not, you'll have to round off your calculated figure.)

RECOMMENDATION:

If the number you get is higher than the number of salespeople you now have, do some field travel with your people. Perhaps the daily call rate you figured is too low. A recent reduction in the number of lines you sell, for example, may have changed the duration of each call.

Chapter 10

TAX ISSUES

WRITING OFF CASUALTY LOSSES

· · · · ·

Casualty losses may be caused by earthquakes, floods, storms, fires, burglaries or even sonic booms. But they have to be sudden and unpredictable, not the result of a mysterious disappearance, a steady decline or the progressive weakening of a structure by the weather.

Although some taxpayers have been able to prove successfully that "fast-eating" termites caused major damage, despite regular and thorough inspections, the IRS generally regards termite damage as progressive deterioration.

When it comes to theft, the hardest point to prove is usually that the property was really stolen, not simply lost. Once you do prove theft, the cost of recovering the property is deductible as an added loss.

The amount of a casualty loss, whether business or personal, is the lesser of the difference between its fair market value immediately before and immediately after the event, or the adjusted basis of the property immediately before the casualty.

AVOID STATE TAX TRAPS

· · · · ·

When you're planning a merger, acquisition or reorganization, it can pay to check out the state tax consequences beforehand.

All too often, companies focus solely on federal laws, which may or may not work out to their advantage. Thus, they may suddenly find themselves facing tax liabilities that can run into millions of dollars, or they may reap a windfall because some states are actually more generous than the federal government in treatment of dividends.

Nearly a score of states have restrictive or confusing rules on dividends, net operating losses and carryovers, real estate transfer taxes and the like, which could prove costly. To complicate things further, many states make it hard to get reliable information in advance on such matters as how they handle reorganizations that are tax free on the federal level.

RECOMMENDATION:

To avoid the chance of being hit with taxes that might have changed your mind if you'd known about them, make it a point to press the state hard for a private letter ruling.

SAVE TAXES WHEN YOU BUY OR SELL A BUSINESS
■　■　■　■　■

Whether you're buying or selling a business, you can earn big tax savings by allocating the price carefully among the assets.

Part of the Tax Reform Act dictates the use of one system for the allocation process —the "residual method."

The law, Code Sec. 1060, also requires buyers and sellers to file reports with IRS on how they allocated the purchase price.

Under the residual method, you allocate the sale price among four classes of assets:

• *Class I.* This includes cash, demand deposits and similar bank accounts.

• *Class II.* This takes in certificates of deposit, government securities, readily salable stocks and securities, and foreign money.

• *Class III.* This covers other assets such as furniture, equipment, land, buildings, accounts receivable and noncompetition agreements.

• *Class IV.* This is where you put intangible assets, such as goodwill and going-concern value.

In practice, you first subtract all Class I assets from the purchase price, then Class II, followed by Class III in proportion to their fair market values. Whatever is left over is allocated to Class IV assets, which aren't depreciable. Further, because there's no longer a low capital gains tax rate, this category is no particular help to the seller.

Obviously, as a buyer you want to get as many assets into Classes I–III as possible. Customer lists, for example, can be an amortizable asset under certain conditions. If the seller transfers a patent, its value can also be amortized.

If the seller provided some essential service to the business, both parties may want to draft a noncompetition agreement, a consulting contract or a management agreement. This not only benefits the buyer, but it also serves to defer income to the seller into later years.

ACCOUNTING FOR GOODWILL

Besides the tax angle, there are good accounting reasons for keeping the value of goodwill to a minimum when you buy a business.

Rules adopted by the Financial Accounting Standards Board (FASB) require you to write off goodwill over a numbered period of years. But since it's not depreciable or amortizable for tax purposes, there's no tax write-off.

> **EXAMPLE:**
>
> You buy a company for $1 million, and you can allocate $900,000 to tangible or intangible depreciable assets. The remainder is goodwill, which you'll have to write off on the company's books over a period of several years. If, for example, you chose to write off the goodwill over a 10-year period, you would charge off $10,000 against earnings each year.

OBSERVATION:

The result can make corporate earnings under generally accepted accounting principles (GAAP) look lower than they really are. That, in turn, can have a depressing effect on the price of the company's stock.

One way you can minimize this distortion is to put out a cash-flow statement. In many cases, it gives a truer picture of the company's health.

REDUCE YOUR DEBT WITHOUT TAX PAIN

· · · · ·

If a creditor cancels a debt that you owe, you may be able to avoid having to pay to the bank any taxes on this reportedly "imputed" income.

Generally, the rules work this way: Say you owe the bank $20,000 and you suddenly realize that you're having cash-flow problems. The bank doesn't want to throw you into bankruptcy, so it does you a favor and cuts the debt by $5,000. The reduced payments can save your business, but at the end of the year you'll find that you owe tax on the $5,000.

Here are some exceptions:

• *Reduction of debt owed to a person who sells you property.* As long as the property can be specifically identified, reduction of the debt owed to the seller is considered a price adjustment.

> **EXAMPLE:**
>
> You buy a computer system for $15,000, paying $3,000 and giving the seller a note for the balance. He later reduces the amount you owe him by another $3,000. That's not income to you.

• *Bankruptcy.* Discharge of a debt under a bankruptcy court decree, or under a plan the court has approved, isn't income to the debtor.

• *Insolvency.* If your debts exceed the value of your assets, cancellation of part of the debt won't be income. However, this out is limited to the difference between the value of your assets and the total amount originally owed.

> **EXAMPLE:**
>
> Suppose your debts total $200,000, and your assets amount to $196,000. A creditor reduces the amount you owe by $6,000. Your debts are now $194,000, so you're solvent again. The $4,000 needed to bring you even isn't income, but the additional $2,000 of debt reduction is.

• *Debt that's a deductible expense.* If you run your business strictly on the cash basis, a canceled debt that would ordinarily produce a deduction if you paid it isn't considered income.

EXAMPLE:

Say you owe $5,000 for supplies used in the business, and the supplier forgives $1,000 of the debt. If you already included the $1,000 in income, it would then be offset by $1,000 in business expense. Since the transaction is a "wash," no income has to be reported and no further losses would result.

On the other hand, the situation is different if you're on the accrual basis. Under that method of accounting, you'd have deducted the $1,000 of forgiven debt along with the rest of the expense at the time when you incurred the liability. Consequently, to prevent a windfall from happening, you'd have to report the $1,000 of canceled debt as income.

CHECK 'TAX ATTRIBUTES'

Note that the Tax Code requires you to apply the amount of canceled debt against the following "tax attributes," which might produce future tax benefits, in the order listed:
• Net operating losses or NOL carryovers from previous years.
• General business credit carryovers.
• Capital losses or capital loss carryovers from previous years.
• The basis of property.
• Foreign tax credit carryovers.

CHECK LEASING PROCEDURES TO GET TAX BREAKS

· · · · ·

Whether you're a landlord or a tenant, checking *all* the tax angles before you sign a lease can save you money and avoid future problems.

Suppose, for example, that a landlord gives you a bonus for signing a lease. That bonus is taxable income to you and a tax deduction for the landlord. However, if the landlord gives you a period of free rent, there's generally no tax cost to you as the tenant.

IF YOU'RE A LANDLORD

Make sure that the lease specifies that security deposits are called exactly that, not advance rent payments. As long as they're segregated from other income, security deposits generally aren't income. If they're advance rent payments, they're taxable. If security deposits are forfeited by the tenant, they are rental income to the landlord the year they are forfeited.

IF YOU'RE A LESSEE

If you're planning to use a simple lease with an option to buy, you should make sure that the IRS can't later claim that it's really a sale and not a lease. That would mean that you, as the purchaser, wouldn't be able to deduct your rent payments, although you would be able to deduct depreciation. If you're the landlord, you are not allowed to take depreciation.

Here are some things to avoid, because they are among the important factors that indicate to the IRS that the lease is really a purchase in disguise:

• The agreement specifies that payments are applicable to the purchase price, if the option is exercised.

• The tenant gets title to the property after payment of a specific rent.

• The lease specifies payment of a substantial part of the purchase price early in the life of the arrangement.

• The monthly rental is demonstrably higher than fair rental value.

• Some of the required payment is designated as interest.

When you and the landlord are related in some way, whether by blood or marriage, the IRS may try to say that the rent is really a gift. Thus, it's important to make sure that the deal is an "arm's-length transaction," like one you would enter into with a total stranger.

OBSERVATION:

The same applies to situations where you're a principal stockholder and you lease property to your firm. You should have a valid business purpose and charge a fair market rent. Otherwise, the IRS could say the rent payments are really nondeductible dividends from your company, instead of deductible business expenses.

PROPERTY: CONDEMNED OR DESTROYED?

· · · · ·

Depending on circumstances, if you're unlucky enough to lose your property to some natural calamity, or to condemnation by the government, you may have as long as

three years to decide what to do with the compensation you get.

• **Destroyed.** If your property is "destroyed," the law gives you two years to find a replacement before you have to report and pay tax on any capital gain from the settlement.

• **Condemned.** But if the property is used in your business, or held for investment, and you lose it in a condemnation proceeding or due to the threat of one, you have up to three years to replace it.

THE PRINCIPALS IN ACTION

Through no fault of the landowner, a dangerous chemical was released onto his property. The government decided that contamination levels were so high that affected residents would have to relocate.

The government bought the property for the appraised value, without adjusting for the contamination. Just to make sure that its offer would be accepted, the government passed an ordinance that authorized the taking of the affected properties by eminent domain, if necessary.

• **IRS reasoning.** The IRS said there were two principal questions to consider: Was the property "destroyed," and was the sale made under a "threat of condemnation"? In either instance, the gain on the so-called "involuntary conversion" of the property to cash can be deferred.

However, the deferral period for a conversion because of government condemnation, or the threat of it, is three years. If the government decides that the property is "destroyed," the law gives you only two years to replace it with a new property.

The IRS had no trouble determining that the property was destroyed. The chemical spill had made it unfit for use in the foresee-

169

able future. It was also clear that a taking to protect the public health is a condemnation.

• *Measuring compensation.* Normally, the measure of just compensation in a condemnation is the fair market value of the property. If the compensation paid doesn't take into account the decrease in the property's value caused by the destructive force loosed on it, then part of the amount paid is for the taking of the property, and part is compensation for the property's destruction, the agency ruled.

• *Outcome.* So, the property owner has to allocate his compensation. Only the part that represents the fair market value of the property after the chemical spill would qualify for the more relaxed replacement rule. (Rev. Rul. 89-2)

QUICK ASBESTOS DEDUCTION

■ ■ ■ ■ ■

If you own a building with an asbestos problem, you may be able to deduct the cost of replacing the insulation as a straight repair. Obviously, that would give you a big break on your tax return because replacing asbestos with modern insulation is costly. Moreover, if you had to capitalize the cost, you might have to spread the cost of those expenses of the "improvement" to your property over as many as 31 1/2 years.

DEFENSE FOR A DEDUCTION

As yet, there are no regulations or legal decisions on the subject, but you could make a reasonable argument for deducting the cost of asbestos removal in the year you have it done. Here's the argument to support such a claim:

1. You could say that by replacing asbestos with a different type of insulation, you're only returning the building to its former condition, before it was discovered that asbestos is dangerous. That's not a capital improvement.

2. You could argue that correcting hazardous conditions is a repair, not an improvement. It's similar to fixing such building code violations as defective wiring or a backed-up sewer line.

Ultimately, the issue may be resolved by the courts or Congress. But, if you clearly disclose the position you're taking on your tax return, there shouldn't be any question of a negligence penalty applying.

Managing
your
CAREER

Chapter 1

CAREER DEVELOPMENT

HOW TO EARN FAST PROMOTIONS

. . . . .

Your chances of moving up the corporate ladder depend largely on your ability to sell a product—yourself—to everyone, including your competition.

SELF-TEST

Take a self-inventory in the following areas. Questions to which you answer "no" indicate weak areas that you had better strengthen before the next promotion—or the one after that—passes you by.

• *Self-presentation.* Have you successfully created an outstanding presence and profile? Are your written and spoken communication skills as good as they could be? Have you documented your worth to upper management through memos and reports that provide a record of both your ideas and accomplishments?

• *Analytical skills.* Have you solved important problems rather than skirted them? Have your solutions cut costs or increased profits?

• *Follow-through.* Have you supervised projects through to completion? Have you motivated your subordinates to see that things get done?

• *Coolheadedness.* Have you demonstrated your ability under pressure?

• *Ability to set priorities.* Have you consistently completed top management's most important projects before your own?

• *Image enhancement.* Have you undertaken—and completed—projects that showcase your specific skills and strengths?

• *Political savvy.* Have you courted the support of your competitors by pitching in to help get their projects approved or completed? Have you avoided the temptation to bad-mouth them when their projects have failed?

• *Goal definition.* Have you carefully defined long-term objectives? Do you understand the role your current activities play in achieving them?

• *Supportiveness of higher-ups.* Have you supported the ideas and goals of your superiors? Have you kept them out of trouble by pointing out missteps? Have you cheerfully taken on extra work in difficult times?

• *Resilience.* If the promotion goes to a rival, do you have the self-assurance to keep on pursuing your goals with undiminished enthusiasm? It's that kind of backbone that shows you're a leader—and makes you a far more likely candidate when the next chance for a promotion arrives.

ADVANTAGES OF ACTIVE RISK TAKING
. . . . .

Executives should not only take advantage of risky opportunities when they come along, but should also actually create them in order to progress their own careers. Daniel Kehrer, author of the book *Doing Business Boldly* (Times Books, $19.95), has coined a term, "ARTists," for people who are Active Risk Takers. Here's how to become one:

• **Risk from strength.** The comfort level must be right, especially if you're not a frequent risk taker. Start in areas you know well, because you'll be armed with better information to guide you along the way. Also, it's wisest to take risks only in a com-

pany that won't penalize you for doing so—one whose management recognizes that although risks sometimes end in failure, they're also vital for growth.

• **Gather information wisely.** This one's tricky. You can never know when you have enough data. And you can't be sure that what you have is correct.

EXAMPLE:

General Foods thought it had a winner in its Great Shakes drink mix. In extensive test marketing, all flavors sold well. But the product failed.

■ REASON:

The product sold briskly while consumers were trying all the flavors. But they liked none, and eventually stopped buying the product altogether.

It's vital for you to learn the limits of information—that it doesn't always guarantee success. While you must look before you leap, you must eventually stop looking and go for it.

• **Be sensitive to timing.** There are no formulas for determining when to act. It's almost a gut-level decision. Remember, too, that taking a risk doesn't always mean moving forward. It may mean deciding to take a product back into development rather than into the marketplace.

◆ RISK:

You might miss your window of opportunity in the marketplace.

• **Be flexible.** Conditions change. If you're determined to stick with your original plan no matter what, you're not gutsy, you're stupid.

174

EXAMPLE:

When New Coke provoked a consumer backlash, Coca-Cola company chairman Roberto C. Goizueta resurrected the original flavor, which he had insisted he would never do. His flexibility and willingness to offer consumers both flavors (even though that contradicted his original plan) gave the company a larger market share than it had before the introduction of New Coke.

• **Fail successfully.** While your goal in taking a risk is success, you won't always achieve it. To gain positive benefits from failure, you must learn something from your mistake. You must also avoid taking the failure personally.

All this may make the process of risk taking sound like gambling. But Kehrer says there's a big difference: "In gambling, money just moves around. Nothing is created."

SURVIVING A MERGER

∎ ∎ ∎ ∎ ∎

When your company is acquired or becomes part of a merger, upper management will probably tell you that change will come gradually or not at all. Don't believe it. In such situations, it's common practice for firms to hire outside consultants to assess the health of various departments and suggest where cuts should occur. Staffing decisions are going to be made quickly, with sketchy data. You have to think fast if you want to be among the survivors.

Here are some survival tips from Dr. Price Pritchett, head of Pritchett and As-

sociates Inc., a Dallas-based consulting firm that specializes in helping firms minimize the turbulence of post-merger adjustments.

• *Understand that you will face a different corporate culture.* Evaluate the situation: Do you want to buy into it or not? Maintain an open-minded attitude about the new company. Strive to remain positive until all the information is in. Remember, you've got to negotiate for your position through your behavior.

• *Be honest with yourself.* If you really are incompatible with the new regime, staying could be an exercise in frustration that would damage the quality of your life and career. On the other hand, jumping overboard too quickly can be a mistake that causes you to lose out on one of the substantial severance packages that are often given during post-merger shakeouts.

• *Keep cool.* When discussing your department with outside consultants, says Dr. Pritchett, "don't get defensive, don't blow smoke and don't show fits of panic—at least not visibly."

Instead, critique your department in a balanced way. Talk about its strengths, developmental needs and potential. Explain how you would upgrade the department, given the fact that changes are coming. Your best tactic is to take a pro-merger stance and suggest concrete ideas for improvement.

By taking this approach, you'll be sending messages that you are a leader, not a drone. Try to show that you have your subordinates' support and that you are someone who can help make changes, not just a fence-sitter.

• *Don't try a cover-up.* If you know deep down that your job or department is redundant and bound to be eliminated, frankness may be the wisest approach. Think about other jobs you could assume in the revised corporate scheme, and sell yourself.

RECOMMENDATION:
The new powers may not be that concerned with finding a place for you. You'll have to convince them of your worth by showing you're a team player.

• *Don't expect a rapid readjustment.* Be prepared for the merger integration period to drag on. Top managers often think they are helping employees by going slowly and methodically. Actually, they are prolonging the sense of instability.

Dr. Pritchett warns, "The average time frame before the organization is really one unit moving forward together is two years." For some companies it's even longer.

SHOULD YOU GET AN MBA?

. . . . .

If you still believe an MBA assures you of becoming a formidable force in your chosen profession, or of doubling your income rapidly, you may be in for a major disappointment.

▲ FACT:
In many fields, such as finance, an MBA is now an entry-level degree—much like a BA was 20 years ago.

"Those three letters are no longer viewed as an automatic passport to the fast track," says Milo Sobel, a New York-based management consultant and creator of the "MBA in a Nutshell" crash course in business skills.

THE TRENDS

Sobel sees these trends:
• MBA salaries have dropped, especially at the entry level. MBAs no longer enjoy a substantial lead over other job-market entrants.
• The MBA lacks its former cachet—employers are concerned less with glitz than with productivity.
• Recruiters tend to focus primarily on candidates from the top business schools.
• The arrogance often exhibited by new MBAs has caused a backlash reaction against recent business-school graduates.

However, you may still want to consider pursuing studies toward an MBA degree if the following considerations apply to your career or profession:
• It's a written or unwritten requisite for success in your corporation's culture or in your industry.
• It would solidify your position by making you a specialist in a particular area. Some examples are corporate finance and marketing.
• Your employer will pay for it. Many companies are currently sponsoring two-year MBA programs for their employees—typically requiring one full day of class work per week and two weeks of full-time study each summer.

ALTERNATIVES TO AN MBA

• **Certificate programs.** Many top schools and industry associations now offer week-long, off-site programs for working professionals. Certificates are given for studies within a general field (such as human resources development), or for specialized work on a specific skill or discipline (such as compensation). The presence of several such certificates on your résumé will often catch a reader's eye as effectively as the presence of an MBA.

• **Synergy programs.** These let you combine two degrees, such as an MBA with a law degree, or a law degree with one in accounting. Graduates of such programs are currently in demand.

• **Functional skills programs.** Analyze the skills you need to get ahead. Depending on your field, certain courses may be more beneficial than degree or certificate programs. Some examples are foreign languages and computer skills.

WHEN TO MAKE A RISKY MOVE

. . . . .

If you had the chance to move into a senior management position at a company whose future was uncertain, would you trade the security of your present job to take it? While the rewards of such a position could be high, so could the risks.

QUESTIONS TO ASK YOURSELF

• **Does top management view the potential upside for your career the same way you do?** Don't leave questions of future money, status or benefits up in the air. You won't be able to nail down *all* the particulars, but you should have an agreement in principle on what you stand to gain, should the company regain its footing.

• **Is the senior management team talented?** You won't be able to perform miracles on your own. Unless the people you're working with are as competent and

committed as you are, the company's future isn't bright. Spend more time than you normally would talking to your prospective colleagues about their background and experience in dealing with the kind of crisis the company is undergoing. If you have doubts about their ability and it doesn't seem likely the players will change, factor it strongly into your decision.

• **How viable is the action plan?** If you doubt the company's strategy for turning things around, express your reservations and observe how they're received. It may be that management welcomes a fresh view and will alter its plans. If there is no cohesive strategy, find out why and when one is likely to be implemented.

• **How strong is morale?** If the mood of senior executives isn't "We're going to get on top of things," beware. The attitude is likely to reverberate through the ranks. If the company's labor force isn't in a *success* mind-set, its chances of surviving aren't great.

• **How concerned are key outside constituents?** If the company's shareholders, banks or clients are openly nervous about the stability of the company, you should be, too. You can't afford to have major supporters jump ship as you're about to board.

• **Is senior management prepared to give you an employment contract?** You should be offered some financial protection in the form of severance benefits if the company goes under. In addition, the contract should describe your job title and explain its duties, outline the basis on which your performance will be evaluated and when, and delineate your benefits and reporting relationship.

• **Do you have a crisis mentality?** If

you've never before been in a situation that demands solving major day-to-day problems, think twice before you put yourself in a pressure-packed environment. If, on the other hand, you get satisfaction from putting out fires and implementing survival strategies, a floundering company may well be the perfect place for you.

• **What is your financial situation?** Taking a higher-paying position with a company whose future is uncertain isn't a good idea if you're in an unstable financial position yourself. You may find yourself out on the street sooner than you think; and even with severance benefits, you may end up stretching to make ends meet.

HOW TO GET PAST THE NO-RAISE BARRIER
· · · · ·

When reaching for a raise, look on the first *no* as round one, and explore the applicability of other raise-negotiating methods.

COUNTERING FOUR COMMON OBJECTIONS

Objection #1: A raise would put you above your job category maximum.

♦ A D V I C E :

If you're doing outstanding work, point to your industry's pay scale. Don't compare your pay to other managers in your company; cite salaries for comparable positions elsewhere.

You can get a good idea of the numbers by consulting want ads, headhunters, business associates and career centers. Know-

ing—and letting higher-ups know—what you're worth on the outside can help increase your value inside.

Final fallback if the boss still says no? Offer to take on additional responsibility.

Objection #2: You already earn more than anyone else in the department.

● R E P L Y :

"I may be making more than the rest, but don't you agree that if I work harder and accomplish more I should be paid more?"

Objection #3: The company has had a bad year.

♦ A D V I C E :

If true, you should probably be happy with a small raise. But it doesn't hurt to dig deeper if your work is good.

Ask when things are expected to turn around and, if they do, what impact that will have on salaries. Faced with an iron-clad ban, ask about compensation in other forms—e.g., a company car, more vacation time.

Objection #4: I'd like to give you more, but odds are a raise won't be approved.

♦ A D V I C E :

Coming after you've listed your accomplishments, this answer signals an unbridgeable gap for now. So ask your boss to outline specifically what you have to do to get a bigger raise. Then establish a timetable for reevaluation.

R E C O M M E N D A T I O N :
When the bottom line is a definite no, you can still gain something. Use the session as a wedge into next time. The answer should tell you if it's worth retrying.

WINNING THE BATTLE FOR BUCKS

■   ■   ■   ■   ■

Sooner or later, every executive has to ask for money to fund new projects, buy needed equipment or add staff. Most of them go about it very badly.

In today's competitive climate, even small firms are adopting sophisticated methods of determining which projects will yield profits and which will not. "What's the ROI (return on investment)?" is the first question you're likely to hear when asking for funding. If you don't have an answer full of dollars, percents and ratios, you're likely to be treated as a lightweight.

HOW FIRMS ANALYZE INVESTMENTS

Here are some capital-investment analysis methods you may encounter. Consider including them in your written or oral proposal:

■ **The payback period.** If you want to spend $110,000, when do you expect to recoup that money? Measure the capital to be invested, plus costs, against probable cash flow from the investment. The amount of time needed to break even is the payback period.

Say, for example, you want to purchase a machine for $110,000. You expect this new machine to replace one employee who now gets $25,000 per year. Divide the total cost of the investment ($110,000) by the increased cash flow per year ($25,000) to project a payback in 4.4 years. In this case, you have very little risk involved and a short payback period. If your payback period is much longer, your risk is greater, and the

chances of approval are cut proportionately.

There are limitations to this system that may give you an opening to advance your projects. They include:

• *No profit measurement.* Payback analysis measures the time to recoup an investment. It says nothing about new profits that may result.

• *Time limitations.* The system doesn't predict ongoing profits after the date when the investment is returned.

• *Failure to consider money's time value.* In most payback-analysis methods, the same value is given to money received today as to money expected later. Money received now is worth more than money received five years down the road, or even tomorrow.

▲ I M P O R T A N T :

To get your proposal past these caveats, show that your project will increase profits annually, and stress that they will keep coming after the payback period has passed. If no new profits are added, talk about various intangibles, such as keeping up with technology or improving customer service.

■ **Net Present Value (NPV).** This method relies on a technique known as discounted cash flow. This assumes that money received in the future is worth less than money received today, because money received today can be invested to earn future interest.

The projected cash flows from an investment project are therefore mathematically "discounted" to what is called *present value.* The initial cash outlay is subtracted from this present value to yield *net present value.* The net present value must be a positive number for the project to be accepted.

NPV is complicated. To include it in your presentation, ask a colleague in your accounting or finance department to help you make projections. NPV also has some basic flaws:

• *Inaccuracies resulting from failure to forecast cash flow accurately.* Estimates that are only slightly off can greatly impact NPV results, possibly leading to an unjustified rejection—or acceptance—of a project.

• *Failure to project profits.* Like the payback method, NPV does not measure gains in profitability.

▲ IMPORTANT:

If you use NPV and you are asked about profits, show that your project will bring in new and ongoing profits. Because of the emphasis on cash flow, also try to emphasize immediate cost savings.

■ **Internal Rate of Return (IRR).** This method also is based on discounted cash flow. An *internal rate of return* is calculated for a proposed project based on discounted cash-flow measures. This rate is compared to a criterion rate decided on by company management.

This criterion rate is called the *hurdle rate.* Upper management picks a hurdle rate based on the cost of raising capital, and on how risky the project is considered to be for the prospective economic environment. If the internal rate of return for a project exceeds the hurdle rate, the project is accepted.

▲ STRATEGY:

Find out your company's hurdle rate by asking around. There may be a specific number, such as 11%, that your financial people have chosen after years of experience. Use the number in your presentation by saying something like, "I see

our hurdle rate is 11%. I will show you how my project will return 15% annually."

WINNING BY LOWERING RISK

Given a choice between two projects with the same projected return, management will nearly always choose the project with the lower risk—even though promises of higher return may lower management resistance.

Buying a new machine to replace an employee is a low-risk project. Introducing a new product, or entering into a new market, carries a higher risk than any other project.

• *To boost your odds of success,* minimize the impression that your proposal is risky. Be enthusiastic in your presentation, but not overly optimistic.

• *Plan for the unexpected.* Say what will happen if interest rates rise or if sales decline by 10%. That brands you a realist who has thought ahead and planned for contingencies.

ARE YOU TOO GOOD TO PROMOTE?

Doing your job too well can land you in an "excellence rut."

■ SYMPTOMS:

Management refuses to promote you because no one else can handle your duties as capably as you do.

HOW TO MOVE AHEAD

• **Say what you want.** By asking for more responsibility, you become far more likely to move up. Few bosses can resist ambition—it reminds them of their own drive and translates as potential. So be sure to resist the comfort of the *status quo*.

• **Take on new tasks.** Accept new duties with relish.

• **Delegate.** Hand off responsibilities at the same time you assume new ones. Controlling what you do is the most powerful way to steer your career.

• **Stress operational efficiency.** To build confidence that someone else can do your job, show that you've built systems and a capable staff who can operate autonomously. Also, document how someone else could take over.

• **Find your replacement.** Resistance to replacing you will soften when a viable successor is at hand. Look within the ranks of your department—and elsewhere—to spot potential candidates.

▲ S T R A T E G Y :

Get involved in hiring new employees, and stay alert for candidates with the potential to assume your job.

• **Resist praise that stalls you.** "They may say the job you're doing can be done by only you, but you can't fall for it," says one executive. Accept praise, but show how your talents qualify you for greater challenges.

• **Resist stagnation.** When any employee gets too comfortable in a position, management may come to equate him or her with the job, and a change becomes unthinkable. The best defense is to undertake projects that impact well beyond the range of your own department.

• **Capitalize on your ambitious image.** Follow the strategies outlined above and upper management will give you appropriate challenges—or be prepared to

see you walk out the door to seek more rewarding opportunities elsewhere.

● B E N E F I T :

The fear that your successor will not equal you becomes a secondary concern.

YOUR TITLE: THERE IS A LOT IN A NAME

Claiming the right title can be as simple as swapping something shopworn like "data processing manager" for the newer "manager of information systems." But netting a new title isn't always easy.

"Negotiating a new title is a 'both-win' negotiation," says Dr. Virginia Karrass, a clinical psychologist and negotiating consultant at Karrass Executive Seminars in Los Angeles. "To get your boss's approval, you'll have to show that the title change will bring satisfaction to both of you."

IMPROVE YOUR CHANCES FOR A HIGH-POWERED TITLE

• **Fit into corporate culture.** If your company has a rigid hierarchy of titles and positions, you can't mold the system to fit your own aspirations. Make sure your request fits into the firm's structure, or you'll only draw negative attention to yourself.

• **Stress shared benefits.** Show how the new title will underline your credibility with your staff, colleagues, clients and customers—and enable you to do your job more effectively.

• **Document your case.** Bring in sales figures, productivity reports and other materials that show you are already performing the duties the new title entails.

• **Clarify your duties.** Be sure your boss understands what you really do. Dr. Karrass suggests typing up a job description and giving bosses copies to show to *their* superiors in requesting the title change.

• **Suggest a "probation" period.** If you meet resistance, consider asking for several months to demonstrate that you can perform—or continue performing—the duties of the new title you're after. Then your boss can evaluate whether you've done a good enough job to merit the new designation.

CREATIVE PROBLEM SOLVING
· · · · ·

Nearly everyone can unlock creative abilities to help solve career and personal problems in fresh, innovative ways.

◆ S N A G :

Following a systemized approach to a problem usually stifles creative spontaneity. The creative person's hallmark is the ability to adopt different kinds of thinking at different points in the problem-solving process.

A SYSTEM TO HELP YOU THINK CREATIVELY

• **First, be an explorer.** Most computer programmers spend their time talking to other programmers, bankers to other bankers, etc. A better idea would be to get out of your pigeonhole and see what's going on in other fields. Explore ideas from other areas, bring them back to your field, give them a twist and emerge with something innovative.

R E C O M M E N D A T I O N :

Give yourself one day each month to get outside your department or field to seek out and borrow ideas.

• **Next, the artist.** If you want to develop an idea that's really going to set your industry on its ear or dazzle your boss, you have to apply imagination to it. Try spending 5% of your day thinking like an artist, asking "what if" questions and challenging the commonly perceived rules in your field.

Question the old standby, "But we've *always* done it that way." For example, an electronics buyer for a chain of Midwestern department stores repeatedly proposed that his company start marketing fax machines and other business equipment. After being rebuffed many times, he stopped trying. But he realized that the market for such equipment had expanded to the point that he could try again. He compiled and presented some very convincing market data and his proposal was finally accepted.

• **Then, the judge.** If the idea's going to be any good, you must now shift from the "anything goes" attitude of the artist to the "check out everything" attitude of the judge. Is the timing right? What's your course of action going to be if the idea fails?

◆ P R O B L E M :

Being a judge requires balance. If you're too critical, you could discard potentially good ideas. But if you're not critical enough, you might try to implement a lot of garbage.

Develop the ability to focus on the positives. If you determine that an idea is two-thirds good, look for what can be improved rather than discarding the whole thing.

• **Finally, the lawyer.** This may be the most important of the four roles. Like a lawyer, you negotiate and find ways to implement your idea within the rules and conventions of your business or field. Your explorer, artist and judge stages may take a day or a week to come up with an idea, but it may take your lawyer phase six months to pave the way for its implementation.

Know what your objective is, find out who will help you and keep away from people who will step on your ideas. Finally, be persistent enough to sell and push your ideas until you ultimately reach your goal.

MAKING THE PROCESS WORK FOR YOU

As you put this process into motion, you'll probably find that your greatest strengths lie in one or two of the steps—explorer and artist, for example. Find ways to help your weaker characters take shape.

> **EXAMPLES:**
> You can help your judge by relying more on people whose judgment you respect, or help your explorer by joining a new club or working with more diverse accounts.

THE INTELLIGENCE GAME

■ ■ ■ ■ ■

Hundreds of major corporations—including AT&T and Pfizer—maintain staffs of intelligence professionals to watch rival firms. Even if your company isn't following suit, it's to your advantage to start gathering information yourself.

■ **R E A S O N S :**

Inside information will help you advance *within* your company. And it will help you to know when it's time to start working for a better-positioned competitor.

WHAT TO LOOK FOR

Like corporate intelligence departments, you should gather data on competitors' products, services and pricing; profits; customer accounts; hiring patterns; promotional and advertising plans; marketing and distribution systems; new products and R&D; and expansions, mergers and acquisitions.

WHERE TO GET INFORMATION

■ **Your competitors themselves.** Most firms freely give away vital intelligence. Don't overlook:

• *Products.* If possible, buy competitors' products and try them out. Or get a demonstration at a dealer.

• *Trade shows.* Drop by booths to browse, talk with sales representatives, and observe product demonstrations.

• *Press releases.* Contact competitors' public relations departments or representative firms and get on the mailing list. You'll get important information *before* it appears in newspapers.

• *Annual reports and stock-offering prospectuses* are excellent sources of information on finances and long-range plans. They're easy to obtain through business libraries or brokerage houses.

■ **People.** You can learn a lot about competitors by speaking with:

• *Your customers.* If they deal with your competitors, ask how their products and services compare to your firm's.

• *Distributors, retailers.* What kind of volume do competing firms produce? Are shipments up or down?

• *Suppliers.* Salespeople from whom you buy supplies or equipment can tell you about other firms' purchasing volume and patterns.

• *Consultants.* Hire ones who have worked for other firms. It's not illegal to ask about a rival's plans and concerns.

• *Competitors' former employees.* Be sure to interview any who apply for jobs with your firm.

■ **Publications.** Keep current by reading the following:

• *Newspapers.* Read local papers and those from areas where other firms have operations. You'll learn about plant openings, layoffs, etc.

◆ **VITAL:**

Review want ads to learn which jobs your competitor is trying to fill.

• *Specialty publications.* Read business and trade periodicals. Advertising journals can tell you how much competitors spend for advertising and for which products.

DON'T FALL INTO DECISION TRAPS

■ ■ ■ ■ ■

Making the right choice is seldom easy. But when a decision puts your future and your company's success on the line, the added pressures can lead straight into a decision-making trap.

WHAT TO AVOID

• **Making an impulsive choice.** Confronted with a frustrating decision, you seize upon a solution because you feel relieved that one has finally been found.

A variant would be to make a choice by "gut" feeling alone.

◆ **PROBLEM:**

In either situation, you fail to weigh your decision objectively against other available options.

• **Using the process to advance yourself.** Under pressure, you consciously or subconsciously opt for the path that seems to offer the greatest self-advancement. The variant is you select an option that retaliates against people who have offended you.

◆ **PROBLEM:**

If you make the wrong decision—for whatever reason—it will ultimately harm you.

• **Bowing to peer pressure.** It's sometimes unavoidable, but often involves severe pitfalls.

◆ **PROBLEM:**

Trying to please everyone usually results in a plan that is either weak or just plain unworkable.

HOW TO APPROACH DECISION-MAKING

University of California psychologist Irving Janis developed an approach called "vigilant problem solving," described in his book, *Crucial Decisions* (Free Press, $27.95).

• **Outline the problem.** Determine the minimum gains that must result. Also consider the dangers to be avoided and the costs to be contained.

• **Gather information.** Review the

sources of data you already possess and determine what new information (forecasts, market and intelligence reports, etc.) you need to make an informed decision.

• **Analyze the situation and reformulate your approach.** Do the original parameters of the problem still stand? Do the requirements for the outcome still hold? Would additional information reduce the chance of uncertainties?

• **Evaluate your alternatives and make a decision.** After making the decision, review the original problem. Has your solution failed to solve any of the sub-problems it contained? If so, can additional planning solve them?

It's a mistake to stop promoting a decision actively once it's been put into effect.

■ R E A S O N :

People who opposed you will continue to work against its implementation. To defend yourself, continue to gather supporting information that can refute new criticism. To be sure of continuing help from your supporters, invest extra time with them to review the progress your plans are making.

GROUP-THINK VS. YOU-THINK
■ ■ ■ ■ ■

You can distinguish yourself in a team setting without seeming self-centered.

HOW TO GO ABOUT IT

■ **Ask the right questions.** They can contribute to clarifying ideas and sharpen-

ing group focus. Questions should be phrased in a probing, not snide, way.

For instance, says William Iuso of the Michael Allen management consulting firm in Rowayton, CT, don't ask, "How would that work?" because that could sound like an attack. Instead, try, "Could you describe how that would work?"

• Blame yourself for any gap in understanding by starting your question with something like, "I don't know enough about that area," or, "Am I correct in understanding that. . .?"

• The timing of your questions is important, says Marcia Potter Katz of Katz & Associates, Inc., a Berkeley Heights, NJ consulting firm. "Any time a doubt comes up, clarify it immediately," she says.

If you say, "I need something clarified," and then ask your question, it won't be perceived as a criticism and will minimize misunderstandings and delays.

■ **Draw out the others on the team.** One way is to "empower" them, says Mary Rabaut of United Research, Morristown, NJ. Have everyone in the group listen to others. Give each of them an opportunity to contribute ideas. "The more air time you give each individual, the more likely he or she is to listen to you in turn and be open to your ideas," she says.

• Another way to draw out other people: Play down your own expertise to make others comfortable about elaborating on their thoughts. That is the key to getting quality participation from everyone in the group.

■ **"Hitchhike" your ideas.** Give others credit for stimulating your thinking, says Iuso, with a technique he calls "hitchhiking." For instance, preface your own ideas with a comment like, "After hearing what Joe said, it occurred to me that we might also. . ." In this way, the idea becomes a group product, not just your own.

■ **Time your own contributions carefully.** Before you speak, says Rabaut, "listen to the overall direction the team is taking. If you jump in with something that's already been said or done, they'll discount you from then on."

The first time you make a contribution, she adds, "address the larger issue instead of jumping right to the detail. Demonstrate your understanding of the problem, then make your contribution."

OBSERVATION:

People with a talent must offer themselves to their teammates periodically to help them shine. "One who stands out is also gracious about sharing the limelight." The message is "we," not "me."

COPING WITH A HOTSHOT ASSISTANT

Manage this "wunderkind" in a way that helps your career.

• *Try to give the outstanding person highly visible assignments,* where the good job that's done will redound to your credit and to that of your assistant.

• *Propose the assistant for key interdepartmental or ad hoc committees if possible.* The exposure to top executives and heightened visibility may prompt others to propose him or her for additional special projects, thus "inventing" a promotion for the star.

• *Avoid the temptation to call on the superstar for everything.* He or she only seems like Superman, and is as susceptible to burnout as anyone else.

CAUTION

Watch out for knee-jerk negativity.

Almost no idea springs forth from its creator's lips in a perfectly developed state. It's all too easy—especially if you're feeling the least bit threatened—to pick out the negatives in an outstanding subordinate's proposals and dismiss an idea. Try to pick out the positives, to look for the opportunities inherent in an idea, and to encourage your assistant to develop it.

OBSERVATION:

It takes more than one brilliant assistant to make a department. In your enthusiasm, don't ignore the rest of the staff. They may be having difficulties with envy and resentment of the superstar as it is. Give them some good assignments, and don't miss an opportunity to say something like: "I noticed you spent extra time on the X project, and you did a really fine job on it."

BUILDING AN 'OUTSIDE' STAFF

A growing number of successful executives are relying on outside resources—invisible "staffs" consisting of mentors, consultants and freelancers they nurture over the course of their careers—to greatly enhance their own productivity and desirability.

For many of them, being able to draw upon these expert and reliable outside resources has been instrumental in rising to their present positions.

■ REASON:

In today's business environment, no one person has enough data to make fully informed decisions. And within companies, ideas tend to become inbred. So you have to look to individuals on the outside.

HOW TO BUILD A MOBILE STAFF

• **Don't lose touch with good people.** As you change jobs, don't burn your bridges behind you. Networking helps you to keep abreast of legislation, the economy and trends in the marketplace.

• **Seek out new people.** To expand your contacts, keep networking actively. In addition, try out various freelancers and keep using the good ones.

• **Don't keep your contacts a secret.** When negotiating a job with a new firm, point out that, in addition to you, they're getting access to a cluster of talented, knowledgeable people.

HOW TO WORK WITH PARTICIPATIVE MANAGEMENT
■ ■ ■ ■ ■

In many plants, workers set schedules, measure quality, requisition supplies and know more facts about their departments than most traditional managers ever did.

Nor is participation limited to factories. Work teams, task forces and quality circles are taking over planning and decision-making functions. They're developing fresh ideas on improved services or products, cutting costs and doing other jobs

once reserved for managers. Some firms have even told middle managers they won't be needing them anymore.

Actually, they do need you, but you have to show them. Don't sabotage participation, as some managers have done. That's self-defeating. Instead, make participation work for you.

PROVE YOUR VALUE

■ **Adapt to the new climate.** Participation fractures bureaucracy and opens up your career path. Be on the lookout for hidden opportunities.

> EXAMPLE:
> Use the new climate to propel yourself into higher management decisions. They can't object to your raising issues or discussing the problems of your department when employees horn in on your decisions.

■ **Fill the gaps.** Managers can no longer justify their role by controlling the information flow. But they can still manage.

• Two managerial skills vital to participative environments are the ability to build a team and being able to follow up. Other critical gaps you can fill include solving unscheduled problems, such as equipment breakdowns and snags in employee relations.

• If you work in a plant, spend time overseeing preventive maintenance. Make sure people have needed tools and supplies. In the office, upgrade training, organize unstructured tasks, and handle "quick response" situations unsuited to the participative approach.

■ **Cross traditional boundaries.** Grease the skids between work units by communicating directly rather than through channels. Talk with people in purchasing, quality assurance and industrial engineering, and to suppliers, customers, or anyone who can help you identify and solve organizational problems.

■ **Expedite your group's participation.** Say some of your staff members are put on a coordinating task force. Draw on your managerial skills to help them formulate and clarify questions, gather needed data and develop alternative solutions.

Train them to evaluate, think through the consequences of options, weigh their chances of success with each one and develop contingency plans.

▲ IMPORTANT:

Know when to bail out. If you feel participative management leaves no room for you, don't turn bitter. Instead, start your own contingency planning. It may be time to move on to a smaller company that could apply your solid managerial background more effectively.

HOW TO TAKE TIME OFF TO YOUR ADVANTAGE

■ ■ ■ ■ ■

Successful managers plan their vacations to suit their companies as well as their pleasures. Consider these factors before you make vacation plans:

• *Is your company in transition?* Being visible and active is important in the aftermath of a reorganization, merger or downsizing. The more involved you are in the transition, however, the easier it will be for you to take time off once the major changes are in place. If you're a key player, chances are decisions that could affect your department can be put on hold until you return.

If the transition is being handled at levels far above yours, it's smart to talk to your boss. Explain why you'd like to take time off, assess your staff's ability to handle the work, and ask if there will be problems in your being away that you can plan for. (Scheduling time off without an explanation may suggest that you intend to job-hunt.) If your boss's future with the company is still uncertain, taking a long vacation probably isn't wise.

• *Are you going through a "down cycle" with your boss?* Every relationship has its ups and downs, and taking time off when things haven't been great won't improve your standing. If you sense your boss is unhappy or dissatisfied, clear the air before you announce your vacation plans. That gives him or her a chance to tell you what's wrong. If you can make the necessary amends first, you'll be able to enjoy your vacation without worrying about your job.

• *Are you newly promoted?* Even if you were working particularly hard before achieving your goal, you'll lose momentum if you take time off too soon after the announcement is made. When you win a promotion, you attract attention for a while. It's a good time to get a hearing for your plans and ideas.

WHILE YOU ARE AWAY

No matter how carefully you schedule vacation time, a crisis can strike while you are away. You can prevent the situation from getting out of hand by making some contingency plans.

• Put important projects or clients into

the hands of trusted staff members. Make sure they know where to get help .

• Tell your staff what circumstances warrant an interruption. Give your phone number only to the people you want problems funneled to. If you want to keep difficulties that might come up with clients confidential, give the clients your number.

• If your presence might be required in an emergency, pick a vacation spot close to a major airport.

RECOMMENDATION:

No matter how sensitive the situation at work, don't give up vacations entirely. People who don't take some time off often suffer serious stress problems. Too frequently, they end up resting in a hospital instead of on a beach.

BEWARE OF DEAD-END JOBS

· · · · ·

Every corporation, every business has a main profit stream—the shortest, fastest and most visible route to the top jobs and the top rewards. If that's what you're after:

• *Avoid support areas.* Data processing, public affairs and purchasing, while necessary functions in most corporations, rarely lead to the big rewards. According to headhunters and outplacers, they often turn out to be some of the worst career traps.

EXAMPLE:

One study found that over a two-year period, less than 5% of purchasing managers changed jobs while 30% of marketing managers moved on.

Similarly, although public relations managers are often well paid, they spend a long time getting there—and they are always sailing in harm's way. Since they must be totally compatible with the CEO, PR managers are especially vulnerable.

If you do find yourself trapped in one of these situations, you are not helpless. Your editorial and financial skills could be applied in sales, marketing or development work. Or an advanced degree in management or technology could be a ticket into the mainstream.

• *Don't overspecialize.* Data processing can be a problem area for aspiring young managers, because your skills don't translate anywhere. Moreover, if you're doing a good job with your specialty, there's little incentive for management to move you away.

So expect to do your own searching for other outlets for your special skills. If you know your way around the data banks, focus on those that are especially important to your managers—financial data—and try to use them to your advantage in a shift to the comptroller's office. Also, take some courses that will broaden your special skills.

• *Never swim alone or far out.* Your progress in the mainstream will be slow if you try to go it alone. The operating reality here is that you need a power base for advancement. For example, you may do a great job in a staff or foreign assignment, but lose your place in the chain of command.

But never say "never." Instead, carefully weigh the risks of venturing alone or outside the mainstream. Much will depend on the assignment or the particular business you're in. Doing a great job anywhere may give you some points. If you'd like to say no but can't, try to get a time commitment and a promise (recorded) about your next assignment.

It's a fact of business life that the fast tracks rarely run through the support departments. So if your eye is on the gold, you are well advised to serve your apprenticeship in the line operation.

WHEN YOU NEED A JOB OVERHAUL

• • • • •

Knowing the elements that lead to job satisfaction and finding ways to work them into your job can eliminate the need to dust off your résumé and walk out the door, advises Cynthia Scott, coauthor with Dennis Jaffe of *Take This Job and Love It* (Simon & Schuster, 1230 Ave. of the Americas, New York, NY 10020; $9.95).

WHAT MAKES A JOB ENJOYABLE

• **Feeling committed to what you are doing.** If you feel your job—no matter how small—is essential to the overall success of your company, it's easy to get excited about your work. There is a purpose to your work and your contribution is valued.

• **Having control over your job.** Being given the flexibility you need to make changes within your job or department shows that your company trusts your judgment and values your ideas, enabling you to keep your job skills fresh.

• **Feeling challenged by your work.** Knowing that you're working to your full potential provides a great sense of personal accomplishment.

• **Feeling connected to your job and co-workers.** Because you spend more time at work than at home, having good professional relationships and believing in what you're doing impacts strongly on your happiness. If you are not getting along well with co-workers or disagree with the way your company does business, it is very hard to feel strongly connected to what you're doing on the job.

HOW TO REVAMP A FRUSTRATING JOB

• **Join committees that directly impact on your company's overall image.** Working on the United Way campaign or blood drive makes you feel more a part of the organization and also puts you into contact with new people. This increases your visibility and leadership role in the firm.

• **Ask for what you want.** If there is some project you'd like to help out with or organize, let your boss know as soon as possible. If you have an idea that could make your job or your company more efficient, present a proposal.

• **Create a positive inner climate.** The way you perceive yourself influences the way others see you. If you feel you will never move up the career ladder, you probably won't.

▲ IMPORTANT:

Even if you aren't very confident in your abilities, *act* as if you are. As others begin responding to you in a more positive way, your confidence will increase.

• **Set a vision for what you want to become and move toward it.** When you can see a payoff in the long run, it's much easier to view each job as a stepping-stone to that end, rather than a life sentence that merely pays the bills.

GETTING OFF A PLATEAU

. . . . .

Most people hit predictable plateaus during their careers. These deadlocks often result from a numerical "narrowing" effect that occurs as people move upward. For example, many young executives' careers grow quickly for the first few years after they get out of college. They assume they're on the fast track to the top.

But after that, the pace of progress slows because of the smaller number of upper management positions available and the large pool of eager, capable people competing for them.

DON'T GET STUCK

To calculate your chances of getting off a career plateau, assess the following:

• *How large and/or stratified is your organization?* A large structure can offer opportunities—or, conversely, may limit mobility between divisions or departments. Review the promotions at your level that have occurred over the last several years to analyze the patterns of movement within your firm's structure.

• *How fast is the firm growing, and by what means?* How good is the current market for the goods or services it provides? How do your firm's offerings stack up against what the competition is selling? Is your firm aggressive enough to make it in the marketplace?

Has your firm acquired other companies, or is there a likelihood of such acquisitions taking place? More opportunities are generally created through internal growth than through acquisitions. Buy-outs only bring in new staff and increase competition for advancement.

• *What percentage of promotions is filled internally?* Some companies routinely select their top managers from outside. Speak with people who have observed the workings of your firm over a long period of time—either company old-timers or outside industry contacts who actively follow developments within your field.

BREAKING STALEMATES

Analyze the above factors to get a clearer picture of what has stalled your upward progress. In planning your course of action, first try to identify promotions that you can aim for in your firm.

Explain to your boss that you're ready to move up, accept more responsibility and make a greater contribution. If you don't have a specific move in mind, ask your manager how he or she would suggest that you proceed.

If there are no possibilities within your company, it's time to consider moving into a position of more responsibility with another firm. Or consider a lateral move within or outside your firm.

● N O T E :

Lateral moves within corporations are generally not offered to employees. If an interesting slot becomes vacant, you will almost certainly have to ask for it.

The benefits of a lateral move can be great. You can boost your value to your firm and to other potential employers. And, because you have diversified your skills, it's far more likely that you'll be the candidate of choice when a major opportunity for advancement comes along.

CAUTION

Because recruiters will be curious about why you are considering a parallel move, be prepared to explain why your company's structure has blocked your progress, and stress your eagerness to broaden your base of expertise.

ARE YOU IN A NEUROTIC ORGANIZATION?

■　■　■　■　■

Look around your workplace. If you perceive widespread patterns of aggressive, submissive or other destructive relationships, the odds are that you've found your way into a neurotic organization.

SOME COMMON NEUROTIC STRUCTURES

• The executive who withholds or distorts information to foster dependency or insecurity in the people he or she supervises.

• The subordinate on your staff who needs to feel hated—just because you're in a position of authority.

• The boss who feels that every action by a subordinate is a test of loyalty, rather than a simple procedure.

• A manager whose desire to be liked outweighs the necessity of reprimanding chronically late subordinates.

• A saboteur who monkey-wrenches projects hours before deadline, then gets everyone involved in last-minute efforts to save the day.

TRICKLE-DOWN NEUROSIS

While individual neuroses can be spotted and analyzed, what makes an entire organization turn neurotic? Dr. Danny Miller, author of *Unstable at the Top* (New American Library, $4.50), explains that an organization's neuroses usually reflect those of one or more people in top management.

Neurotic organizations are nearly everywhere, says Dr. Miller. He recently conducted a study of large companies and found that 40% of them showed signs of fostering widespread neurotic behavior.

When trapped in unhealthy relationships, you may have trouble realizing what is happening because you're too close to the problem. However, if you experience any of the following, you may be caught up in a neurotic web:

• A desire to rebel or escape.

• Excessive feelings of envy.

• An unrealistically lowered level of self-esteem.

• Extreme concern with other people's opinions of you.

TAKING POSITIVE ACTION

If you're a top-level manager at a neurotic company, you may be able to institute positive change by encouraging healthy, independent relationships among colleagues and subordinates, and by building such relationships with others yourself. These strategies may also prove effective:

• *Call in outside help.* Organizational consultants, some of whom also are practicing psychologists, can prove effective. Supervised off-site employee focus groups can often improve negative relationships.

• *Solve the problems indirectly.* If widespread neurosis is affecting profitability, try instituting cost-saving incentives or other programs to redirect energies toward positive goals.

◆ ALTERNATIVE:

Share the bleak outlook by distributing unacceptable sales statistics, etc., and say that the company faces serious cutbacks unless teamwork results in a turnaround.

• *Restructure.* Stir the managerial pot by reorganizing work cells, changing reporting relationships or terminating the visible offenders.

RECOMMENDATION:

If you are a middle-level manager in a neurosis-filled environment, "it's often better to flee than to fight," advises Dr. Miller. Unless you're in a high-ranking position, making fundamental changes in a neurotic company's culture is often very difficult.

Your best personal defense may be to realize that the problems you're experiencing are not your fault. Renew your own self-esteem, and seek a healthier environment where your career can prosper.

ARE YOU IN THE WRONG CAREER?

■ ■ ■ ■ ■

Nella Barkley, president of Crystal Barkley in New York City, a career counseling organization for executives, outlines common symptoms that may point to the need for a change of career direction:

• Difficulty in concentrating and finding motivation.

• A growing indifference toward work activities.

• Euphoria when Friday arrives and depression on Sunday evening.

• A deep, nagging sense of having unfulfilled career goals.

ASSESSING THE PROBLEM

If the signs outlined above are familiar to you, follow these steps to evaluate the problem and to determine a course of action:

• *Pinpoint the problem.* Are you dissatisfied with your career, or just your job? "If you feel enthusiastic about the potential for moving ahead in your field, but unhappy about current roadblocks, the problem is most likely your job," says Barkley. "If, on the other hand, you cannot summon enthusiasm for new projects, or can't even identify any, you are definitely in the wrong career."

• *Look at your colleagues.* Do your values jibe with those of others in your field? Generally, people in a given field—whether it be advertising, retailing, journalism or whatever—tend to have a number of shared values and interests. "If you do not feel comfortable with the prevalent set of values that you encounter in your field, regardless of your particular employer," notes Barkley, "it may be time to look for a new career."

• *Examine your outside interests.* What do you most enjoy reading about and discussing during your leisure time? "If you are in the right career, you will probably enjoy pursuing job-related interests during your off hours," explains Barkley. If your attitude toward your job is, "Out of sight, out of mind," look at the topics you do enjoy. Subjects that intrigue you are clues to possible career choices.

• *Review your abilities.* Does your career allow you to do what you are best suited for? "First, review your skills and aptitudes, either by yourself, with a book or with a counselor," suggests Barkley. A review of your skills and abilities should point to fields you might enjoy. Research educational requirements, the types of jobs available, and salary ranges for fields you might want to enter.

• *Put your fears in perspective.* Does the prospect of leaving a career to which you have devoted years of time and effort frighten you? Don't let unfounded fears keep you from acting. "Careful research leading to knowledge of yourself and your field of interest can eliminate most of the unknowns," says Barkley.

WHEN TO JUMP SHIP

Even though you've survived a cutback and/or a reorganization, it pays to ask yourself how secure your company really is.

INDICATORS OF TROUBLE

• **Lack of decisiveness** on the part of senior management. Particularly worrisome is an inability to discern "both the drones and the destructive achievers and get rid of them." If this failure of leadership is unusual for your firm, it is even more serious.

• **Loss of focus.** Ask yourself whether the company still understands its mission.

• **Who's leaving? Staying? Coming?** There's a certain amount of politics in every company, but you should be taking note of the people who are being let go, those who have resigned and the ones being promoted. Also examine new managers who

are being brought in. Will they reinvigorate the company, or are there implications of politically shoring up one faction?

• **Market position.** If you observe the company losing market share year after year, it's not going to remain a factor in its industry. Ask yourself what's being done about quality and other problems. If new products are important to your firm, explore what's in the pipeline. Is there competitive activity outside the company? Does that look more exciting than what your own people are coming up with? If you think so, customers probably will also.

• **Adjustment to change.** In many industries, technology is transforming the way business is conducted. Computer-integrated manufacturing (CIM), for example, is revolutionizing companies like General Motors. But the jury is still out on how successful this change will be. Still, if your company doesn't have the resources or the will to keep up with state-of-the-art developments, its days are numbered.

NONCOMPETITION CLAUSES

An increasing number of firms are asking their employees—and not just those at the most senior levels—to sign noncompetition agreements. You're usually asked to agree not to use the skills and knowledge you acquire on the job to enter into competition with the firm after you leave.

"Employers are losing more cases that involve oral contracts, so they're using written employment contracts, many of which have boiler-plate noncompetition clauses that aren't enforceable," says Darien A. Mc-

Whirter, a lawyer and author of *Your Rights at Work* (John Wiley & Sons, $14.95).

WHAT TO CONSIDER BEFORE YOU SIGN

• **What is the firm protecting?** Court decisions about whether an employee is in violation vary from state to state, but the key question being addressed in suits brought by employers against employees is, "What interest is the employer trying to protect?"

EXAMPLE:

An Illinois court found that noncompetition clauses were enforceable if an employee had a personal relationship with customers, or access to confidential information that would harm the former employer if the employee shared it with a competitor in a new job.

An increasing number of courts are concluding that the employer has to have a viable protectable interest at stake for a noncompetition clause to be enforceable.

• **What are your rights?** Talk to a lawyer who specializes in employment or labor law before you sign an agreement or employment contract.

• N O T E :

Noncompetition clauses often appear in fine print or are hidden in the language of protecting trade secrets.

"I always advise people not to agree to noncompetition clauses," says McWhirter. "You have to weigh whether it's worth the possibility of not getting the job or the promotion," he adds, "but remember that

employers often don't mind taking out no-compete provisions."

• **How will you leave?** Get legal advice before you give notice. It used to be the case that an individual could go to the boss and get a pat on the back and best wishes. But now an employee whose new job is perceived to be a threat may get a letter from the company lawyer instead.

Consult a lawyer to assess whether the noncompetition clause you signed is likely to be enforceable in court. The more narrowly drawn such a clause is, the better its prospects of withstanding a potential legal challenge.

EXAMPLE:

The Alabama Supreme Court ruled that a television station was within its rights to say its salespeople couldn't sell TV ads within a 60-mile radius if they left the company.

• **Negotiate.** If you have reason to believe that your employer may sue you, encourage your lawyer to have a friendly discussion with your ex-employer's lawyer. "It's more difficult to negotiate when the rules are changing, which is the case today," says McWhirter, "but there are strong incentives for both parties to resolve the matter out of court."

JOB HONEYMOONS

When you get a big promotion, win a great new job, or do something really extraordinary at work that you can be proud of and eager to boast about to your friends or family, the weeks that follow the exuberance can be a heady time.

Honeymoon periods are risky—at the same time you're being praised, you're also being scrutinized. It's a bad time to stumble, because you have that much further to fall.

EXTENDING THE HONEYMOON

• **Plan your next moves.** If you score a win, begin to look for the next big opportunity or challenge. If you've been waiting for the right moment to ask to take over a new project or territory, or to look for support for a pet project, now may be the time.

If that isn't appropriate, think about what you would like to do next. Then start planting seeds. Take advantage of management's confidence in you. You might say, "Now that you know I can successfully handle my own department, how about letting me help out on Sam's new project, too?" Use subtle words such as "help out" and "lend a hand" when asking to work on a new project or share someone else's responsibility. Avoid terms like "take over" or "give me responsibility for."

Astute players in political and corporate arenas know when to ask for power and when to ask for money. Asking for power during this honeymoon era is fine. Asking for a raise (if you haven't gotten one already) to accompany your new role may be tacky.

• **Don't misrepresent yourself.** It's natural to want to build on the positive image you've created. But if management gets a distorted picture of what you can do, you may find yourself in a no-win situation.

> ### EXAMPLE:
> A human resources manager knew only a little about computers, but he did know that networking the PCs in his department would streamline operations. After the network was installed and work efficiency increased, upper managers started to ask him more involved questions about computers. He figured that reinforcing the impression that he was a computer expert would help him, but he went forward with a project and bought the wrong equipment.

In short, he really fouled things up, both for the company and himself. All of the good from his first success disappeared because he let his ego get in the way.

■ **LESSON:**

Don't fake it. Your first few mistakes may be tolerated, but your honeymoon—and even your tenure in a position—may be cut short if you fail to live up to people's distorted beliefs about your capabilities.

• **Take a fresh look at what matters to management.** The ability to produce results that will be looked on favorably can prolong a job honeymoon while simultaneously securing you a firm place in the corporate hierarchy.

In many cases, senior executives don't know what they want until they see it. Rather than asking members of the top brass what they expect, take a look at the accomplishments and personal styles of company stars. Try to emulate them, and you can probably cap your success with another one.

RECOMMENDATION:

Look for new challenges, and don't try to extract all the nectar from what you've done. Putting your last success behind you allows you to be seen as a risk taker, and makes you all the more likely to be tapped for an opportunity with built-in chances for success.

TAKING YOUR CLIENTS WITH YOU
■   ■   ■   ■

You are planning to leave your current employer to strike out on your own or start working for a competitor. You've been working with a number of clients. Now that you're leaving, you are thinking about approaching them and trying to take their business with you. Is this ethical? Is it legal?

LEGAL IMPLICATIONS

The first thing you need to consider are any legal obligations you might have to your employer.

• *Trade secrets, proprietary documents, marketing lists and the like are company property protected by law.* Did you sign an employment contract that explicitly stated that client names are also assets to be considered "company property," and not to be appropriated by employees? If so, you'd better be extremely careful. Although you may be able to overturn such a contract in court, you are on shaky ground if you've already agreed that clients belong to the company.

If you can show that such a contract endangers your livelihood, the courts may be reluctant to uphold it, according to Tom Dunfee, professor of social responsibility at The Wharton School. Courts will also look at employment contracts on a case-by-case basis to see if restrictions are limited by time and space, and if your contract was reasonable.

• *Even if you do not have any binding contractual obligations,* there are still some hazards to consider. Courts generally recognize that companies have a legitimate claim to physical and intellectual property. Also, according to Harvard Business School Professor Kenneth Goodpaster, verbal promises to your employer can constitute a legal obligation.

• *You are at great risk if you approach clients for future business while you are currently working for your present employer.* Such activities could precipitate a conflict-of-interest case where the employer would have a legitimate claim against you. Dunfee also adds that you should be sure not to disclose any confidential company information to prospective clients, even after you leave a firm.

ETHICAL CONSIDERATIONS

Once you get past the legal questions, ethical considerations come into play. The experience and skills you acquired on the job legitimately belong to you, says Professor Manuel Velasquez, director of the Center for Applied Ethics at Santa Clara University. However, your employer did invest dollars and resources in obtaining clients.

One consultant in Georgia who worked for a pharmaceuticals firm before striking out on her own decided it would be fair to wait one year before approaching any of her previous clients. Consider the impact your actions will have on your employer. It's to your advantage to maintain cordial relations with everyone in your field.

HOW TO WIN THE BATTLE OF THE SEXES

· · · · ·

Competing one-on-one against someone of the opposite sex can turn you into your own worst enemy.

■ **REASON:**

Chivalry, subservience and other attitudes you were taught when growing up have no place in business—and they can take you right out of the running.

Most of today's executives grew up when society's views regarding acceptable male and female roles were vastly different from today.

COMPETITION TODAY

Kathy Kram, associate professor at Boston University's School of Management has studied workplace relationships extensively and offers these observations:

• *Male and female managers are generally feeling more positive about working and competing* with peers of the opposite sex, learning to accept it as part of today's business landscape. Problems often arise, however, when a man ends up working for a female boss—still an unusual situation in most companies.

• *Women in middle management* seem to be getting over the feeling that they shouldn't compete with men. Younger women who are entering business today compete quite effectively, possibly because they grew up with the idea that they would pursue careers.

• *Women who compete with women* often experience difficulties. Because it's still quite difficult for women to move into senior management positions in most companies, problems between female colleagues may be currently more visible than those that may occur between men and women.

• *Companies,* such as Digital Equipment, are starting programs to help employees deal with troubled work relationships—male/female, interracial, manager/employee. Some are starting to offer workshops on gender relations in recognition of the fact that there are problems that must be addressed.

CONQUERING COMPETITIVE QUALMS

• If you're experiencing difficulties in competing with someone of the opposite sex, talk with a colleague you can trust about your discomfort—someone of the same or opposite sex, whomever you feel more comfortable with. Also ask people who have been in similar situations how they dealt with them.

• Take the time to examine your attitudes toward competing with the opposite sex. Are you up to date or behind the times? In this labor-short climate, only the fullest development of all human resources will result in any company's success. This depends on every person's ability to cooperate—and also to compete—with a high degree of effectiveness.

Chapter 2

FITNESS

HOW TO TAKE FITNESS ON THE ROAD

. . . . .

Business trips can be draining, both physically and mentally. But physical activity and good nutrition can help you maintain high energy and vitality—even with a hectic travel schedule.

GETTING THERE IN GOOD SHAPE

Long flights can take a toll on the body. Sitting for hours causes blood to pool in the legs, resulting in stiff, tight muscles and swollen ankles.

■ S O L U T I O N :

Try these exercises while you're strapped in your seat:

• *Flex your feet* and rotate your ankles. This stimulates circulation in the feet.

• *Simulate walking* by lifting your knees lightly and shifting weight from leg to leg. This exercises the hip joints and the muscles located on top of the thighs.

• *Stretch your arms* over your head as though you were climbing a ladder, alternating right and left arms.

• *Stretch your neck* by tilting your head from side to side and dropping your chin to your chest.

FOOD FOR FLIGHT

To arrive at your destination feeling energized rather than depleted, watch what you eat on the plane.

• *Avoid alcohol and coffee.* Pressurized cabins are dry. Liquor and coffee tend to dehydrate you even more.

• *Say no to salty snacks* like peanuts. They cause you to retain water and feel bloated.

• *Call ahead to order a low-cholesterol, low-calorie or low-sodium meal.* Most airlines offer seafood, fruit plates and vegetarian selections.

• *Drink plenty of water and juice.* But avoid salty tomato juice.

PLANNING FOR FITNESS

Do some pretravel investigating. Many hotels now have pools, exercise rooms and tennis courts. If not, ask if the hotel is located near a health club, gym or YMCA.

If you attend an exercise studio or health club in your home city, find out if it has a branch where reciprocal privileges will be honored.

To pack efficiently for your fitness routine, bring these things along:

• *Cross training shoes,* which are good for tennis, running or aerobic dancing. They save space and give you several options.

• *A swimsuit, pair of shorts or sweats.*

• *Dynabands™* or other rubber exercise bands that offer resistance. Or pack the new lightweight plastic weights that can be filled with water. (These products are advertised in fitness magazines and mail-order catalogs.)

• *Exercise music.* If you've been exercising to a tape, bring it along with your cassette player. If you use an exercise video, ask the hotel if it has rooms available with VCRs.

WHERE TO GO, WHAT TO DO

If you're a jogger, call the Chamber of Commerce in the destination city for advice on safe places to run. Or check with the local branch of the Road Runners Club for recommended running paths or group runs that you can join.

ADDITIONAL SOURCES

International Dance Exercise Association, 619-535-8979; Aerobics and Fitness Association of America, 818-905-0040.

If you opt to do aerobics in your hotel room, make sure they are low-impact.

■ R E A S O N :

Most hotel rooms put carpeting on top of a concrete base. Any kind of jumping or running in place could cause discomfort.

Many business trips consist of wall-to-wall meetings that leave little time for sleep, much less exercise. Be realistic. If you simply can't find the time to exercise, don't worry. Walk whenever you can, even if it's just a few blocks, before flagging down a taxi. You can go a couple of days without losing the fitness gains you've made.

▲ I M P O R T A N T :

Travel is the time to maintain, not to make, fitness gains.

HOW TO ADAPT TO LESS SLEEP
• • • • •

When you're traveling on business or working late hours to prepare a special presentation, you're likely to lose one or two nights of adequate sleep.

■ R E S U L T :

You're fatigued and irritable at the very time you most need to be in top form.

Sleep researchers, however, have developed some techniques to help you adapt to short-term sleep deprivation, according to Dr. Richard Bootzin, professor of psychology at the University of Arizona's Sleep Disorders Center in Tucson.

THINGS TO AVOID

• **Caffeine.** It adds to the irritability that sleep deprivation brings. Natural and environmental stimulants—a brisk walk or a shower—work much better.

• **Heavy meals.** Large meals—especially those containing high levels of fat and carbohydrates—don't make you stronger or more aware. They cause your digestive system to work harder, using up what little energy you have left after a poor night's sleep. Also, carbohydrates produce insulin, which depletes the bloodstream of amino acids and causes drowsiness.

• **Alcohol.** Don't take a late-night drink to help you sleep. Alcohol *is* a depressant that causes you to feel sleepy, but it also prevents you from sleeping very deeply.

SPECIAL TECHNIQUES

• **Traveling through different time zones.** Traveling west is generally not much of a problem, because you gain time and merely feel you've stayed up a little too late. But when you travel east, particularly if you go from the U.S. to Europe, your body clock has to adjust to a loss of four or more hours and it's much harder to become acclimated.

RECOMMENDATION:

Get up earlier than usual for several days before you leave and eat meals in accordance with the new time schedule. When you arrive, engage in stimulating activities such as walking outdoors or interacting with others.

▲ IMPORTANT:

Make sure that your meals contain plenty of protein, which stimulates the neurotransmitters in the brain and leads to arousal.

• **Avoiding sleep to complete a project or prepare a presentation.** The day after can be extremely difficult, especially late in the day.

RECOMMENDATION:

The day after, take frequent short breaks to restimulate your senses with social interaction or a quick walk around the block. If feasible, listen to music while working. And make sure the lighting and temperature in your office are comfortable.

Adrenaline will usually get you through the presentation, no matter how sleepy you are. But experiment with these techniques as well: Before the presentation, listen to relaxing music for 15–20 minutes, then take a shower or splash water in your face. A short 15- or 20-minute nap works well for some people and poorly for others. Try it and see.

ON-THE-JOB STRETCHING
• • • • •

"Unless you compensate for long periods spent in cramped positions, you're going to feel stiffness or tightness on a regular basis and, in the long run, your posture will change for the worse to compensate for it," says Bob Anderson, who has taught flexibility and stretching to U.S. Olympic teams and professional football teams (including the Denver Broncos and the New York Jets) and is the author of *Stretching* (Random House, 201 E. 50th St., New York, NY 10022; $9.95).

Stretching for as little as five or ten minutes a day can combat common office-related aches and pains as well as stiffness of the shoulders, neck or back. It is also a great way to reduce stress.

Unlike other forms of exercise, stretching can be done at your desk, in an airplane seat, or even when you're watching television—and it is not painful. When done correctly, it should feel as natural as yawning. Anderson advises holding a stretch only for as long as it isn't painful. With regular practice, your muscles will become more flexible and you'll be able to comfortably increase the duration of a stretch. Here is a sampler of stretches that can easily be done in your office:

ARMS, NECK AND UPPER BACK

• **Interlace your fingers,** then stretch your arms out in front of you with palms forward. Hold the stretch for 20 seconds. Repeat the stretch twice. Using the same technique, put your arms over your head, turning palms upward. Repeat three times, holding each stretch for ten seconds.

• **Extend your arms overhead** with palms facing forward. Holding the outside of your left hand with your right hand, gently pull your left arm toward your right side, bending your upper body slightly. Keep your arms as straight as is comfortably possible. Hold for 15 seconds. Repeat on both sides.

• **Extend your arms overhead.** Hold your right elbow with your left hand; then gently pull that elbow behind your head until you feel an easy tension stretch in your shoulder or the back of your upper arm. Try to hold for 30 seconds. Relax for 30 seconds; then repeat on the other side.

• **Interlock your fingers behind your head,** keeping your elbows in line as much as is comfortably possible with your shoulders. Gently push your elbows back, as if your shoulder blades were being pulled together. Hold this position for eight to ten seconds. Repeat several times, relaxing between each repetition.

• **With your arms hanging at your sides,** grasp your right arm just above your elbow with your left hand, then gently pull your elbow and arm across in front of you toward your left shoulder as you look over your right shoulder. Hold for ten seconds. Rest, then repeat on other side.

FACE AND NECK

• **Sit in a comfortable position.** Very slowly roll your head around in a full circle as you keep your back straight. Hold a stretch at any place that feels tight, but don't strain. Repeat, rolling your head the other way.

• **Raise your eyebrows** and open your eyes as wide as possible. At the same time, open your mouth to stretch the muscles around your nose and chin and stick your tongue out. Hold for five to ten seconds.

Chapter 3

INTERPERSONAL RELATIONS

SEVEN WAYS TO SAY GOOD-BYE
• • • • •

If you sometimes feel awkward when ending a conversation, it's possible that you haven't chosen the *right* way to say good-bye.

HOW TO END IT

Psychologists have identified at least seven different ways to terminate a chat:

• *Supportive.* If you want to continue or increase contact with the person in the near future, use a good-bye that both expresses your satisfaction with the present discussion and anticipates your next contact:

"This has been very informative for me. Let's talk again soon."

• *Summary.* When you expect results from a conversation, remember that the last remark made is the one that is most likely to be remembered. Use a good-bye that not only clarifies but also pins down what you've both talked about: "So we'll begin training on the 15th."

• *Continuance.* To save time, you make the date for your next discussion right then and there.

• *Legitimizing.* When you want to end your discussion, put a final seal on your talk that justifies your ending it. For instance, "Well, that's the last item on the agenda," or "If that's all, I've got to run."

• *Appreciative.* For a simple, upbeat

203

ending, express your satisfaction: "I really enjoyed talking to you."

- *Downshift.* You've finished your business, and want to end on a friendly note: "By the way, how's your family?"
- *Filling.* Your conversation started a little tensely but is now ending in an amiable spirit. An irrelevant, light close is appropriate: "Say, before I go, did you hear the story about. . .?"

MAKING SMALL TALK COUNT
. . . . .

Small talk is underestimated and its value downgraded, asserts Deirdre Boden, an assistant professor of sociology at Washington University in St. Louis, MO. But it is one of the best ways to get to know someone in a brief amount of time. It sets the stage and paves the way for what's ahead, making conversation easier.

GETTING STARTED

- **Ask questions that initiate a conversation.** "A good question is a topic initiator," Boden explains. "It triggers a complex answer." A poor question elicits a one-word answer and brings the conversation to a dead stop. Some examples of poor questions: *Question:* "Do you come here often?" *Answer:* "No, I don't," or "Yes, I do." *Question:* "What do you think of the terrible weather we've been getting?" *Answer:* "I think it's awful and I can't wait for it to get better."

An example of a topic-initiating question is: "I don't agree with the lead speaker. I think he missed the point, and should have concentrated on issues that concern the division managers. How do you feel about it?" *Answer:* "I didn't think it was all that bad, although I certainly think you have a point. . ." etc. The later question elicits a lengthy response that makes it easy to ask many more questions. It also triggers questions and opinions from the person with whom you're speaking.

- **Ask questions that build intimacy.** "Questions that reveal something about yourself establish a comfortable rapport quickly," says Boden.
- **Lighten the conversation with humor.** Laughter is a marvelous tension reliever, says Boden. "As we laugh, it relaxes others. Even a friendly smile makes conversation a lot easier."
- **Give the other person time to answer.** Don't monopolize the conversation. People speak at their own rhythms. Allow the other person plenty of time to gather his or her thoughts and respond.

SWITCHING TO SERIOUS TOPICS

There is no formula for when to change the tone of the conversation and move it to serious issues. Once the conversation is moving along at a comfortable rhythm, and you sense that the other person is at ease, you can change topics.

> EXAMPLE:
> "I know that you love the California climate, but how do you think the line supervisors in our central office will feel about relocating there? I see problems down the road that we ought to be thinking about right now. What do you think?"

PREPARING FOR THE EVENT

If small talk is difficult for you, and you feel awkward about striking up a conversation with people you don't know, prepare for the event, suggests Boden. Think up topic-initiating questions that are suitable for the occasion, plus ways to comfortably shift the conversation from small talk to meaningful talk. If you're getting together with engineers, buyers, product managers, supervisors or architects, decide beforehand what information you are looking for and the best way to get it. Finally, create imaginary conversations. The real thing will be very different, but the exercise will open you up to a variety of conversation scenarios.

FEAR OF CRYING
■ ■ ■ ■ ■

A subordinate who cries is probably releasing simple frustration or anger rather than trying to achieve anything specific. But a manager may misunderstand and feel manipulated.

HANDLING THE SITUATION

• **Maintain your professional relationship.** Don't act like a parent or a friend and become overly solicitous. Let the employee use her own resources to regain her composure.

• **Stand your ground.** If the criticism is realistic, don't yield. However, make it clear that you are criticizing the problem at hand and not the person. Then try to move to a structured plan that you and the employee can jointly work out to prevent a recurrence of the problem or to improve the situation.

• **Bring in a buffer.** Often, crying comes as a complete surprise to the manager. But if you know that the person is highly sensitive and is likely to cry at emotional situations, arrange to have a respected staff member—preferably female—sit in on the conversation.

• **Know when to stop.** If a worker is unable to compose herself or the session becomes hostile, the best action is to end the conversation and resume it when emotions have cooled down.

• **Don't make rash judgments.** A single incident of crying should not be taken to mean that an employee is too emotional and cannot handle her job.

Open communication remains the top priority. If you avoid criticizing a female employee because you fear she may cry, you'll both suffer from the lack of communication. The employee may see the lack of feedback as a sign of "a climate inhospitable to women's talents and abilities," says a study from Catalyst, a New York City research organization that works with corporations to foster the career and leadership development of women. This may result in loss of morale, impaired productivity and possible attrition of valued employees.

SUCCESS-SELLING TECHNIQUES
■ ■ ■ ■ ■

In negotiating and closing sales, successful salespeople use basic techniques that get people interested in what they have to say, build on that interest, and culminate in a final agreement. You can use the same techniques when you have something to sell at work, be it a key project or your need for a new staff member.

STRATEGIES TO GET TO THE 'YES' YOU WANT

■ **Pique interest**—and underline the value of the time you'll take. State your objective briefly in an interesting way.

> **EXAMPLES:**
>
> "I've outlined a number of ways I think we can boost profits in our group—enough to make the time you give me pay off well."

■ **Build yeses.** Get the listener in a positive mode by starting with questions you know will trigger positive responses.

> **EXAMPLES:**
>
> "I'm sure the idea of increasing our efficiency and cutting costs is attractive" or "We'd all like to get more out of the time we put in here, don't you agree?"

■ **"Sell" benefits.** Put the proposal in terms specifically beneficial to your prospect.

> **EXAMPLES:**
>
> "Mary, if you put me in charge of that project, I'll put in all the time that's required, without regard to the clock. I'll draw on every bit of marketing knowledge I have to make sure that the customer is satisfied, and I'll get my entire staff personally involved."

Also, mention corollary benefits.

> **EXAMPLES:**
>
> "This is good for the company. . .and it won't do our image as division managers any harm, either."

■ **"Close" the sale.** This is the equivalent of a salesperson asking for the order. For you, it means asking for what you're after. But the phrasing is crucial. The following are some examples:

• A smart retail salesperson doesn't say "Do you want these shoes or not?" He or she says, "Will this be cash or charge?" In business, you need an approach—one that gives your prospect an easy way to say yes.

• "The best way for me to get started on the project is to start coming in at 7:30 every morning. Is that all right with you?" Once you've met with success, you can apply similar closing techniques to win the support you need to complete the job.

• "The mail room clerks can help me with the clerical tasks on either Tuesday or Wednesday each week. Which day is lighter for them?"

GET AN HONEST OPINION ON YOUR BRILLIANT IDEA

• • • • •

When you come up with a report, plan, proposal, speech or the like that is not just a rerun of an old idea, you are likely to feel both pleased and apprehensive. It is common then to want another's opinion—but to hesitate to expose your ego by asking.

If you overcome your hesitation and ask, you'll have to make clear that you want a candid opinion or you won't get it. You'll get strokes instead—a waste of time.

HOW TO GET THE TRUTH

• **Ask early in the process.** Don't wait to ask your assistant—or your spouse—for a critique as you are about to leave for the meeting at which you will deliver your speech. You will be told it's "just great," which is what your timing is asking for.

• **Avoid the macro approach.** "How do you think it adds up?" or "Do you think the point it makes is valid?" may draw affirmative responses that are honest, but prevent the person from offering the "Yes, but" opinion that he or she really holds.

● BETTER:

"I'm confident that the approach I'm suggesting is new and correct. But please tell me whether I've included enough backup arguments. Do they follow in a logical sequence and support my conclusion? Or do some of them go off on a tangent?" Now you are inviting a line-by-line critique, and you have a better chance of getting it.

• **Open yourself to complete disagreement.** Even after you've asked for a detailed review, you may not have uncovered some strong reservations. Therefore, add: "OK, thank you for helping me rephrase those points. Now I'm going for broke. Even though I believe that you agree with the whole concept here, I have one more question. Is this the way you would have written the proposal if I'd asked you to do it for me?" Then, repeat the person's points to make sure you understand them.

CAUTION

Be sure that you really value the person's opinion before you ask that last question, because you may hear "No," and find yourself looking at the need to rewrite your whole proposal. But that is an inherent hazard of original thinking.

RECOMMENDATION:

Don't ask for opinions unless you intend to abide by them—or have a good reason to offer as to why you will not. Otherwise, cross the person off your "He always gives me an honest opinion" list. If you don't follow through, the person won't take you seriously the next time. Be sure, too, to allow yourself the time to rework your presentation as needed.

HOW TO SAY 'I'M SORRY'
■ ■ ■ ■ ■

Effective apologies clear the air and set the tone. They help build a new and risk-taking climate as employees realize that mistakes—yours and theirs—are not the end.

But if you don't make your apology the right way, it can go unnoticed or even backfire on you.

MAKE 'I'M SORRY' AN EFFECTIVE MANAGEMENT TOOL

• **Apologize face to face** if at all possible. A personal apology comes across as more sincere than a note and stresses that you care about the individual's feelings.

• **Never apologize while angry.** Cool down first. Recover from your own chagrin. Otherwise you'll sound insincere, and that is self-defeating.

• **Be specific.** Regrets couched in generalities make you come off as wimpy. Pinpoint the action you took—or didn't— that you now regret.

• **Don't spread the blame** to the whole department, company or group. That makes it too diffuse, even if you know that others were involved. Take responsibility for your part in the problem and apologize for that.

• **Follow up an apology** with a plan to avoid future misunderstandings. But don't rush in with a quick fix. Show the other person that you've taken the problem and the trouble it caused seriously.

• **Don't overapologize.** Every minor misstep does not need to be excused. Use the "I'm sorry" sparingly for the greatest effect.

Chapter 4

JOB HUNTING

HOW TO CONDUCT EFFECTIVE JOB SEARCHES

. . . . . .

Certain techniques must actively be used to find the job best suited to your career goals:

• *Set a clear objective.* Don't say, "I want to go into marketing and sales." In today's climate, you must narrow your goal.

Know what salary range you want, too. If that differs greatly from your current salary, have a good rationale for why you merit it.

> EXAMPLE:
>
> You did a long-term, difficult project that increased your skills and your old company's profits.

• *Formulate a strategy consistent with your objective.* Three main strategies exist for finding jobs: going through a network of contacts and referrals; marketing yourself directly through a mail campaign and follow-up calls; and using intermediaries, such as want ads and executive search firms to find the jobs you want.

▲ IMPORTANT:

Find out how jobs in your desired field are usually filled and devote most of your time to that method.

• *Create structures to support your objective.* Have a polished résumé and build a list of strong references. If referrals are an important source of job leads for you, keep them organized and somewhere readily available.

TODAY'S SALARY NEGOTIATIONS

When you land the job you want, be organized in negotiating your new salary. Here are some strategies to get the compensation you want:

• *Educate yourself before your interview.* Talk to industry contacts, or the new firm's current or former employees, to find out about compensation practices. Does the firm view itself as a high-paying leader in the industry? What's the compensation package as a whole? Are bonuses or stock options part of the compensation picture?

• *Discuss compensation during the initial interview.* While it's best to let the interviewer bring up money, don't fail to pin down the salary range. One technique: Rather than asking what the job pays, state the salary range you're looking for. If the money they're offering is very different from your goal, they should tell you—and you should deal with the discrepancy right away.

• *Enter final salary negotiations only after you've been offered the job* and decided to accept it. You've already pinned down the salary range, and the stage has been set to finalize your compensation. Before final negotiations, amass as much information as you can.

If all has gone well, you can assume that the company wants you so much that stretching the budget for you won't be a problem. Rehearse your presentation and have a well-defined rationale to back up your request if it is called into question.

◆ REMEMBER:

Negotiating a higher starting rate is far easier than winning raises later on.

• *Don't fail to talk about bonuses.* Ask about bonuses—when the company pays them and how much you can expect. If you will be giving up an upcoming bonus at your current job, ask for a "signing bonus" from your potential employer. This means that the new firm will pay you for the bonus you will lose.

EXAMPLE:

If you have six months before you get your old firm's annual $4,000 bonus, ask for an additional $2,000. Your agreement will depend on how soon you will receive a bonus at the new firm, and on the amount.

While you may not get financial compensation for lost bonus money, the company may offer extra vacation days instead, or may agree to give you a bonus after six months on the job instead of one year. Odds are that it will be up to you to begin bonus negotiations.

STALKING A BIG JOB
■　　■　　■　　■　　■

More and more middle managers are competing for fewer upper-management jobs. To put yourself ahead of the pack when you interview for one, avoid the following mistakes:

• *Lack of focus.* In your first interview, stick with just the big issues. Try to learn as much as you can about the job and what the work entails. Then discuss your prime motivations for seeking it, and clearly present your skills and experience. Introducing secondary concerns too soon weakens your image.

EXAMPLE:
Asking about access to the executive dining room—even as a tension-breaker—pegs you as someone who is more interested in status than in getting the job done.

- *Talking money too soon.* Don't discuss pay until you're confident that you are under serious consideration for the job. Then look beyond salary and consider total compensation. Top jobs often offer packages that include stock options, incentive payments, pension packages and other components.
- *Mismatching your style.* If you come from a Silicon Valley company where jogging shoes and T-shirts are the norm, don't expect a conservative company to make exceptions in its style or policies just for you. Dress in a businesslike fashion at interviews to show that you understand style differences and that you are willing to adapt.
- *Mistargeting questions.* Ask a vice president about a manufacturing process or your job responsibilities, but save questions about benefit programs for the personnel manager. If negotiations are well along and important questions have not been answered, ask to speak with appropriate personnel who can provide answers.
- *Parading your current company.* Most interviewers quickly tire of hearing "At my company, we do it this way. . ." The result is that you seem inflexible—or even condescending.
- *Dragging out negotiations.* Be decisive enough to know when it is time to stop negotiating and accept or reject the job. Prolonging the process only makes you appear indecisive.

CHANGING INDUSTRIES

An increasing number of job-hunters, including many top-earning executives, are discovering that their skills and experience transfer across industry borders.

A recent study by Right Associates, an international outplacement firm headquartered in Philadelphia, found that 57% of the clients it counseled in the last two years had changed industries. In the process, they scored salary increases of 10%. Those who stayed within the same industry actually experienced average salary *decreases* of 4% after adjusting for inflation.

PREPARING FOR THE CHANGE

- **Do a self-analysis.** Determine what you can offer employers outside your industry. The key is to identify proven skills—not just knowledge areas.
- **Show a grasp of industry problems.** Not all employers are receptive to candidates whose backgrounds are in different fields. You'll have to show them that you understand the problems the company (or industry) is facing and explain how your skills and credentials can help solve them. Read trade and professional publications and interview people in the new industry for information and advice.
- **Learn to speak the language.** If you can comfortably plug in industry buzzwords or acronyms, you'll come across as more of an insider.

WHAT ARE YOUR CHANCES?

People who work in human resources and training, communications/public relations, EDP/information services and engineering research were among the most likely to change industries, according to the Right Associates survey. The *least likely* were those in general management, technical support and operations/production.

The older you are, the *more likely* you are to make a move to another industry. According to the survey, 55% of those under the age of 50 had changed industries, while 63% of those between the ages of 50 and 59 and 78% of those over age 60 had made such a change.

OPPORTUNITIES FROM ABROAD

While the ability to converse fluently in the language of a foreign employer is a big plus, it's not always necessary for gaining employment. What is essential as an American, however, is adjusting your behavior to avoid coming on too strong.

BRIDGING THE CULTURAL GAP

■ **Arrange for a proper entrée.** More so than in the U.S., a personal introduction provides a common entryway for many people hired by foreign businesses. If you learn of a foreign firm's plans to open an office here and you want to be considered for a position, look for a reputable intermediary to introduce yourself.

• College connections are highly valued in Europe, South America and the Orient. If you went to a large college or university, check alumni organizations for fellow graduates who work for the firm. Whether they are based here or abroad, write them

directly, stress school ties, and ask for an introduction to those who are hiring.

• Other possible intermediaries include banks and law or accounting firms that have relationships with the company.

● N O T E :

Many foreign companies retain search firms because they lack networks here. Call the foreign firm to ask if a headhunter is handling the staffing process. If you're a qualified candidate, headhunters will be glad to present you.

■ **Understand cultural expectations and values.** If you've had no previous experience dealing with the culture of the prospective employer, give yourself a crash course. Start by talking to clients or colleagues with that ancestry for general cultural guidelines. But bear in mind that specific customs may have changed over several generations.

People who have done business with that culture are a good source of information, particularly on questions of etiquette. A meeting with a language instructor from a local college or language school also may provide tips on clothes, interviews and business protocol.

■ **Sell the whole person.** In most foreign countries, the hiring process focuses on a person's interests and knowledge, in addition to what's required on the job. Share your views on art, architecture, literature, history—it's likely to enhance your image and status as a job candidate.

■ **Understate your accomplishments.** In America, overstressing your personal accomplishments has become a prerequisite to getting hired. In most other cultures, it's likely to be met with suspicion. Even using the word "I" too frequently can be considered rude.

● BETTER:

Stress your firm's accomplishments; share your knowledge of the industry.

■ **Pay attention to your body language.** A handshake is an almost universal greeting, but other gestures can get you into trouble. Pointing and using your hands to emphasize what you're saying makes people in most Eastern and northern European cultures uncomfortable.

● SAFEST:

Take cues about body language and voice modulation from the person with whom you're interviewing.

■ **Don't go overboard.** Bowing rather than shaking hands with Japanese executives who are accustomed to doing business in the U.S. is a blunder. Remember, you're being considered because you're an American and know—or come across as knowing—how the company can best operate in the U.S.

HIT HOME-RUN ANSWERS AT INTERVIEWS

■ ■ ■ ■ ■

Stinging questions have become part of nearly every interviewer's arsenal. Usually he or she first asks a series of reasonable questions, then suddenly stuns you with something particularly difficult or unsettling.

EXAMPLE:

"Tell me something terrible you've heard about our company."

RESPONDING TO TOUGH QUESTIONS

• **Expect to be stunned.** When you anticipate that one or two zingers will be thrown at you during an interview, you have an edge.

• **Understand the purpose of hardball questions.** The main purpose is to determine whether you can keep your head under pressure. Keep cool, and you'll win points—even if your answer falls this side of being brilliant.

• **Be sure you understand the question.** The most common stress-induced error is answering a question that's different from the one that was asked. Asking for clarification buys extra seconds and shows that you're treating the process with appropriate seriousness.

HOW TO PREPARE FOR CURVEBALLS

There are few questions that can unsettle you if you practice ahead of time. Sit in a chair, imagine that you're in an interview, and rehearse—aloud.

■ REASON:

Just thinking about answers won't teach you to talk things through convincingly.

Many of the curveballs you're likely to encounter will be variations on the following questions:

• *Where does your current employer think you are right now?* You don't want to say that you lied to your current boss, or put time pressure on the interviewer by claiming that you're on lunch hour. One escape hatch is to say that you took a personal day to handle several personal matters, including the interview.

• *Tell me something terrible you've heard about our company.* Use this as an opportunity to show off the research you've done about the firm.

▲ STRATEGY:

Explain that you wouldn't have come for an interview if the company had a spotty reputation. Then talk about your view of how the company is positioned in the market, or make some other demonstration of your analytical skills. If you're pressured to say something negative, cite something about the firm you believe needs improvement, then show how you can help get it done.

• *Your boss probably said something negative about you in your last review. What was it, and how did it make you feel?* This is your chance to show that you take criticism well and use it to improve your performance.

EXAMPLE:

"Since I can't watch myself working, I've always seen reviews as a source of objective information about my work." Then go on to mention something you improved upon based on criticism you received.

• *Your last company seems to be in a lot of trouble. Do you think it's going to survive?* This is an attempt to trick you into bad-mouthing your previous employer—always a mistake at interviews.

■ TACTIC:

Bring the question into focus by asking exactly why the interviewer thinks your old firm is in trouble. Then, without divulging any inside information, give a bal-

anced view of the problem he or she cites.

• *You don't seem very enthusiastic. What is your reservation about taking a job with this company?* Go ahead and point out a problem, but then go on to show how you plan to solve it.

EXAMPLE:

"I'm worried because the department I'd be heading seems to be understaffed. But if the firm is willing to work with me on revising operational procedures, the situation can be brought under control."

• *Why have you changed jobs so frequently?* If you have been a job-hopper, stress that you were quickly able to accomplish what was required of you in different positions, and that new challenges were not forthcoming.

▲ STRATEGY:

Throw the question back at the interviewer by asking about challenges that his or her firm can provide. This shows that you're growth-oriented—that you'll go the distance if the challenges are sufficient. Because every interviewer thinks that challenges abound, this ploy will nearly always work.

HOW TO CHARM A SILENT INTERVIEWER
■ ■ ■ ■ ■

You're ready to field any tricky question in an important job interview. What you didn't anticipate was a passive interviewer.

It happens often, yet few job applicants are prepared for such a situation, says

Stephen K. Merman, coauthor with John F. McLaughlin of *Outinterviewing the Interviewer* (Spectrum Books, a division of Prentice-Hall, Rte. 9W, Englewood Cliffs, NJ 07632; $8.95).

Your goal is to make a good impression on this person by telling important things about yourself. But you need to keep the meeting cordial and relaxed.

HOW TO BEGIN

• **Strategy #1:** Walk in prepared with a general statement about yourself that sets a businesslike tone and invites questions.

> EXAMPLE:
>
> "I have been in banking for 20 years. I started out as a teller and worked my way up to district manager. I was responsible for automating my branches, which increased our profits by more than 40% over the first two years. There are other marketing innovations I would like to discuss. . ."

• **Strategy #2:** Toss the ball back to the interviewer by asking questions.

> EXAMPLE:
>
> "Now that you know something about me, I'd like to learn a little bit more about your organization."

• **Strategy #3:** Give the interviewer a choice of subjects.

> EXAMPLE:
>
> "Would you prefer to hear about my current job or would you be more interested in my career goals and how they can fit into your organization?"

BUILD RAPPORT

Realize that your interviewer may be as uncomfortable with the interview process as you are. The faster you can break out of the rigid question-and-answer format and get a comfortable conversation going, the more easily information will flow.

A good technique for opening up a silent interviewer is to get this person to talk about himself or herself, suggests Jim Kennedy, author of *Getting Behind the Résumé* (Prentice-Hall Information Services Div., 235 Frisch Court, Paramus, NJ 07652; $35.00). "Most people loosen up and relax when they're asked questions about themselves," says Kennedy. "Here's an easy way to establish a better rapport which can make information gathering very comfortable. You might say: 'While I'm here today, I'd be interested to learn something about your background with the company. Have you been here long?' "

When the tension eases and there is a relaxed exchange, you can shift the conversation back to the company. "What are some of the competitive pressures your company is under right now?" "What kind of people best fit into your corporate culture?"

ASK OPEN-ENDED QUESTIONS

• **Avoid starting questions with a verb,** cautions Kennedy. "More likely than not, you'll get a one-word or a short-phrase answer," he says.

> EXAMPLES:
>
> "Are there many chances for advancement?" *Answer:* "Yes." Or, "Do you fill your jobs internally or from the outside?" *Answer:* "We use both methods."

Instead, begin questions with *I*, *what*, *when*, *where*, *why* or *how*.

> **EXAMPLES:**
> "I'd love to know about the advancement possibilities in your company" or "How do you fill your job openings?"

But while *what*, *where*, *when*, *why* or *how* questions can pave the way for more questions, don't overuse any one of them. This is especially true of *why* questions, says Kennedy. A series of these fired in rapid succession can put the interviewer on the defensive.

> **EXAMPLE:**
> "Why is turnover so high? Why has the company reduced its product line?"

CONFRONTATION TACTIC

If you try these strategies and still feel resistance, you may find that you have no choice but to put your cards on the table, according to Kennedy. You can say: "I am here today because I am interested in the job opening. I believe I can make many contributions to your company. I have suggested four or five things that I can tell you about myself, none of which has sparked any interest on your part. Is there something about our interview that I should be aware of, because I am finding it difficult to move in any direction?"

There is nothing wrong with speaking your mind, adds Kennedy, as long as it's done respectfully. You can be assertive, but at the same time, professional and polite, so that you do not offend the interviewer and cloud your chances of being considered. If you handle a difficult interview, you will have scored some hard-earned points.

RECOMMENDATION:
Just being qualified for a job is not enough, cautions Kennedy. Walk into an interview prepared for a variety of scenarios.

Chapter 5

LEADERSHIP/ COMMUNICATIONS

EARNING RESPECT: A GUIDE FOR NEW MANAGERS

. . . . .

Here are six tips for winning respect and loyalty from those who work with you, without using methods that instill fear and resentment:

• *Demonstrate the work ethic you expect from others.* No manager should ask people to work harder than he or she is willing to do. If you expect your workers to put in 10 hours a day, put in at least that much or more yourself.

• *Be evenhanded.* Don't play favorites among subordinates.

• *Set high ethical and moral standards,* and live up to them conspicuously. That will send a clear message to others about the level of performance you expect.

• *Don't grandstand.* Refrain from lecturing, praising or humiliating subordinates in public. Keep all communications between individual employees and yourself private. If they want to talk about it, that's their decision, not yours.

• *Always keep your word.* It's wiser to under-promise and over-deliver to your staff than vice versa.

• *Share the spotlight.* Don't hog the credit for every bright idea that emerges from your department. Give credit where credit is due. You'll find that much of it will reflect back on you.

HOW TO SAY WHAT YOU MEAN

■　■　■　■　■

To master the art of communication, you should be aware of the subtleties that affect how accurately people grasp what you mean. Consider the following:

• *Your understanding of your listeners.* Sensitivity to others' points of view is vital to getting your message across.

EXAMPLE:

Your assistant has to revise her market report substantially. You've learned that she's easily hurt when you order changes, so you temper what you say to reduce the sting: "It's my fault for not being more precise."

• *Your means of communication.* Written messages are often misinterpreted. The reader, unable to ask questions to clear up meaning, is forced to interpret them without any assistance—sometimes incorrectly.

On the other hand, formal messages are best presented in writing to ensure that they are not taken too personally.

EXAMPLE:

If you want to issue a formal policy against sexual harassment, a memo is best. A verbal pronouncement might leave people wondering, "Has someone complained about being harassed?"

• *Your tone or body language.* Consider this message: "Bob, I want to talk to you in my office about the Leonard deal." Now see how that message would be interpreted

with two different sets of signals from the executive: (1) a smile and an enthusiastic voice; or (2) dead eyes, a frown and a serious voice. In the first case, the invitation seems friendly and positive; in the second, potentially threatening.

• *Your feelings about the content.* Your personal bias can distort a message. For example, top management instructs you to cut down on employee tardiness, but you feel that the problem is being exaggerated. You dutifully make the announcement about coming to work on time, but employees sense no conviction behind what you say. If higher management is serious, you could be doing employees a disservice and leading them and yourself into trouble.

• *Your feelings about people.* The way you feel may come across more clearly than the information you try to give.

EXAMPLE:

You don't like Doris, and you don't hide that fact when you attack her idea for a new customer service. Your sarcasm, however, puts off others, so they don't hear the facts you cite against Doris's proposal.

• *The complexity of your message.* Elaborate instructions must be given slowly to be received accurately.

EXAMPLE:

In a rush to a lunch appointment, you quickly instruct a typist on how to format a report. Don't be surprised if you find it's not done exactly as you wish.

RECOMMENDATION:
Before blaming others when they misunderstand your messages, look at

the six factors cited here as possible culprits. Use them to frame your instructions more clearly.

SECRETS OF CHARISMA
· · · · ·

It seems today that major careers cannot be built without the personal magnetism possessed by people like Lee Iacocca or Steve Jobs. If you lack natural charisma, you can adopt those personal traits that build a charismatic image, which you can use to advance your career.

WHAT CREATES CHARISMA?

Dr. Jay A. Conger, professor of management at McGill University in Montreal and author of *The Charismatic Leader* (Jossey-Bass, 433 California St., San Francisco, CA 94194; $28.95), believes that outstanding charismatic executives have four recognizable key traits:

• *They possess vision.* They perceive present affairs as unacceptable and offer instead an inspiringly idealistic—yet believable—vision of the future.

One example would be Steve Jobs. In building his company, Next, he didn't ask his staff to build a computer that would meet a list of technical requirements. Instead, he set a specific goal—to give high school students a $10,000 machine capable of simulating the machinery in a $10 million DNA laboratory—and challenged his employees to create a machine that would revolutionize the way people learn. Technical requirements were met because of his motivational vision.

• *They communicate masterfully.*

Charismatic leaders formulate dreams that others can believe in. And they portray their vision of the future as the only path to follow. They often use strong metaphors to depict a current situation as unacceptable and to present an inspiring alternative that acts as a magnet, attracting employees to move in that direction.

> **EXAMPLE:**
>
> Lee Iacocca did *not* tell his employees at Chrysler, "You're basically doing a good job." He used military metaphors, portraying Chrysler's situation as a battle in which the company would lose some people but would nevertheless prevail in the long run. This is the imagery behind Chrysler's turnaround.

• *They inspire trust.* Charismatic leaders inspire such confidence that subordinates are willing to put their own careers on the line in order to pursue their chief's vision of the future.

Charismatic leaders don't wait quietly for recognition to come their way. They make sure that their accomplishments are noticed by colleagues, subordinates, even the press. In this way, they use their activities effectively to strengthen the perception that they are leaders.

• *They motivate people.* Charismatic leaders build feelings of potency in their subordinates.

> **EXAMPLE:**
>
> In one common technique, the leader first lets people achieve success on relatively straightforward projects, then praises them and raises the stakes.

PUT THE FOUR TRAITS TO WORK FOR YOU

• **Recognize that emotional persuasion is more effective than rational persuasion.** The best bosses lead by stirring their employees' emotions, not by appealing to logic alone. Don't stand up and talk about statistics or about increasing profits by so many percentage points. Describe your goals in visionary terms, and speak with passion.

• **Strengthen your communication skills.** Businesspeople today are generally poor speakers. But charismatic leaders recognize the critical importance of words and language. Review the guidelines on page 219, and try putting them into practice. Tape yourself to see how you're doing. If your skills still need improvement, consider hiring a communications coach.

• **Empower your employees.** This is the most important part of charisma. To become charismatic, it's vital to give people the feeling that they are actively involved in attaining a shared set of goals. Try putting these effective empowerment techniques into action.

• **Build one-on-one contacts.** Directly expressing your confidence in subordinates can have dramatic results.

E X A M P L E :

When a man became president of an unprofitable, large corporation, he visited all 250 regional offices to meet individually with each manager. He told them he believed they could turn the firm around. That simple act roused people to action, and profits rose.

• **Hold events.** Be they playful or dramatic, motivational sessions—such as company dinners, retreats or special awards ceremonies—can work. Use them as opportunities to publicly thank your people and praise their achievements. This will counter individuals' feelings of being lost in a large company or department. Suddenly, they become important.

DIRECTIVE LEADERSHIP: IS IT RIGHT FOR YOU?
· · · · ·

Directive leaders tell subordinates exactly what to do, and let them know who's boss. Group members have the secure feeling of knowing exactly what is expected of them. Nondirective leaders seek the opinions of group members, consult with them in planning and decision making, and sometimes even put issues to a democratic vote.

MIX AND MATCH

• Neither approach is appropriate at all times. In general, directive leadership will be more appropriate with low-level employees, and a more participative style with upper-level ones.

• The directive leadership approach assumes that the leader knows exactly what needs to be done.

A problem can occur when the leader doesn't have a clear picture in his or her mind of what the desirable course of action is. In such cases, participation is called for. Also, when a leader is nondirective, it's more likely that group members' intellectual abilities and technical knowledge will contribute to the task.

• The participative style has important

bonuses. It makes subordinates feel autonomous, a proven motivator for many personality types, and it gives them the opportunity to develop their skills.

In deciding between the two methods, also consider: Can I expect subordinates to implement a decision if they don't participate in making it?

A COMPATIBLE STYLE

If one style or the other feels uncomfortable to you, don't be surprised. While many theories assume that all managers will be equally adept at any behavior presented, a considerable body of research shows that leaders have personal styles that they habitually prefer to use.

• Managers who are very concerned about relationships, and about acceptance by subordinates, lean toward the participative style. They place a greater emphasis on morale. Thus, if it's very important to you that people like you, you can expect some difficulty with the directive style.

• Managers with a high need for order and a very strong desire to accomplish a task as efficiently as possible frequently favor a directive approach.

Knowing which style your own boss or your colleagues favor can help you work with them more successfully. Suppose your boss is highly directive. You may be bitterly resentful, and say to yourself: "He thinks I'm a dummy. That's why he's always telling me what to do." In contrast, if you understand that he has a highly directive personality, you can say, "Well, this is just his style." That will depersonalize and defuse the situation.

• Colleagues will interact differently, depending on their styles. Two directive leaders will often find themselves in con-

flict about whose directions should be used. Two relationship people, on the other hand, may want to avoid conflict so much that they don't have clear communication and, therefore, waste a lot of time. People need to understand their own inclinations, in order to recognize situations that might lead to an impasse.

OBSERVATION:
Managers should be on their guard against falling back on their favored style when it's highly inappropriate. If you've just been hired as an expert in a particular area, you must be directive to put that knowledge to work—no matter how much you may favor the participative approach.

HOW LEADERS ARE MADE
· · · · ·

Leadership skills are not as rare or as elusive as many managers think. "Everyone is capable of demonstrating leadership to some degree," says Barry Posner, director of graduate education at the Leavey School of Business and Administration at Santa Clara University and author of *The Leadership Challenge—How to Get Extraordinary Things Done in Organizations* (Jossey-Bass, 350 Sansome St., San Francisco, CA 94104; $22.95). "It's like basketball—not everyone will be an NBA player, but everyone can be better."

While there is no magic prescription, good leaders share the following six behavior patterns:

• *They challenge the process,* search for opportunities to institute change, and are restless to make things better.

▲ ASK:

How curious am I? How up-to-date do I want to be? Do I challenge the business-as-usual environment? Many prospective leaders are less-than-ideal team players, since they are not always content in a follower's role.

• *They are good learners* who aren't afraid to err, and then adapt accordingly.

▲ ASK:

Am I willing to make mistakes? If not, you won't take the risks that leadership demands.

• *They inspire a shared vision* and get other people excited about their ideas.

▲ ASK:

Can I communicate new ideas in a stimulating way? Can I tell inspirational stories—and are the stories about heroes and achievements?

• *They enable others to act* by making other people on the team feel powerful, and win *followers* rather than mere subordinates. They don't always insist on having their way, even when they are right.

▲ ASK:

Do I openly acknowledge other people's good ideas? In discussing a project, do I use the plural "we" rather than the singular "I"?

• *They serve as models,* realizing that they are always on stage—that leadership is a dramatic art.

▲ ASK:

Do I have credibility? Do I carry through on projects? Am I generally trusted? Do I do homework and keep company interests at heart?

• *They encourage the heart* and display the courage to persist and continue. They are unabashed to be cheerleaders for their projects, to thank people for their contributions, or to build camaraderie. And they show the ability to balance the demands of work with their social and personal lives.

▲ ASK:

Do I have a sense of humor? Can I smile to break the tension? Do I help initiate office lunches—or a round of drinks—to celebrate team accomplishments?

Chapter 6

OFFICE POLITICS

THE SMART SHOOT-OUT

Office politics can resemble a shoot-out at the O.K. Corral. But the rules are different and the fastest man on the draw often loses.

Clinical psychologist William J. Knaus offers some advice on the intricacies involved in such managerial competition.

■ **On competing one-on-one:**

Even when a fight seems imminent, resist the idea that you're competing *against* someone. You're more likely to win if you sight *beyond* your opponent and work toward a goal.

Competing one-on-one places an upper limit on your development. You end up obsessing over your adversaries rather than improving your performance.

■ **On comparisons:**

The secret is to make *wise* comparisons. For example, you can't let yourself be thrown off balance if a newcomer seems to be on the inside track with upper management. Take the long view, continue to build on your strengths, and you'll be unstoppable in time.

Competition for its own sake is limiting. You had best have a personal mission, such as achieving power, influence, security, knowledge or the ability to help people. With a clear mission, action becomes more powerful because you do something (specific actions) for something (your long-range mission).

■ **On achieving goals:**

Let's say you've decided to be a sales manager. Have you considered the day-in, day-out duties the job entails? Be sure you track toward activities that are right for you—not titles that sound glamorous. Try to do what comes naturally to you.

Where do your talents lie? If you build on your strengths, you'll have interest, ability, incentive and drive on your side—a very tough combination to beat.

OTHER WAYS TO COMPETE

• **Stay organized.** On top, things get simple. On the way up, complexity increases. Organizations have systems for controlling complexity. Analyze what they are in your company and adhere to them.

• **Don't concentrate only on becoming more capable in your current job.** Also prepare yourself objectively for the next level up.

• **Confirm your beliefs.** Solid advancement comes from your ability to question your own assumptions—to consider the opposing view and try to disprove your own ideas. In this way, you gain distance, get less ego-involved and become much harder for rivals to beat.

• **Keep positive.** Upper management wants people who can contribute to the benefit of everyone—not finger-pointers, excuse makers or cranks.

• **Accept stress—but the right kind.** Tension that arises from overcoming obstacles as you advance in a valid direction—effort stress—is healthy.

• **Concentrate on people skills.** Upper management values them highly. You'll get further by working with people than by butting heads with them.

• **Present your plans and proposals in supportable terms.** Consider the things that other people are trying to accomplish, and make them part of your plans and projects. Go for mutual advantage wherever possible. Thereby, everyone is supportive and everyone wins the competition.

COMPANY PARTIES

Some management experts claim that company holiday parties are opportunities to advance your interests and increase your visibility within the organization; others argue that politics and office business are best left at your desk.

THE 'PROMOTE YOURSELF' POINT OF VIEW

People who are always interested in getting ahead in their careers always look for chances to introduce themselves and talk to those who are in a position to help them. Nothing you do or say is going to make wonderful things happen overnight, but meeting the right people and acting friendly toward them will certainly help you in the long run.

■ These experts advocate making a list of six to eight people you'd like to speak with and rating them in terms of priority, since you may not be able to cover your entire list in the course of several hours. If you have had contact with those on your list on the telephone or through company correspondence, it's relatively easy to approach them and identify yourself.

■ If you've had no previous contact with members of senior management or your CEO, make a "thank you" part of your approach. You might say, for example, "Hello, I'm Mark Smith from the research division, and I just want to let you know that I and the people in my department are enjoying the party."

■ Another possibility is to get involved in the planning of the event so that you have a legitimate reason for easy access to top management. You may need to consult senior executives about the event or their appearance during it.

CAUTION

While making yourself known is advisable, being overly enthusiastic can be a problem.

You should not, for example:
• Make a specific request regarding business matters or your career. Much better is suggesting the two of you get together at some future date.
• Pursue a business topic that is likely to make the other person feel uncomfortable or put him or her on the spot.
• Corner someone for more than a few minutes, unless it's obvious that he or she wants the conversation to continue.
• Discuss any other person in a negative way; your comments could be overheard or backfire if the person you're speaking with is an unknown ally.

'JUST ENJOY YOURSELF' SCHOOL OF THOUGHT

"The point of top managers having a party is to show employees they appreciate their efforts during the last year, so it's inappropriate to use it to further your own career," says George Rossi, partner and director at Heidrick & Struggles, a Boston-based international executive search firm. "People who go with the intention of participating in the festivities are much more likely to be thought of as team players."

■ While Rossi sees nothing wrong with introducing yourself to people you haven't met or with whom you've had dealings, he advises against discussing business at a company social gathering.

■ **REASON:**

The executive may be unable to focus on what you're saying because of the typical interruptions to party conversations. Or he or she may hold back expressing an opinion because it may be overheard by the wrong person.

■ Just being friendly—and being yourself—is more than enough, Rossi advises. Talk about current events, athletics or any other topics that you would ordinarily discuss in a social setting. If you've noticed the type of car that someone drives to work every day, you might ask how he or she likes its performance. (For tips on making small talk, see page 204.)

■ Finally, he advises volunteering to work on a party committee because you feel you can make it a better party and because you enjoy that kind of activity, not because it's an "in."

RECOMMENDATION:
Regardless of whether or not you enjoy company social gatherings, keep in mind that it's important to attend them to show your support for top management and to set an example for your staff.

DEALING WITH BACKSTABBING
■ · · · · ■

Backstabbing often increases during a stormy period, but it can occur even in a normal business climate. Therefore, it pays to be on the lookout for colleagues or superiors who may be out to undermine you so that you can decide when and how to respond.

MOTIVES

Backstabbers' actions are usually triggered by several different things, says Bill Werther, Jr., professor of executive management at the University of Miami.

• *A sense of insecurity,* which may be heightened during a period of transition, is most often the reason why someone tries to discredit you. You may exude an air of competence that the underminer perceives as threatening.

• *Your responsibilities may overlap territory the backstabber regards as his—or hers—alone.* During a restructuring, you may in fact be seen as a real threat to someone who is willing to resort to devious means to get rid of you. Even in stable companies, healthy competition among peers for the few top management spots can turn sour.

• *You inadvertently said or did something that was misinterpreted.* The result: Someone is now out to get you.

TACTICS

Backstabbing is like guerrilla warfare—the enemy's actions are often invisible, but the results aren't.

• *One of the most common tactics is bad-mouthing.* It can happen in meetings when an enemy says something disparaging about you—but neither you nor an ally are there to dispute it. Clever backstabbers often badmouth their victims to superiors who are their allies. The information is then often passed along from a "neutral" source to your mutual boss.

• *Spreading rumors about your personal life* is another favorite strategy of backstabbers. But they run the risk of digging their own corporate grave if they're found out to be the source. So a smart back-stabber is likely to avoid this tactic.

• *Sabotage is another tactic.* Backstabbers have been known to steal mail and memos, scramble computer disks, change important times on computerized calendars, and fail to pass along important messages they promised to give you.

• *Backstabbers can also create roadblocks to your doing a good job.* They may withhold critical information, sit on reports you submit, or even try to set you back by pointing out flaws in your work to important people.

REMEDIES

Once you realize that someone is trying to undermine you, analyze the situation before reacting.

• *The first time a backstabber attacks,* you may be better off ignoring it, especially if the stakes aren't that great. The advantage of letting your work speak for itself and appearing unflustered is that the back-stabber may retreat because you haven't provided any fuel for the conflict. On the other hand, he or she may perceive you as being cowardly and escalate the mischief.

• *When the stakes are great,* or the backstabber's actions are damaging, it's best to confront him or her, preferably in private. You don't have to make accusations. It's often sufficient to let the person know that you're aware of what's going on. You might say, "Someone has been saying untrue things about my work. I don't know who it is, but if you hear anything, I'd appreciate your letting me know." If you deliver the same message to others, it's likely that you'll neutralize the backstabber's actions because they're likely to catch on to his or her tactics.

• *Confronting someone directly* can be

effective if this individual has made no attempt to hide his or her campaign. But threatening to go to your mutual boss is likely to backfire. A backstabber can defuse this by telling your boss that you are out to get him or her. Then when you do come in with a complaint, your boss may question whether it's legitimate.

Defending yourself to management, in any event, should be done carefully. It's in your best interest to be cool and to have objective proof of the backstabber's ploys in hand. If you don't, you're better off alerting management that someone is undermining you and that it's not doing you or your staff any good. Then ask them to let you know if they hear where it's coming from.

OBSERVATION:

The best preventive measure is to make allies who are likely to alert you to potential underminers or defend you against your detractors.

WHEN TO PUT IT IN WRITING
. . . . .

The written word is a two-edged sword—it can build you up or undermine your position.

WHEN YOU SHOULD PUT IT IN WRITING

• **To establish ownership of your ideas.** Put your suggestions and proposals in dated memos, so you can demonstrate where ideas originated.

• **To praise people.** Praising subordinates in a memo to your boss is a powerful motivator that helps you advance capable people you want to groom for promotion.

• **To keep your boss informed.** In addition to copies of external memos you originate, consider sending your boss copies of important internal memos—particularly those that make you or the department look good or that discuss unusual projects.

WHEN NOT TO WRITE IT DOWN

• **When you're being set up.** One manager's colleague sent him a memo, asking for his thinking on a new sales plan. The colleague knew the manager had negative views and wanted him to put them on paper.

Knowing such a commitment wouldn't help his career, the manager conveniently "lost" his conniving colleague's missive.

• **Any time you're angry.** When you're fuming or otherwise upset over some slight, don't put your feelings in writing under any conditions. Postpone any communications on the subject until you've cooled down and can think without emotional distortion. Then, if you still decide to write a memo, you'll make it more effective.

• **When face to face is better.** One executive was asked by his company's CEO for his written reaction to a lengthy report that the CEO had drafted. "I hesitated," this executive says, "because I wasn't clear on a number of points in the report, nor was I sure of his conclusions." Instead of writing his response, the executive arranged lunch with the CEO. "It made all the difference. If I had gone off half-cocked, I would have made some stupid suggestion. As it was, I offered some useful ideas."

• **When there's a memo war going on.** Such a duel occurs when two or more executives take sides on an important issue and start issuing written broadsides against each other to back up their position. The best advice is to stay out of it.

SORTING MYTH FROM REALITY IN COMPANY GOSSIP

■ ■ ■ ■ ■

Savvy managers cultivate the grapevine by getting to know key people on it and exchanging confidential information with them. Studies show that these nets are fast and surprisingly reliable sources of company news. But they can also be sources of half-truths and outright fabrications. Learning to tell the difference between myth and reality can be vital.

HOW TO USE THE GRAPEVINE

• **Know whom you can trust.** Use many sources, so you can verify information. And learn to sort out what's true and useful from mere gossip.

• **Act as if you already know the facts.** Try to get a higher executive to spill what he or she already knows by stating what little information you've gathered about a situation and pretending to know more. For example, "Too bad about the layoff, isn't it?"

• **Guess out loud.** If you want to check out a suspicion, bluff your way and hope the other executive will pick it up and corroborate. For example, "Looks like there'll be a reorganization."

• **Name-drop.** If you've overheard a passing comment by a higher executive, mention it during a conversation with a

knowledgeable colleague and act as though the overheard comment was spoken directly to you.

• **Take a direct approach.** If you think you have a trusting relationship with a key person, test it by directly asking for information. If you've gone out on a limb for others, they're likely to do the same for you and share information.

DON'T PUT UP WITH PUT-DOWNS

■ ■ ■ ■ ■

It's natural to feel angry and respond instinctively when you're attacked. But it is possible to exert control over the situation.

WHERE TO BEGIN

The first step is a review of the event to determine:

• *The context.* Whether the insult occurs in private or in front of others could make a big difference in how you respond. If no one else heard it, you can often be confrontational and direct. If, on the other hand, it was said at a meeting or in any type of group, you'll want to weigh the potential consequences of how you react more carefully. Do you want to address the person who insulted you, or those who overheard the offensive remark as well? Ask yourself if saving face outweighs saving the relationship.

• *The importance of the relationship.* How well do you know the person, how often do you have contact and what is your position relative to hers or his? All of these considerations could affect how you respond when attacked. Obviously, the more important your business relationship, the more vital it is to handle the situation properly.

• *Your state of mind.* Just as you're more susceptible to colds when you're run-down, you're more vulnerable emotionally if you're under pressure or off keel. So, it's usually better to think about it than to react impetuously.

AVOID PASSING JUDGMENT

This works well in one-on-one situations, particularly when you want to preserve a working relationship with the person who's insulted you. One technique is to repeat what you heard without passing judgment on the content.

An example might be: "You said, 'No professional would ever do what you did.' " Explain, for example, that the comment was incorrect, uncalled for or that it made you feel embarrassed and angry. At this point, it's possible that the offender will back off and say one of several things: that you misconstrued the remark; that it "slipped out" and he or she is sorry; or that the wrong words or situation were chosen to express dissatisfaction.

CONFRONTATION

If the employee doesn't acknowledge the insult or offer an apology, tell him or her exactly what you want. For example, "I don't want you to speak to me like that again in front of clients."

Finally, tell the person what you intend to do if it does happen again.

EXAMPLE:

"I'm not going to bother asking for your input again." The offender may not change his attitude, but he may change his behavior.

If there's no question that the comment was intended to be a put-down and you care more about what others think than you do about your relationship with the insulter, try coming back with a witty rejoinder. Your object, however, should not be so much to "strike back" at the offender as to keep the audience on your side. If, for example, a colleague accuses you of being a sloppy memo writer, you might say, "I bet he circles every misspelled word we write."

CAUTION

You've got to be quick on your feet to attempt this kind of response. You don't want to begin a shooting match that you can't win.

If there's an "audience" to the insult, you can even set the insulter up as the "bad guy". Try thanking him for his criticism and telling him that you appreciate his comments and corrections. The more outrageous his remark, the more ridiculous he'll appear.

THE NONVERBAL RESPONSE

Whether you're with others or alone, your best option may be to say nothing and let your body language speak for you. A cold stare or frown—or walking away—can indicate your displeasure (and can also be handy if you're too overwhelmed to think of a good verbal response). If others are present, smiling or shaking your head and shrugging your shoulders communicates that you don't take the insulter seriously, and neither should they.

OBSERVATION:

If you're successful in parrying an insult

or offensive remark, you will often end up handling an apology. Remember that your graciousness, or lack of it, in accepting the apology could be just as critical to how you are perceived as the way you handled the insult in the first place.

COLLEAGUE SEEKS ADVANCEMENT AT YOUR EXPENSE
■ ■ ■ ■ ■

John Ahearn has been burned twice now by someone he had long considered—well, not a close friend, perhaps, but a close colleague who, in the past, could usually be counted on for counsel and support when Ahearn needed them.

If you find yourself in just such a situation, how can you best deal with it?

• *Assess your position.* There is always the possibility that, somehow, you may be viewing the situation from the wrong perspective or be out of step with current conditions in the organization. In John Ahearn's case, for example, his proposal may have had some major flaws—after all, top management did buy his colleague's unflattering dissection of it.

• *Maintain at least a surface cordiality.* There is really very little to be gained in cutting off every semblance of what was previously a friendly relationship. For one thing, it might be viewed as a lack of confidence in your own ability. For another, it would close off an important line of communication. It's difficult to know what someone else is doing and thinking if the two of you are not speaking. So, at least outwardly, preserve the amenities—the "good morning," the pat on the back, the

casual comments. However...

• *Keep your own counsel.* At this juncture, it's probably wiser not to discuss your thinking, your plans, or your work in any in-depth way with your colleague. You aren't sure what this person's motives are and you don't know the reasons for the change, so a certain amount of caution is definitely in order.

OBSERVATION:
What you really need is some idea of what's going on. You may be able to get this by asking discreet questions, doing more listening than talking and putting bits and pieces of conversations together. Just be wary of giving your own hand away.

• *Buttress your defenses.* Like John Ahearn, you may have been able to count on a close colleague for counsel and support in the past. But, at present, you cannot. That means that you are going to have to look elsewhere when you need assistance of one kind or another. This is the time, then, to look for new and stronger lines of support.

It is also the time to put your best foot forward—in the work that you do, in the ideas that you contribute, in the plans that you propose, in the dealings that you have with people up the line. The better you look, the less you have to be concerned about the possible harm in a change in relationships.

• *Stay attuned to change.* Personal relationships—good or bad—are an intrinsic part of any organization. But they can seldom be taken for granted. That is why, when a long-time relationship begins to change, you have to be alert to prevent yourself from viewing the change as necessarily working to your disadvantage. You'll find the change might be for the better.

Chapter 7

PRESENTATIONS

OVERCOMING PODIUM PANIC

• • • • •

Surveys have found that Americans fear public speaking even more than they fear death or taxes. Here are some pointers that may make the task less fearsome and more successful:

PREPARING FOR A SPEECH

• **Focus your ideas.** "People can only assimilate two or three major points in a spoken presentation," says Jay Ludwig, dean of the School of Arts and Communication at William Paterson College, Wayne, NJ. "A speech should be organized around those major points, with the rest of the material supporting them."

• **Choose a striking beginning.** Open with a vivid observation or—if you are good at storytelling—an anecdote that makes a point. A speech should grab the audience's attention right away.

• **Rehearse.** Practice your speech several times out loud. Running over it in your mind is a supplement, not a substitute. Dean Ludwig advises against rehearsing in front of a mirror, because it will make you too aware of yourself. "You need to be able to forget yourself," he says. "A speech is a conversation with the audience."

• **Listen to your rehearsals.** Tape-record and critique your speech. Listen especially for dropped syllables that sometimes appear under stress. Keep practicing until you've picked them up and dropped any "ums," "ahs," and other distractors. Ask others to critique your diction.

While some experts recommend videotaping your rehearsals, Michael Good-

231

man, director of the Master of Arts program for Corporate and Organizational Communication at Fairleigh Dickinson University, Madison, NJ, feels that rehearsing with a video camera is usually less effective than rehearsing with a small group in your office. "You are giving a speech to people, not to a camera," he says. "Ask colleagues to watch for distracting mannerisms, such as hands in your pockets, gripping the podium, or speaking away from them when you turn to charts." Choose colleagues who will feel comfortable evaluating your performance.

ONCE YOU ARE UP THERE

• **Keep visual aids and handouts in their place.** Use slides or charts to highlight your points, not to compete with them by supplying overdetailed information. If possible, avoid turning out the lights—it breaks the rhythm of the talk and encourages drowsiness, especially in the afternoon. Wait until after your speech to distribute handouts.

• **Once in front of your audience, establish eye contact.** This is the most important step in building rapport. If looking directly at someone makes you uncomfortable, Goodman suggests that you focus on a spot one inch above the bridge of the nose. Be sure to move your glance around the room to make contact with as many people as possible.

If public speaking is likely to become a regular activity for you, or if your speaking engagement is particularly important to you or to your company, consider coaching with a pro, joining a Toastmasters International chapter, or taking a Dale Carnegie course. Call the drama or communications department of a local college if you want a public speaking coach and none is listed in your phone book.

LIVEN YOUR TALKS WITH FLIP CHARTS
· · · · ·

Flip charts can make your talks go a lot more smoothly and effortlessly, with only a modicum of preparation.

TIPS ON USING THEM

• **Prepare your talk first.** Because a flip chart should only emphasize or illustrate the most important points of a talk, you can't plan the chart well until you've got that presentation down.

• **Make sure everyone can read it.** Select a writing pad that's at least 22″ × 32″, but not cumbersome to carry or handle. To determine the most visible lettering size, follow this rule: two-inch lettering for rooms up to 30 feet deep, four inches for rooms up to 60 feet. Beyond that size, flip charts aren't appropriate; use slides instead.

• **Keep it simple.** Use bar graphs and other visual aids as much as possible to illustrate your data. Write only a few key words on each page rather than writing complete sentences.

• **Use the chart early and often.** Your audience will be expecting you to use your chart, so don't keep them waiting. Plan each page so you won't linger over it more than a couple of minutes. If you want to spend some time on one point, devote a whole page to it.

• **Let the chart do some of the talking.** If you fit the talk and chart together well, the chart will become part of the flow of your speech. That way, you won't have to keep drawing your audience's attention to the chart and repeating what's there.

• **Practice.** Experienced speakers keep looking at the audience, not at the chart.

With practice, you can flip the chart without breaking eye contact. Learn to use a pointer. It keeps you facing the audience and off to the side, where you won't obstruct the audience's view of your chart.

HOW TO SURVIVE POST-SPEECH 'Q&A'
■ ■ ■ ■ ■

Danger often lurks in the question periods following an oral presentation. During those moments, speakers relinquish some degree of situational control to their audience. As they do, their vulnerability to embarrassment rises. Muff replies to questions, and you can undo any favorable impression created by your formal remarks.

"Most audiences are friendly," says Dr. Edgar T. Thornton, a Chicago educator and human relations trainer, "but tough, hostile questions do get tossed and it pays to be ready for them."

HOW TO MINIMIZE 'Q&A' RISKS

■ **Make an ally of the program chairman.** Let him or her know how you prefer to handle audience follow-up. If you feel more comfortable taking questions in written form, ask the chairman to collect and screen them for you while you talk.

■ **Plant questions.** An old stratagem, but even U.S. Presidents use it. It's a way to ensure that the questioning will at least begin with something you're well equipped to handle.

■ **Pass it along.** If you find yourself on a panel of speakers, and someone in the audience hurls a tough query at you—one you don't feel competent to answer—ask a fellow panelist to field it.

■ **Be prepared.** In his book, *Talk Your Way to the Top* (McGraw-Hill, 1221 Ave. of the Americas, New York, NY 10020; $4.95 paperback), longtime White House speech writer James C. Humes cites a number of ways to deal with post-speech toughies from the floor.

The most foolproof defense, he says, is to sit down the night before your talk and think of hostile or tricky questions that might be asked. Then, frame a brief answer to each on paper.

Just the process of writing them out will commit the gist of an effective response to memory, Humes explains.

RECOMMENDATION:

If someone zaps you with a controversial question, or something for which you don't have a ready reply despite your preparation, smile and ask for time to look into it. Promise to get back to the person later on, and be sure to do that. With most questioners, and most audiences, this will be perceived as a graceful gesture.

It doesn't hurt to admit that you don't *know* an answer, as long as you don't do it too often!

'YAK' YOUR WAY TO SUCCESS
■ ■ ■ ■ ■

The best way to improve your public speaking style is to hire a professional who can train, videotape and critique you. Failing that, here are some tips from an expert in verbal communication to help enhance your presentation skills:

• *Analyze your audience.* What are they there for: to be informed, trained, persuaded or entertained? Whenever you can, it's smart to talk beforehand to some people who'll attend the meeting to find out what they need and want to know.

• *If you're on a program, know when you'll speak.* Make your speech short if you're on late and your audience will be "listened out." Also, find out what the speaker ahead of you is going to say, so you can tie your opening remarks into the prior comment.

• *Rehearse.* Thanks to videotape, you can record and critique yourself. But it helps to try out your remarks before a friend or colleague who can give you a candid review.

• *Be ready for the unexpected.* As contradictory as that sounds, there are surprises you can prepare for. Develop an alternative presentation in case your projector breaks down or your visual aids are lost in transit.

And don't get flustered if you're informed at the last minute that you must cut 10 or 15 minutes. Be ready with a shorter version, and have your close down pat so you can make a smooth switch.

• *Should you read it verbatim?* That depends a good deal on your confidence. Generally, though, you should speak from notes when talking to a small, informal group. Use a text if you're working a large audience or must talk within a tight time frame. Try to capture a conversational tone as you rehearse to avoid vocal monotony.

Make sure that your speech is easy to read. That helps you maximize eye contact with the audience. Have it typed either in all-capital letters or, if available, the "speech" ball of an IBM Selectric.

Number each page in the upper right-hand corner, indent each paragraph, and triple space between lines (six spaces between paragraphs). Pencil in "bullets" or arrows to highlight points you want to stress.

• *Some nervousness is natural, even beneficial,* because it helps prompt a better performance. If you're extremely uptight, stop concentrating on yourself; focus on what you want to say and how to say it best.

Chapter 8

SELF-DEVELOPMENT

INTUITIVE PROBLEM-SOLVING

• • • • •

Problem solving is generally perceived as a product of conscious thought. In fact, the subconscious can often be more efficient at the task.

HOW TO TAP INTO YOUR SUBCONSCIOUS

• **Don't think in compartments.** While the conscious mind is processing an idea, other concepts and ideas are blocked out. This inhibits solutions. For example, you may believe that the only way to approach your service problem is to do something about your staff—you're not tapping into other solutions or approaches.

To break through, do some free associat-ing. List all the components of the problem. Next, reel off a list of words as they come to mind. Jot down the words as they flow, and review them later to see if any of them point you in new directions.

• **Replace negative beliefs.** The conscious mind's preconceptions inhibit creative problem solving, so try to feed your subconscious positive messages that contradict negative stumbling blocks.

If you feel that you lack technical expertise, make a list of the resources you have that can solve the problem—imagination, contacts, publications, etc.

• **Incubate.** The late English economist Graham Wallas, who researched thought processes, found that answers appear suddenly, when least expected. Often, a period of incubation precedes such a breakthrough.

To let problems incubate, put them completely out of your mind for a preset time period—hours or days, depending on your deadline. Avoid the temptation to think about them and the answers may occur— seemingly from out of the blue.

'MULTI-MEDIA' VISUALIZATIONS
· · · · ·

Before making an important phone call or presentation, do you ever psych yourself up by visualizing success—only to sabotage your efforts with a critical inner voice?

If so, you may doubt the value of visualizing. The problem lies not with the technique itself, however, but with your application of it.

"For self-validation to work, you need to do it in all the senses," says psychologist and sales consultant Donald Moine of the Association of Human Achievement Inc., Rolling Hills Estates, CA.

CREATE POSITIVE 'MULTI-MEDIA' IMAGERY

"Often, people visualize a positive performance but say negative things to themselves," says Dr. Moine. Such mixed signals confuse your subconscious and undermine your power.

We give ourselves mixed messages in many ways. Some examples include:

• You say to yourself, "I'm going to make ten cold calls today" (Positive). But you dwell self-critically on the fact that yesterday you didn't make any (Negative).

• You mentally rehearse handling a certain objection (Positive). But you fear it and hope no one brings it up (Negative).

• You tell yourself you're going to come across wonderfully in a meeting (Positive). But you walk in with a slightly stooped posture, displaying your lack of confidence (Negative).

When you mix your negative thoughts, feelings and images together with your positives, you will end up feeling like a cart being pulled in different directions by an uncoordinated team of horses. For effective visualizing, "all of your sensory programming needs to be on the same track," says Dr. Moine.

HOW TO MAKE IMAGERY TOTALLY POSITIVE

"We are programming ourselves every day," observes Dr. Moine, "and each part of the programming is either positive or negative. Realize that you can change the inner pictures, the self-talk and the feelings to be the way you want them to be."

How? Consciously create the desired impression in each dimension of your mind. The following are several examples:

• *Self-talk:* Say to yourself over and over, "I'm going to make a great presentation."

• *Visualization:* Imagine yourself erect, smiling, relaxed, confident, and saying the right things.

• *Sound imagery:* Imagine the sound of your voice and the voices of your audience as vividly as possible. Hear your success as well as see it.

• *Emotions:* Create, in your imagination, a warm glow of confidence, well-being, friendliness and optimism.

Once you get all your mental "horses" pulling in the same direction, you will be primed to act the way you want to. Thus, your chances of giving an excellent performance will be greatly enhanced.

Totally positive multi-media "visualizing" is hardest after a setback. That's when negative self-talk and imagery bubble up "on their own" to sabotage your best efforts to psych yourself up.

● THE FIX:

Doggedly redirect every element of your wayward, multi-dimensional mind to focus on your next success.

SLASH YOUR READING TIME
■　■　■　■

Here are some effective techniques to keep on top of your reading and remember more of it:

● *Preview each item to be read.* Check the table of contents in the front of books and magazines to get a quick preview of what they all have to offer. Then, before reading each article or chapter, read the first few paragraphs and skim the rest of the article, reading subheads and highlighted quotes. Finally, read the last few paragraphs in depth.

● *Control your eye movements as you read.* If you feel somewhat exhausted after a few hours of reading, it's probably because your eyes jump from word to word instead of moving smoothly along each line. Practice moving your finger along the lines at a constant, rapid pace and making your eyes follow your finger steadily. You may miss a few words at first, but you will find you still easily understand the full meaning of the paragraphs.

● *Develop the habit of reading at a rapid pace.* Many people argue that speed reading is not for them, because they claim they must read slowly to understand what they're studying. But it is actually more difficult to understand and remember if you read a passage slowly.

Try to read as quickly as you can comprehend, then double-check your comprehension at the end of each paragraph by summarizing its main point aloud. This exercise will quickly speed up your ability to absorb information.

● *Jot down important concepts.* Even if you never reread your notes, the act of writing them down will help you remember the key points.

● *Never underline as you read.* Most people underline too many words, because they don't understand what the most important points are until after they've read all the way through. Instead, go back and highlight what is really important *after* you've read an entire section or chapter.

● *Schedule reading time to your best advantage.* There are many busy executives who keep a manila folder filled with articles and information that they carry with them everywhere they go. They read these articles during downtime, such as on line at the bank, waiting for a lunch partner, sitting in a traffic jam or commuting to and from the office.

● *Be selective.* You probably don't need to read every journal and report that crosses your desk. Have an assistant read some of them for you. You'll kill two birds with one stone: You groom your assistant for a higher position that requires a solid knowledge and understanding of your field, and he or she can pass on to you only the articles you shouldn't miss.

YOUR EXECUTIVE IQ

. . . . .

Executive intelligence—the ability to apply practical rather than academic knowledge in a business setting—is a key component of career success today.

Dr. Robert J. Sternberg, IBM professor of psychology and education at Yale, explains that the bulk of such intelligence is just common sense.

> EXAMPLES:
> Knowing how much time a project is worth; when to use humor to defuse a situation; how to get along with people.

However, it's often hard to use this intelligence effectively. Roadblocks, many of them self-imposed, get in the way. Dr. Sternberg lists 20 of them in his book, *The Triarchic Mind* (Viking, $19.95).

BEWARE OF ROADBLOCKS YOU BUILD YOURSELF

• **Using the wrong abilities.** Many people don't know their strengths. Successful managers do. They capitalize on them and find ways around their weaknesses—often by delegating.

• **Not translating thought into action.** Great ideas aren't enough. You must act to get them implemented. Often, that involves knowing how things get done in your particular company.

> EXAMPLES:
> Does your superior prefer a personal visit or a memo? Does he or she want only the big picture—or a step-by-step analysis?

• **Emphasis on process, not product.** Looking busy, even being busy, all the time isn't enough because "you are judged by the products, not the processes."

> EXAMPLES:
> Don't expect to be rewarded for a report just because you spent 15 hours preparing it. Only the report's quality matters.

• **Fear of failure.** People who fear failure won't accept a challenge that could lead to advancement. Sometimes the company culture creates that fear, says Dr. Sternberg. The message—overtly or subtly—is that if you fail, you will be fired.

Fear of failure makes sense when failure could be devastating. But Dr. Sternberg adds, "In most cases we learn from our mistakes, and we will never learn much unless we allow ourselves to make them."

• **Spreading yourself too thin or too thick.** Many people habitually bite off too much, thus have trouble getting it all done—and what does get done is of poor quality. Others put so much effort into one project that they have no time for anything else. You must know how much work you can do.

BETTER MINGLING

. . . . .

Do you anticipate conferences, industry association meetings and work-related cocktail parties with resignation and dread?

Here are some suggestions on how to work a room with confidence—and even have some fun in the process.

■ **Prepare thoroughly.** Call ahead and find out who will be there or what industries will be represented.

■ **If you wear a name tag, make sure it can be easily seen.** Bring along a thick marker and write your name so that people can easily read it. Place your name tag on your right-hand side, in order to be in line with your contact's line of vision when you shake hands.

■ **Pause in the doorway and look around the room.** See where people are congregated, and find out where the bar and buffet tables are located.

Look for someone you know, so that you can join in and be introduced. Also, standing in line for a drink is a good way to start talking to people.

■ **Look for the person everyone is trying to talk to.** Chances are, that person holds some power or is worth meeting for some reason. Otherwise. . .

■ **Look for the person no one else is talking to.** He or she is probably more uncomfortable than you are and would welcome a friendly conversation.

■ **Don't strive for great opening lines.** A smile and a "hello" are the best ways to begin. People will respond in kind. Though many people don't realize it, "small talk" is the most important talk you can make—it helps establish your commonalities.

Try these simple approaches:

• *An observation.* For example, "There certainly are a lot of people here."

• *A question,* such as "Are you a member of this organization?"

• *A self-disclosure.* For example, "It took me 30 minutes to find a parking space. Did you have any trouble?"

CAUTION

Be careful that the question is not too personal or something that will make the person feel uncomfortable.

■ **Circulate.** Don't talk to only one person. You have been invited to meet a number of people. The best way to make contacts is to move around according to a schedule. After 10–15 minutes of talking to one person, excuse yourself and move on.

◆ **PROBLEM:**

Most people find it far more difficult to end a conversation than to initiate one.

▲ **SUGGESTION:**

You can say that you see someone you need to talk to.

One veteran conference attender says that he often brings the person he is talking to over to someone else he knows in the room. He then introduces them and leaves them together after a few minutes, while he moves on to another person.

■ **Be a good, interested listener.** It's vitally important to share the moment with the person you are talking to. Make eye contact, and listen attentively to what he or she is saying. Interrupting and looking elsewhere is insulting and off-putting.

OBSERVATION:

We often think of working a room as the old political back-slapping scene. But it really means meeting people and communicating with them, establishing contact and rapport. The best way to do that is to listen actively.

■ **Ask for a valuable contact's business card.** Most often, the person will ask for yours in return. Write some mnemonic device—something you discussed or something memorable about the contact—on the back to help you remember the person. *Also:* Carry the card and "live with it" for a while before you file it. This will help to imprint the contact firmly in your memory.

■ **Follow up.** No one signs a deal with sweet and sour sauce on his or her fingers. It is in the follow-up that most business is done. A lot of businesspeople miss the boat on this. If you promised to call or have lunch, do it soon.

■ **Cultivate the ability to circulate and communicate.** It's seen as a very powerful skill.

OBSERVATION:

The leaders of industry are the ones who feel comfortable mingling, who extend themselves and enter into conversations gracefully.

IF MEMORY DOESN'T SERVE
· · · · ·

The fear of fading memory is growing among America's success-oriented, fast-track executives, says Dr. Joseph Mendels, chief psychiatrist at the Philadelphia Medical Institute's Memory Center. He gets several hundred calls each month from individuals asking to have their memories checked.

However, he has found that "the problem for most people who seem to have trouble remembering things is not memory, but concentration when registering a name or a piece of information."

RECALL TECHNIQUES

• If you have trouble remembering people's names at a business conference, concentrate on each individual you meet,

and repeat the name to yourself. Pick out a prominent facial feature, such as bushy eyebrows, and make a connection between the feature and the person's name.

• Write down the information you will want to recall.

• For unrelated items, create old and familiar associations. One technique used by a famous Russian with a photographic memory: He created a picture in his mind of the main street of his home town. To remember a list of 50 unrelated items, he placed each item in appropriate and familiar locations along the mental street, such as cucumbers in the vegetable market.

There are about a half dozen memory-enhancing drugs being evaluated in Europe and the U.S. Dr. Mendels says one recent patient showed dramatic memory improvement after being administered one of the drugs, but approval for use by the population at large is still many years away.

COPING WITH A CONFIDENCE CRISIS
· · · · ·

How do you deal with a job crisis—short deadlines, sudden assignments, overdue reports. Try the following:

• *Slow down, literally.* Take a deep breath, push your chair back, and begin to look around as though you're in a slow-motion movie. Breathe slowly to prevent yourself from racing to get things done in a frenzy. Then resume working at a slower pace.

• *Paint a worst-case scenario.* Consider what would *really* happen if you sat there and didn't do a thing. Would your boss fire you, or would he or she extend the deadline to get the work done?

- *Remind yourself of what's important.* Remember that you're dealing with simple work pressures. Think of something that's really central to your life—your children safe at school or your spouse at work—to remind yourself that what's *really* important is safe and not in jeopardy.
- *Take positive action.* Remember that trouble brings opportunities. The crisis might serve as a warning to you that you're becoming a workaholic and need to hire more staff or implement more efficient delegation systems.
- *Use the crisis for leverage.* Make a list of everything you do, and decide whether you can use the fact that you're overworked to pressure your boss for positive change. If you frankly admit you're overworked and express a willingness to come up with creative solutions that will get the job done, chances are you will get support—not tantrums—from your boss.

SOUND MORE AUTHORITATIVE
■ ■ ■ ■ ■

To get your message across more forcefully, take the time to correct unconscious speech patterns that may be diminishing your impact.

SPEECH PITFALLS TO AVOID

- **Upward inflections.** Ending statements on a rising pitch conveys the impression that you're questioning yourself.

■ S O L U T I O N :

Even if you *are* looking for approval, drop your voice definitively at the end of your

declarative sentences. Don't anticipate objections. Let others take issue if they question your ideas.

- **Sing-song speech.** Regularly accented speech can make your message sound more like a jingle than a statement.

■ S O L U T I O N :

Accent only the most important words in any sentence.

- **Mumbling.** If you don't enunciate, you'll seem to lack self-confidence. Do you rush over difficult-to-pronounce words, or slur words at the end of long sentences?

■ S O L U T I O N :

Look up the pronunciation of words you're unsure of and shorten your sentences to a comfortable length.

- **Poor projection.** If you were your company's genius CEO, you might get away with speaking in a soft, low voice. When the rest of us do it, people tune us out.

■ S O L U T I O N :

Speak from your diaphragm, not your throat.

- **Speeding.** Don't talk so quickly that people can't digest your thoughts. The best indicators that you may be speeding are comments from your listeners, such as "I'm not following you," or "Could you go over that again?"

■ S O L U T I O N :

Practice speaking more slowly. You might also ask family members or trusted staff members to let you know when you need to slow down.

• **Hesitation.** Even a silver-tongued speaker occasionally has to pause to reach for the right word. But if you hesitate too frequently, you'll seem to lack confidence.

■ SOLUTION:

Pace your speech flow to avoid starting and stopping sentences as you collect your thoughts.

Don't use "ahs" and "ums" during pauses. If you're a chronic "um-er," you may find it helpful to remind yourself of your habit with a note card or sign posted near your phone.

RECOMMENDATION:

Make a tape recording of an upcoming presentation or of the ideas you'll bring up at a meeting. Then listen for these speech pitfalls and take steps to correct them.

NETWORKING TUNE-UP
▪ ▪ ▪ ▪ ▪

Networking is not a one-time task. In fact, maintaining and strengthening ties to older contacts is just as important as collecting new business cards—perhaps even more so.

BRUSH UP YOUR SKILLS

• **Be prepared.** Keep your cards and your company materials handy. Before any function, take a few minutes to think about what you want to achieve, and bring along appropriate materials.

• **Never pass up an opportunity.** You never know when the card you collect casually today may lead to something use-

ful. Make as many contacts as you can and keep track of them as valuable assets.

◆ VITAL:

Keep your records organized in a notebook or computer file so that you can easily review them.

• **Rate your contacts according to what you need**—not just their position or clout. It can be a mistake to view the highest-ranking people as the most valuable. Strive instead to bring the potential value of each contact into focus.

EXAMPLE:

A company president may be valuable if you're going to make a pitch for a new job, but a technician or salesperson can be worth just as much when you need information.

• **Don't be afraid to say what you want.** Don't call a contact and expect him or her to know your needs. Be specific. And don't be shy. Remember that networking is a team sport, and asking for assistance will free your contact to profit from your knowledge and network of contacts.

• **Follow up.** Let your contacts know the outcome of what they did for you, and remember to thank them.

• **Give without expecting an immediate favor in return.** If you give a favor in order to receive one, people will usually sense an ulterior motive.

◆ BETTER:

Instead of engaging in one-for-one trades, give and take freely.

• **Set realistic goals.** Make sure your contact is really able to make the introduction you're asking for, or that you're really qualified for the job you're asking about. And don't expect too much from a single reference or introduction. Just because a contact makes a call for you doesn't guarantee you'll get a job or even an interview.

• **Commit to doing whatever it takes.** Don't expect instant results from your networking efforts, and don't lose your sense of humor. Successful long-term networking requires patience and persistence.

As an exercise, decide whether people in your network are "maintainers," who help you get your job done effectively, or "propellers," who can promote your career advancement.

▲ A S K :

What are my goals in the next six months? The next five years? What support do I need? Can I get that support from the contacts currently in my network, or must I add new members to accomplish my aims?

BALANCING WORK AND WEEKENDS
■ ■ ■ ■ ■

Weekends are a problem for many people because they are like a mini-vacation. If work is the only thing that matters in your life, a day away simply represents wasted time.

Dr. Steven Berglas teaches clinical psychology at Harvard Medical School, runs Boston's Executive Stress Clinic and is the author of *The Success Syndrome* (Plenum Publishing, 233 Spring St., New York, NY 10013; $19.95). He thinks there is some-

thing more basic bothering executives who have trouble coping with weekends: "They are probably stressed by the obligations of interpersonal contact.

"Sunday in particular is a day when you are 'required' to interact with family members and others with whom you have a significant relationship," he explains.

WHY WEEKENDS ARE HARD

• **Your body and your mind need time to taper off.** Just as it took time to gear yourself up for a 14-hour workday, so it takes time for you to adjust to a slower pace. It's not possible, for example, to sneak in two hours of work on Sunday morning and then expect to relax with the family for the rest of the day.

Once you've activated the system, your body pumps adrenaline and you're in fighting mode. You can't turn off that arousal like a light switch in order to play with a child or enjoy a leisurely Sunday dinner. Physiologically, you need to shut down on Saturday afternoon in order to be able to relax on Sunday. Even then, you may not be *psychologically* ready. What really counts is not where you are or what day it is, but what's occupying your mind.

• **Relaxation is a process, not a product.** And it is an individual process. One person's relaxer is another one's stressor. Moreover, learning to relax requires weeks of time and effort. Too many executives demand immediate solutions, says Dr. Berglas. When they hear that learning to relax is going to take time, they say, "Oh, just give me a Valium." However, Dr. Berglas refuses for two reasons: First, it's addictive. And second, it's totally worthless for stress based on your own negative thinking.

LEARN TO RELAX

While praising techniques like meditation and yoga, Dr. Berglas cautions against a cookbook approach. Rather than buying self-help tapes or anything else that's available over the counter, he urges investing in two or three sessions with a trained specialist in behavioral psychology. To find one in your area consult the Association for the Advancement of Behavior Therapy, 15 W. 36th St., New York, NY 10018.

Expect to spend five to six weeks learning how to actively relax. While learning to relax is important, you may also need to learn to relate to family and friends. Some suggestions:

• *Seek group support.* Churches, YMCAs, YWCAs, Little Leagues and other community groups can help people relate comfortably to children, says Dr. Berglas. By volunteering to help in programs for young people, you can gain valuable experience and insight.

• *Find ways to be a team member and not the leader.* Most executives get plenty of experience being on top, explains Dr. Berglas. "What they need is to get back in touch with reality by taking part in activities that cast them in the role of participant." He tells the story of a manager whose wife threatened to divorce him unless he participated more in family activities, such as going to church. The manager responded by becoming a deacon. His wife went ahead with the divorce.

• *Question company values.* In her book, *Workaholics* (New American Library; can be obtained in libraries), author Marilyn Machlowitz says that even though employers say they want people with balanced lives and outside interests, in fact many company value systems encourage employees' workaholic tendencies.

It is expected, for example, that young Wall Street lawyers and investment bankers will spend 68–80 hours a week on the job. The pay is excellent, but what these professionals lose is a sense of balance between work and the rest of their lives.

• *Reevaluate your own priorities.* Try to find an objective friend who can give you accurate feedback about your life situation. Have the courage to take a long-term perspective on your life and recognize that it is your family and interpersonal relationships that will sustain you over the years. Investing five minutes in self-evaluation now will pay big dividends later on. Strive for real empathy with family members, not just joint TV watching.

• *Diversify your goals.* Set a variety of goals for yourself in both your personal and professional life. Remember not to sacrifice your family for finances.

CONSTRUCTIVE COMPLAINING

Carefully construct a strategy for voicing complaints, rather than letting pressures drive you to a hotheaded outburst. Presented the right way, complaints can make you look like a team player dedicated to your firm's success.

Before you register a complaint, ask yourself: Is raising this issue worth the trouble it may cause me? Will it damage my future with this company? If the problem is severe or management is traditionally unyielding, would another option—such as asking for a transfer or job hunting outside the company—be better for my career?

MAKE COMPLAINTS WORK FOR YOU

• **Formulate a plan.** While it's very tempting to get a problem off your chest immediately, you'll be more successful if you plan a logical strategy. Figure out which individuals can help you solve your problem, and how to approach them.

• **Don't go it alone.** Discreetly ask colleagues if they've also experienced this problem, and if they would be willing to sign a group memo asking department heads or company officers to look into it. It's much easier for uncooperative managers to trivialize a lone person's complaint than to disregard a responsible group of employees with a serious concern.

• **Let your boss be the first to know.** Even if the problem is your boss's fault, make sure that he or she is well aware of your concern. Going over your boss's head will doubtlessly challenge his or her authority, and it may make others question the legitimacy of your complaint by asking, "Why are you bringing this to me instead of to your boss?"

• **Check your perspective.** Your opinion of what you're doing and what someone else thinks you are doing may be very different.

• **Present a balanced view.** Giving management your overview of what's good as well as bad in your department shows that you are a thinker rather than a griper.

• **Request that a meeting be scheduled.** Just the fact that time is set aside to address your complaint gives it legitimacy and implies that the company may be in agreement with you.

• **Don't be a "genius."** Never present a problem as "here's what you did wrong and here's how *I* plan to fix it." Instead, describe the problem as a shared dilemma and ask for help in fixing it. Be specific about what you would like to see happen, but avoid making it sound like an ultimatum.

• **Focus on the company.** Stress how a solution will make the company stronger and more productive as a whole. Make management want what you want. Emphasize the positive consequences of getting the problem solved, rather than the negative results it has caused so far.

• **Nominate yourself to be the problem fixer.** By showing that you're willing to take on more responsibility, you connect yourself to your next position on the corporate ladder.

MAKE YOUR OFFICE WORK FOR YOU

Most people don't have office spaces that maximally suit their communication needs. However, office clutter and disorganization can be quickly corrected.

A CREATIVE OFFICE SYSTEM

■ **The area right in front of you**—almost to the limits of your peripheral vision—has to remain empty. It is a space reserved exclusively for your creative activity. If you procrastinate or have trouble managing your time (like almost everyone), you probably get distracted by whatever is in your field of vision. So you need to remove papers from your creative space as soon as you are done with them.

In addition to eliminating distractions, this layout also serves to generate a healthy tension that motivates you to continue working on the project in front of you, says Teri-E Belf, a personal productivity consultant with Success Unlimited Associates, Annandale, VA.

■ **An efficient office lets you review and process documents quickly.** Since mail and other materials come from many sources and must be dealt with differently, one of the most time-efficient and cost-effective things you can do is to have someone else open and sort your mail according to your predetermined priorities.

ORGANIZING YOUR PAPERS

Whether or not this is possible, the following system for organizing your paper flow will greatly enhance your productivity:

Keep a stack of three horizontal trays near your phone, which can be on either side of your desk. Organize the boxes in the following way:

• *In-box.* Make the top tray your in-box. If you have a support person who sorts your mail, he or she should be the *only* person allowed to put anything in there. Others should put communications in your support person's box.

Go through your in-box two or three times a day. The first time you touch a piece of paper, decide what to do with it, and move it to one of the following locations:

• *Action box.* Place any letter, memo or other document that requires written action in the middle tray. Put the most urgent things (due today or tomorrow) on the top. Use a highlighter pen to indicate the date by which a response is due.

• *Pending box.* In the bottom tray, keep papers on which you will defer action until you obtain additional information or receive a return phone call. When a call comes in, the papers you need are right by the phone.

MANAGING YOUR WORK

Put a standing vertical file with about six dividers on the side of your desk opposite the telephone. This is the center from which you will manage your projects and your staff. Organize your work into three main categories:

• *Active projects.* These are the projects you will actually be working on within the next three to six weeks, with each project's documentation in a separate file folder. If a project requires oversized material, include a note indicating where the rest is filed. To avoid overlooking any projects, be sure that each is represented by a folder, even if it is temporarily empty.

• *Staff.* Keep one folder for each person on your staff, and when you need to communicate, make a note and put it in his or her file folder. Keep one for your boss as well. In addition, have one folder for ideas and projects to take with you to staff meetings.

• *Resource/reference material.* This section contains reference books, phone directories, schedules and other frequently used resources.

OUT OF SIGHT

Keep three more box trays on a table or shelf near the door.

• *"To read" box.* This is the place for journals, newsletters and other documents you don't have to read immediately. If someone opens your mail for you, ask that person to place these items here rather than in your in-box.

• *Out box.* This is the point from which papers leave your office, so it should be near your door.

• *"To file" box.* This is a holding pen for all papers on their way to your file drawers.

Make your office an inspiring place by adding color, plants, art, etc., so that you look forward to coming "home" to a space that supports you in doing what you need to do in the most effective way.

OVERCOME BLOCKS TO FOLLOW-THROUGH

▪ ▪ ▪ ▪ ▪

Most managers know the frustration that can set in when a project stalls. But you *can* follow through on your plans and get things done. The first step is to recognize obstacles of our own making, says William Knaus, author of *Do It Now: How to Stop Procrastinating* (Prentice-Hall, Rte. 9W, Englewood Cliffs, NJ 07632; $11.95).

ARE YOU INVOLVED IN SELF-SABOTAGE?

• **Fantasies.** The mind can instantly envision how well a plan will work when implemented. When you prepare to install a new assembly machine in a factory, you happily picture the machine humming away while productivity soars. Because this fantasy is far happier than overseeing a lengthy implementation process, your mind tends to dwell there rather than concentrate on pressing the project to a conclusion. To get results, you have to set the fantasy aside and get your hands dirty.

EXAMPLE:
Edison had a vision of how a light bulb would work, but he had to build over 1,000 of them to make it work.

• **Fear of failure.** Often, people fear that results will fall short of expectations and that they'll be judged accordingly. Fears tell us that it is safer to let a project die quietly than to live with results that are less than we expected. Perfectionists are attracted to this trap because of their lofty standards.

• **Invisible ruts.** A common pitfall is mindlessly following old habit patterns. If the company founder (who may have retired 20 years ago) never implemented anything without first taking each of the five vice presidents to lunch, you may feel that you also have to go through these steps. But to be a decisive manager, you have to ask whether anyone cares about stale protocols and be ready to bypass them to get things done.

• **Comforting mythologies.** If you believe "everything is fine as long as everybody is busy," you may overlook the urgency of new projects.

• **Egotism.** Thinking that your own intuition and insights are infallible—the "If I feel something strongly enough, it must be true" mentality—cuts you off from your colleagues' ideas. Review all suggestions objectively, including your own, and implement the best ones regardless of their source.

• **Failure to delegate.** Your ego may tell you to shoulder the whole burden because nobody else is as effective as you are, or because you don't want your colleagues to share credit when the project is done. Either way, you put your project at risk.

Your odds of success increase greatly when you take on only the tasks that suit your abilities best. Let other people take on the rest. You may be surprised that a duty that seems onerous to you may be the very thing someone else enjoys.

• **Inflexibility.** When an approach is not working, substitute something more positive. For example, if your staff is not implementing your ideas for meeting a particular goal, let them develop their own plans and put those into action. Flexibility often requires taking a step backward, but in the end, it is far more productive.

• **Love of intrigue.** Everybody thinks certain people are "on their side" in a project, and that others are "against them," blocking progress. Put aside petty intrigues and enlist help from everyone. If you love intrigue more than progress, become a spy instead of a manager.

DOING GETS IT DONE

When a project stalls, making a new beginning can provide the spark that lets a project catch fire.

• *Use the five-minute system.* If you're stuck, agree with yourself that you will start working on a task at a particular time and will continue for five minutes. At the end of the five minutes, determine if you want to continue for another five.

Make the same determination again, and so on. This enables you to take focused action, rather than viewing the project as a behemoth. And that immediate action builds immediate follow-through.

Chapter 9

TIME MANAGEMENT

WHY ARE YOU ALWAYS TAKING WORK HOME?

• • • • •

On the whole, taking work home because it simply must be finished is a commendable act. But if it's been going on for a prolonged period, with few layoffs, perhaps you'd better take a long look at the reasons why.

QUESTIONS TO ASK YOURSELF

• **Is it an emergency?** The word is defined as "an unforeseen combination of circumstances that calls for immediate action." If you face an emergency every day— a daily management crisis, say—perhaps, consciously or otherwise, you are always on the lookout for fires to put out. If that seems to be the case, you may need to do more planning on a regular basis.

• **Is it "just something you do"?** For some people, so is smoking too much or driving too fast—habits they know they ought to break, but don't. This take-work-home habit is just as bad in its way for you and your family, and it deserves the same treatment—a complete wipeout.

• **Does it "go with the job"?** Chances are that no one—read "your boss"—ever told you that you'd be expected to work at home on a regular basis. If your workload is really so heavy that you simply cannot get it done in the course of the work day, does your boss realize it? If he or she doesn't, and your standing as a manager is high, it may be time to sit down and talk over the situation with the boss. Some people are Simon Legrees, but if your boss doesn't fit that mold, he or she might well find a way to take

249

some of the burden off your shoulders.

• **Is a compromise possible?** Perhaps your job really cannot be done in a normal work week. But maybe working *every* night isn't necessary. Lay out your tasks for the week. Put off those that can wait until next week, and then see if the remaining overload can't be done in just one or two nights at home. That's a vast improvement over five—or five-plus weekends.

O·B·S·E·R·V·A·T·I·O·N :

Bringing work home at night may be inescapable at times. Some of those times, you probably feel a sense of fulfillment as you push back your chair; the job is done—and done well. But as daily fare, it will ultimately give you occupational burnout and emotional indigestion.

HOW'S YOUR MANAGEMENT TEMPO?
■ ■ ■ ■ ■

Your ability to use time well controls how well you use all your other management skills, explains Stephanie Winston, author of *The Organized Executive* (Warner Books, New York City; $8.95). That's why you should review your time-management methods regularly, particularly your style of dealing with:

■ **Interruptions.** To find time for working on your foremost tasks:

• Find a hiding place. Use the office of someone on vacation, an unused conference room, the public library, or even a nearby coffee shop, where you can work uninterrupted when you need to.

• Angle your desk away from your door, so people walking by your office can't easily catch your eye and converse with you.

• Politely ask unexpected visitors if you can meet them later. Don't be abrupt, but try to guard the time you've set aside for lengthy tasks.

■ **Telephone time.** To keep your conversations businesslike:

• If you call, avoid starting with idle chatter. Begin by saying you have a couple of questions.

• If you're called, promptly ask what you can do for the caller after a brief greeting. This is a courteous way to get the party right to the point.

• Return calls shortly before lunch or just before the end of the day, when you'll be more likely to catch the person you want to talk to.

■ **Meetings.** Don't meet if a written memo or a quick phone call will produce the same results. In addition:

• Always have a written agenda. Even if you call a sudden meeting, jot down the two or three points you need to cover and stick to them.

• Have a note-taker on hand to keep track of who is to do what.

• Don't meet unless all concerned parties can attend. Otherwise, you'll wind up having to meet with whomever was absent at a later time and repeat what you said at the previously scheduled meeting.

■ **Waiting time.** When you find yourself with a spare five or 10 minutes between tasks, be prepared. Use the time, for example, to:

• Make an appointment.

• Prepare a tentative agenda or a list of meeting attendees.

• Make a phone call or two.

• Organize papers on your desk.

• Read business or news articles you've set aside for just such a moment.

COPING WITH CHRONIC DISORGANIZATION

■ ■ ■ ■ ■

Should you suspect yourself or one of your staff of suffering from chronic disorganization, uncover the reasons as a first step toward a lasting cure. Look for these symptoms:

■ **The dependably late.** Why are some people chronically late for meetings? Often, it's a way of getting attention or asserting their importance. But there may be other, more subtle reasons.

For example, you may feel insecure or nervous because you're ill-prepared for the upcoming meeting. Or you could be sending a "passive-aggressive" signal of job dissatisfaction or annoyance at having to attend it.

Whatever the cause, be aware that your co-workers will resent your tardiness and may even balk at working with you, especially when deadlines are tight.

RECOMMENDATION:

Recognize that being late is rude, unproductive, and dangerous to your career. Set up some practical prods to help you be more punctual:

• If you think it will take only 10 minutes to get to a meeting, allow 20.

• Set an alarm clock on your desk to remind you when it's time for your next meeting.

• Ask a punctual co-worker to "pick you up" on the way to a meeting, or have your assistant or secretary give you advance warning.

■ **Too busy to breathe.** You're involved in so many projects that you run around the office looking like you're directing the invasion of Normandy. Although some managers like to act frenetic because it makes them look and feel important, most do so because they haven't learned to say no, or fear that turning down an assignment will hurt their careers.

RECOMMENDATION:

Train yourself to say no. You may even want to plant a small "think twice" sign on your desk as a reminder.

Use a note pad to keep a careful inventory of your current projects. Set priorities, and review them with your boss occasionally to make sure you're both in sync. Try not to get distracted by other tasks in the works, however enticing and easy they might sound.

■ **The phoenix.** Like the legendary bird that rises out of its ashes, you always seem to be able to make order out of the chaos that is your office. At least, you know where everything is and how you can get it quickly.

Unfortunately, others don't have that same visual gift. And you may be harboring an unconscious wish to control others by forcing people to search you out personally for information.

RECOMMENDATION:

Get together with the people who may need to find documents in your office when you're away. Make it easier for them by keeping your budget figures in a green folder, for instance, or always stacking sales reports on the right side of your desk.

One person's mess may be another's system. But if yours is making problems for you or others, examine the reasons that you work the way you do.

PRODUCTIVE PROCRASTINATION

▪ ▪ ▪ ▪ ▪

One of the best ways to achieve our goals is to procrastinate selectively, according to Charles R. Hobbs, author of *Time Power* (Harper & Row, 10 E. 53rd Street, New York, NY; $16.95). "If you have mastered the 'fine art' of procrastination, chances are you can turn it to good advantage because, believe it or not, procrastination is essential to effective time management," says Hobbs. "All you need to learn is how to procrastinate on the Cs and Ds and how to avoid procrastination on the As and Bs."

MAKE PROCRASTINATION PAY OFF FOR YOU

• **Do tomorrow what you could not do today.** Even with the best intentions, you may have to put off something on your A list. What's important is starting each day by establishing priorities. What was on your A list yesterday may be on your C list tomorrow.

• **Prepare a "grass-catcher" list** and use it to feed your daily list. This list includes all the projects—important and not so important—that are tossed your way each day. (It's akin to the grass-catcher on a lawn mower that captures grass, flowers and weeds.) You must sort through these items and decide which deserve your attention.

• **Place your A1 item in the center of your desk for tomorrow.** Clear your desk the night before, leaving only the project that you want to get started on first thing in the morning.

• **Select the best time of day for the work required.** If you write best in the morning, don't waste the early hours making phone calls or holding meetings.

• **Use blank spaces of time constructively.** Whenever you leave your office or house, take a book, a report or some project from your A list with you. If you end up waiting in line somewhere, you'll have something to work on.

• **Commit to a deadline.** Set deadlines for high-priority items. Don't however, set deadlines for low-priority projects. "To procrastinate effectively, you must remove the urgency from all trivia," says Hobbs.

• **Start with the tough part.** Put off doing the easy part until you've made headway with the problem. That's productive procrastination.

• **When bogged down, take a break.** If you've reached the point of diminishing returns, it's time to start something new.

• **Turn difficult tasks into games.** Prepare an action list so large it will be a challenge to finish. If you do get through it, you've won. If not, you'll still have accomplished a lot and have something to aim for next time around.

WORKING EFFICIENTLY WHEN YOU'RE ON THE ROAD

▪ ▪ ▪ ▪ ▪

When traveling on business, your day is likely to be peppered with periods when you're killing time in a hotel room or waiting for appointments or travel connections. The following suggestions are designed to help you make productive use of that time:

• *Cluster appointments.* If you have a number of appointments in a city, plan to be at the most important ones first. Then schedule less important appointments around them, using a map of the city to check locations. If in doubt, ask your contacts how long it takes to get from one place to another, and have them recommend the best modes of transportation available.

• *Use "downtime."* Before a trip, organize prioritized folders containing papers, reports, memos and correspondence that need attention. You can relieve the pressure on your first day back at work by writing follow-up letters and organizing projects that have developed because of your trip. Consider hiring a temporary assistant through the hotel or a local agency to help with these projects.

• *Reflect.* Traveling alone provides a break in routine—a good opportunity to think about current issues and problems and to develop innovative ideas.

• *Treat yourself well.* You'll be in a more positive frame of mind if you don't overeat or overdrink—and get some exercise. Many hotels have pools, tracks, exercise equipment and exercise videos. Some even hold classes. Remember to pack gym clothes, running shoes, socks and a swimsuit. A brisk walk in a new city will give you the chance to go over what you plan to accomplish while you're there.

ARE YOU EFFECTIVE...OR JUST EFFICIENT?

Efficient people work hard at scratching a large quantity of items off their "to do" lists. Effective people get the *right* things done, and usually don't work as hard. In the end, effectiveness wins the race.

HOW TO WORK EFFECTIVELY

• **Align your priorities with management's.** Don't waste time doing an excellent job on projects that aren't a top management concern. Your hard work will only end up in file folders and go largely unnoticed.

● BETTER:

Throw your weight behind the projects that you know are the pet concerns of your superiors.

If you want to convince people that one of your key projects is worth supporting, don't throw work at the problem.

● BETTER:

Explain the idea's value in one or two sentences, and build in ways other people can further their own aims by supporting you. Work is not a tool of influence.

• **Install a mental "wide-angle lens."** Rather than focusing exclusively on one or two pressing problems, keep all your projects in view.

■ TECHNIQUE:

Organize your workload in a way that keeps track of your progress *visually*, such as on a large calendar, on ledger paper, or through one of the new time-management software programs that provide printouts of work in progress.

■ REASON:

Studies have shown that it's easier for people to remember and track information that they've stored visually instead of conceptually.

• **Don't confuse process and product.** The success of any project is judged by what it achieves—not by how hard you worked on it. Before starting any project, get a clear vision of what the results should be—right down to a clear image of how they should look. Then chart the simplest path to them, and avoid unnecessary work.

● B O T T O M L I N E :

Increase the amount of visible work you put in and eliminate any time-wasting dead ends.

HAPPY PHONE HANG-UPS

■ ■ ■ ■ ■

To keep your incoming calls brief, but not blunt, here's the last word on telephone etiquette:

• *Be businesslike.* Avoid time-wasting pleasantries, but try for an opening a bit warmer than a brusque "What can I do for you?" Try saying simply, "Good morning, Helen," with a friendly inflection. Then wait for your caller to get down to cases.

• *Keep it moving.* Begin by announcing that you have only so many minutes to talk. As the call proceeds, refer subtly to the passage of that allotted time.

● A P P R O A C H :

If a conversation seems to drag, adopt a more staccato tone of voice. Or feign confusion and request clarification: "I'm sorry, Helen, I'm lost. Can you give it to me in a nutshell?"

• *Bail out politely.* Unless you're talking to your boss, it's OK to interrupt to request that the person phone you again. Or ask when you might return the call. This is more polite and gives you more control of your time.

If you don't mind harmless lying, you can also manufacture excuses: "My hot line is ringing," or "My overseas call is about to come through."

Or if you really can't talk, say so. But don't be too abrupt. Give callers about 45 seconds to state their business.

• *Pass the call to your secretary or assistant.* Before you do so, however, ask the caller's permission. Don't hang up until you've introduced your assistant to the caller and thanked your assistant.

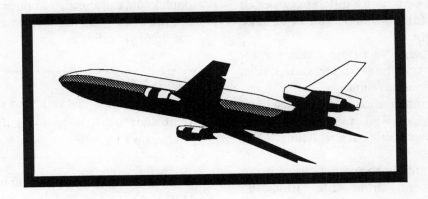

Chapter 10

TRAVEL &
ENTERTAINMENT

WINNING AT AIRPORT BINGO

■ ■ ■ ■ ■

Some business travelers describe getting bounced from airline to airline in search of a flight as "airport bingo."

HOW TO TAKE PAIN OUT OF THE GAME

■ **Reserve early and fly during off-peak hours** (midday or weekends). Flights are up to 50% cheaper, and you avoid long delays. You can also get a good seat with elbow room (next to an exit window) or near the front of the plane for a quick exit.

■ **Avoid flights or connections** through hub airports, including Chicago's O'Hare, Atlanta, Denver and Dallas–Ft. Worth. You're more likely to be delayed

■ **Take a nonstop flight.** While more expensive, chances of delays are half that of connecting flights.

■ **If you must take a connecting flight, book with the same carrier,** and allow at least an hour between connections. Avoid stopovers (flights that leave four hours or more after your arrival); they cost more than straight connections.

■ **Take along carry-on luggage only.** Remember that only two carry-ons are generally allowed and sometimes only one.

■ **Have an alternate travel plan ready** in case you're delayed, bumped, or canceled:

• Ask to be put on a different carrier, or request a full refund if you can't take another flight.

• Ask about the airline services available—free telephone, telegrams, meals, beverages or hotel rooms.

• Get compensation. Airlines must compensate travelers who can't be rebooked to within an hour of original arrival time. They pay up to $200.

• If you are put on another carrier, make sure the bumping airline writes "Rule 240" on your ticket. This means that you have been involuntarily rerouted and can't be charged extra.

• Keep track of any expenses due to your being bumped. They are reimbursable up to a reasonable amount, so save receipts.

RECOMMENDATION:
For meetings that you must make, consider paying extra for a private flight to your destination.

RESTAURANT SAVOIR FAIRE
■ ■ ■ ■ ■

A meal at a fine restaurant can help set the scene for successful negotiations. But making the arrangements and carrying it off require some expertise. Here are some suggestions on how to be in control and at ease at any elegant restaurant:

■ **Minimize the unknowns.** If possible, choose a restaurant you know quite well—and one where you are known. That will boost the odds of getting an "A" table, and minimize the odds of encountering a haughty staff or other unwelcome surprise.

• If you must dine in a restaurant you don't know, call ahead, introduce yourself to the manager or maitre d', and explain the nature of your dinner.

> EXAMPLE:
> You're closing a deal and need an elegant ambiance to discuss business. Butter him or her up a bit.

• To be safe, visit an unfamiliar restaurant ahead of time. If you can't dine, arrive before your guests and look at the table and menu. Get the waiter or captain to explain items that are unfamiliar to you.

• You can also ask the maitre d' beforehand to let you pay the bill privately. (Explain that you will leave the table and pay the bill, rather than having it brought to the table.) This adds elegance to the meal, enhances your role as host, and prevents squabbles over who will pay.

■ **Don't grease the maitre d's palm up front.** Advance tipping for a good table marks you as a patsy and may signal to restaurant personnel that they can add special items to your bill.

● BETTER:
If you had a nice table and good service, tip the maitre d' on the way out. When you return, service should be superb.

■ **Don't be intimidated by menus printed in a foreign language.** Use them as a way to build rapport with the waiter or captain, who can point you in the direction of a good meal if you're inquisitive and interested.

Since food should not be the focus of attention at a business meal, stick to safe bets like lamb, beef or chicken at a French restaurant, for example. You don't want to appear too finicky or too much the gourmet.

■ **Don't write off hotel restaurants.** When hosting a business meal in an unfamiliar city, you may want to try the hotel dining room. While it may not be the best in town, it's usually set up to accommodate the business traveler, offering a sumptuous setting and tables spaced far enough apart for you to talk and hear what your guests are saying. Some of the best restaurants in town may not have those amenities.

O B S E R V A T I O N :
Some of the best restaurants in many cities are located in hotels—and you may be surprised to learn that your business guests have never bothered to try them before.

HOW TO RELAX WHEN ORDERING WINE
■ ■ ■ ■ ■

The next time you find yourself hosting a business lunch or dinner in a restaurant, you can grasp the wine list with assurance and order with authority by keeping a few simple suggestions in mind:

• *Keep light wines with light foods.* The sauce and the way a dish is cooked should determine the type of wine you order—more so than the old "white wine with fish and poultry, and red wine with red meat" rule. (That rule's not *completely* wrong, though.)

There are different wines to choose, however. With a light-flavored chicken dish, you would want a light white wine. A chicken dish in a heavier sauce might call for something more robust—perhaps a rich, buttery white Chardonnay that can stand up to it. White wine is often the best choice with

fish—but with oily fish such as salmon or tuna, a light red wine would be equally fine.

WINES TO KNOW

• **Chardonnay.** White wines produced from the Chardonnay grape are the most popular of all varietal wines.

● N O T E :
The term "varietal" denotes all wines produced from one type of grape. They range from French Burgundy to California Chablis. French Chardonnays are more acidic, leaner and austere, while the California wines are richer and fruitier with bigger flavors.

• **Light Burgundy, Beaujolais and Pinot Noir.** Popular, light red wines that go well with light foods, such as chicken, veal and fish dishes. *Note:* Beaujolais, though red, is often served slightly chilled.
• **Cabernet Sauvignon.** A good, heavier red wine that comes mainly from the Bordeaux region in France, but is also grown in lesser quantities in Italy and California.
• **Merlot.** Softer than a Cabernet, this is a new choice with a luscious quality to it. Even young Merlots are easy to take—the odds are high that the wine you order will be excellent.
• **Sparkling wines.** A good premeal aperitif choice that goes well with hors d'oeuvres. Good sparkling wines come from France (Champagne), Spain (Cavas) and California.

ORDERING WITHOUT FEAR

• **Ignore vintages.** Unless wine is your hobby, you won't be aware, for instance, what 1987 was like in the Napa Valley.

● BETTER:

Understand the basics of wine ordering outlined above, and rely on the restaurant for guidance about what years are best.

• **It's all right to ask for help.** Explain what you're having and what you think you'd like. Then let the sommelier or wine steward suggest some wines.

● BOTTOM LINE:

It's far better than trying to look like you know what you're doing when you really don't.

• **Smell the wine, forget the cork.** Sniffing the cork is pretentious and doesn't really give you any information. Smell the wine and taste it.

Here's how to do it: Give the wine a swirl in your glass to mix in some oxygen and then give it a sniff—our sense of smell is more acute than our sense of taste.

If the wine smells dull, it has become oxidized. If it smells sour—a little like vinegar—it has become too acidified. You can usually tell by smell whether the wine is off. Have a taste to confirm what your nose tells you.

If the wine is oxidized or sour, ask the person in charge to give you another bottle.

◆ PROBLEM:

Wine should not be sent back if you decide upon tasting that you simply don't like it or feel it won't go well with your food. If you're not sure about a particular wine, it's best to ask the waiter or wine steward before ordering.

• **Don't rule out house wine.** It's never a great choice, but it's usually a good one. It's unlikely that you'll get a really bad house wine—and you can order by the carafe or glass.

• **Learn to adapt when everyone at the table is having something different.** This calls for compromise—perhaps a rich, flavorful Chardonnay or a light red, such as Pinot Noir. Both will work pretty well with either heavier or lighter entrées.

Or order wine by the glass, a growing trend as many restaurants increase the quantity and quality of the house wines they make available.

• **Don't select by price.** More expensive wine is not always better. You do not have to order something expensive to get something good.

• **Experiment, relax and enjoy.** Wine should be no more intimidating than food. If you are ordering a second bottle in a restaurant, try something different from your first.

Learning about wines simply has to do with finding what you like. Keep trying different things. Remember, it's rare that you will have a bottle of sour wine or a disastrous wine-food combination. So relax and enjoy.

SOME TIPS ON TIPPING

■ **Restaurants.** The usual amount is 15%–20%. In some of the more exclusive restaurants in larger cities and in the evening, 20% is more common. In any case, the amount should reflect the quality of service you think you were given. Most authorities agree that the tip should be figured on the basic bill *before* tax.

■ **Hotels.** Don't tip the door attendant just for opening the cab or car door for you, but do tip anywhere from 25 cents to a dollar if he or she hails a cab on your behalf.

• The person who carries your luggage generally gets between 50 cents and one dollar per bag. A dollar is typical in the larger cities.

• The housekeeper who cleans your room generally gets 50 cents to one dollar for each day of your stay, although more than a dollar would be in order if the room requires extra attention because of a party or meeting.

■ **Personal services.** Cab drivers get about 15%, or one dollar for a six- or seven-dollar ride.

• For an employee of a valet parking establishment, 50 cents to a dollar is generally sufficient. In some parking garages, this amount can be trimmed or eliminated if all the employee actually does is shuttle your car to you in an assembly-line fashion.

• For hairdressers, about 10%–12% of the bill is sufficient—typically $3–$4—with another dollar for the person shampooing your hair. You do not generally tip the owner of the hair salon.

• For barbers, one dollar is probably the most frequent tip. For a two-dollar shoe-shine, tip from 25 to 50 cents.

GUIDE TO HOTEL SAFETY
■ ■ ■ ■ ■

While hotel fires are not an everyday occurrence, the occasional disaster should alert travelers that they can't take safety for granted. There are sensible precautions that can be taken ahead of time and some rules to know during an emergency.

THINKING AHEAD

• **Ask about safety features before you book.** Does the hotel have a sprinkler system, room windows that open and a smoke tower for escape? Ask for a room on the first four floors. The clerk's responses will tell you a lot about how concerned the hotel is with safety. If you are not reassured by what you hear, try another hotel.

• **Insist that a bellhop or clerk escort you to your room.** Check that no one is hiding there, that any sliding door to the outside can be locked and that the hall door has a peephole.

• **Keys are worth more than a quick glance.** The worst are the ones with the room number and hotel name engraved on them. Unless you refuse to take the room, your only alternative is to take special precautions not to let the key out of your control. The best keys are cross-coded—the number on the key is computer-coded to the room.

• **Bring along your own safety kit,** including a flashlight, portable smoke detector and a whistle.

• **Take the time to read the safety instructions posted in most rooms.** Go into the hallway and count the doors to the nearest exit. Check that it's unlocked. Is there a stairway to the roof? That may be your escape route if your room is located on a high floor.

• **If you hear an alarm or smell smoke,** don't open your door until you have felt the frame and knob for heat, as well as checked for smoke by looking through the peephole. Remember that more fatalities are cause by smoke inhalation than by flames. If the door is cool and there's no sign of smoke, leave your room (and take your key because you may have to return if all escape routes are blocked) and head for the nearest exit.

• **If your door is hot,** do not open it: Your room may be the safest haven. If smoke is coming in, fill the bath tub, soak towels or bed clothes, and use them to block the door crack. Signal from the window, if possible, to show where you are. But don't open or break the window; increased oxygen will feed the fire.

• **If your room gets smokier,** cover yourself with a wet blanket. Don't give up hope or panic. The fire fighters may be only seconds away.

Chapter 11

YOU & THE BOSS

DARE TO SPEAK UP TO YOUR BOSS

· · · · ·

If you do it right, confronting the boss can help you keep your self-respect *and* your job. Approach the problem *not* by worrying about what could happen to you if you do speak up, but rather about what will happen to your job satisfaction if you don't.

CHALLENGING THE BOSS

• **Take an honest look at your gripe.** You may be overreacting. Be sure you have enough information to judge your boss's behavior; it could be the result of pressure from his or her superiors. Ponder, too, whether it's a case of two different management styles clashing. If so, you may be the one who has to change your approach out of

deference to your boss's position.

• **Give your boss the benefit of the doubt.** Chances are, whatever your superior did was unintentional. Bringing the matter up will probably lead to change.

• **Prepare for your confrontation.** Think through exactly what you want to say. Rehearsing your argument lets you clarify your message as well as vent your emotions. Thus, you'll be more likely to keep your composure when you sit down to talk.

• **Try the good news, bad news approach.** Say something favorable to your boss before bringing up the troublesome situation and your feelings about it: "I've heard a lot of positive comments about your talk last week." Then get down to the nitty-gritty of why you came.

• **Watch out for loaded words.** Avoid *you* statements. Instead of saying "You really ly messed me up when you switched suppliers without notifying me," put your grievance in *I* terms: "I look pretty foolish when I don't know what's going on."

Be careful of your choice of terms, too. It's better to say you're "uncomfortable" rather than "upset"; "concerned" rather than "angry" or "bothered." The wrong words can make you sound like you're whining or spiteful.

• **Treat the case as a mutual problem.** You're not trying to pin the blame on anyone. So don't say, "This would never have happened if you had told me first."

● B E T T E R :

"I know you're trying to cut costs. But is there some way you can notify me ahead of time so I don't lose my credibility?" This gives the boss a chance to solve the problem without losing face.

O B S E R V A T I O N :

Even if your conversation goes nowhere, at least you'll have gotten the matter off your chest, in a manner to which your boss can't object. The fact that you spoke up is a partial victory in itself.

KEEP THE BOSS INFORMED AND GET WHAT YOU NEED

∎ ∎ ∎ ∎ ∎

If you feel you are losing the battle to get your job done on a paltry budget, here is a way to get top management to give you the resources you need:

■ **Make top management's uncertainty work for you.** The top brass know they can make mistakes. If they've recently

made cutbacks, you can bet that, right now, they're worried that they have thinned out resources too much.

■ **Fill the information gap.** Keep the boss filled in on your day-to-day operations. Don't, however, be a constant harbinger of bad news. If you keep up a stream of cheerful facts, higher executives will be more receptive to the unpleasant ones. Ways you can provide this information:

• *"FYI" copies of your memos* to people within your group, if they are complimentary or discuss unusual tasks.

• *Encourage employee suggestions.* Have your staff put their good ideas in writing, and then pass them on with your cover memo to the boss.

• *Staff meetings.* When you expect an impressive show, invite the boss.

• *An employee newsletter,* prepared monthly by your assistant, discussing who in your unit is working on what, along with achievements and plans.

• *Bulletin board.* Make it lively, and change information frequently. Post it where the top brass will see it, and fill it with good news.

In addition, update the top boss at least weekly on projects completed or still underway, and new ones assumed.

■ **Don't suffer in silence.** When the boss tries to squeeze more work out of your group, subtly remind him or her of what you're already doing: "Should I tell Larry to hold off on the customer survey, or can this assignment wait?"

■ **Keep pressing for more.** When you keep the top boss informed, it becomes easier to say, "If we had one more person (copying machine, computer or whatever), we could turn this around much faster."

■ **Speak top executives' language.**

When asking for additional resources, speak in terms of return on investment, increased sales projections or ultimate cost savings. And express your request so it's seen as helpful, not a complaint.

WHAT TO DO WHEN YOU OUTSHINE YOUR BOSS

Few situations are more frustrating than working for a superior who is your intellectual inferior. You must balance your desire to excel against the need not to show up your boss.

HOW TO COPE

• **Don't hide your intelligence.** You'll resent the constraint and sour quickly on what may be a good job. Ultimately, that hurts your career.

• **Avoid being overly aggressive** in fighting for recognition of ideas you know are good. Being right is important, but so is being a team player and acknowledging organizational charts.

• **Never surprise the boss or oppose him or her in public.** Tell the boss you have different ideas before a meeting, and ask if he or she minds your presenting them.

• **Don't criticize subpar work** your boss presents to clients or to other company departments. Shoddiness always shows through, but it will be perceived as the boss's, not yours.

• **Let your boss take credit for your good work** without protesting. You'll have many opportunities for showing your stuff without alienating him or her.

• **Stress teamwork, and then achieve.** Convince your boss of your total support and commitment before asserting yourself. Once your superior trusts you not to steal his or her thunder, your boss will encourage you to use your brains.

• **Praise your boss** whenever you can do so in good conscience.

• **Cover the boss's mistakes only if it's best for the company.** If he or she blows it and you can save the day, do it in a low-key way and without doing the boss's job. Otherwise, he or she will resent your interference.

• **Don't ever tell anyone that you're smarter than your boss.** It could get back to the executive, which could only hurt you.

• **Try to do some work independently,** without threatening the team framework. That downplays any glaring difference in intellect, and makes it easier for you to get some credit.

• **Finally, leave before conflict becomes unresolvable,** and while you can still salvage an unresentful reference.

MAGNIFY YOUR CLOUT

One prescription for frustration, if not outright failure, is to have heavy management responsibility and not enough authority to make good on it. To get the authority you need:

• *Make your case vividly.* Without clout, complaining won't help. But walk into the boss's office with six defective parts that have gone through the system as OK, and you'll get a fair hearing.

Think of similar visual aids—a pile of customer complaint letters, a graph depicting sales or production problems, for example—that will help dramatize whatever point you wish to make.

• *Push for the right environment.* A poorly designed work setting has a serious effect on efficiency.

For example, a wire-and-cable company had several departments split up on different floors. Managers had become so used to this that they never complained. Then a major customer came by and exclaimed, "How can you people get anything done with such a setup?" Top management called in a consultant, who drew up a new, more logical arrangement. Productivity soared.

• *Manage the right people.* If the quality of your subordinates is high enough to require little supervision, you and your assistants will have more time to think and develop new ideas. Make it a constant concern to train your people so they'll work to their full potential.

• *Give them the control they need.* Just as you need clout, make sure you give assistants the power they need to support you effectively.

• *Don't take on more than you can handle.* There is a limit to how many people you can manage. Your effective span of control consists of no more people than you can know personally, in terms of their strengths and weaknesses.

MISSING: YOUR BOSS

When decisions must be made at once, nothing can be as infuriating as an inaccessible boss who has to approve them first.

It's a situation that leaves you with two grim options:

• Stick your neck out and endanger your career by making the decision yourself.

• Miss a potentially good opportunity and end up looking ineffective.

HOW TO COPE WITH A WANDERING BOSS

• **Keep a clear list of "what ifs."** When you can pin the boss down, discuss some hypothetical situations that you think could arise in his or her absence. Then ask how they should be handled, and by whom.

• **Maintain a running list of questions and issues** that arise during the boss's absences. That way, you won't waste time at your next meeting shuffling through notes and trying to remember what you wanted to discuss.

• **Set up a regular meeting.** Make it clear that you need a chance to talk over current projects on a weekly basis.

• **Establish emergency procedures.** Find out (1) who should be consulted when the boss is unreachable, (2) what decisions you can make in an emergency, (3) when you should get approval from another manager at your boss's level, and (4) when only the boss can authorize action.

• **Ask for prototypes.** Models of budgets, schedules, presentations and reports can answer hundreds of questions that come up when you first tackle a similar project on your own.

• **Talk to others in your department.** Find out how they deal with the problem boss. Use techniques they've employed successfully. You'll probably get their moral support, too.

• **Make sure everybody knows that decision-making information should be routed through you.** One way to handle an elusive boss to your advantage is to gather all of the information needed to make a decision, outline all of the options, and choose one that seems best to you. Then, when you present the information and the option you favor, you'll save the boss's time and energy—plus impress him or her with your ability to think critically and make decisions—while still checking for an OK.

• **Communicate creatively.** Find in-between times for meetings—drive your boss to the airport and talk while waiting for his or her flight, or meet for breakfast or late evening drinks. Send questions—and receive answers—via fax machines, tape recorders, overnight mail, etc.

● BEST BET:

Compose memos in which options can simply be checked off. Frame questions so you can act after receiving a yes or no.

BOSS ON YOUR BACK?
· · · · ·

The boss who regularly hovers over you—checking your work, offering direction you don't need—takes all the joy out of your job. He or she can also hurt your career.

HOW TO RESPOND

• **First, look at yourself.** If you've had a problem with hovering bosses in other jobs, you could be projecting an insecure image, unconsciously implying that you need constant checking.

As a check, ask yourself: Do I often ask the boss for reassurance that I've done a good job? Do I seek his or her advice too often? On the other hand, have I failed on certain tasks because I *neglected* to ask the boss for advice when necessary? If your answer to any of these questions is yes, you

may have failed to convince the executive that you can be left alone.

If you're not sure whether you're to blame for your boss's attitude, check with your colleagues. Do they have similar problems with this superior?

• **Then look for other causes.** Your boss may be insecure for a variety of possible reasons: Your predecessor might have been incompetent. Or perhaps your boss preceded you in the job you have now, and may be simply unwilling to let go.

• **Response strategy.** Pry your superior's sticky grip loose by using these preemptive moves: Go to your superior often to check up on your progress, send memos filling him or her in on decisions you've made, and copy the boss on all correspondence he or she might be even remotely interested in. As time goes on, this executive should come to trust your ability and decision making.

• **If that fails, see your boss.** Without accusing or criticizing, simply point out the detrimental effect this excess monitoring has on your performance.

Focus the meeting on formulating ways your boss can back off while still feeling some control over what gets done. Redesign your tasks so that he or she has an impact on the product, not every detail of how it is produced.

Most companies now judge managers not only on their departments' output, but also on their ability to help their subordinates develop and become even more productive, management experts say. So such criticism should hit home if your superior has any sense of what's needed to be a good manager.

OBSERVATION:
If all these measures fail, you're not like-

ly to help your career to develop by staying where you are. Start looking for a new position where your ability to shine won't be dimmed by your boss's shadow.

YOUR SUBORDINATE IS NOW YOUR BOSS

■ ■ ■ ■ ■

How do you face a role reversal in your career that has you reporting to your former subordinate? The first rule in such situations, management experts and clinical psychologists agree, is keeping your "cool." Don't blow up. Don't let your anger, humiliation or self-pity show. And take your time in deciding what you want to do and how you are going to do it.

QUESTIONS TO ASK YOURSELF

• **Why were you supplanted?** Was it style, personality, work habits or ability that made top management put a subordinate over you?

Use this knowledge to decide whether the company is still right for you and, if so, what changes you might make to put your career back into forward gear.

• **What's your real status now?** Does the company really want you to stay or is it only paying lip service to the idea? A good clue is how the switch was handled. Derogatory comments from on high, reported through the grapevine, for example, are not a good sign.

• **Can you negotiate a comfortable reporting relationship** with your former subordinate? Arrange a prompt meeting. Avoid platitudes, but be pleasant. Find out what your new boss expects from you, and how he or she sees your personal and professional relationship evolving.

• **How does this affect your career?** Take a hard look at your professional goals and plans in light of what has happened. They may not be as adversely affected as you think.

RECOMMENDATION:

Get objective counsel. The human resources department of your firm is a good source. A senior official may know what happened and understand the underlying dynamics and politics involved. You can ask this executive for advice both on and off the record.

OBSERVATION:

Such a reversal is emotionally draining and can lead to depression and self-doubt. If it does and you don't snap out of it, consider counseling. Many companies have Employee Assistance Plans (EAPs) that will pay all or part of the cost.

COPING WITH A BAD BOSS

■ ■ ■ ■ ■

A bad boss can hinder your career progress—or halt it entirely. If your boss fits into one of the following five categories, you'll need special tactics to survive.

• *Superachiever.* This boss insists on overseeing every detail of everyone's work and refuses to delegate responsibilities. He or she tends to be a vacillating perfectionist who makes frequent changes as projects progress. This causes delays, confusion and resentment.

▲ STRATEGY:

A younger manager who doesn't delegate may still be flexible enough to learn. Try a simple, "Let me write that marketing report and bring it back for you to check on Friday." But a confirmed, lifelong superachiever is very hard to change.

• *Milquetoast.* This shy, pleasant boss just wants everything to go smoothly and never makes demands. He or she has a hard time delegating or giving clear instructions, and will not go to bat for you with upper management. Your projects take second place behind those from departments with stronger managers. You may even have a hard time getting raises and reviews.

▲ STRATEGY:

A boss who is afraid of subordinates is certainly scared of his or her supervisors. Use this to your advantage by suggesting that you pitch your ideas and suggestions directly to upper management. Chances are that your boss will be relieved.

• *Credit-grabber.* Through real or feigned memory lapses—or outright thievery—this boss lays claim to all your good ideas.

▲ STRATEGY:

Submit all suggestions as memos with copies to all staff members involved, including your boss's superiors. If your boss has already stolen an idea, write a memo with more suggestions: "Another thought on the project I suggested for Denver..."

• *Bully.* This abrasive boss has nothing but contempt for staff members, who toil away while trying to anticipate the next skirmish. This boss *does* delegate—but as a dictator. Making suggestions is like setting out bowling pins to be knocked down.

▲ STRATEGY:

Don't be intimidated. Continue to make suggestions—a habitually gruff person is not necessarily evil, and good work may still penetrate a crusty exterior. If the situation does not improve, transfer or find a new job. There's no reason to endure suffering and hardship you don't deserve.

• *Incompetent.* Your boss is learning from you—and enjoying a higher salary and title. The more you help, the more secure this boss becomes—and the more dependent on you.

▲ STRATEGY:

Keep supporting your boss, but expect credit—and advancement—for your expertise. Keep records of your suggestions and ideas. If this boss starts stealing your ideas, see the instructions above for a *credit-grabber.*

WHEN YOUR BOSS FALLS FROM FAVOR
■ ■ ■ ■ ■

When your boss is on the outs with top management, his or her fate will inevitably affect your own. You must decide whether to increase your support or defensively distance yourself from the situation.

ASSESS THE SITUATION

Try to verify your suspicions that your boss has fallen on hard times.

- *Feel the matter out indirectly with a senior-level person* with whom you have a good relationship.

● BEST BET:

Rather than asking how your boss is seen by upper management, inquire about how your *department* is seen—its current performance and its role in the company's overall plans.

- *Ask your boss about an issue related to the loss of power.* For example, ask why a project he or she proposed didn't get funded or why your department is not represented on a key committee. Your boss may address the question of lost status directly. If not, you should be able to get insight based on the explanation—or lack thereof.
- *Examine your boss's situation to see how his or her status may have changed.* Look for a shrinking staff, a smaller budget, a loss of membership on old committees or the failure to be included in new ones.
- *Rely on the grapevine* to give you perspective on the situation, especially if you are new to the firm. Does the company motivate managers by alternately encouraging them and then throwing them into the doghouse? Does your boss have a history of trips there? If the answer to either of these questions is yes, then your boss's loss of status may be a temporary setback, rather than the beginning of the end.

THE INEFFECTIVE BOSS

Based on the information you've gathered, decide whether senior management's actions against your boss are warranted. Past performance that's not up to par *is* your boss's responsibility if he or she has had adequate staff support.

▲ IMPORTANT:

Take steps to protect yourself. If you're not in the habit of making your accomplishments known to people who count, it's time to start. The less you're tied to your boss's image of failure, the better.

THE GOOD BOSS UNDER SIEGE

If, on the other hand, your boss is a victim of circumstance, you must decide on what role to play. Your choice depends on your concern for your job and whether your loyalty belongs to your firm or your boss.

- If your boss is a strong, dynamic manager and your relationship with him or her has been good in the past, continuing your support can benefit you in the long run. The odds are good that your boss may bring you along to another company. And there's always the chance that upper management may notice your continuing support and reward you accordingly.
- But there are dangers to being supportive. You may be risking your own paycheck.

OBSERVATION:

When top management stops supporting a staff member, the underlying meaning is that *change* is taking place in your company. Management is setting new company goals that require different managerial approaches or personalities.

Try to get a handle on *trends* and position yourself for them. If you find out that your organization is becoming more market-driven, look into the possibility of a transfer to the marketing department before the ranks of your own department are diminished or decimated. Consider taking courses to build skills in newly important areas if necessary.

Chapter 12

YOUR IMAGE

MAKING A SUCCESSFUL TELEVISION APPEARANCE

· · · · ·

Television appearances are often turning points in careers. If handled competently, they can powerfully advance your status. If bungled, they can do considerable damage. Knowing what works and what doesn't will keep you from coming across negatively or appearing less intelligent or educated than you are.

TO PREPARE

• **Formulate answers to questions you know you'll be asked** and rehearse them aloud so they sound natural.

• **When you practice, learn to pace yourself comfortably.** Read your script as though you're savoring it, even if you're not. Excessive speed implies that you find your ideas unimportant, and your TV audience will probably agree.

• **Practice hand gestures** to accentuate important points or illustrate ideas. Gestures do more than look good—they also burn off nervous energy and actually improve the quality of your voice.

ON-CAMERA SUCCESS

• **When being interviewed in an office,** don't remain seated at a desk. It makes you look stiff and formal.

● BETTER:

You and your interviewer should sit in two chairs placed in a corner, or perhaps at a coffee table. This gives a greater level of physical comfort and builds rapport between you and the reporter.

• **Sit in the front third of your chair,** plant one foot slightly in front of the other, and lean slightly toward the reporter. This puts you on an equal footing with the reporter and keeps you from suddenly leaning forward and looking defensive when a tough question is thrown your way.

• **Maintain eye contact with the reporter when answering questions,** rather than looking upward while thinking.

• **Keep your answers short** to reduce the risk that your statements will be distorted by later editing. If you're giving a full interview, spend no more than 45 seconds on one answer. If you're on a local or network news program (for which the average sound byte is between eight and 18 seconds), stay under 30 seconds.

• **Be interesting and concise,** and say things the audience can relate to. Spice up your answers with "sparklers," such as anecdotes, statistics and analogies that clarify your most important points.

• **Limit television interviews to 20 minutes,** and preferably 15. This will give the reporter adequate time to cover the topic, but not enough time to go into areas you're unprepared to discuss.

• **When being interviewed in a studio setting,** watch the program beforehand to get an idea of what the interviewer is like—aggressive, insinuating, a pussycat, etc. Determine how aggressive you must be to get in what you have to say.

Anticipate the tough questions that are likely to be asked and formulate your answers ahead of time. Write down all the positive points you want to make and review them before going on the air. Espe-

cially important: Assume the microphones are on the minute you enter the studio.

• **Read the day's newspapers and listen to a news program** before you go on camera, no matter how early in the day you must appear. This will help keep you from being surprised by a question that may have come up within the last few hours, or by an interviewer's reference to a recent event.

• **Dress conservatively** so that the audience's attention is focused on what you're saying rather than on what you're wearing. It's best to stick with comfortable clothing in medium blue tones, with a little dash of color (such as a maroon tie for men or a silk scarf for women). Women should avoid wearing heavy jewelry that can reflect light or clink against the microphone.

• **When being interviewed outdoors in a setting where you're standing,** rest your hands lightly at your sides rather than putting them behind you or in your pockets.

▲ **IMPORTANT:**

If you're at the scene of a problem situation (a strike, environmental problem, etc.), don't allow the interview to take place with that scene in the background. Instead, stand away from the scene so that you and your company won't be directly associated with the problem.

UPDATE YOUR IMAGE
■ ■ ■ ■ ■

Visual impact is 85% of the message sent when you first meet somebody; what you say is only 15%. So even if you're on top of all the new developments in your field, you'll still seem out of date if you don't keep your visual image current.

• *Don't dwell in the past.* Many people remember a wonderful period in their lives—college, the army, a year overseas—and lock themselves into "those were the days" dressing.

EXAMPLE:

Children of the '60s with too-long hair or sideburns.

• *Review your wardrobe every three years.* During that time, clothing usually needs refurbishing and styles change. Men's pants, for instance, are constantly adding pleats or cuffs or changing leg widths.

◆ MISTAKE:

Trying to piece things together rather than taking in fashion as a whole. You can't add your 10-year-old slacks to this year's sports jacket and expect the look to work.

• *Review new styles.* Men can flip through the pages of *GQ* or *Esquire* and look at the ads for menswear. Or check out a company's annual report. What hair styles are in vogue? What ties, shirts, suits, shoes and accessories?

Women can check *Glamour's* "Job Strategies" column, *Savvy* and *Working Woman*, as well as clothing ads, to see how up-to-date businesswomen are dressing and wearing their hair.

• *Invest in yourself.* The cut and fit of your clothing are more important than how much you spend. Think of it as marketing. Successful companies have found that when they pay as much attention to the packaging as to the product, they can command the best price.

YOUR SILENT IMPACT
· · · · ·

Whenever you enter a room, people react to more than your physical appearance alone. They also have a strong emotional response to your mannerisms—your habitual way of standing, sitting, walking and using your hands.

By increasing your awareness and mastery of these habits, you can gain control of the impression you create—and stand a far better chance of building a relationship from a position of strength.

THE IMPRESSION YOU MAKE

• **What are your gestures saying?** There's no such thing as a good or bad gesture—any one of them can convey different meanings depending on its force, speed and context. Problems arise only when your accustomed movements cause reactions that work against what you are trying to accomplish.

EXAMPLE:

People who complain of not being taken seriously often unconsciously use hand movements that are light, airy and delicate—giving the impression of tentativeness rather than self-assurance. And people who favor emphatic gestures may lose out when negotiations require tact and diplomacy.

• **What does your posture convey?** People who hold their spines erect and people who slouch send different messages. Straight posture can connote formality, stiffness or strength—it depends on what the rest of your body is "saying." A supple spine can show openness, but can also imply that you're weak or not to be taken seriously.

> **EXAMPLE:**
> The TV sleuth Columbo, played by Peter Falk, slouches in order to seem bumbling—someone to be ignored. People underestimate him, making it easier for him to nab the bad guy.

CHANGING MANNERISMS

Before you can take control of the process, you need to understand your habitual mannerisms. You'll be able to pick up some of them just by watching yourself, but more ingrained ones will be harder to discern.

• Ask a friend or your spouse—someone who is honest enough to say things that may not be flattering—to comment on how you walk, sit and hold yourself.

• When trying to eliminate counterproductive habits and build better ones, practice first in a nonstressful situation, not when the stakes are high. Trying to make changes when you're under stress will cause you to go back to what is familiar and habitual.

● **NOTE:**

If trying to change a movement is particularly difficult, you can be pretty sure you have come close to one that is connected to strong feelings.

One example is a man who habitually walked with his toes turned out because it gave him a feeling of being easygoing and gentle. When he straightened his feet in an

effort to bolster his image, he began to feel more aggressive. He became so uncomfortable that he reverted to his old style of walking.

• Watch other people closely and see how you react to their movements or posture. Make a mental note of which mannerisms convey strength, assurance or friendliness. See how the same mannerisms work for you.

> **EXAMPLES:**
> A quiet attitude—with a minimum of hand fluttering, eye movements or fiddling with objects—gives an impression of calm competence.

Also, external calm makes you feel more centered within yourself. You therefore give an impression of greater power.

• Consider how you wish to present yourself in different situations. You may want to appear serious in certain business situations, yet remain more open and receptive with your staff and in your personal life.

CHECK YOUR ATTITUDES

• **What are your attitudes?** We all make mistakes in our human relationships, but some of us consistently give off bad impressions. For example, some let their emotions hang out; some think only of themselves; and some are blinded by ambition. If you fall in line with any of those, you have little chance of creating a useful image.

Instead, consider whom you are trying to impress. Elwood Chapman, author of the authoritative *Your Attitude is Showing* (Science Research Associates, 1540 Page Mill Road, Palo Alto, CA; 94304, $11.95), reminds us that we are not the same person to every one we meet. Because everybody sees you differently, you have to try to make good impressions with different people differently. You rarely make good impressions on two people in the same way.

• **Work toward attaining a confident speaking manner.** A steady voice, some conviction and plenty of specifics are bound to impress others. Avoid verbal signals that suggest subordination or insecurity, such as turning statements into questions and qualifying what you say with "I think" or "sort of."

• **Be positive.** Co-workers you meet for the first time appear to have little radar sets finely tuned in to your attitude. If your attitude is positive, they receive a friendly, warm signal and they are attracted to you. If your attitude is negative, they receive an unfriendly signal and they try to avoid any contact with you.

• **Be human.** Often, the small daily attentions and courtesies—sharing a joke, discussing family plans—can have a big impact on the impression you make. Being human also means being sensitive to the feelings of others—to their concerns, their griefs and their joys.

OBSERVATION:

Those who want to make a good impression become attuned to the ways others react to them. In other words, your perception of how others see you will improve with the effort you make.

An encouraging note for the socially anxious: Research shows that we are liked by others far more than we assume.

EXECUTIVE DINING

· · · · ·

If your table manners belong in a high-school cafeteria rather than the executive dining suite, you could be damaging your professional image and chances for career advancement. To be safe, take this quick refresher course on dining basics from Elizabeth L. Post, director of the Emily Post Institute in Waterbury Center, VT.

• *Selecting a restaurant.* If you're invited to dinner and your host asks you to suggest a restaurant, the safest bet is to select one in a medium price range. A pricey menu may put the host in an awkward situation, and an inexpensive one may reflect negatively on you.

● OPTION:

Come up with several ideas, include price in your description of the restaurants, and let your host decide.

• *Ordering.* Don't select a dish you're unfamiliar with—you may end up not liking it or not knowing how to eat it. There's nothing wrong with asking a waiter to explain how a dish is prepared or making a special request, such as sautéing the entrée with olive oil rather than butter.

Whether you're the host or the guest, it's best not to comment on menu prices. If you're the host, it's cordial to place the order for yourself and your dining companion, even if you're both of the same sex. If there are more than two of you, each person should place his or her own order.

• *Conducting business.* Try to cover as much ground as possible before the entrées arrive. This makes conversation and eating more pleasant and relaxed, and is less likely to result in a two- or three-hour meal.

PICKING UP THE TAB

If getting together was a mutual decision rather than an invitation, and seniority is not defined by rank or relationship, it's best to suggest splitting the bill if the waiter puts the check near you. Another possibility is suggesting you pick up the tab this time, and that your dining companion pay the next time.

OBSERVATION:

If your selections were considerably more costly than the other person's, it's courteous to offer to pay your share rather than split the bill in half.

Finally, if you need a record of what you spent, don't hesitate to ask the waiter to divide the bill between two credit cards.

MANAGING
your
FINANCES

Chapter 1

ESTATE PLANNING

BLUNDERS TO AVOID

· · · · ·

If you want to pass your hard-earned wealth to your heirs instead of Uncle Sam, you'll need a good estate plan. Avoid these nine common errors:

1
NO LIFETIME GIFT PROGRAM

You can give up to $10,000 per recipient free of federal gift tax each year. A married couple can dispense $20,000. Lifetime gifts remove the assets from your estate (and your control).

The sooner you set up a gift program, the more you can pass along. Suppose a married couple transfers $10,000 annually to their newborn child. After 14 years, the child has $210,000 ($140,000 of principal, $70,000 of income, assuming a 6% aftertax return).

The best assets to give away are those likely to appreciate significantly over time, such as stocks and real estate. If and when they sell the assets, the recipients will incur a capital gains tax based on the donor's original cost, but the tax rate (currently 28% in most cases) is lower than the estate tax rate.

2
OWNING ALL
PROPERTY JOINTLY

An estate includes half of all jointly held assets in addition to what's in your name only. And if a surviving spouse sells jointly owned property that has appreciated in value, he or she may face a stiff capital gains tax.

Splitting ownership is a way for a married couple to shelter up to $1.2 million of assets. They can fully use each other's unified gift and estate tax credit of up to $192,800, which exempts estates worth $600,000 or less.

3
LEAVING EVERYTHING TO A SPOUSE

The unlimited marital deduction lets you do this free of estate tax, no matter how large the estate. But when the second spouse dies, the estate amount over $600,000 will be subject to tax.

Instead, minimize taxes by setting up a marital bypass trust for your spouse (see page 283). Fund the trust with $600,000, and give the spouse trust income until death. Then the trust assets pass to your children. They receive the money tax free, because it is within your estate's tax credit and isn't included in your spouse's estate.

4
NOT COORDINATING ESTATE AND PENSION PLANS

Many otherwise excellent estate plans are ruined because they don't properly account for pension money. By law, your spouse is automatically the beneficiary of your profit-sharing account at your death. In the case of a pension, your spouse receives the payout in the form of an annuity. To opt out of these rules, you must sign a waiver with your spouse's notarized signature.

5
ACTING AS CUSTODIAN OF YOUR CHILDREN'S TRUST ACCOUNTS

Anyone who sets up a trust can have the trust assets excluded from his estate only by giving up control over the funds, such as the power to distribute trust income. In most states, this is also the case with custodian accounts for minor children. Consider naming your spouse or another trusted person.

6
NOT CONSULTING HEIRS ABOUT YOUR PLAN

Discuss everything in advance so there will be no unpleasant surprises or legal challenges. You and your heirs can develop alternatives on the best way to distribute assets.

7
CHOOSING THE WRONG EXECUTOR

He or she has the time-consuming task of collecting estate assets, paying out any obligations and distributing the rest to your heirs. In some instances, this requires more than run-of-the mill financial savvy. For example, if you own a small business, the executor must keep the business running profitably until a sale is negotiated.

Many people routinely select their spouse or a close friend as executor, without considering whether this person has the financial expertise required. If necessary, consider hiring a bank trust department for complex estates. The fee, typically 5% of estate assets, may be more than offset by the benefit of professional management.

8
NOT UPDATING YOUR PLAN PERIODICALLY

Many well-designed plans become useless because of frequent law changes. There have been five major pieces of tax legislation since 1981, so periodic reviews are definitely essential.

Changes in your life may also necessitate revisions. Events that might require a review include your marriage or divorce, changes in your financial situation, your move to a new state, the birth or marriage of a child or grandchild, and a family member's death or disability.

9
CHOOSING THE WRONG ASSISTANCE

The greater your assets and the more complicated your estate planning situation, the more you need a professional, not a salesperson.

CAUTION

Don't go overboard to avoid estate tax. Otherwise, you may lose some flexibility in handling your own assets as you wish.

PROTECT ASSETS FOR HEIRS WITH SURVIVORSHIP INSURANCE
■ ■ ■ ■ ■

Taking normal estate taxes into consideration, you would need in the neighborhood of some $4,783,950 of before-tax assets in order to leave $1,000,000 net to your grandchildren. But with the benefit of some sharp estate planning, you can leave $1 million net on the basis of just a little more than $1 million.

How? By purchasing one of the so-called "survivorship," or second-to-die plans. They're sold by more than a score of companies, including State Mutual of America, Mutual of New York, Manufacturers' Life and Sun Life of Canada.

Each insurance company has its own name for this kind of policy, but the basic principle is the same.

By stipulating in the policy that two deaths must occur, the premium outlay is smaller and a family can afford a larger policy to pay estate taxes on the money and property that will eventually go to grandchildren or other heirs.

NOT JUST FOR THE RICH

Even people whose estates are relatively modest in value now should bear in mind how easily their net assets could grow to be worth well over a million by retirement time.

Just the increase in home equity, a certain amount of inflation and normal prospering of some stock investments could add up to that. That's truer even if you have company profit-sharing plans or stock options. Those who own a small business can make the jump even faster.

Jumping in now and letting the time value of money work for you is the way to pay with pennies on the dollar.

> **EXAMPLE:**
> A husband aged 45 and his wife of 47 decide to start on a second-to-die policy. At their ages, they can buy a $2 million plan for an annual premium of $16,000, payable for 10 years.

START EARLY

This means that even if estate taxes amount to as much as $2 million, they'll be paid by the insurance company rather than the estate.

OBSERVATION:

Few people are foresighted enough to start at age 45. Let's say they wait 10 more years, until he's 55. By then, a $2 million survivorship policy will cost them at least $43,000 annually.

SURVIVING SPOUSE CAN BENEFIT TOO

Up to now, most survivorship policies have been of the older, whole-life variety. Now the newer universal life concept has been introduced—and given the brand name "Inheritage" by one company. Such plans offer a good deal of flexibility in death benefits and policy values as life situations change.

This makes it simple for a surviving spouse to borrow a part of the accumulated policy value to help with living expenses. Yet the basic second-to-die death benefit will stay there to pay off liabilities after death and pass the basic estate on to the heirs, almost untouched by taxation.

PROTECTING YOUR ESTATE FOR A NONCITIZEN SPOUSE
· · · · · ·

Noncitizen spouses aren't eligible to inherit an unlimited amount of property free of federal estate tax. They're limited to $600,000 free of estate tax.

On jointly held property, generally only the half of the property held by the deceased spouse would count toward this $600,000. Thus, jointly held property worth well over $1 million probably could pass, tax free, to the surviving spouse.

For potentially larger estates, the law offers choices. For example, you can give as much as $100,000 a year to an alien spouse without being subject to the gift tax. You can also set up something the law describes as a "qualified domestic trust." The law specifies that such a trust must meet four conditions:

• All the trustees must be either U.S. citizens or domestic corporations.

• The noncitizen spouse must be entitled to all the income from the trust, and it must be payable at least annually.

• The trust must provide that there'll be enough assets to pay the estate tax when the noncitizen spouse dies.

• The trustee must make an irrevocable election on the marital deduction when filing the estate tax return.

SPECIAL PROTECTIONS FOR YOUR CHILDREN
· · · · · ·

You may want to make special provisions to protect assets that are earmarked for your children or other heirs by considering these trust options:

Q-TIP TRUST

This ensures that children from a former marriage aren't disinherited by a surviving spouse and/or that an inheritance remains safe if the latter remarries. Your spouse gets the trust income (and access to some principal) after your death. When your spouse dies, the assets go to your other heirs.

Property placed in a Q-TIP trust qualifies for the marital deduction, if the executor elects it.

● N O T E :

If estate tax is paid at once, the property's cost basis is stepped up to current market value, which reduces the heirs' capital gains tax liability when they sell the assets at a future date.

E X A M P L E :

Your $1.8 million estate is divided into three parts—one-third left outright to your wife, another third in trust for your children and the other third put into a Q-TIP trust for your wife. The one-third to your children isn't taxable (under the $600,000 estate tax exemption). The $600,000 left to your wife outright isn't taxable because of the marital deduction. The $600,000 to the Q-TIP trust can either be taxable (possible if the wife has a substantial estate of her own) or designated marital deduction property.

MINORS' TRUST

You can set up a testamentary trust in your will, to go into effect when you die, that will manage assets bequeathed to your children until they reach a specific age. If you and your spouse divide assets in separate testamentary trusts, you can pass on up to $1.2 million tax-free to other heirs. Both trusts can be structured so that the surviving spouse receives the proceeds from the other's trust.

Through instructions to the trustee, you can control when, how and for what purpose trust funds are distributed to your heirs. You pay a one-time fee to a lawyer to set up the trust. This is usually $500 to $2,000, or higher in complicated cases. At death, law firms usually charge an additional, relatively modest fee to execute the trust. There are no ongoing fees.

R E C O M M E N D A T I O N :
Get a lawyer who is willing to set up such a trust—not all are—and who has plenty of experience with them. Ask about the fee and what it covers. It's wise to give the trustee discretionary powers, including the right to draw on the principal in an emergency.

GETTING YOUR ESTATE OUT OF PROBATE
■ ■ ■ ■ ■

You're inviting trouble for your heirs if you let your estate go through probate.

■ R E A S O N :
Depending on the size of your estate and your state's law, they could lose 4%–10% of everything you've worked for and saved during your lifetime. Adding insult to injury, you'll also be handing control of your financial affairs over to the legal system. Moreover, during the probate process—possibly six months to two years long—your money may not be available to your loved ones, and their hands will be tied when making decisions about your estate assets. This will be particularly disruptive if your estate holds few liquid assets.

• *Other disadvantages:* A probated will can easily be tied up by challenges from relatives and others, and every probate asset you own becomes public record.

The best alternatives to probate include:

1
NAME SPECIFIC BENEFICIARIES

Name beneficiaries for your life insurance, Individual Retirement Accounts, and Keogh or company retirement plans. Then they'll pass directly and automatically to those people. But if your estate is the beneficiary, the proceeds will go through probate.

2
CONSIDER JOINT PROPERTY OWNERSHIP

This can be used to transfer personal property to an intended heir outside of your will, avoiding probate. There are three different ways to hold assets jointly:

• *Joint tenancy with right of survivorship.* Both parties have access to all of the property, but each owns only half of it. If one person dies, his or her share goes automatically to the survivor(s), outside of those stated in probate.

• *Tenancy by the entirety.* This is similar to the above for estate-planning purposes, but exists between husband and wife only.

• *Tenancy in common.* When one party dies, half does not automatically go to the other person but whomever the will states.

The biggest potential problem with joint ownership is the potential estate tax liability. An estate includes half of all jointly held property in addition to what's in your name only. If both owners die at the same time, joint tenancy doesn't help avoid probate.

CAUTION

Survivorship rights are restricted or have been abolished in some states. Joint ownership isn't a good idea in a shaky marriage, and possibly, not if you and your spouse have a large estate.

3
SET UP A LIVING TRUST

Whatever assets you put into it stay out of probate, and you specify how the holdings will be handled after your death. A living trust is challenge resistant, and it keeps your affairs private. Used with other estate-planning tools, it can also reduce federal estate tax. Note that only individually owned property can go into a trust.

A living trust doesn't have to be complicated. And you can be the sole trustee, thereby avoiding management fees. But picking a suitable successor trustee is crucial because, in avoiding probate, you also forfeit court supervision of your estate. Be sure you trust whomever you designate.

OBSERVATION:

In many cases, a living trust should be used in addition to, but not instead of, a will. You may want a will, for instance, to name a guardian for minor children or another specific purpose. If so, don't mention in the will any assets that are in the trust.

TWO TYPES OF LIVING TRUSTS

• **Revocable trust.** This lets you keep considerable control over trust assets. You can be the trustee, receive trust income and change or terminate the trust at any time. When you die, the trust assets go directly to your beneficiaries and aren't included in your probate estate. There are no inherent tax advantages, however, because you only pay tax on trust income during your life, and trust assets are included in your taxable estate.

OBSERVATION:

A revocable living trust is also useful for protecting your financial affairs if you become incapacitated. A successor trustee named when you form the trust would take over management of the trust assets.

• **Irrevocable trust.** This can save significant sums in federal estate tax because you effectively pass on control of the assets. But—and a big but—an irrevocable trust cannot be changed during your lifetime, although a well-planned trust can take care of most contingencies.

EXAMPLE:

You can provide that, in case of divorce, your spouse should be treated as if he or she has predeceased you and is therefore not entitled to the benefits of the trust.

WHEN A LIVING TRUST ISN'T A GOOD IDEA

· · · · ·

You don't need one if: most of your estate will automatically pass outside of probate; your estate is modest; your heirs won't need money from your estate right away; or you have no reason to keep the proceedings private. Also, be sure to check the laws in your state before deciding whether a living trust is right for you.

WAYS TO LOWER ESTATE TAX

· · · · ·

The estate tax rate starts at 37% for estates of over $600,000. It climbs to a whopping 55% above $2.5 million. So you have to plan aggressively if you want to pass as much of your accumulated estate as possible to your heirs.

GIFTS

During your lifetime, to reduce estate tax, you can give up to $10,000 per person each year (or $20,000 per person for a married couple making a joint gift) free of gift taxes. Amounts over those limits are subtracted from your estate tax exemption of $600,000.

BYPASS TRUST

This lets you shelter assets that would otherwise be taxed when your spouse dies.

EXAMPLE:

You have an $800,000 estate and your spouse has one worth $300,000. If you leave your spouse your entire estate outright, it will be exempt from federal tax when you die. But on your spouse's death, he or she might have a $1.1 million estate, of which only $600,000 would be protected.

A bypass trust could hold up to $600,000 of your estate, with $200,000 given directly to your spouse—all free of federal tax. Your spouse would receive income from trust assets, possibly with access to the principal. When he or she dies, the remaining trust assets go to your children. Uncle Sam doesn't get any of the money since the assets aren't part of your spouse's estate. Meanwhile, that estate of $500,000 ($300,000 plus the $200,000 given in your will) falls within the federal exemption.

● N O T E :

Some states allow the unlimited marital deduction, which lets you give as much property as you wish to your spouse tax-free. A bypass trust can be doubly beneficial for couples living in those states.

R E C O M M E N D A T I O N :

Both you and your spouse should provide for a bypass trust so that one will be set up no matter who dies first. An optional trust could go into effect only if the surviving spouse decides it's necessary.

GRITs

Suppose you want to give more than $600,000 to a nonspousal heir. Consider a grantor-retained income trust (GRIT). It's really a gift with a tax advantage.

E X A M P L E :

You put income-producing assets into a GRIT for up to 10 years, during which time you receive all trust income. Then, either your heirs receive the financial assets or they are placed into another trust. The longer the term of the trust, the greater the monetary discount below the gift's current market value. A 10-year delay reduces to just $600,000 (the amount of the lifetime exemption) the taxable value of a $1,540,000 gift. If you die before the trust expires, however, the assets are subject to estate tax.

PAPER TRAIL AVOIDS TROUBLE

The importance of keeping complete records of *all* your property dealings is spelled out in a recent Tax Court case. The problem surfaced after the deadline for filing an estate tax return had passed. The executor hadn't filed a return because there didn't seem to be enough in the estate to trigger a tax.

Later, he discovered that the deceased had left a farm, by an oral agreement, to a couple in 1969, retaining the right to its income for life. With the farm included, it turned out that the estate owed $82,518.

The estate was willing to pay the tax owed, but argued that a late-filing penalty wasn't appropriate because there was no "willful neglect" by the executor.

The Tax Court disagreed, saying failure to file was "intentional and without reasonable cause. The executor knew the obligation to file, but didn't, assuming no tax would be due. He took the risk that the assumption might not be correct." (*Clinton v. Commissioner*)

HOW LIFE INSURANCE CAN HELP

Life insurance proceeds can provide a good-sized estate at a low cost because of the modest premium, the tax-free buildup of insurance cash values and tax-free death proceeds. Your beneficiary receives cash—liquid property that doesn't require specialized training to handle, as would real estate, securities or a business interest.

HOW TO REMOVE LIFE INSURANCE FROM YOUR TAXABLE ESTATE

· · · · ·

The proceeds of an insurance policy on your life generally are included in your estate if (1) the proceeds are payable to, or for the benefit of, your estate; and (2) you have "incidents of ownership" in the policy, such as rights to change the beneficiary or borrow against the policy.

Consider these alternatives if you wish to leave your children the death proceeds of an insurance policy on your life, without the cash being counted in your taxable estate:

HAVE THE KIDS INSURE YOU

If your children own the policy, the proceeds won't be part of your estate. Have your children apply for insurance on your life and be sure they are listed as the applicant/owner on the application. Then when the policy is issued, you simply make a gift of the annual premium to your children.

CAUTION

Paying the premium directly to the insurance company raises the risk of an IRS challenge. Don't use an existing insurance policy because it will be counted as part of your estate if it's transferred to your children within three years of your death.

SET UP AN IRREVOCABLE LIFE INSURANCE TRUST

Transfer ownership of your life insurance policy to an irrevocable trust. There'll be no estate tax on the insurance proceeds because you or your spouse no longer own the policy.

At your death, the trust gets the proceeds. Your spouse receives lifetime income from the trust, and some principal if required. When he or she dies, the trust assets go to the policy's beneficiaries.

◆ DRAWBACKS:

When you transfer the policy, you give up all ownership rights, including borrowing against it and changing beneficiaries. If you die within three years of the transfer, the policy is included in your estate.

Because of the three-year pullback rule, you should create the trust, give it cash and have the trust buy the policy. Then the only asset that can be brought back into the taxable estate is your cash gift—and then only if it's more than the $10,000 annual exclusion.

CAUTION

Life insurance proceeds are the best source of cash to meet immediate financial obligations after a death. You must either make the executor of your estate the beneficiary of the policy, or you must authorize the executor to borrow from the beneficiaries.

MINIMIZE ESTATE TAXES FOR BUSINESS-RELATED ASSETS

· · · · ·

Company stock and group life insurance can be important parts of your estate. Handle them correctly and you'll minimize the estate-tax bill for your heirs.

COMPANY-PAID LIFE INSURANCE

You're the controlling stockholder of a closely held corporation. You want your company to own and pay for an insurance policy on your life, with the proceeds payable to your spouse or another beneficiary.

Treat the premium paid by the company as additional taxable income to you. Then the death benefit will not be treated as a gift from the business to your heirs, which would incur gift tax.

STOCK IN A CLOSELY HELD BUSINESS

This is valued for federal estate-tax purposes when you die. To lower your tax, have the corporation redeem your shares at a predetermined specific or formula price. Insurance on your life can be used to fund the purchase.

OBSERVATION:

If your stock in the company represents more than 35% of your gross estate, you may want to have your business pay your estate taxes. With a "Section 303" stock redemption, your estate can tender enough shares to the corporation to pay federal estate tax (and certain other estate expenses) without paying ordinary income tax on the cash paid by the corporation for the shares.

KEY-MAN INSURANCE

When a corporation owns insurance on the majority shareholder's life, the proceeds are payable to the corporation. They increase the value of the decedent's estate to the extent that they inflate the value of the stock. So have the company pay your personal insurance premium (while you retain the right to name your personal beneficiary). Under a "162 bonus plan," the company will grant you bonuses equal to the annual premium. Since the bonus is considered additional compensation, it's deductible at the corporate level.

DOLLAR PLAN

Use this to divide the "protection" and "investment" elements of any permanent life insurance contract between the business owner and the corporation. The corporation can buy the policy and contribute to an amount equal to the investment element (cash surrender value), while the business owner pays an amount equaling the protection element (term insurance premiums).

At death, the corporation recovers its outlay and the business owner's heirs receive the balance of the death proceeds. Split-dollar plans may be arranged to use corporate dollars to provide for personal estate liquidity. Other split-dollar arrangements can provide good retirement income for key executives or shareholders.

Chapter 2

FINANCIAL PLANNING

PICKING A FINANCIAL PLANNER

· · · · · ·

There are 250,000 to 400,000 people in America who call themselves financial planners. While the Securities and Exchange Commission (SEC) and many states regulate investment advisors, financial planners are not yet covered by federal or most state laws. It's an open arena for snake-oil peddlers and swindlers. Some dishonest ones have taken investors for millions. How do you find someone you can trust?

FINDING A PLANNER TO FIT YOUR NEEDS

Financial advice comes from many places. Some life insurance salespeople call themselves financial planners, but offer only a limited selection of insurance products. And only limited numbers of securities brokers are trained as financial planners.

▲ IMPORTANT

The offerings of financial planners probably will be colored by their backgrounds and training. A CPA, for example, probably wouldn't suggest the same investments as a life insurance agent. Also, be aware that the best financial planners are as careful in choosing clients as you should be in selecting a planner.

POINTS TO CONSIDER

■ Your investment philosophy. Are you comfortable with a high degree of risk, or do you prefer safer, more conservative ventures? A good planner should be diversified enough to understand different investment strategies.

■ **Investment plans.** Flush out those pushing a limited line of products by asking for an alternative investment strategy. Insist on a clearly written and detailed plan, and be sure that all securities investments are registered with the SEC and state agencies.

■ **The background of the person.** Check with the state attorney general and state securities regulators for any action taken against the planner in your state or any state in which he or she has done business. Ask for references from several clients, and check for past complaints with the Better Business Bureau.

■ **Specific credentials.** Ask about training, certification and any continuing education program the planner has gone through.

A planner may also have taken courses and exams to earn one of the following titles. Check with the organizations listed below to review certification requirements, and be sure your planner has met them.

• Chartered Financial Consultant (ChFC)—American College, 270 Bryn Mawr Ave., Bryn Mawr, PA 19010; 215-526-1000.

• Chartered Financial Analyst (CFA)—Institute of Chartered Financial Analysts, P.O. Box 3668, Charlottesville, VA 22903; 804-977-6600.

• Certified Financial Planner (CFP)—International Board of Standards and Practices for Certified Financial Planners, Inc., 5445 DTC Parkway, Englewood, CO 80111; 303-850-0333.

■ **Fees and charges.** Some planners make money from commissions on the products they sell. Others operate on a fee-only basis. Get a complete statement of fees and charges, and find out how they're computed.

♦ **WARNING:**

Never give a planner discretion to execute trades without your permission. Always review any prospective investments, as well as all transactions and paperwork.

FINAL PLANS: FUNERAL EXPENSES

Funerals are among the largest expenses most families will have to face during their lives, exceeded only by the costs of housing, college educations and automobiles. Yet, many people avoid making plans that can spare their heirs considerable expense and indecision when funeral plans must eventually be made.

▲ **FACT:**

The basic choices regarding funeral services have an immense impact on cost. According to the National Funeral Directors Association in Milwaukee, costs range from $2,500 to over $8,000, with most falling between $2,700 and $5,500.

PLANNING AHEAD

Speak with several funeral directors to compare costs and find someone with whom you and your family feel comfortable. Since 1984, funeral directors have been required by the Federal Trade Commission (FTC) to furnish written price breakdowns of their services and the goods they market. Current price information is also available from the 175 nonprofit, nonsectarian memorial societies in the U.S. that assist in preplanning of memorial services.

● TO LOCATE ONE:

Contact the Continental Association of Funeral and Memorial Societies, 1828 L St. NW, Washington, DC 20036.

● *Control costs* by deciding what type of memorial services you desire and whether you favor cremation (now chosen for 14% of all funerals in America) or burial (grave or mausoleum). According to the FTC, cremation services average $1,054—less than half the average cost of a closed-casket service and burial. It is also possible to save more money by having a body transported directly to a crematorium without passing through a funeral home.

● *Ask about the legal requirements in your state.* For example, embalming—which most people assume is required by law—is usually only required when death was caused by certain contagious diseases or when the body will be transported across state lines.

FINANCIAL PLANNING

Prepayment is risky—there is the chance that you will move out of state or that the funeral home will go out of business. It is a better idea to save the money you will need ahead of time.

● *Totten trust.* This is a special account set up with a bank and earmarked for funeral expenses. It is administered by an executor of your choice after your death.

● *Savings account designated for funeral expenses.* To be sure that funds will not be frozen at the time of your death, it may become necessary to open the account in the name of a trusted family member or friend.

● *Other sources of financial assistance.* Social Security currently makes burial payments of $255 to relatives of persons who have paid sufficiently into the system. The Veterans Administration pays up to $450 toward all funeral and burial expenses of veterans who served their country during wartime.

Since more consumers began demanding to know funeral expenses ahead of time—and the FTC began to regulate the system—there have been fewer disputes with funeral directors. However, if problems arise, contact the Conference of Funeral Service Examining Boards, P.O. Box 497, Washington, IN 47501; 812-254-7887.

TEST YOUR FINANCIAL PLANNING SKILL
■ ■ ■ ■ ■

How good are you as a financial planner? The International Association for Financial Planning (IAFP), Atlanta, GA, has developed a quick quiz to help you check your standing.

For each question, pick the appropriate response from the list below. To determine your "Financial Planning Quotient," add up the numerical values for your answers and refer to the ratings at the end of the quiz.

5—Yes (always, absolutely)

4—Pretty much (generally, most of the time)

3—Somewhat (about half the time, 50% of the way)

2—Not really (rarely, not very good)

1—No (not at all, never)

☐ Do you have a budget and do you stick to it?

☐ Do you have money left over every month after expenses?

☐ Have you adequately planned the

funding of your child's education?

☐ Will your current savings plan provide you with a comfortable retirement?

☐ Do you have enough insurance set aside for your family in case of a life or health crisis?

☐ Are you satisfied with your net worth?

☐ Are your investments diversified?

☐ Do your finances permit an annual family vacation?

HOW DO YOU RATE?

34–40: You're an excellent planner.

29–33: You're on the right track, but there's room for improvement.

21–28: You need financial help.

15–20: You've got problems that need early attention.

14 or less: You're in urgent need of help; a crisis is impending.

Chapter 3

INSURANCE

INSURANCE SHOPPING FOR EXECUTIVES

▪ ▪ ▪ ▪ ▪

Many executives spend at least a few thousand dollars a year for various kinds of insurance without realizing that it is possible to improve coverage while cutting premiums.

POINTS TO CONSIDER

• **Buy comprehensive coverage only.** Spend your money on policies providing broad coverage and stay away from narrow policies—cancer policies, car rental, etc.

• **Take the biggest deductibles you can afford.** Rather than trying to protect against all financial loss, protect yourself only against what you cannot afford. Premiums drop sharply when you accept larger deductibles.

• **Find out about discounts.** Insurers offer these with every kind of coverage, but some provide more than others.

• **Shop for the best coverage.** Premiums for identical coverage from reputable insurers vary widely—sometimes by more than 100%.

RECOMMENDATION:

Before buying, look at your present coverage. You probably have good health insurance provided by your employer.

GUIDELINES FOR BUYING DIFFERENT COVERAGES

▪ **Life insurance.** This is designed to protect your dependents from financial hardship in case of your untimely death. You should have enough coverage to maintain their standard of living or meet major expenses, but not to provide more than they would really need. You probably don't require any coverage if you have no dependents. Rather than basing the amount you buy on your annual salary, determine the future income needs of your dependents. Your life insurance requirements generally will decrease as you age.

• Term insurance is by far the least expensive form of life coverage available, even though the cost of premiums may rise each year. Other kinds of coverage, such as whole life, universal life or adjustable life, have various investment and tax deferral features at extra expense.

■ **Disability.** Many employees do not get this coverage as a fringe benefit. Yet it is essential because an executive between ages 35 and 65 is far more likely to suffer a work-preventing disability than to die prematurely. Social Security disability benefits are payable only if you cannot do any work at all. And your employer's medical plan may cover only the first one to three months that you are out of work.

• Experts suggest getting long-term coverage that pays at least 60% of your income (perhaps up to a specific maximum). The policy should pay off as long as you cannot return to your own occupation. It should also be guaranteed renewable and noncancelable.

■ **Homeowners.** You need coverage for at least 80% of your home's replacement value to get full reimbursement for a lesser loss. One hundred percent coverage can be costly, considering that total losses are rare. Nevertheless, you may want full replacement value coverage on the contents of your home. The standard policy covers only actual cash value, which typically is far less.

• Since insurers set limits on specific categories of destroyed or stolen valuables, consider buying a separate rider for furs or jewelry, for example.

• Liability coverage is becoming increasingly necessary. Most homeowners policies include up to $100,000 of coverage. But a $300,000 limit costs only a few dollars more annually. (For more specifics, see "Get more household coverage for your money," page 304.)

■ **Auto.** Liability is the most important part of this coverage: you need to protect your assets. That probably means getting coverage of at least $100,000 for injuries to one person in an accident, $300,000 for all injuries in an accident and $50,000 for property damage.

• You might cut your collision and comprehensive coverage—or drop them entirely if your car is more than five years old. Even with a total loss, your insurer would pay no more than the car's market value, which could be low.

■ **Umbrella liability.** Such a policy provides protection past the limits of your homeowner and auto policies. You can usually get $1 million of coverage (the minimum) for under $125. However, some insurers give you this only if you buy other coverage from them.

SAVE BIG ON LIFE INSURANCE WITH LOW-LOAD COVERAGE
• • • • •

Knowing what type of insurance you want before you buy can save you a bundle and get you a better policy.

Insurers increasingly are offering low-load coverage that reflects savings in marketing and sales expenses. To get these bargains, however, you must contact the company yourself and decide which policy is best for you.

BENEFITS OF DIRECT BUYING

• **Choice without bias.** Insurance salespeople have an inherent conflict of interest. Their livelihood depends solely on selling a line of products, some of which generate higher commissions than others. Most salespeople are ethical and professional. But they must weigh these virtues against their income needs, which sometimes get higher priority than customers' needs.

• **Better insurance or lower cost.** Your dollar savings will depend on the type of coverage you buy and how much. On cash-value life policies, commissions can represent the first few years of premiums— $1,500 on a $500 annual outlay, say. Or, for the same dollar amount, you can buy more coverage.

CAUTION

Just because a policy is sold directly— that is, not by an agent—doesn't automatically mean it's cheaper or of better quality than a regular policy. Although the average low-load policy is a better choice, inferior low-loads do exist. In general, insurance advertised on television or via direct mail is more expensive than, and/or inferior to, a comparable agent-sold policy. In addition, some insurers merely replace the load with surrender (back-end) or other charges.

• **Cancellation advantage.** When insurers set premium rates on agent-sold policies, they assume that about 15% of their customers will cancel after the first year, and 40% or so within five years. However, since none of the low-load premium goes to pay a commission, policyholders get back most of their money if they cancel in the first few years. With interest-paying policies, they may even get more than they paid.

LOW-LOAD OPTIONS

Eight national companies offer good low-load insurance policies.

• *Term life insurance.* This offers the smallest savings over commissioned policies. Most regular insurance companies consider term policies a loss leader, designed to draw customers so that they can market high-profit products. Three insurers offer low-load term: American Life of New York (212-581-1200), Lincoln Benefit (1-800-525-9287) and USAA (1-800-531-8000).

• *Cash-value insurance.* Savings on this expensive coverage can be substantial. Companies offering fixed-interest policies: American Life of New York, Ameritas (1-800-255-9678), Colonial Penn (215-988-8000), Essex (201-325-3655), John Alden (813-874-5662), Lincoln Benefit and USAA.

• *Annuities.* Fidelity Investments (1-800-343-3079) sells variable policies (including single-premium) that enable you to invest your cash value in mutual funds. Essex, John Alden, Lincoln Benefit and USAA offer fixed-rate annuities.

R E C O M M E N D A T I O N :

Most of these companies also offer agent-sold policies. When you contact them, specify that you want low-load.

WHERE TO GET INSURANCE ADVICE

If you're buying a lot of coverage, consider hiring an independent insurance agent as a consultant—not to sell it, but to advise which low-loads are best for you. A good consultant will charge $50–$100 an hour, but you'll be amortizing this expense over many years of lower premiums.

Independent agents are listed in the *Yellow Pages*. Ask friends or a financial advisor for recommendations. A financial planner or accountant may also be qualified to help.

An excellent book is *The Individual Investor's Guide to Low-Load Insurance Products*, by Glenn Daily (International Publishing Corp., 625 North Michigan Ave., Chicago, IL 60611, 1990; $19.95).

FINDING THE BEST DEAL IN TERM INSURANCE
. . . . .

Premiums on whole-life insurance and its variations are notorious for wide price differences. Even premiums on plain-vanilla term coverage carry a wide range of prices, despite relatively few and minor differences among products.

Term insurance provides simple death protection at the lowest cost. Premiums increase as you get older, but by the time they exceed the cost of other kinds of life coverage, your insurance needs probably will have declined substantially.

Term premiums can vary by 300% or more because companies adjust their rates based on their own mortality experience, investment income, expenses and other factors. And insurers often compete aggressively for only certain segments of the market. For example, a company with low rates for smokers is unlikely to have a good deal for nonsmokers.

SAVING MONEY ON POLICIES

• **Compare premiums.** Look beyond the first-year cost. If you expect to keep the policy for a long time, especially if you're concerned about your present or future health, look at the total estimated premium for that period. Many insurers will provide a projection of future premiums based on their current experience. A cost of $1,000 of coverage, which declines as the amount of coverage increases, is the key measure.

However, the most competitively priced policies generally carry a guaranteed rate for one, three or five years. If you're in good health and don't anticipate medical problems, your best bet may be to get a good rate for a few years, then go shopping again.

• *Look at features.* Any term policy you buy should be renewable, meaning you are guaranteed continuing coverage, regardless of health, until age 65 or older. You may also want a policy that is convertible to other types of insurance should your needs change.

• *Other factors to consider.* For an additional fee, insurers offer a waiver of premium. This enables you to retain coverage even if you become disabled and cannot work. But in most cases, you'll do better to spend the money on adequate disability insurance that covers all your needs.

Some policies pay dividends, which are really a partial refund of your premiums, if the company's experience, expenses and investment returns meet projections. Since premiums on these participating policies typically are higher than on nonparticipating policies, factor in the effect of dividends on the premium only if the company has a long dividend-paying history.

• **Check out the insurer.** The stability of the insurer is also important. A company's financial problems could cause worries about your coverage or delays in settling claims. *Best's Insurance Reports*, published by A.M. Best, contains ratings of insurers, which you can also get from individual insurers or agents. Buy only from one of the many companies rated A-plus or A.

• **Shop around for the best price.** A good starting point is companies that usually charge highly competitive rates such as the following five: Bankers National Life (201-267-4000), Jackson National (517-394-3400), Lincoln Benefit (402-475-4061), Midland Mutual (614-228-2001) and Old Line Life (414-271-2820).

In addition, five rate-screening services can be a big help in getting the best deal. Insurance Information (1-800-472-5800) doesn't sell insurance, but it will refund its $50 fee if you don't save that much the first year. Instead of charging a fee, the other four receive a commission if you buy: InsuranceQuote (1-800-972-1104), LifeQuote (1-800-521-7873, 1-800-843-1768 in FL), SelectQuote (1-800-343-1985) and TermQuote (1-800-444-8376).

WHEN TO SWITCH FROM TERM TO WHOLE LIFE

· · · · ·

If you are approaching age 50 with term life insurance, you may want to switch to a whole life policy. It's worth considering if you expect to need life insurance for at least 15 years and you can afford to pay a higher premium now.

FACTS ABOUT WHOLE LIFE

Whole life, the most common form of cash-value insurance, is also a tax-shelter investment. You generate income at a fixed interest rate on a tax-free basis. You pay income tax on these cash-value earnings only if and when you finally decide to cash in the policy.

You can also borrow against the policy's cash value without paying tax. Since you needn't repay the loan, you're getting what amounts to a tax-free withdrawal. The death benefit may be reduced, however. Since the cash value reverts to the insurer at your death, you should plan on using this asset while you're alive.

ADVANTAGES OF WHOLE-LIFE COVERAGE

Most term policies allow you to switch to one of the insurer's whole-life products without a medical checkup. Once you change, whole-life policies, unlike term, usually don't require periodic medical exams unless you want to increase your coverage.

Unlike term, whose cost rises as you age, a whole-life policy carries a fixed annual premium. The younger you are when you sign up, the lower the premium. Most whole-life policies pay dividends, which are refunds of premiums and are based on the insurer's investment and actuarial results.

Most policyholders pay annual premiums for as long as they hold the policy.

◆ ALTERNATIVE:

With a vanishing premium policy, you make larger annual payments that stop after several years. By paying more now, while you can afford it, you finish your payments well before you retire. The estimated dividends cover future premiums while adding to your cash value.

SAVING MONEY WITH WHOLE LIFE

"Buy term and invest the difference" was long a financially shrewd life insurance strategy. Whole-life policies paid low dividends, and you were typically better off just stashing the savings from term coverage in a money market fund. In addition, term usually is the better buy when you're young because it's the cheaper way to provide death protection.

Now, despite higher initial premiums, the net long-term cost of a good whole-life policy usually is lower because you're salting away a modest portion of your assets for a steady return in a tax-deferred account.

The annual cost of term rises sharply from $300 or so for a $250,000 policy in your early 30s to roughly $700 at 45, $1,200 at 55 and perhaps $3,000 at 65. At 70, coverage may be unavailable, except as part of a group package. Whole life's appeal has risen in recent years because of major product improvements and tax law changes that cut back the tax benefits of other investment vehicles.

The break-even point—when the benefit of tax-free cash value accrual outweighs the liabilities of high policy premiums and company expenses—depends on each policy's cost, the whole-life policy's net interest rate and dividends, and your likely returns from investing the annual savings from term coverage. Your break-even point is likely to come between nine and 20 years. Then your cash value grows rapidly.

WILL YOU NEED ALL THAT LIFE INSURANCE WHEN IN YOUR 60s?

That depends on the number and ages of dependents who would suffer financially if you die, and on your other financial assets. Life insurance, unlike most other assets, can be easily kept out of your taxable estate; so your beneficiary would not be taxed on the proceeds.

RECOMMENDATION:
If your insurance needs will probably decline, switching to whole life isn't necessary. Stick with term coverage and look for a lower-cost policy every few years.

POINTS TO CONSIDER WHEN SHOPPING FOR A POLICY

• Company illustrations aren't guarantees. When you shop for a whole-life policy, agents will present computer-generated illustrations that project cash value, death benefit and surrender values over many years. These are based on various assumptions about interest rates, dividends and the insurer's expenses. You'll have to decide whether they're realistic or too optimistic.

● COMMON FALLACY:
Assuming that current trends will continue indefinitely, good investment results and major improvements in life expectancy may be less frequent in the future than in the recent past.

• The guaranteed interest rate and cash value growth—what the insurer says it will pay no matter what—and the "current" numbers, based on the various assumptions, can be widely different.

• Companies that have paid top dividends over the last 20 years (according to A.M. Best Co.)—a good indication of low-cost coverage—are Northwestern Mutual Life, State Farm Life, Guardian Life, Massachusetts Mutual Life, Central Life of Iowa, Principal Mutual Life, Phoenix Mutual Life, Home Life, Sun Life of Canada and Country Life. Any insurer you choose should have an A.M. Best rating of A+.

RECOMMENDATION:

Since costs vary widely, you should shop around for the best policy. Have different agents run illustrations using various assumptions about interest rates, dividends and policy charges.

UPDATE ON SINGLE-PREMIUM LIFE INSURANCE

• • • • •

While single-premium life insurance (SPLI) is no longer the tax shelter it once was—tax-free loans against policy accumulations are no longer allowed—SPLI still carries the benefits of long-term asset accumulation and family protection.

INTRODUCING THE MEC

There are two classes of life insurance for policies bought after June 20, 1988. One passes a "seven-pay" test: You can't pay premiums faster than you would to get a paid-up policy over seven years. This precludes a single, up-front investment, but you can take tax-free policy loans.

Policies where premiums are paid faster fall into the other class: modified endowment contracts (MECs). These include single-premium policies.

MECs are subject to the same distribution rules as annuities, so they're less liquid than seven-pay life insurance. They are also subject to LIFO (last-in, first-out) taxation on distributions (loans or withdrawals), to the extent of investment income. If you're under age 59 1/2, there's also a 10% penalty tax on income distributions.

Aside from the tougher distribution rules, MECs are treated like regular life insurance policies. Your premium compounds tax-free. If you die, your beneficiaries owe no income tax on the proceeds they receive.

EXAMPLE:

Suppose you buy an MEC for $50,000 at age 50. If your money earns 8% per year, your premium will grow to $100,000 of "cash value" in nine years. By the time you're 68, you'll have $200,000. Then, assuming a continuing 8% return, you could borrow $16,000 ($11,000 after tax) per year indefinitely. In addition, your heirs stand to receive $150,000 or more, exempt from income tax, at your death. Since policy loans reduce the death benefit, there will be more insurance coverage for your heirs if you don't need loans for your retirement.

IS AN MEC RIGHT FOR YOU?

It is if you meet these criteria:

• *You want life insurance.* Buy an MEC only if there's someone else you want to provide for. Some insurance companies offer MECs that insure both spouses.

RECOMMENDATION:

To shelter assets for your own retirement, you're better off with a deferred annuity. Despite the same tax deferral and distribution rules, the inside buildup is greater due to no insurance to pay for.

- *You can make a substantial investment.* You should invest at least $25,000 to enjoy real tax savings. Many MEC buyers invest $40,000 or more.
- *You have taxable investment income.* If you now hold CDs or taxable bonds and you don't need ready access to your money, you might want to invest through an MEC.

EXAMPLE:

You hold $40,000 in CDs and corporate bonds, probably earning over $3,000 in annual interest. Switching to an MEC will save you more than $1,000 a year in taxes because earnings won't be taxed until withdrawal. With tax-deferred compounding over the years, the difference can be considerable.

- *You're middle-aged or older.* The closer you are to age 59, the smaller your risk of incurring the 10% penalty tax. In either an MEC or seven-pay policy, you can choose a fixed return comparable to that of municipal bonds, with a big difference: Your return of principal is guaranteed, rather than risking loss of principal if interest rates rise.

Or you can choose variable life, with a choice of investment portfolios. There's no guaranteed return of principal, but the tax-free buildup can be greater with good funds.

RECOMMENDATION:

Choose a solid insurance company—one with an A.M. Best rating of A or A+. If you're shopping for a fixed-rate policy, ask what rates the insurer is now paying on older policies. For variable life, get the track record of the investment portfolios.

LIFE INSURANCE IN SICKNESS AND ESTATE PLANNING
· · · · ·

Traditionally, life insurance provides for a breadwinner's family in case of untimely death. Now, new types of life policies are being developed to meet other needs. One kind can help you pay for a dire illness. The other will help your heirs fend off the IRS.

TYPE #1: 'LIVING' INSURANCE

This coverage can pay off while you're still alive. Suppose you take out a $100,000 universal-life or whole-life policy with a living benefits rider. After a short waiting period, you may then have access to a chunk of the face value in case of a serious illness or a long nursing-home stay.

In contrast, borrowing from a regular cash-value life policy typically isn't feasible until the assets have built up over many years. Of course, tapping the death benefit early means your beneficiaries will collect less later. But premium costs are then reduced proportionately, and sometimes premium payments are waived.

■ **Coverage of specified illnesses.** If you suffer from certain designated conditions, such as heart attack, stroke, kidney failure, coronary bypass surgery or life-threatening cancer, you can typically collect 20%–30% of the policy's face value—or

$25,000 or so on a $100,000 policy—in a lump sum. In most cases, the money needn't be used for medical expenses; you can do whatever you want with it.

Two companies sell life insurance with catastrophic coverage: Jackson National Life (1-800-227-8755) and Transamerica Occidental Life (1-800-633-8584).

■ **Payment for nursing-home care.** In a typical life policy with this feature, you can tap 2% or so of the face value per month—$2,000 per month on a $100,000 policy, say.

▲ IMPORTANT:

Don't confuse this coverage with a regular long-term care policy, which pays only if you go into a nursing home. This is a lower-cost alternative, and your beneficiaries ultimately will collect whatever death benefit you don't take in advance.

Three companies selling life policies with nursing-home coverage: National Travelers Life (515-283-0101); First Penn-Pacific Life (1-800-323-1746), and ITT Life (1-800-541-6757).

■ **Benefits vs. costs.** Access to your own life insurance will cost you 5%–25% more than ordinary life coverage. Suppose you could buy a $100,000 universal life policy for $1,600 per year in premiums. A comparable policy with a "living benefits" feature might cost around $1,800.

• Your situation will determine whether the extra coverage is useful. These policies are worth a look if you're worried that medical problems could also endanger your financial health. But if you already have top-quality health and disability insurance, plus a large pool of liquid assets, you probably don't need it.

• Be sure to check the conditions of coverage carefully. For instance, some policies with nursing-home riders pay off only if you go directly from the hospital to a nursing home and/or the home provides skilled medical care, which you may not need.

• Shop carefully before you buy any life policy because prices and features vary widely.

What does the IRS think? Life insurance is the only way to pass money to heirs tax-free. The insurers say that pre-death payments, like payments from a health insurance plan, don't constitute taxable income. These policies are so new that the IRS hasn't issued any rulings yet.

TYPE #2: PREPAYING ESTATE TAXES AT A DISCOUNT

"Second-to-die" or "survivorship" life actually has been around since the 1950s. But recent tax law changes have boosted demand, and insurers have issued less expensive policies.

The twist here is that the policies don't pay off after you die. Instead, they insure two people and pay only after the second death. Usually, the policy insures a married couple, with the proceeds going to their children.

The main goal of second-to-die insurance is to pay estate taxes. Even with the best planning, a married couple with over $1.2 million will owe plenty.

While $1.2 million may sound like a lot, when you add up the value of your home, maybe a second home, personal property, retirement plans, investments and any business interests you own, you'll be surprised at the total.

SECTION · 4

EXAMPLE:
Suppose you estimate $2 million worth of assets. That leaves $800,000 exposed to taxes, and a likely estate tax bill—in cash—of $265,000 for your heirs to pay. In the case of a family business, a sale may be necessary just to pay the tax man. Enter second-to-die life. A 71-year-old man and his 62-year-old wife, for example, might want to reduce this tax burden on their children. They buy $300,000 of coverage for about $6,500 annually for eight or 10 years, until it's fully paid up.

■ **Avoid double taxation.** If not handled properly, the $300,000 life insurance proceeds will wind up in the estate of the second spouse to die. Instead of an $800,000 taxable estate and a $265,000 tax bill, the heirs might inherit a $1.1 million estate and a $385,000 estate tax bill. Even with the $300,000 cash from life insurance proceeds, there would be a large shortfall.

• Avoid this potential problem by getting the policy out of the parents' estate. The children can own it, and the parents might give them $6,500 per year to pay the premiums.

• Another possible solution is an irrevocable life insurance trust, which will hold the policy, collect the proceeds and provide funds to pay estate taxes. It's a complex, possibly costly, planning technique—you'll need to work with a good lawyer. Such trusts may appeal to parents who don't want their kids to have outright control of the life insurance policy.

Second-to-die life insurance is available from: The New England (1-800-343-7104); The Guardian (1-800-482-6474); and Phoenix Mutual Life (203-275-5000).

AVOID TAX ON GROUP-TERM LIFE

On the first $50,000 of group term life insurance provided by an employer, you needn't report the premium as taxable compensation. But group term above that amount is an expensive way to build your estate.

■ **REASON:**
The insurance protection's economic benefit is taxable—and based on an inflated government schedule.

EXAMPLE:
Suppose you're the 52-year-old owner of a company with a group-term plan. Your current benefit is $250,000, so you'll have to pay tax on $200,000 of protection. At age 52, each $1,000 of protection imputes income of $5.76, or $1,152 of additional taxable income. Yet at age 52, you could buy a $200,000 individual policy for about half that amount, assuming that you're in good health and insurable at standard rates.

OTHER WAYS TO AVOID EXCESS GROUP-TERM COVERAGE

• **Accidental death benefits** are not subject to the $50,000 limitation. Thus, an employer may provide coverage with travel life insurance, or with accident-and-health policies that include a special life insurance feature.

• **Executives' Death Benefit Only** (DBO) plans are nonqualified; so they

300

aren't subject to nondiscrimination rules, and the company can choose the participants. You avoid imputed income during your life. The company agrees to pay death benefits to a named beneficiary at your death.

Since this tax-deductible payment is taxable to the recipient, many companies "gross up" the payment so that the beneficiary receives the full aftertax amount. Most DBO plans are funded by company-owned life insurance.

RECOMMENDATION:

Consider strategies for particular assets in terms of their effect on your overall estate plan.

WHAT DEPOSIT INSURANCE REALLY COVERS

■ ■ ■ ■ ■

Just because accounts at your bank are insured up to $100,000, don't assume all your money is covered. Close inspection may reveal that it isn't.

FACTS ABOUT FDIC AND FSLIC

Insurance under the Federal Deposit Insurance Corp. and the Federal Savings & Loan Insurance Corp. covers all types of accounts, including checking, savings, certificates of deposit, money market and other accounts. You're covered for up to $100,000 in individual accounts, and up to another $100,000 for your portion of joint accounts. IRAs, Keoghs and trust accounts are considered separately.

EXAMPLE:

Suppose you had $100,000 in an individual account, a $100,000 account with your son, and a $100,000 account with your spouse—a total of $300,000. Technically, you would be insured for $200,000, your son for $50,000, and your spouse for $50,000. That's because owners of joint accounts are considered to be equal owners unless otherwise specified. All joint accounts owned by the same combination of individuals are added together and the *total* is insured for up to $100,000. If two people have a joint account with $130,000, each person is *not* insured for $65,000, but for $50,000 each, which means that $30,000 is uninsured.

WATCH THOSE JOINT ACCOUNTS

• **Checking/savings accounts.** If a husband and wife have two accounts, one checking and one savings, each with $100,000, they could not divide the two accounts, allotting $50,000 to each and come out with $100,000 each. Instead, when the same combination of people have an account or accounts, they are considered as one entity, just as an individual would be. Thus, the couple would only be insured for a total of $100,000.

• **IRA and Keogh accounts** are considered separately from regular accounts. However, the FDIC and FSLIC differ on whether such accounts are separate from each other. Check with your bank.

• **Trust accounts** are also handled separately. Such accounts are considered to be those of the beneficiaries, and are insured up to $100,000. However, all trust interests created by the same person in the same bank for the same beneficiary are lumped together for insurance purposes.

• **Testamentary accounts** which pass to a named beneficiary upon the death of the owner are insured separately as long as the beneficiary is a spouse, child or grandchild of the owner. If the beneficiary is someone other than those relatives, the funds would be added to other individual accounts of the owner.

If two people establish such an account, the money is insured up to $100,000 for each of them. So, you and your spouse could establish a testamentary account of $400,000 for your two children. You would be insured up to $100,000 for *each* child, as would your spouse, giving the account total coverage of the $400,000.

MEDIGAP: DO YOU REALLY NEED IT?

· · · · ·

"Medigap" policies are private, supplemental health-insurance policies for seniors that are designed to cover (1) much of the deductibles and copayments not covered by Medicare insurance, and (2) most Medicare-eligible expenses after Medicare's limits have been reached.

HOW MUCH HEALTH INSURANCE DO YOU NEED?

Many people end up with too much health insurance that they pay too much for.

RECOMMENDATION:
Buy one comprehensive policy rather than others with overlapping coverage.

FACTORS TO CHECK WHEN BUYING EXTRA COVERAGE

You should receive an explanation of the policy's benefits, limitations and exclusions and how they relate to Medicare. In addition, you should have the right to renew a policy automatically. Also check for:

• *The loss ratio.* This is the ratio of the policy's benefits to its premium. The higher the ratio, the more the company pays in benefits relative to the policy's cost. A loss ratio of at least 60% is required by law.

• *Preexisting condition exclusions.* These affect health problems for which you have received medical advice or treatment. The phrase "no medical examination required" doesn't exempt you from the rule. Medigap policies must pick up preexisting conditions after six months. Look for a policy that waives the condition or has a shorter waiting period.

• *Coverage of all Medicare deductibles and copayments* (possibly with a policy deductible of up to $200).

• *Benefit increases* that keep up with changes in Medicare charges.

• *A full refund if you're not satisfied* and you return the policy within 30 days.

FINDING AN INSURER

Listed below are 10 highly regarded Medigap insurers. To find which companies offer policies in your state, call your local Social Security office or write to the Health Insurance Association of America, P.O. Box 41455, Washington, DC 20018. Insurers usually offer more than one plan.

• Bankers Life and Casualty (1-800-777-5775).
• Colonial Penn (1-800-523-4000).
• Equitable Life and Casualty (1-800-633-3480).

- First National Life (1-800-289-3654).
- Golden Rule (317-297-4123).
- National Home Life (1-800-356-6271).
- Pioneer Life (1-800-950-0084).
- Prudential/AARP (1-800-523-5800).
- Pyramid Life (913-722-1110).
- Standard Life and Accident (405-232-5281).

EVEN PEOPLE WITH MEDICAL PROBLEMS CAN GET INSURANCE

Although you suffer from high blood pressure, heart problems, excess weight, diabetes or other medical problems, you can obtain life, health and disability insurance—often at standard premium rates or a modest markup:

• *Look for insurers who specialize in coverage for those with particular problems.* While a specialist might consider as a standard risk average blood pressure readings of 140/100 for a male aged 50–59 who is already taking medication, a general insurance company probably will view the same applicant as a high risk and tack on a high surcharge to its normal premium.

To find out which insurers handle coverage for particular medical problems, occupations or other special situations, you can order *Who Writes What in Life and Health Insurance* (1989 edition) for $18.95 from National Underwriter Co., 420 East 4th St., Cincinnati, OH 45202. Or you can ask the American Council of Life Insurance, 1001 Pennsylvania Ave., Washington, DC 20004-2599; 202-624-2000.

• *Buy additional group life insurance if it's available.* Some employers that provide group insurance as a fringe benefit allow employees to buy additional coverage. If you are a principal or key executive in a small corporation, you may be able to get a substantial amount of group coverage at a considerable saving. For example, a 10-employee corporation might get $250,000 of guaranteed issue (no medical exam or medical information required) per employee.

• *Accept a three-year "deductible."* Some companies offer up to $250,000 of individual coverage on a guaranteed-issue basis, with this proviso: If death occurs within the first three years, your beneficiary gets only the premiums paid plus interest. However, the full coverage takes effect if you live beyond that.

• *Buy a "rated" policy.* You'll pay extra premiums. But if you live for a certain time (15 or 20 years, for instance), you'll get that money back, albeit at no interest. For example, an executive with a heart condition pays a $5,000 yearly premium instead of the standard $2,500 for $100,000 of coverage. After 15 years, he gets a $37,500 refund.

• *Know how to pass an insurance medical exam.* A detailed exam is required for larger insurance amounts and/or older applicants. Getting "bad marks" can mean you'll have to pay a higher premium if you are accepted. Furthermore, the results are available to other insurers.

The best time and place to take a medical exam is a weekend morning at the doctor's office. Avoid taking it during a hectic business day or at your office. Prepare for the exam by cutting down on or eliminating drinking, smoking, coffee and high-cholesterol foods weeks in advance.

Don't be put off by an initial failure. When the doctor and equipment are different, a person can show radical differences from one medical exam to another.

RECOMMENDATION:
Submit a "John Doe" application. An experienced insurance agent may be able to submit a medical exam plus all other pertinent applicant information (except the name of the insured) to an insurance company underwriter with whom he has done substantial business. If the client is turned down, there is no unfavorable record.

GET MORE HOUSEHOLD COVERAGE FOR YOUR MONEY

• • • • •

Some insurers have introduced comprehensive policies that provide more coverage per dollar than if you add various riders to a standard policy.

REPLACEMENT-COST COVERAGE

Because of soaring property values over the years, your coverage generally should be based on replacement value—what it would cost to rebuild the home. Adding replacement-cost coverage to your policy guarantees the same materials and workmanship.

● ANOTHER OPTION:

Guaranteed replacement cost offers even more protection. The insurer agrees to rebuild your house even if the cost exceeds the dollar amount of your coverage. For that guarantee, though, you usually must buy the replacement-cost coverage the company specifies—$200,000 instead of the $170,000 you request, for instance.

OBSERVATION:
The value of land makes up a much higher percentage of home values than it used to. Since land needn't be insured, you should be able to lower the amount of guaranteed-replacement cost coverage by largely excluding the land value.

PROTECTING VALUABLES

Suppose your home doesn't warrant replacement-cost coverage, but your personal property does. With a typical policy, coverage on damaged or stolen personal property is limited to 50% or less of the coverage on your home, and is paid at "cash value"—replacement cost minus depreciation. What's more, set limits for specific types of objects typically are extremely low, such as $1,000 for jewelry and furs. Switching to replacement-cost coverage gives you a much higher overall personal property limit—at least $125,000, with higher limits on individual categories.

◆ ALTERNATIVE:

Personal articles coverage. You can boost coverage, either with a separate policy or as a rider to your basic policy, on individual categories such as art, antiques, jewelry, stamps, coins or a wine collection. Hard-to-replace objects require a property appraisal.

LIABILITY PROTECTION IS VITAL

Homeowners insurance covers personal liability, medical payments for injuries to others and damage to other people's property. It usually applies to family members living in your home, and typically up to $100,000. You should probably have considerably more coverage. Boosting it to $300,000 costs only a few dollars more annually. A separate umbrella liability policy provides coverage of $1 million and up, is relatively cheap and may be essential in your situation.

TOP-OF-THE-LINE POLICIES

If you own an expensive home and valuable personal property, you may want to obtain a comprehensive replacement-cost policy. This option provides features that either cost less than if you add them to a standard policy, or are otherwise unavailable. Your coverage automatically rises as the value of your home goes up, and these policies are easier to tailor to individual needs than are standard policies.

• *Other policy features:* Guaranteed replacement-cost coverage; up to 75% coverage on personal possessions with higher category limits; reimbursement without having to replace a damaged or stolen item; coverage for part-time business activity in the home, losses of computer software or damage from the backup of sewage and drains; and no limit on housing expenses if your home becomes uninhabitable. Some policies also include umbrella liability and auto coverage.

• *Some top-of-the-line policies:* Allstate Deluxe Plus, Chubb's Masterpiece, Continental's Link Plus, Fireman's Fund Prestige Plus and State Farm Homeowners Extra.

MAKE SURE YOU'RE GETTING THE MOST FOR YOUR PREMIUMS

• Analyze your home's construction and your possessions with your agent to see what types of coverage make the most sense.

• Buy all your policies from one good agent to get yourself thorough coverage at a price break, with little or no duplication.

• Boost your deductibles. On a $100,000 home, for example, an annual premium of $600 with a $100 deductible could be reduced about 10% with a $250 deductible and 20% with a $500 deductible.

• Ask about discounts for installation of locks, smoke alarms and other safety devices.

• Review your policy at least every three years to make sure it keeps up with the value of your house and its contents. You may need periodic appraisals of your valuables.

• Compare insurers' premiums every few years, even if you're happy with your current company. Prices vary widely even within the same locality.

O B S E R V A T I O N :

In one recent survey, price differences totaled up to $380 or 45% in individual cities among the five leading insurers: Aetna, Allstate, Nationwide, State Farm and Travelers.

LIGHTS! CAMERA! INSURANCE INVENTORY!

Most people know that they should keep an accurate inventory in case belongings are stolen, damaged or destroyed by fire. But that doesn't necessarily mean that they do it.

Many insurance agents distribute special inventory books or forms to clients who buy homeowners policies, and several computer software companies put out "home inventory" programs, organized by room, with blanks to insert descriptions of belongings and their worth. With either method, the problem of taking photographs still remains. Appraisers estimate that it may take thousands of snapshots to accurately document the entire contents of a typical home.

VIDEO YOUR VALUABLES

A quick and easy way to document your belongings is to videotape them. Take the following steps:

• *Do a complete pan of all rooms, plus the grounds, garage, etc.* This helps to prove the caliber and style of the home itself (e.g., expensive wallpaper, rugs, books, artwork, landscaping, etc.).

• *Take close-ups of all valuable items.* You should tape artwork, jewelry, antiques, etc. Remember, however, that you'll also need appraisals of such possessions. A videotape alone won't be acceptable for insurance companies should losses occur.

• *Zoom in on serial numbers.* These provide positive identification if thieves try to resell such items as televisions and stereos.

• *Record an audio commentary.* As you photograph, describe details about objects that might not be apparent from pictures.

If the idea of making your own video inventory does not appeal to you, you can hire a video company to do it for you.

▲ C O S T :

$100–$225, depending on the size and contents of your home. Ask your insurance agent to recommend such a service. If you want to do your own taping, but don't have a video camera, rent one.

CAUTION

Don't take an unknown video maker you find in the *Yellow Pages* on a guided tour of your home.

Last, but certainly important, store your inventory videotape in a safe place, such as a locked file cabinet at your office or in a bank's safety deposit box. And be sure to include a snapshot of the video camera if it's your own.

O B S E R V A T I O N :

"Video documentation is most useful when there is a partial loss of items, not total destruction of the home and its contents," says Ken Olsen, vice president and general manager of the Forsythe Insurance Agency in Lincoln, NB. "Say you report a robbery and list all of the items stolen. Then, six months later, you discover that the family silver and your electric power drill are also missing. The video can prove that you had the items before the robbery, and it can also act as a checklist you can use to check for things that wouldn't be immediately missed."

Chapter 4

INVESTMENTS

HOW TO SPOT INVESTMENT POTENTIAL

• • • • •

Every day, just driving to work, you may look with only passive interest at new retail outlets that represent a small new chain with a hot concept. You may stop for a sandwich at a new fast-food business that's destined for big things.

People in Washington, DC still remember when Willard Marriott set up a small root beer bar and began to expand it rapidly into the hotel/restaurant giant it became.

TALK TO 'INSIDE-OUTSIDERS'

If you're serious about finding new opportunities, make it a point to talk with as many leading people in your area as you can contact about it.

• *Your own banker* often knows how certain new ventures are doing, and perhaps is even helping to finance them. He or she probably knows a lot about how they manage their financial affairs.

Without the slightest impropriety, the banker can say, "I'm very impressed with these fellows who've started A-to-Z Data." Or if you bring up a name that the banker thinks poorly of, you may get just a shrug to let you draw your own conclusions of his personal opinion.

• *Your lawyer, your accountant* or even a real estate broker you know can often pass along names and ideas that spark thoughts in your mind. Even if they don't prove to be of direct value, they may mention someone else who you might possibly discover will be very useful.

HOW TO CHECK OUT INVESTMENT IDEAS

Your stockbroker's office has directories that may include basic facts about the companies you are interested in. If the firms are too small to be on those pages, your broker can usually call on someone who keeps tabs on the so-called "pink sheet" stocks—usually smaller stocks traded over-the-counter.

By talking with other brokerage houses that actually make a market in the particular stocks you're asking about, you can often find someone who has followed those companies closely.

CAUTION

Brokers who have this kind of special interest in certain firms may have their own reasons for wanting to see the stocks rise. So listen for any information they have, but don't be panicked into buying hurriedly by any glowing talk of a last-chance opportunity.

TEST IT OUT YOURSELF

If the firm is in a consumer line, try its product. Eat at the new restaurant chain, shop in the new retail chain, buy the mouthwash, the small appliance or whatever it sells to the public.

If it appeals to you, it has a good chance of winning other followers. Your early enthusiasm can often be an unconscious forecast of how well it will succeed. Just be a little more conscious about it, and you may find yourself with a low-priced foothold in a surging enterprise.

WINNING BIG WITH SMALL STOCKS

Investing in lower-priced stocks can build your wealth much faster than the blue-chip route. The risk is a trifle higher, while the reward can be much greater.

This small-stock phenomenon was found by academic researchers some years ago, but got scant attention because of its scholarly background. Now some savvy Wall Streeters see it as a bonanza.

The principle is this: In a falling market, stocks priced at $10 to $20 a share drop only 7% more than the biggies. But in bullish times, they rise from 2 $1/2$ to 4 times as fast.

■ REASONS:

One hot new product or patent makes little impact on a giant company's stock, but it can double a small stock. The smalls usually get less government interference. And it is easier, marketwise, for a $15 issue to hit 60 than for a $150 stock to climb to 600.

As a result, investors who consider themselves "conservative" because they stick to the higher-priced issues are less prudent than they think.

PRACTICAL POINTERS

• There are various ways to define "small." It can be small capitalization, small company size, or just a low-priced stock. All three usually go together, and each method of selection works well if you stick to it and don't bail out when the smalls lag for a time. Over a recent 15-year span, $10,000 invested in a small-stock index would have become $132,000—three times the S&P Index rise in that period.

OBSERVATION:

You have to be well diversified for the idea to work. Otherwise, you may wind up owning two or three cheap stocks that stay in the basement. If you don't have the time and capital to pick 50 companies with low-priced shares, look at mutual funds. Several mutual funds are building their programs on this idea, some of them basing their holdings almost entirely on it. Others have 50% to 70% in small stocks—and are among the leaders in the industry. Ask your stockbroker for prospectuses that will identify the ones with that philosophy.

OTC STOCKS ARE WORTH CHECKING OUT

■   ■   ■   ■   ■

Checking out some sparsely traded over-the-counter (OTC) stocks is like digging for a well-buried treasure—tough but very lucrative.

Such stocks never appear in the daily newspaper listings. Instead, you must look in the batch of "pink sheets," so-called because of their color, that brokers keep.

Included there are some closely held firms that are seldom traded. They range in price from pennies to thousands of dollars per share. They have one characteristic in common: a scarcity of information about them.

Obviously, this can be treacherous, because a sick situation may be totally hidden. But it can also be very rewarding, if you're able to learn the facts behind the facade.

EXAMPLE:
A new product, a merger or some other great development may be about to triple the stock's value, and only the secrecy has kept the shares from soaring.

If you have time to put extra effort into your investment activities, it can be worth your while to do some digging.

HOW TO BEGIN

• Start by finding a broker who has the interest and the flair for smoking out hidden situations and tell him to keep you posted on anything he gets wind of.

• When you get a likely prospect, gather all the facts you can from the corporate directories in the broker's office (probably not much), call the company's officers and try to sense what might lie behind their evasive answers.

• Ask some of your business contacts, such as your bank, financier, lawyer, CPA, etc., whether they have any clues to the inside facts. This approach works especially well in learning about a company in your own locality.

• Additional pointers on the subject can be found in the book: *Trading Stocks on the Over-the-Counter Market*, from the New York Institute of Finance, Two Broadway, 5th Floor, New York, NY 10004 (January 1989; $21.50). The institute also publishes *Trading in Options on Futures* (February 1990; $34.95), and *The Affluent Investor: Investment Strategies for All Markets* (April 1990; $24.95).

INVESTING FOR VALUE EARNS STOCK PROFITS

· · · · ·

Can you make money in a market that high-roller institutions and fast-gun speculators have turned into a frenzied financial craps shoot?

Yes, if you can be an investor instead of a speculator. An investor is in the market for the long haul. Thus, if a company's fundamentals are right, it can make sense to buy even when you think the market may be in for a decline. That's provided you have the stomach and the patience to wait out short-term price drops.

▲ FACT:

Over the long term, stocks with a low price/earnings ratio tend to outperform those with a high p/e. According to one study, 80% of low p/e stocks have scored better than average returns.

When owners of high p/e stocks grow disenchanted with performance, they quickly dump them, dropping the prices sharply. With low p/e stocks, the first solid indicator of better earnings tends to force a sharp upswing in price.

WHERE TO LOOK

• Consider investing in stocks with a conservative 5–10 p/e ratio, in well-managed, noncyclical companies. Look for a consistent history of rising or constant dividends long term, debt of less than 35% of capitalization and plenty of depreciation write-offs, among others.

• Check out companies that aren't in the Dow Jones Industrial Average, whose individual stock prices are constantly twisted and prodded out of shape by the gamblers.

• Look in your own area as well as elsewhere for solid companies that trade only on regional exchanges. Cosmetics companies, for instance, tend to hold up well in hard times. Well-run utilities can provide safety, income and growth.

HOW YOU CAN PROFIT FROM A CHANGING AMERICA

· · · · ·

A dramatic shift in the U.S. population leading up to the year 2000 and beyond will directly influence your investments in the 1990s. You can make big money if you choose, but ignore this demographic reality at your peril.

THE AGING POPULATION

The baby-boom generation, far and away the most important force in the country, is getting older. The 76 million babies born from 1946 to 1964 now account for almost one-third of the U.S. population.

By the year 2000, the 35–54 age group will climb 40% from 1987, the U.S. Census Bureau estimates. The 45–54 group will jump 56% and the 35–44 group 29%. Also to rise dramatically is the number of people over 75—up 40%, with a 62% gain among those 85 or older.

Younger age groups, though, will actually decline in number because overall population growth is currently just 1% a year and slowing. The under-25 age group will fall 17% and the 25–34 group, 15%. There are already more people over 65 than there are teenagers.

WHAT THESE CHANGES MEAN

- The buying power of those aged 35–54—years of peak earnings—will soar an estimated 70%. The affluent 55–74 age group, while growing just 5%, will see a 40% hike in discretionary income.
- More Americans than in the past will be saving for their children's college educations and their own retirements.
- Overall, Americans will probably spend more time at home and traveling, and less time in fancy restaurants.
- We'll also see expanding markets for products and services for senior citizens.
- Bond yields will tumble as Americans save and invest for income. As the ratio of young buyers to older savers continues to drop, so too will consumer spending growth and demand for consumer credit. Inflation will remain low to moderate.

The increasing realization by investors that the long-term interest-rate trend is down could set off a scramble to lock in rates on long-term Treasury bonds, which cannot be called away by their issuers when rates drop. Yields on 30-year Treasury bonds could fall to 5% by 1993. A 9% T-bond due in 20 years would then appreciate 50% or so, plus interest payments.

WHERE TO PUT YOUR MONEY

Companies with solid market niches in growth industries should prosper from the changing population mix in the 1990s. Look at these industries:

- *Financial services.* As the 35–54 group expands, it will spend more on annuities, life insurance, mutual funds and other financial products.
- *Vacation travel.* The 35–54 group travels the most and the 55–64 group takes the longest trips.
- *Home furnishings.* Even after baby boomers stop buying homes, they'll be remodeling and redecorating them.
- *Health care.* Probable growth areas include drug manufacturers and drug wholesalers. Also consider drugstore chains, vitamin/health-food retailers, medical product suppliers, and home and health-care service.
- *Education and vocational training.* More people will retire than enter the work force. Businesses will need more employee training to alleviate the shortage, especially in low-paying, labor-intensive industries.

REAL ESTATE OPPORTUNITIES

Home prices generally will climb at a slower rate than in the 1970s and 1980s. Most baby boomers have already bought homes, and the baby-bust group following them is much smaller. But look for a boom in vacation homes as aging baby boomers hit the prime buying age.

Fast-growth areas will see higher home prices too. California, Texas and Florida will gain the most new residents by the year 2000, accounting for more than half of the nation's total population increase. In Florida alone, the likely population gain in the 1990s will be a stunning 58%—from retirees and from younger people who can't afford housing in the Northeast.

● BEFORE INVESTING:

Demographic investing is strictly a long-term strategy. And predictions involving spending, saving and investment habits aren't cast in stone. Anything could change the expected patterns, especially a major economic event like the energy crisis of the 1970s. Remember that even a company in the right place at the right time may be dragged down by inferior products or services.

STICK WITH LOW-COST MUTUAL FUNDS

. . . . .

The best mutual funds for you are those that match your investment objectives, are managed by top pros with a good long-term record, and are cheap to buy and hold.

In anything less than a roaring bull market, a fund's costs can make quite a difference in your investment return. In a lackluster market and over the long run, the fund fees you pay may be surprisingly high. Since no fund can guarantee what performance it will deliver, it's up to you to keep your costs down.

The confusing combination of fees can leave you vulnerable to getting your pocket picked. Many funds charge front-end loads of 1%–8.5%, and some carry back-end loads or sliding redemption charges. All funds charge an annual management fee, usually ranging from 0.05% to 2% of fund assets, that lowers your shares' net asset value. If a fund has a 12b-1 plan, a portion of assets—usually 1% or less—goes toward marketing and promotion expenses. Both management and 12b-1 fees can climb with fund assets.

FACTS ABOUT NO-LOAD AND LOW-LOAD FUNDS

As a rule, no-load funds with low annual fees are your best buy, followed by low-load funds.

■ REASONS:

Up-front charges reduce your investment at the outset. But even no-load funds can take a good cut of your profits.

EXAMPLE:

You invest $10,000 in a no-load (no sales charge) fund with an annual management fee of 1%, a 12b-1 marketing fee of 1% per year and a redemption charge of 4% after three years. If the fund appreciates 10% annually and you sell out then, total expenses will cut your gross profit by 35%—from $3,310 to $2,162 before taxes.

What's more, net fund performance (after deducting all fees) is the key factor. A top fund may be worth a high load, while a no-load laggard with high annual fees is no bargain. What's more, full-load funds don't have 12b-1 plans, and sometimes have relatively low management fees.

▲ RULE OF THUMB:

If you expect to keep a fund for five years or less, bypassing the up-front load while paying annual fees (and possibly a redemption charge) usually costs less. But an up-front load usually is cheaper if you stay in the fund for many years.

FIGURING OUT THE ACTUAL COSTS

Analyzing a fund's fees is relatively easy to do. Funds must assemble the expense information in a table published in the prospectus. The table shows what all the fund's fees would add up to on a $1,000 investment over one, three, five and 10 years, assuming a 5% annual return and redemption at the end of each period.

In newspaper listings, *NL* in the pricing column means no front-end sales charge. A *p* next to the fund's name means it charges a yearly 12b-1 fee and an *r* stands for a redemption charge. Either a *t* or a *p* and *r* together mean both fees.

HOW TO LIGHTEN THE LOAD

If you own full-load funds, they usually offer several ways to cut your long-term investment expense. To qualify for a discount, you're usually allowed to include separate purchases by your spouse and children, as well as retirement and trust plans.

While a fund family may levy an 8.5% sales charge on purchases under $10,000, the fee might drop to 7.75% on the second $10,000, then gradually to 3.5% over $100,000 and 1% over $1 million.

Once you've paid the load, you can shift among the group's other funds at no additional cost. Most (not all) load funds levy no sales charge on reinvestment of interest, dividends and capital gains distributions.

A cumulative purchase privilege enables you to include the original cost or current net asset value (whichever is higher) of your fund shares. Suppose you've invested $100,000 in a family's funds over the years. If your shares are worth $225,000 and you invest another $25,000, the sales charge is based on $250,000.

STOCKS: KNOWING WHEN TO GET OUT

· · · · ·

It's all too evident by now that the stock market is capable of frighteningly fast declines. That means you may not be able to get out in time if you sense trouble. What's more, market risk clearly has risen as signs of a possible recession keep growing. Still, avoiding stocks altogether isn't the answer; their long-term record is too good.

■ **Ironclad rule #1: Cut losses and let profits run.** Avoiding big losses is essential if you want to build wealth at moderate risk.

■ **Ironclad rule #2: Forget about trying to sell at the top.** It's better to get out early than run the risk of staying "married" to a tumbling stock, telling yourself it will "come back." A stock may go higher after you sell. If you're not a money manager whose livelihood depends on beating the averages, why take on unnecessary risk?

WHEN TO UNLOAD A STOCK

• **To keep your losses down.** Set a stop-loss point—a specific price at which your shares will be sold. Even though you may miss a rebound, it's safer to accept a small loss than to take the risk it will mount.

The stop price to set—10%–25% below the current price—depends on the stock's volatility, market conditions and what loss you can accept. Move up the stop as the stock rises.

• **Other unfavorable action in the stock.** One warning is when the stock lags behind others in its industry group, or the group falters. Another is if the stock falls below a major support level—one at which past declines have ended. Such stocks often tumble much lower.

Moving averages of stock prices help you stay attuned to the long-term trend and spot reversals. When a stock drops below a key moving average—such as a 39-week or 200-day average—it often enters a significant decline, especially if the moving average itself turns down.

• **When the stock rises to your target price.** Set a goal at which you will sell. Reexamine the company's prospects at that level, asking yourself if you would still buy the shares. If not, say good-bye.

If a stock has had two years of good appreciation, consider selling at least half your position. Also, sell and don't look back if a stock has shot up 50%–100% in a few months, especially if "everybody" is talking about it.

• **An expected favorable development occurs.** It may be a big earnings increase, a major new product or a takeover offer. Sell on the good news, or if the event occurs and the stock doesn't go up.

• **Significant deterioration in the company's prospects.** Watch out for shrinking market share, unit growth, profit margins or sales/earnings growth rate. In today's market, heavy debt is potentially a big negative. Also a sale candidate these days is the stock of a company whose profits start to fall short of analysts' projections; such surprises tend to repeat themselves.

• **When a stock's price/earnings ratio seems high.** Find out the average p/e ratio of the stock and its industry over the long term relative to the average for the Standard & Poor's 500. Suppose the stock historically has sold at a p/e 20% lower than the S&P average. If the S&P 500 carries a p/e of 12, you might sell when your shares' p/e reaches 10.

• **If you've found a better place to put the money.** Weed out laggards with lesser prospects because they'll be particularly vulnerable in a weak market. By reinvesting in a stock that seems undervalued, you may increase your profit potential while cutting your risk. But don't put off selling just because you don't know where to reinvest the money.

CAUTION

Investors often sell stocks for tax purposes. As a rule, your tax situation shouldn't dominate what's largely an investment decision.

FIND INVESTMENT OPPORTUNITIES WITH YOUR COMPUTER

■ ■ ■ ■ ■

Although profitable investing is pretty tough these days, there are money-making opportunities out there. Using computer software is a good way to find them.

▲ FACT:

Computers are becoming increasingly indispensable for investors who make their own investment decisions, spend several hours a week managing good-size portfolios—$50,000 or more, say—and/or are active traders.

WHAT'S OUT THERE

Some 300 software packages costing from $30 to $1,000 or more can give you quick access to a wealth of investment information, news and analysis. Software programs fall into five categories: financial databases, portfolio management, fundamental market analysis, technical analysis and trading.

• *On-line financial database.* Used with one or more other programs, this is your source of current and historical information—news items, prices, financial data, brokerage reports and much more on companies, industries, individual stocks and the financial markets. Each service offers different features.

Database usage charges vary depending on the program, how much you use it and when. Many services have monthly minimums. Get the information you need, store it in your computer and get off line quickly.

• CompuServe, 5000 Arlington Centre Blvd., P.O. Box 20212, Columbus, OH 43220; 1-800-848-8199, 614-457-8600 in OH.

• Dow Jones News/Retrieval, Dow Jones & Co., P.O. Box 300, Princeton, NJ 08543; 1-800-522-3567, 609-452-1511 in NJ.

• National Computer Network, 1929 North Harlem Avenue, Chicago, IL 60635; 312-427-5125.

• NewsNet, 945 Haverford Ave., Bryn Mawr, PA 19010; 1-800-345-1301, 215-527-8030 in PA.

• Telescan, 2900 Wilcrest, Suite 400, Houston, TX 77042; 713-952-1060.

• *Portfolio management.* These programs range from simple bookkeeping (not worth the expense) to ones that can sort your entries in various ways—by type of security, size, performance, industry group, etc.

● BEST BET:
Programs that provide portfolio rate of return vs. the broad market.

• *Dollars and Sense,* Monogram Software, Inc., 21821 Plummer St., Chatsworth, CA 91311; 818-700-6200.

• *Managing Your Money 4.0,* MECA Ventures, Inc., 327 Riverside Avenue, Westport, CT 06880; 203-226-2400.

• *Market Manager Plus 2.0,* Dow Jones & Co. (see above).

• *Fundamental analysis.* These programs help you evaluate companies and in-

dustries using such norms as return on equity, earnings growth, dividends, assets, debt and price/earnings ratios. You can screen lists of stocks for those that meet specific criteria you set. Most programs cover 1,000 to 6,000 companies, giving you flexibility in setting up screens and spreadsheet capacity.

• *Active Investor,* Jeffers Computerized Investor Center, P.O. Box 2105, Danville, CA 94526; 415-736-7670 in CA.

• *Market Microscope,* Dow Jones & Co. (see above).

• *Stockpak II,* Standard & Poor's Corp., 25 Broadway, New York, NY 10004; 212-208-8581 in NY.

• *Value/Screen II,* Value Line Software, 711 Third Avenue, New York, NY 10017; 1-800-654-0508, 212-687-3965 in NY.

• *Technical analysis.* This software focuses on market and individual securities' prices, volume, moving averages, indicators and other technical factors, presenting data in charts and graphs.

CAUTION

Avoid software that covers only individual stocks, not the broad market and investor sentiment.

• *CompuTrac,* CompuTrac, Inc., 1017 Pleasant Street, New Orleans, LA 70115; 1-800-535-7990, 504-895-1474 in LA.

• *Market Analyzer Plus,* Dow Jones & Co. (see above).

• *Technical Investor,* Savant Corp., 11211 Katy Freeway, Suite 250, Houston, TX 77079; 1-800-231-9900, 713-973-2400 in TX.

• *The discount connection.* Several discount brokers offer a trading service via personal computer. You have access to database, portfolio management and analysis programs; your computer places the order.

● LEADING SERVICES:

Fidelity Investments Express (1-800-225-1799), Quick & Reilly's Quick Way (1-800-634-6214), and Charles Schwab's Equalizer (1-800-431-3112).

BUYING SOFTWARE

Most software works with IBM, IBM-compatible and Apple personal computers, which cost $1,500 and up. Get as much computer memory as possible to handle the investment software, but you don't need state-of-the-art hardware. You'll need a modem ($150–$500) to tap into a database over telephone lines. The faster your modem, the lower the database access time. A printer ($400 or less) is necessary if you want paper copies of any information.

RECOMMENDATION:

Investment software runs from simple and inexpensive to complex and costly. Before buying, make sure the package can access a database, has the features you need and is easy enough to use. Can you modify or add programs to it? Does the manufacturer have a support system of people to answer customer questions?

WINNING WITH 'WASH SALES'

The "wash sale" rule was devised to protect the government and not the taxpayer, but there's a twist to its use that can work in your favor.

Under the rule you have to delay taking a deductible loss on securities, if you bought the same ones (or other securities substantially like them) within 30 days of that date.

You can take that loss only when this new purchase is liquidated. But this could be used to your advantage if you sell at a loss, then get new information and repurchase within 30 days after the sale.

> EXAMPLE:
> You hold 100 shares of ABC Data, now worth $2,600, down $1,200 from the $3,800 price you'd paid two years earlier. Your broker hears that a tender offer may send the stock higher, and you buy quickly at the $2,600 price. In two weeks, the stock goes up six points, and you sell the old shares at $3,200.

Since there's no difference between the old and new shares, this is like a gain of $600 on the new transaction. Yet there's no current tax liability, because the "wash sale" rule says the gain can't be recognized until the new shares are sold.

If you do sell a year later, your overall tax liability depends on where that second sale occurs. If it's at, say, $4,000, the tax man sees it this way: There was a previous gain of $600 and a gain of $200 on the original shares, for a total taxable profit of $800. Your tax cost has not been diminished, but deferred—the money stayed in your pocket longer.

WHAT YOU SHOULD KNOW ABOUT BOND YIELDS

Yields are the yardstick to use if you want to compare returns on several fixed-income bond investments.

TYPES OF YIELDS

■ **Coupon yield.** This is the stated interest rate, a percentage of par value. An 8% bond selling at par (face value) yields 8% and pays $80 annual interest ($1,000 × .08).

■ **Current yield.** This is the bond's fixed annual interest payment divided by the bond price. When you buy a bond at par ($1,000), its current yield equals its coupon yield—8%, say. As bond prices fluctuate because of interest-rate fluctuations and other market factors, the current yield does too. Thus, if you instead buy that 8% bond for $1,125 after rates drop, the current yield falls to 7.11% ($80 divided by $1,125), even though you receive the same income.

Conversely, if you bought the bond at a lower price—$900, say—after rates rise, you'd receive the same dollar amount of interest, but a higher current yield of 8.88%. Remember, though, that your yield is based on how much you paid for the bond, not the prices at which it later trades.

■ **Yield to maturity.** This is more useful because it combines coupon income with the premium or discount spread over the life of the bond. For the 8% bond selling for $1,125 (a premium above par), the yield to maturity is lower than the current yield because at maturity you will get back only $1,000 for the bond, not the $1,125 you paid. So you will suffer a capital loss. On a 20-year bond, for example, the yield to maturity is 6.94%. Here's how to calculate it:

1. Subtract par value ($1,000) from the purchase price ($1,125). Total: $125.

2. Divide $125 by the maturity (20 years). Result: $6.25.

3. Subtract $6.25 from annual interest ($80). Result: $73.75.

4. Add par value ($1,000) to the purchase price ($1,125). Result: $2,125.

5. Divide $2,125 by 2: $1,062.50.

6. Divide $73.75 (from Step 3) by $1,062.50. Result: 6.94%.

To calculate yield to maturity for a bond selling at a discount, or at less than par, subtract the purchase price from the par value in Step 1. In Step 3, add the result from Step 2 to the annual interest. The other steps remain the same. Thus, if you bought the bond above for $900, its yield to maturity would be 8.94%.

■ **Yield to call.** This is important if you buy corporates or municipals that trade at a premium and are callable.

Most are callable: The issuer may retire them before their maturity date, generally after a specified number of years, by paying either par value or a stated premium above par. Issuers usually call high-coupon bonds when rates drop so they can issue new bonds at the lower rates. A bond call shortens its maturity, so your yield to maturity on a premium bond declines.

To calculate what you'll earn if the bond is called, use the number of years after which the bond can be called in Step 2 instead of the actual maturity. Thus, if the premium bond in the example is callable after 10 years, your yield to call is only 6.35%.

RECOMMENDATION:
Be sure you understand what rate of return you can expect on your bonds.

FINDING A QUALITY BOND FUND

A bond fund or a fixed-income fund sounds so solid it overrules the usual forms of analysis. If an investor finds that one bond fund yields 8% and another, 12%, he may see little sense in considering the former.

◆ PROBLEM

There can be a great difference in the quality of the inventory of bonds in each case. A fund that achieves a high yield while selecting mainly fine quality bonds is truly doing a great job. But if the cash payout is achieved by accumulating junk, it is no great financial feat—and it will probably damage you in the end.

SPOTTING THE DIFFERENCE

The way to tell the quality of a fund's bonds without spending endless hours in studying or becoming a do-it-yourself manager is to look at its total return. That means counting not only the income provided by the fund, but also the changes in price of the fund's holdings.

● GOOD NEWS:

You don't have to figure that for yourself. Just call the toll-free numbers of the funds you want to compare and ask each one its current yield and its total return over a five-year period.

If you call some of the funds with fancy yield figures, you may learn that they had total returns of only 30% to 45% over five years. With a few, however, you'll find a total return over 100% in five years. A good many others will be in the 80% to 90% range.

◆ REMINDER:

The fund's bonds are your money, too. And the increase in their value is part of your profit. So never buy solely on the current yield. If the bonds aren't sound, the value of your investment could drop. As a result, your total return might be less than you'd get by investing in a fund with a somewhat lower initial yield.

PICKING THE BEST BOND FUND FOR YOU
▪ ▪ ▪ ▪ ▪

Put part of your investment capital into a bond fund and the managers will handle the details of picking the inventory.

The hard part is selecting the right fund in the first place, because you must have a clear idea of what the categories are and which funds excel whenever certain economic conditions prevail. There are zero bonds that pay no current income but guarantee a lump sum at a future time, and junk bonds that have a substantially higher yield than normal, but also a higher risk.

But what about the maturity dates of the bonds that each fund specializes in? It's important to be very clear on that before you choose.

LONG, SHORT AND INTERMEDIATE BOND FUNDS

● **Long-term bond funds** concentrate on bonds that have a maturity of from 10 to 30 years. In normal times, these give investors a higher return to repay them for the extra risk of betting on a longer leap into the unknown future.

But there are times when the Federal Reserve's tightening of money policy sends short-term rates abnormally high. Then three-month Treasury bills can actually yield more than 30-year Treasury bonds.

● **Intermediate-term bond funds** usually deal in maturities of three to 10 years. If interest rates rise, these can be hurt, but not as much as the long-term bonds. So the intermediates can be a good way to play safe.

● **Short-term bond funds** hold a portfolio of less than three years' maturity. They usually engage in more trading than the longer-term funds do, and so they go after a high level of current income. This is a conservative strategy that's particularly appealing when the economic crystal ball is cloudy.

BUILD YOUR STRATEGIES AROUND SOME BASICS

If you're convinced that interest rates are going to go higher, stay out of bonds because they could drop sharply in value.

If rates seem about to peak, the long-term bond funds have the best chance of gaining value for you as rates decline. But bear in mind that fear of inflation can play a part too. If that's a factor, the intermediate-term bonds are apt to outperform those that mature over a longer period.

If you want current income, however, the short-term bond portfolios usually offer your best chance of getting it steadily, with fewer and smaller swings.

HOW TO AVOID HASSLES WITH YOUR BROKER

· · · · ·

"The time to head off trouble with your stockbroker is at the beginning. Also in the middle and at the end."

That's the considered opinion of Hartley Bernstein, an attorney with the New York law firm of Brandeis, Bernstein, who specializes in representing investors in their many disputes with brokers.

Bernstein points out that most disputes are automatically subject to arbitration, in accordance with the agreement that you generally sign when you open a new account.

These agreements aren't always in your best interest, but you usually can't avoid them, because most brokerage firms won't open an account unless you do.

What you can do, however, is be alert to every word and act that takes place, so that you hold all the right cards, if you're unfortunate enough to get to the arbitration or litigation stage.

CHOOSING A BROKER

• **Be very cautious about selecting the broker who's right for your needs.** Be particularly wary of choosing someone who wants to put you into investments you're uncomfortable with.

• **Read every word of what you are given to sign.** It may look innocuous, but it won't seem so if a dispute arises.

• **Make sure that every piece of information and every number you give is exactly right.** Very often a broker or an office manager urges you to give slightly inflated figures on income, assets and net worth—all in order to get the account approved. Those involved may laugh it off at the time, but it won't be funny if trouble arises. Then it will come back to haunt you: You signed it, so you'll be in the wrong.

• **Read every piece of paper the brokerage firm sends you, such as confirmations of trades.** Some otherwise sensible businesspeople sometimes boast that they never open those broker's envelopes. They're very unwise on that score. If you find evidence of trades you never made, insist on instant corrections. If you meet resistance, go over the head of your broker to the office manager. If need be, go over the manager's head to the director of compliance. Any delay will be used to indicate that your negligence contributed to the problem.

• **Be equally careful with each monthly statement.** It has to be 100% right. If it's wrong, insist on having it fixed immediately.

• **If you find yourself doing something totally new, perhaps at the broker's suggestion, be very skeptical.**

EXAMPLE:

You may have been used to doing about ten stock trades per year. Suddenly, the broker's suggestion that you trade stock options has you making twenty trades a month. Maybe it's a perfectly sound technique to follow, but it's a different league. So before you even start, be sure you understand it thoroughly and can handle it.

RECOMMENDATION:

If a deal is offered you through the mail that either sours or seems suspicious, there's a special way to act on it: Send full details of the matter to the Chief Postal Inspector, U.S. Postal Service, 475 L'Enfant Plaza West, SW, Washington, DC 20260-2100. If the case seems urgent, call them at 202-268-4267.

USING A DISCOUNT BROKER

You can take advantage of the competition for retail brokerage commission dollars that has intensified in recent years.

• **Discount brokers have expanded,** and many investors have moved to mutual funds or the sidelines. The result: Overall commissions are low, and the discount rates charged by full-service brokers have widened to as much as 75%.

Inexpensive trading costs are the discounters' main selling point. But there's actually a wide spread in the bargain rates they charge you.

Most brokers set commissions based on the transaction's dollar amount, while others base their results on the number of shares traded. The latter method tends to boost the commission on a large number of low-priced shares.

RECOMMENDATION:

No single broker offers the cheapest fees for all kinds of trades you may wish to make. Review yours for a pattern in terms of shares/price or total dollar amount. Then determine which discounter is likely to offer you the best deal.

• **Commissions aren't the only factor distinguishing one broker from another.** Some discounters provide more beneficial services than others, such as IRA and Keogh plans, mutual funds and precious metals trading, and home brokerage via personal computer.

You may or may not want any of these extras. The one service you do want, however, is quick, accurate execution of your orders. If you don't get it, your loss will more than offset any commission advantage.

OBSERVATION:

All discounters carry at least the minimum account insurance from the Securities Investors Protection Corp., and some offer additional coverage. SIPC meets claims up to a $500,000 maximum (including $100,000 cash) and provides for account transfers from failed brokerages.

TREASURIES: SAFETY, LIQUIDITY AND TAX BREAKS

· · · · ·

Investors the world over consider the securities issued by the U.S. Treasury just about the safest investments available anywhere, a buffer against economic and governmental uncertainty.

That's because the interest rates they pay are attractive and they're backed by the "full faith and credit" of the United States. In other words, they're guaranteed 100% by Uncle Sam.

ADVANTAGES

• **You can buy and sell Treasuries virtually at will,** which isn't always true for other kinds of securities. So, you can stay agile by investing in short-term Treasuries or lock on to an attractive rate for a longer term.

• **You don't need a broker to buy one.** You can buy Treasuries through one of the 12 Federal Reserve banks, their 25 branches, or through the Bureau of Public Debt, an arm of the Treasury. Of course, if you wish, you can buy through a brokerage firm or commercial bank, which will charge a fee of $35–$50 per security.

If you think you may want to sell the securities before maturity, buying that way may be the more convenient way to go, because the transaction then can be handled quickly.

If you buy directly from the government and want to sell early, you'll have to transfer your securities to a broker or bank for sale in the open market.

• **For U.S. investors,** there's a little-noted feature that can give Treasuries a special shine: They're exempt from state and local taxes. Higher aftertax yields make them especially desirable if you live in a high-tax state, a category that more and more jurisdictions are falling into these days. That's because your aftertax yield can be substantially greater than for a fully taxable investment that pays a somewhat higher interest rate.

TYPES OF TREASURIES

• **Treasury bills,** so-called T-bills, are short-term investments sold at discount from face value with maturities of 13, 26, and 52 weeks. One drawback: The minimum face amount is $10,000.

• **Treasury notes** are sold in maturities ranging from two to 10 years and interest is paid every six months. You receive your principal when the note matures. Minimum investment is generally $5,000, although they're available in amounts as high as $1 million.

• **Treasury bonds** carry maturities of 10 to 30 years and pay interest every six months. They're issued in denominations of $1,000, $5,000, $10,000, $50,000 and up.

DEBT PREPAYMENT: A SAFE, HIGH-YIELDING INVESTMENT

· · · · ·

One type of investment, often overlooked, pays a higher yield than any good-quality, fixed-income vehicle available today. And there's absolutely no risk. This investment is called a debt prepayment.

The next time you think about rolling over a CD at 8% or so, think again. If you have debt outstanding, you may do better to pay it off if there are no serious prepayment penalties. In fact, paying off credit-card debt and lines of credit is just about the best investment you can make today.

If you haven't paid off your Visa or MasterCard balances, for example, you're likely paying 18% or more in annual interest. A few years ago, that interest was fully deductible. In the 50% tax bracket, an 18% credit-card loan cost you only 9%.

PAYING OFF CREDIT CARDS

In 1990, only 10% of your credit-card interest is deductible, and starting in 1991, you won't be able to deduct one cent. In such a situation, taking money from a CD and paying off your credit card balance will save you a great deal more a year (after taxes) than you'd earn on the CD.

PAYING OFF HOME MORTGAGES AND EQUITY LOANS

The case for prepaying credit-card debt is clear cut. With home mortgages, second mortgages and home equity loans, the answer is less sure because interest rates are lower and interest is fully deductible. Yet prepayment is still an attractive option in many cases.

O B S E R V A T I O N :
You can build wealth through home mortgage prepayment because it will speed your equity buildup. The higher the rate on your home loan and the lower your tax bracket, the greater the aftertax payoff from prepayments.

On even a 10% mortgage, your aftertax cost ranges from 6.0% (40% federal/state

bracket) to 7.2% (28%). That's better than earning 8% on a CD, where you'll net 4.8%–5.76%. Municipal bond yields may be comparable to what you'd earn from prepaying a home loan, but then you're exposed to investment risks.

On a 30-year, $100,000 mortgage at 10%, your monthly payment would be $878. Over 30 years, you'd pay a total of $316,080—$216,080 in interest. Suppose you make the equivalent of one extra mortgage payment per year. That is, you add about 8% to each monthly payment, which then rises to a total of $948. Now you can pay off your mortgage in 21 years instead of 30. By prepaying an extra $840 annually for 21 years, or $17,640, you wind up ahead of the game by $77,184 because your payments will total just $238,896.

You might start out prepaying $25 a month, for example, then raise it to $50 or $75 a month as your income increases. Another approach is to "double up": Add on a month's payment of principal to each regular payment. This is relatively painless early in a mortgage's life, when principal payments are small.

Prepaying a high-rate home equity loan almost always makes sense. For a mortgage, the key question is whether you'll stay in your home long enough to benefit from the accelerated equity buildup. If you move within five years, quicker payments won't make much difference.

CAUTION

A possible drawback to prepayments is the lack of liquidity: Once you've made them, it's hard to get your money back unless you refinance later. So don't prepay with money you might need later.

Most lenders now permit prepayments. Check with yours and ask about the best procedure to follow. Be sure, too, that your mortgage carries no prepayment penalty.

After you've made a few prepayments, ask for a statement to make sure that they have been reflected in your principal balance.

DISCOUNT MORTGAGES: HIGH YIELDS AND GOOD CASH FLOW

■ · ■ · ■

It would be tough to come up with any other moderate-risk investment that can pay yields even close to those you can get from discounted mortgages.

If you're already a real estate investor, you can draw on your experience when buying mortgages. Because of their bond-like qualities, mortgage investments can pay off even when property values aren't appreciating in your area. If you're not a property investor, this is a good way for you to start.

BEST BETS

Your safest investment is a first mortgage secured by a good, easily salable property, preferably a single-family house. Here, you can expect an annual yield of at least 13%–15% in today's market. A well-secured second mortgage is a moderate-risk investment on which you should be able to collect 15%–18% or more.

Getting your high yield has nothing to do with lending money at exorbitant interest rates to borrowers who likely will be unable to pay off the loan.

■ R E A S O N:

The loan has already been made; your yield comes partly from purchasing it at a discount.

EXAMPLE:

Suppose you can buy an existing $20,000 second mortgage from a home seller who took the loan back to sell his home. The borrower pays 12% annual interest with monthly payments of $286.94 for 10 years. Suppose you want to earn a 20% annual yield. You offer to buy the loan for whatever amount will result in that return on those monthly payments of principal and interest. In this case, it works out to $14,848. The best way to calculate a discounted mortgage's yield is on a financial calculator.

DISADVANTAGES OF MORTGAGE INVESTMENTS

• **Risk of foreclosure on a mortgage you hold.** But if you use your savvy and buy right, this is a big plus because you may acquire the underlying property at a huge discount.

• **You might not be able to shelter your high mortgage income from income tax.** You can do so only if you hold the paper in a retirement plan.

• **Lack of liquidity.** This means you'll have a hard time selling mortgages before maturity. However, you can borrow against mortgages you hold.

• **Good discounted mortgages can be hard to find at first.** This is mostly because relatively few people know about them, which actually gives you an edge.

FINDING DISCOUNTED MORTGAGES

Individuals hold most mortgages that can be purchased at a discount. They would often rather have cash, even if they won't get the full mortgage's face value.

• **Reporting services, public records.** In some counties, reporting services list property sellers who carried back loans. Or you can go to the courthouse to check recent sales and get individual lenders' names and addresses. Loan holders who don't want to sell their loans now may want to later. The older a loan, the more anxious the owner may be to cash in.

• **Owners** of loans facing possible foreclosure often don't want to go through that process because they don't want to buy the property or be paid off by a low-ball bidder at the foreclosure action.

• **Other sources** of discounted mortgages include classified newspaper ads you place, real estate and mortgage brokers, local lawyers, title/escrow companies, home builders, investors and neighbors.

WHAT TO LOOK FOR

• **A low loan-to-value ratio.** A conservative rule of thumb is to buy discounted loans only if the total loan-to-value ratio is 70% or less. In other words, don't buy a second mortgage if the owner's equity in the property is a relatively small percentage of the total effective loan amount.

Start small because you'll make more mistakes on your first deals, then fewer later. As an example, say a house is worth $100,000. It has a $50,000 first mortgage and you're offered a $35,000 second; the loan-to-value ratio is a dangerous 85% ($50,000 + $35,000 to $100,000). However, if you can buy that second mortgage for only $20,000, then the total loan-to-value ratio is a much safer 70% ($50,000 + $20,000 to $100,000).

• **A favorable loan position.** A second or third mortgage is less secure than a first. If the borrower defaults on the other loan(s), you should be able to make the necessary mortgage payments to avoid foreclosure and loss of your investment.

CAUTION

Don't buy a small loan that's "behind" a big one.

EXAMPLE:

A $10,000 second mortgage on a $115,000 house with a $90,000 first mortgage. If the borrower falls several months behind in $900 payments, say, you'd have to pay $3,600 (plus legal and other fees) to protect your $10,000 loan. Since you might not hear about nonpayments for many months, your risk could be even higher.

• **Check the mortgage contract and payment record carefully.** Late charges encourage prompt payments and hike your return if the borrower pays late. While a prepayment penalty can boost your income, it also discourages early payoff. A due-on-sale clause, by requiring full payoff if the property is sold, dramatically raises your total return because you get your money back before maturity.

• **Buy mortgages only on properties you wouldn't mind owning if the borrower defaults.** Stick with easily salable properties, such as single-family houses. At first, you may decide you want to stick with local loans.

• **Don't borrow to buy.** If the borrower stops making payments, you'll no longer be getting the cash needed to pay your own loan. Also, you won't be able to buy the first mortgage to protect your investment, if necessary. Instead of borrowing, sell part of the note to an investor who'll accept a lower yield than yours.

• **Get to know the borrower.** Knowing about his character, life-style and occupation, along with his credit history, helps you evaluate the risk.

• **Always obtain title insurance on your mortgage investments.** Otherwise, just one mistake, such as a forged signature or an undiscovered tax lien, could wipe out your mortgage investment. The title insurance company that insured the loan for the seller often will assign the title policy to you at low cost.

• **Change the loan terms to speed up the payback.** The sooner the loan is paid, the higher your total return. To encourage the borrower to pay off earlier, you might lower the interest rate in return for a higher monthly payment, waive a prepayment penalty, or offer a discount.

FOR ADDITIONAL INFORMATION:

• *Invest in Debt*, by Jim Napier, $13.50 from Jim Napier Inc., P.O. Drawer F, Chipley, FL 32428.
• *Investing in Paper*, home study course by John Schaub, $129 to Pro Serve Corp., 1938 Ringling Blvd., Sarasota, FL 34236.
• *The Number 1 Real Estate Investment No One Talks About*, by Sanford Hornwood and Lucretia Hollingsworth (Prentice-Hall, $14.95).
• *Smart Trust Deed Investment in California* (Barr-Randol Publishing Co., $21.50).

HOW TO FIND THE BEST FRANCHISE FOR YOUR MONEY

Franchising is today's most successful way of doing business. Some 10,000 franchise outlets account for more than one-third of all retail sales, says the International Franchise Association. What's more, just 10% of franchises fail within 10 years, vs. 80% of all small businesses.

Choosing a franchise is a complex task, and buying one usually requires $40,000 or more in fees and other startup costs. Although franchisers help you get started and provide some ongoing advice, you're responsible for the day-to-day operation. This requires a long-term commitment and hard work—10–12 hours a day, six or seven days a week.

Also, franchising isn't for free-spirited entrepreneurs, because you must be willing to comply with many requirements set by the franchiser. Indeed, a key question is whether you could run such a business yourself without buying a franchise.

Business trends will affect your franchise buying decision. The Commerce Dept. recently cited these fast-growth franchise industries: maid and cleaning services, business services (accounting, collections, personnel, tax preparation), temporary help, fitness and weight control, hair salons, and automotive repairs and services.

PICKING A FRANCHISE

• **Investigate before you invest.** Once you've narrowed down the possibilities to a few, consider each franchise's product or service. Is it a fad item or does it have long-term potential? Does it taste good, look good or work well? Is the field wide open or already overcrowded?

A franchiser that's growing modestly in one region may be a better bet than one that has embarked on a rapid national expansion. And the lower the percentage of franchises the company runs itself, the more interested it will be in its franchisees.

CAUTION

Steer clear of a franchise if, after several years of operation, the company still makes more money from franchise fees than from royalty payments.

Unless you're already familiar with the industry in which you want a franchise, look for a franchiser that offers intensive management training and perhaps employee training.

The franchiser must provide the names of at least 10 franchisees near you. Unannounced, visit as many as possible to see how business is. Then meet with the owners to ask about franchiser support, expenses and earnings, and other operating questions.

REVIEW THE FRANCHISER'S REQUIRED DISCLOSURE DOCUMENTS

The Federal Trade Commission and most states accept the Uniform Franchise Offering Circular (UFOC), which discloses all the franchiser's requirements. These are the most important:

• *Payments you must make to license the franchise.* Consider what a franchise promises to do in exchange for your payments. Most promise free training, but some don't. Some provide free on-site help,

but others charge consulting fees.

• *Ongoing royalties and fees.* Most require a percentage of gross sales—the average is 6%–8%—plus an advertising fee, often 2%–4%.

• *Territory guarantees.* Determine how exclusive territories are defined and how large an area or population you'll have to draw on. Franchisees often complain about encroachment.

• *Site location.* If you must select the site, does the franchiser give you demographic data and help with lease negotiations?

• *Required purchases/leases of equipment and material.* You may have to buy tens of thousands of dollars in equipment and supplies from a list of approved suppliers.

• *Operating restrictions.* These run from strict quality controls to just following the operations manual.

• *Terminations.* Franchisers often list many reasons they can cancel your agreement. Many make it tough for you to cancel.

Also, in the disclosure papers, carefully examine the franchiser's detailed financial statements and information on the franchiser's management and on any lawsuits. Unless the franchiser's people have experience running their franchises, they won't understand your problems. Make sure none has been involved in franchise bankruptcy, fraud or lawsuits. Also ask about any disputes settled out of court.

HOW TO AVOID FRAUD

• **Make sure the franchiser and its salespeople are legitimate.** Check that the franchise is registered in your state, and with credit agencies and local Better Business Bureaus.

• **Consider the franchise name.** Some franchisers use names similar to major national franchises to confuse potential buyers.

• **Be wary of franchisers with high rates of "conversion"** (when a franchiser buys out or helps sell an outlet) or failure.

• **Avoid franchise salespeople who "guarantee" high profits.** Giving earnings guarantees is illegal and dumb.

FOR MORE INFORMATION:

• *Franchise Opportunities Handbook,* published by U.S. Department of Commerce. Send $15 to U.S. Government Printing Office, Washington, DC 20402 (GPO Reference No. 003-008-00201-3).
• International Franchise Association, 1350 New York Ave. NW, Suite 900, Washington, DC 20005. A publications catalog is available by calling 1-800-543-1038.
• *Source Book of Franchise Opportunities* by Robert E. Bond (Richard D. Irwin, Inc., 1818 Ridge Rd., Homewood, IL 60430; $27.95).
• *1990 Franchise Annual* (Info Franchise News, 728 Center St., Box 550, Lewiston, NY 14092; $34.95).
• *Directory of Franchising Organizations* (Pilot Books, 103 Cooper St., Babylon, NY 11702; $6).

TAX-SMART PATH TO VENTURE INVESTING

■ ■ ■ ■ ■

When backing new business ventures, it's important to touch the three legal bases that will give your investment the tax advantages of a "trade or business," in case the venture unexpectedly goes sour.

To give an example, Willard Newman's primary business was a grocery store. But he had the local reputation of being a risk-taker, who would finance and help in the startup of small businesses.

Over a 15-year period, he spent 30%–50% of his time in a series of diverse business ventures, the majority of which were successful.

Newman's standard procedure was to invest "seed money" in a startup venture, aid it with promotion, bookkeeping and the like, and then sell his interest to his co-venturer when the business was on its feet.

This approach didn't work with one would-be entrepreneur, and Newman ended up losing over $58,000. He took the loss as a business bad debt, deductible in full as an ordinary loss.

The IRS, however, claimed the loss was a nonbusiness bad debt, which is deducted as a short-term capital loss. As a result, he would have been able to deduct only $3,000 a year against his ordinary income.

Newman beat the IRS in Tax Court. The court said his activities met the three-part test to establish that a taxpayer is in the trade or business of promoting businesses:

• Compensation from the venture is other than a normal investor's return. The taxpayer's income is the direct product of his services, not an indirect product of the enterprise's success.

• The taxpayer works for a fee or commission, or intends to quickly sell out at a profit, in the ordinary course of his working business.

• The taxpayer has a reputation in the community for promoting, organizing, financing and selling businesses. (*Newman v. Commissioner*)

STEERING CLEAR OF SCAMS

· · · · ·

You're self-confident, willing to take a risk, sure of your judgment—and quite possibly a professional con artist's ideal victim.

HOW TO KEEP FROM BEING CONNED

• **Always think twice about an offer that promises a phenomenal return on your investment.** While such a deal does exist, it usually comes in the way of wealthy individuals. If you're an average investor, consider it unlikely that anyone will be offering you a legitimate bonanza.

• **Investigate the proposer, not just the proposal.** Con artists get their sobriquet because they inspire confidence. They are nice, dress well and use imposing titles like investment counselor or head of syndicate. They reel off past triumphs and give you the name of someone who sounds like a high executive with an office at a prestigious address, whom you can phone for a reference. In a Ponzi scheme (where the money taken in today is used to pay off yesterday's investors, until the whole structure collapses), they may give you the names of people who are already collecting big loot—for now.

● WHAT TO DO:

Check with Dun & Bradstreet or other personal credit bureaus. Call the Better Business Bureau in any city where the person who wants you to invest has had a business before.

• **See the investment with your own eyes,** particularly if it involves land. Once on the spot, look for flaws. See what you can find out at the county courthouse. Who holds title to the land? Are there liens on it?

Consult the city or county planning or development authorities. Find out about any upcoming developments that could affect the value of the land, positively or negatively.

• **Keep asking questions.** For instance, how much will it cost to get, and keep, this new business in operation? How much time will you personally have to invest in it? Who will be managing the project?

• **Seek advice from an objective expert,** such as your attorney or accountant (provided this person is not involved in the deal). The more you feel you don't want such advice, the more you need it. Your emotional involvement makes you all the more vulnerable to deception.

• **Don't be rushed.** Always ask your attorney to review any papers you are asked to sign. Ignore warnings that you'll lose out by waiting—they're an old ploy.

OBSERVATION:

Every swindler appeals to greed, which you may not want to see in yourself. It takes a lot of maturity to say to yourself, "I'd like to make a fast buck, but is that what this person is trying to make off me?"

INVESTING IN YOUR HOME

· · · · ·

Remodeling or improving your own home is an investment. This is true even if you plan to live there for many years.

As a rule, you'll fare best in the home remodeling/improvement game by keeping would-be home buyers in mind, so that you'll get back most of your investment in a sale. Some improvements will return their cost, assuming you stay in your home for at least five years. But remodeling generally doesn't turn a profit; so be happy if you recoup 80% or more of your cost.

OBSERVATION:

Buying a house to renovate, strictly as an investment is another matter. It can pay off quite handsomely. (See "Six ways to get rich in real estate," page 339.)

• *If you're debating the merits of remodeling vs. moving,* note that in many areas (though far from all), the cost per square foot of adding on has dropped way below the equivalent cost of trading up to a new home. And with housing starts off sharply nationwide, some home builders are seeking remodeling work, which keeps a lid on prices.

Before you fix up your home, consider the two cardinal rules of home improvement:

• *Remodel only if local property values are relatively stable vs. the national averages.* Don't pour your money into a depreciating asset.

• *Don't overimprove.* The best returns will come if your home is now among your neighborhood's least expensive and you're adding standard features. If your home would be pushed above the neighborhood price range when you sell, remodeling won't pay financially.

RENOVATIONS THAT PAY

Most buyers want modern, good-quality features, but in a traditional setting. If you rearrange floor plans or add rooms, hire an architect first.

• *A brand new kitchen* easily costs $25,000 or more. But a typical renovation runs $8,000–$15,000. This expense can re-turn 90% or more of your outlay if you have an older home with the original kitchen. Kitchen size is also important: It should be large enough to justify the investment.

• *Modernizing an old bathroom or adding a second one* probably will repay your full investment. On the average, a new bathroom costs $8,000 or so, while refurbishing one can cost under $2,500 or less. Expect to recover 90%–100% of your outlay when you sell.

• *A fireplace* is likely to return your full investment—and then some—if most homes in your area have one. Typical cost: $4,000–$6,000.

• *Other worthwhile improvements or additions* include closets, a home office, a porch or deck, central air conditioning (especially in the South) and insulated windows (in the North).

RECOMMENDATION:

Ask a good real estate agent for an estimate of the resale value of your proposed renovations.

DEALING WITH CONTRACTORS

• **Get bids** from at least two or three. Quotes are free, the contractors will probably offer some useful ideas, and the price differences may surprise you.

• **Buy experience.** The contractor you use should have several years of experience in your area, and he should provide customer references. Check with the Better Business Bureau too.

• **See that you have the following**: a signed contract that includes a fixed price; detailed plans and specific materials/appliances; startup and completion dates; a reasonable payment schedule (one-third each at the start, middle and end of the project); a guarantee that the contractor carries liability and workers' compensation insurance; and a clause that you won't pay the contractor in full until you get signed waivers of liens from all subcontractors and suppliers in the project.

SHOULD YOU INVEST IN ART?

· · · · ·

With art prices rapidly climbing out of sight, does it still make sense to consider buying art as an investment? That depends on how much you know, or the access you have to those who do. Without professional knowledge or guidance, buying art is like playing the gaming tables at Las Vegas or investing in stocks you heard about at lunch.

Investment analyst Andrew Tobias offers this advice: "Buy what you like. Display it out of the reach of children and pets. Don't count on its appreciating."

Elizabeth Blagbrough, president of the American Society of Appraisers, agrees: "I advise my clients that if they are going to acquire an item, to acquire it because they love it and want to live with it. If it increases in value, that's a plus."

Still, art has risen steadily over the years. Works by well-known artists fetch all-time high prices now, especially since most auctions are still denominated in dollars, and the cheap dollar makes art less expensive for owners of yen or marks.

Paintings can thus be investments as well as pleasures. The best advice, therefore, is to learn about art values.

One guide is "Sotheby's Art Market Trends" in *Forbes*, which tracks percentage changes in its art index over one, two and five years. It covers art from the old masters to the impressionists.

• *If you buy at auction*, look at paintings before you consider a bid. If pictures have expensive price tags, get them appraised beforehand.

• *To find a qualified appraiser*, write the American Society of Appraisers, P.O. Box 17265, Washington, DC 20041. Ask for the personal property directory. It's free.

• *Don't expect cheap art to appreciate.* Pictures bought for under $100 are usually reproductions or seascapes sold in hotels. They look nice, but they are not a good investment.

● OTHER TIPS:

Don't buy pictures that need restoration. Don't plunge on contemporary artists who are hot at the moment—they can plummet like stones. Don't expect quick appreciation.

DON'T THROW IT OUT—SELL IT

· · · · ·

We've all heard about people who struck it rich when some neglected possession turned out to be priceless—like the Brooklyn man who learned that old knickknacks were Faberge eggs made before the Russian revolution and worth $50,000.

Windfalls that big are rare, but taking stock of what you have is worthwhile.

Sam Small, publisher of *The Where-to-Sell-It Directory* (Pilot Books, 103 Cooper St., Babylon, NY 11702; $4.95), says it's wise to proceed slowly in determining an object's value: "Go to the library first and read some books or magazines concentrating on the type of collectible you have."

The Where-to-Sell-It Directory lists dealers for the following items you might have lying around:

- *Americana.* American flags with less than 48 stars.
- *Automotive.* Shop manuals, spark plugs, radiator caps, insignias.
- *Beer.* Old cans, bottles, coasters.
- *Dolls.* Barbie dolls, ceramic doll heads, Kewpie dolls, Cabbage Patch Dolls in original boxes with papers.
- *Electronics.* Old audio equipment, telephones, marbleized plastic radios from the 1950s, old radio tubes.
- *Glassware.* Beads, perfume bottles, nursing bottles, orange-juice reamers.
- *Handicrafts.* Quilts, hooked rugs, needlework samplers.
- *Household items.* Banks, doorknobs, figural Christmas light bulbs and ornaments, corkscrews, coffee grinders, thermometers, kerosine lamps.
- *Jewelry.* Antique costume jewelry, old school rings.
- *Memorabilia.* World's Fair and Olympic commemorative items; political campaign souvenirs; items depicting Shirley Temple, the Dionne quintuplets, Howdy Doody or the Lone Ranger.
- *Miscellaneous.* Boy and Girl Scout badges; cigar bands; tire-shaped ashtrays; Cracker Jack prizes; old lottery tickets; pre-1900 handwritten letters or railroad timetables.
- *Musical.* Phonographs with outside horns, player piano rolls.
- *Photographic.* Old photographs, very large or small antique cameras.
- *Publications.* Serial children's books, such as Horatio Alger or Tom Swift; early TV Guides; mail-order catalogs.

SELLING COLLECTIBLES

Getting the best price for collectibles—artworks, antiques and other specialty items—takes personal involvement. Turning it over to the most prestigious gallery or dealer you can find is likely to net you far less money.

GUIDELINES FOR PROFITABLE SELLING

- **Establish the value.** Check classified and dealers' ads in specialized antique newsletters and magazines. If you suspect you have something of greater value, it's worth spending several hundred dollars to have it appraised and/or authenticated. Contact the International Society of Appraisers (485 W. Berkley Lane, Hoffman Estates, IL 60194; 708-882-0706) for help in finding a trained appraiser in your area.

● N O T E :

Appraisers are not certified or regulated by the U.S. government.

- **Sell it directly to a collector.** They will pay near-retail prices for items in good condition. In contrast, galleries and dealers either charge a 50% sales commission to sell your object or try to buy it for as little as possible.

A private collector may offer $4,000 for your $5,000 painting. If that seems low, consider that a top dealer will sell it for $5,000—and then give you $2,500. To find collectors, place a classified ad in a newsletter or magazine that specializes in what you want to sell. If that fails, place an ad in a newspaper published in a large city where there are likely to be collectors. If you live in a prosperous area, advertise locally.

• **Investigate local outlets.** Local dealers—even amateurs who organize fund-raising events or antique shows—are often open to bargaining. You may be able to negotiate a commission of 10%–20% instead of 50%.

Also, contact local auction houses. They don't often net the highest prices, but you may get them to accept a lower commission.

CAUTION

When selling through an auction house, *always* get a minimum bid agreement in writing. Without one, your object may be sold for an absurdly low bid.

• **Negotiate hard with a high-status gallery.** If other methods haven't worked, consider taking a hard line on commissions with a high-status gallery or dealer. The more valuable your object, the greater your bargaining power.

Insist on an itemized statement of fees ahead of time. You don't want to learn at pay-up time that they've deducted the costs of restoring, authenticating or advertising your object.

• **Hold it.** If your object is not going to bring the amount it's worth and you're not pressed for funds at the moment, wait. Remember that it only takes *one* collector to buy what you have.

Chapter 5

PERSONAL FINANCE ISSUES

SAVINGS ADVICE FROM THE PROS

· · · · ·

According to a U.S. government study, 95% of Americans who retire at age 65 are not financially independent. To avoid becoming part of a cash-short majority, you need to get control of your savings. Here are some tips from financial planners:

• *Put your change into a "burglar-resistant" bank.* Rhoda Israelov, a vice president of Shearson, Lehman Hutton in Indianapolis, advises emptying your pockets of all coins each day. Put them into an empty soft drink can, she says. The cash will be hard to retrieve, but by the end of the month you'll have $25–$40 to take to the bank. And it's money you won't miss.

• *Set reachable goals.* For a quick taste of success, go for achievable results. Jeffrey Levy, general manager of Independent Financial Services in Garden City, NY, advises that if you can't save for a $2,000 vacation, try for something easier—but not too easy. For example, shoot for $200–$400 to buy a microwave oven in two months. Once you buy the oven for cash, you will have tangible proof that you are capable of saving. Then set another, tougher goal.

• *Become your own creditor.* When you sit down to pay bills, put yourself at the top of the list. Treat the payment as a bill, and make it religiously. The Foundation for Financial Planning recommends putting

5%–15% of your gross income into such an account, and paying it before any others.

• *Massacre credit-card debt.* Paying finance charges on a number of credit cards is like being under siege by enemy soldiers, says Levy. But if you kill them off one by one, you gradually eliminate interest, freeing up cash for savings. The easiest way to do this is to pay off your smallest bills first, while continuing to make partial payments on the others.

• *Treat credit-card buys as current expenses.* If your budget is thrown off balance by credit-card bills, Israelov recommends this approach: Attach a colored pen to your checkbook and, every time you make a credit-card purchase, use the pen to enter it as a debit. When the bill comes in, you will have the money to pay it immediately, thereby eliminating interest on the purchase.

THE ADVANTAGES OF LEASING A CAR

· · · · ·

Leasing may be more practical than buying if (1) you trade in your cars at least every three or four years, (2) you want to drive a costlier car than you want to buy, or (3) you prefer to use the down payment required for a purchase elsewhere.

Bear in mind that monthly lease payments usually are lower than monthly car-loan payments. Moreover, a car is an asset that starts to lose value as soon as you buy it. You might limit your capital investments to assets you expect to appreciate.

COMPARING LEASES

The maze of leasing fees and creative financing can present a major drawback: It's tough to compare the available deals and to determine your real cost. In fact, the cost is sure to be considerably higher than the advertised monthly payments.

▲ IMPORTANT:

As when buying a car, you should negotiate the best lease deal you can. Consider the following:

• *Length of the lease.* Most leases run 48 months, although they can vary from 12 to 60 months. The longer the lease, the lower each payment. In most cases, you may buy the car at the end of the lease for a price that is determined when you sign up—usually 30%–40% of the sticker price after four years. Make sure a specific price is set; don't rely on vague promises like "fair market value."

• *Limitations.* All leases carry limitations on the number of miles you may drive without extra charge. The lower the number of miles you expect to drive, the lower the monthly cost. But anything above the limit— 60,000 miles over four years, say—will cost 8–15 cents a mile extra, depending on the lessor. Note that this fee is negotiable.

• *Payments.* Leasing programs usually offer various payment options that affect both the size of your monthly payment and your total leasing cost. For instance, some monthly payments are artificially low because they are followed by a large balloon payment and/or sharply higher payments later in the lease.

You will have to put up a security deposit or a nonrefundable up-front payment. The deposit is usually equivalent to one or two monthly payments, and it should be refundable. Also, determine whether you will receive interest on the deposit and at what rate.

• *Damages and penalties.* Make sure the definition of "normal wear and tear" is clear. It will affect any payment for damage you must make at the end of the lease if you don't buy the car. Stiff penalties for giving up a lease before its due date are standard.

• *Maintenance and insurance.* These cost extra. You may want to compare the fee with the cost of getting them on your own. Lessors sometimes can provide less expensive insurance, but be sure it covers the lease as well as the car. Otherwise, if you have a bad accident or the car is stolen, you may have to make payments even after the company is reimbursed for the car by the insurer.

CAUTION

The maintenance charge may be excessive since the car is new and already has some warranty protection.

• *Beware of options.* Loading up the car with options will also boost your cost. Be sure the lease contract specifies that all the options you want are included.
• *Other costs.* Various fees are tacked on to auto leases. The most common are title/registration fees and a disposition fee to cover the company's cost of selling the car when you're through with it. The latter should be under $250, and it shouldn't apply if you buy the car.

WHERE TO LEASE

Check with new-car dealers and independent auto-leasing firms. General Motors, Ford and Chrysler offer leasing programs that may cost less than those from regular leasing concerns.

OBSERVATION:
While most people still come out ahead financially with a purchase, the gap is

shrinking. A lease on a $20,000 car may cost an extra $2,000 or so over four years, and on a $30,000 vehicle it may make a $3,500 difference.

WHAT YOU SHOULD KNOW ABOUT HIRING A LAWYER
. . . . .

Your lawyer should be honest, have good credentials and provide good service. He or she should be genuinely interested in your case, and should look for easy rather than complicated ways to solve your problem.

HOW LEGAL FEES WORK

The cost of legal services varies widely. Factors include the lawyer's education, experience and reputation. Lawyers who specialize usually charge more than generalists. You may need a specialist for complex and/or big-dollar situations. A generalist will suffice for the typical house closing or for a straightforward will.

Some specialties command higher fees than others. Lawyers in big cities charge more than those in small towns, and big firms may also charge more than small ones in the same city.

Usually, you won't know in advance exactly how much you'll have to pay. But you should get a good idea of a law firm's hourly rates and the approximate number of hours typically required for your situation.

RECOMMENDATION:
Get cost estimates before you decide whether to initiate or defend a suit. Wherever possible, negotiate settlements

rather than taking disputes to court.

• The hourly rate is the most common method of billing clients. Lawyers keep time sheets to determine billable hours. Senior partners charge the highest fees, followed by junior partners, then associates. Find out the billing rates at each level.

• Use of contingency fees—a percentage of a settlement—is largely limited to lawsuits. It remains the same no matter how long the case takes and whether it goes to court or not. If the client loses, the lawyer gets nothing but expenses. Lawyers sometimes work for flat fees, but usually only for short-term projects.

• To their fees, lawyers add expenses. These include travel, photocopying, computerized research, outside experts, staff overtime, meals, messengers, etc.

WAYS TO KEEP THE COSTS DOWN

• **Find out how the work is divided.** You'll probably need a partner to manage your case. However, you shouldn't be charged the partner's rate across the board. Associates often can do research and draw up most documents. Proofreading, photocopying and other administrative tasks should be done by associates or paralegals.

• **Establish fee and expense limits.** Since you're paying the freight, you may be able to eliminate duplication of effort, unnecessary travel, etc. If possible, avoid overtime rates for lawyers and staff, and excess computerized legal research, word processing or secretarial work. If applicable, specify that lawyers traveling on your behalf go coach class, and that you won't be billed for lawyers' personal expenses on the road. Try to settle on an all-inclusive rate that covers expenses as well as services.

RECOMMENDATION:
Confirm your arrangement in writing. For example: $125 an hour, no overtime, and don't go over five hours without my OK.

• **Insist on itemized bills.** "For services rendered" is adequate only for small jobs. Otherwise, you should be told what services were performed, why, by whom and how long they took. Ask about unfamiliar names, charges you don't understand, etc. If necessary, request a look at the firm's records and copies of any research listed on the bill.

• **Get periodic bills.** Never let the tab run until the end of a long-running case. Review each bill carefully as soon as you get it. If you see anything questionable, call your lawyer right away. Regular bills, in addition to tracking costs, give you a chance to evaluate whether you're getting your money's worth.

• **Monitor long-term projects.** You may want to schedule monthly conferences. Review what the lawyer plans to do for you in the coming month, and the results he expects.

A good lawyer will help you achieve your goals. Don't automatically defer to one who tries to talk you into something else.

• **Protect yourself against disreputable lawyers.** A few lawyers steal clients' money.

EXAMPLES:
Misappropriating funds in an estate or a trust, taking cash from an escrow account, settling a personal injury case without passing over the settlement money or simply taking money without performing any service. While some well-publicized thefts involve large sums, many involve routine business matters.

Lawyers who bilk their clients tend to share several characteristics. They are typically middle-aged men who practice alone. Gambling, alcoholism and drug abuse often are involved.

Suspicious behavior that should put you on your guard includes canceled appointments, failure to return telephone calls or long delays in getting legal work done.

RECOMMENDATION:
If you turn money over to a lawyer for any purpose, request a letter of receipt with a statement of the services to be provided. If the money is placed in an escrow account, the letter should provide the bank's name and account number.

SMART WAYS TO SAVE FOR COLLEGE
∎ ∎ ∎ ∎ ∎

It's harder than ever for parents to finance their children's college education. College costs have been soaring at roughly double the inflation rate since 1980.

To avoid taking on a mountain of debt later, you'll want to start saving and investing wisely now. The sooner you start, even with a set amount every month, the lower your up-front cost will be.

STRATEGIES FOR SAVING

∎ **Open a custodian account.** You can do this at banks, mutual funds and brokerage firms, under either the Uniform Gift to Minors Act (UGMA) or the more flexible Uniform Transfers to Minors Act (UTMA), depending on the state. Remember that the child will be legally entitled to do what he wishes with the account assets at age 18 or 21, varying with state laws. For children under 14, the first $500 of annual investment income is tax free. The second $500 is taxed at the child's own rate of 15%. Additional income is taxed at the parents' top rate. The maximum tax on the first $1,000 of income is $75 per year, a saving of up to $255 compared with the parents' tax rate under current tax law.

OBSERVATION:
Parents (or others) may give $10,000 per person to a child annually, free of gift tax. At 8%, $10,000 would generate $800 of low-tax income.

Once your child turns 14, his low 15% tax rate applies up to $17,850. Since there's no tax liability on the appreciating value of an asset, your child can defer income tax until the sale of any gift assets, preferably after age 14. Or you can wait until your child is nearing college age, then give him or her assets to sell.

∎ **Investing the money.** With many tax breaks gone, wise investing has assumed the dominant role in accumulating cash for college. Such money should be invested relatively conservatively. To keep risk down, always diversify your investments.

The younger your child, the more risk you can take, assuming it's prudent risk. For offspring under 14, try to generate at least $1,000 of annual income from assets in their names. Then aim for tax deferral on assets you retain.

After age 14, income becomes the name of the game because of your child's low tax rate, along with the need for safety as college time draws near.

• *Stocks and equity mutual funds.* One approach for a child is to buy top-quality growth stocks or funds that pay low or no dividends. Once your child turns 14, you might switch to higher-income alternatives, such as electric utilities or short-term bonds.

OBSERVATION:

Investing for total return—growth and income—from stocks or funds is a solid long-term strategy, particularly if dividends are reinvested.

• *U.S. Treasury and tax-free zero-coupon bonds.* Zeros sell at a deep discount to face value, so your initial investment can be modest. In addition, you know exactly what your investment will be worth at maturity. Treasury zeros, in particular, are available in a wide variety of maturities, which you can peg to when you will need the money.

Zeros are more volatile than other bonds, so selling before maturity could be risky, depending on interest rates. Taxable zeros are feasible only in a low tax bracket (your child's) because the bondholder is taxed annually on imputed interest. Tax-free zeros, however, could be held in your name.

• *U.S. savings bonds.* These are a good choice for money in a child's name. If your child's income is below $1,000, he can pay the interest annually because little or no tax will be due. Otherwise the child may defer tax payment until the Series EE bonds mature, preferably after age 14. The interest rate is adjusted every six months, with a 6% floor. All interest is exempt from state and local tax.

• *Municipal bonds.* Hold these in your name since the income is free of federal tax (as well as state and local tax on in-state bonds). Most individuals prefer to diversify through a mutual fund or a unit trust.

• *Short-term bonds.* These are a good way to boost low-risk current income of a child over 14. U.S. Treasury notes held to maturity are your safest bet. Also attractive are short-term bond funds.

• *Cash vehicles.* Certificates of deposit can be a good place for money you'll need in five years or less, especially if held in the name of an over-14 child. Money market funds are suitable for short-term money.

• *Single-premium deferred annuities or single-premium life insurance.* Your investment grows tax free. If you hold the annuity or policy, the tax benefit of the deferral is greater than if it is in a child's name. But withdrawals are taxed based on the bracket of the holder, and you will generally be subject to a 10% penalty on withdrawals before age 59 1/2. With single-premium life, if a parent or grandparent dies, the proceeds can go to the child beneficiary.

CAUTION

For either an annuity or single-premium policy, invest any money you won't need anytime soon, and then only as a secondary strategy.

■ REASONS:

Relative inflexibility and possibly high fees.

• *Home equity loan.* Regular consumer loans won't be deductible after 1990 and are only 10% deductible in 1990. But under current law, you can deduct interest on up to $100,000 in borrowings against home equity.

OBSERVATION:

Be certain to keep in mind that your savings strategies will have to change along with any changes in the tax laws that may directly affect save-for-college strategies.

Chapter 6

REAL ESTATE

SIX WAYS TO GET RICH IN REAL ESTATE

· · · · ·

You can make good money in real estate even if prices don't go through the roof. How?

• **Concentrate on your own market.** The best area in which to invest is usually right where you live, since you presumably know this area best. Among the variables to follow closely are job growth and vacancy rates for office, commercial and residential properties.

• **Buy at below-market prices and on favorable terms.** This is the single surest way to make money. What's more, you can usually get better deals in a currently soft market than if you jump into a hot one. It's like buying straw hats in January.

RECOMMENDATION:

Aim to buy for at least 10% under the selling prices of comparable properties in your area. Try to get the seller to take back a loan so you'll avoid costly mortgages from financial institutions.

Motivated or anxious sellers are the best sources of such deals. Telltale signs include an unoccupied or poorly maintained property, especially with out-of-town owners. Foreclosure properties and estate sales are also good possibilities. Find out as much as possible about the seller's circumstances—why he is selling, what he needs from the deal, whether he faces a deadline—so you can structure an offer he may accept.

• **Use conservative projections of property value and rental income.** As a rule, it's wise to avoid negative cash flow; you should be generating profits or at least breaking even before taxes. One exception: if you are rapidly building equity in the property—through a rock-bottom price or a no-interest loan, say—and you have enough cash coming in elsewhere.

• **Buy and fix up houses or apartments.** The ideal property to upgrade has good location, architecture, layout and room sizes, and bad "changeables"—paint, carpets and landscaping. Make only improvements that will increase the property value by more than you spend; aim for a 2-for-1 payback.

RECOMMENDATION:

Don't sink too much into the property, and don't underestimate the cost of labor or your time. The trick is to buy low, renovate fast, then rent at higher levels or sell the property.

• **Buy discounted mortgages.** This can be an easy way to make money because your transaction costs are low, and you don't have to kick the bricks or deal with tenants. Buying existing mortgages can generate annual returns of 15%–50% or more, depending on the perceived risk. The mortgage holder, usually an individual, wants to sell the loan to raise cash or get out of the mortgage business, and therefore is willing to sell at a discount from face value. Your total return is the coupon yield of the mortgage plus your discount amortized over the life of the loan.

Here's the kicker: If your borrower sells or refinances his home, you'll get back the full face amount earlier, thereby boosting your return.

▲ IMPORTANT:

You should like the property securing the note, in the event you have to take it over (possibly by paying off a first mortgage).

A monthly newsletter, *The Paper Source* (8420 Porter Lane, Alexandria, VA 22308; 1-800-542-2270), lists mortgages for sale.

• **Don't be greedy when you sell.** Don't be afraid to take profits if you don't like the prospects for your market. Selling also enables you to lock in net worth, even if you have to pay taxes. Most real estate can be sold quickly if it's priced according to what the market will pay, or slightly below market. You'll still come out of the deal with a healthy profit if you buy right and manage your properties well.

HOW TO CHOOSE REAL ESTATE THAT WILL MAKE GOOD MONEY

• • • • •

Evaluating and buying real estate in this "tax reform" world is far different than the way it used to be. No longer is it reasonable to assume that tax breaks or the price you hope to get when you sell will enable you to make big money. It's essential to focus on today's reality—the deal's current investment aspects—not what may happen in the future.

As a rule, this means you should invest only in properties in which you can avoid negative cash flow. In other words, you should be generating real pretax profits from operations, or at least breaking even.

OBSERVATION:

Even if you know you're entitled to significant tax breaks, it's still not a good idea to let them dominate your purchase decisions because they may not be around forever.

HOW TO PICK
A GOOD INVESTMENT

• **Income/expense ratio.** Divide rental income by total expenses to learn whether the property is at least breaking even. If income is $10,000 a year and expenses total $8,500, for instance, the ratio is 1.176. The ratio of income to expenses must be at least 1. The higher the number the better. Of course, you need to know the property's true expenses, including anticipated maintenance and repair costs.

• **Net operating income (NOI).** This related figure tells you how much income you can expect after operating expenses, but before interest, taxes and depreciation. You should know the multiple of NOI at which the type of rental property you're considering typically changes hands in your area.

> **EXAMPLE:**
> Industrial buildings generally are priced at 9 to 12 times annual NOI. If NOI is $30,000, the sale price is likely to fall between $270,000 and $360,000.

The greater the potential for increasing NOI, the higher the multiple a property will command. A building with long-term tenants may fetch less than one in which leases at below-market levels will expire soon.

• **Price/rent ratio.** This rule of thumb helps determine a reasonable purchase price. Monthly rental income probably should total at least 1% of the purchase price. In most markets, the price should be 5 to 9 times the annual gross rental income. The actual multiple depends on the area, market conditions, type of property and location.

> **EXAMPLE:**
> For a house with $1,000 monthly rent, $100,000 is a more realistic price than $120,000. On an annual basis, $12,000 of rental income translates into a price of $60,000 to $108,000.

• **Cash flow/total income ratio.** By dividing the amount of available cash flow by a property's total income, you can get a good idea of how secure the cash flow is. The higher the ratio, the better. Say, for example, that you're comparing two different condominiums. Condo A now rents for $500 a month and Condo B rents for $800 a month. Each has $100 monthly positive cash flow. However, Condo A's cash flow is 20% of rental income, while Condo B's is just 12.5%.

Both of these cash flow scenarios appear severe. But should you find yourself faced with an unexpected expense—severe damage to the roof as a result of a storm, for example—it would be more likely to wipe out the cash flow in the property with the lower cash-flow margin.

• **Cash flow/investment capital ratio.** This shows your return on investment, aside from property appreciation. Divide annual positive cash flow by your total investment. Even a modest positive cash flow gives you a big leg up on generating a large total return on investment when you sell the property.

> **EXAMPLE:**
> Positive cash flow is $200 a month, or $2,400 a year. If your total investment is $50,000, your annual cash return on investment is 4.8%.

• **Check your AGI before you buy.**
Always keep your present and future adjusted gross income (AGI) in mind when you're evaluating investment real estate. How you'll fare partly depends on how the deal is structured, and your AGI may have something to do with it.

If your AGI is under $100,000, you can deduct as much as $25,000 worth of property losses each year. So you can use more leverage and pursue more risky ventures than bigger earners can. In the 33% tax bracket, your deduction on $25,000 would be $8,250. As your AGI goes over $100,000, your allowable loss declines by $1 for every $2 of income. At $150,000, passive losses are deductible only against passive income.

BARGAINS IN FORECLOSURES

• • • • •

Foreclosed homes can be a worthwhile investment. But because so many investors are on the lookout for these bargains, it's not always easy to acquire them.

WHERE TO FIND BARGAINS

• **Early-stage foreclosures.** Before foreclosing, the lender must publish a notice of default in local newspapers. This gives you time to offer to buy the home from the owner, at a big discount from market value.

• **FHA-backed properties.** HUD often accepts offers well below its listing price. Contact your local HUD office for a list of its properties in your area.

• **Lender-owned properties.** Foreclosed homes that don't sell at auction remain in the hands of lenders, which refer to them as *real estate owned* (REO) properties. Because outstanding liens are paid, REOs don't have title problems. Most are eventually sold to real estate brokers, but it's possible to find out about these properties if you've established a good relationship with the lender.

To find out about REOs owned in your area by the Federal National Mortgage Association, a government-backed corporation, call 1-800-553-4636.

DRAWBACKS TO CONSIDER

• **Potential title problems.** Be sure to hire an attorney who is familiar with buying foreclosed property; and buy title insurance to protect against possible problems. Have the attorney check with the IRS, which may have a lien on the property because of back taxes owed by the former owner. Some states also have a right-of-redemption statute, allowing the original homeowner up to a year to buy back a foreclosed home.

• **Poor condition.** Owners with financial problems may tend to let the place run down for years. Have the house professionally inspected.

• **Squatters.** Be sure the former owner or others don't still occupy the place. If they do, you'll have to evict.

SMART WAYS TO USE YOUR HOME EQUITY

• • • • •

Your home equity can provide more than a roof over your head. It can put dollars in your pocket, educate the kids, and ease you into a comfortable retirement. It is also your best financial cushion to carry you through difficult times, provided you know how to use its potential to the fullest.

- *Home equity loans.* These allow you to borrow against your equity in the house and deduct the interest paid on the loan from your income tax.
- *A reverse mortgage.* A homeowner borrows against his equity in the house and is paid a fixed sum each month, based on the interest rate and term of the loan. The loan can be repaid later, such as when the house is sold or when the homeowner dies.
- *Sale with a leaseback clause.* Here the owner sells the property to an investor. The seller retains the right to live in the house for life as a renter, with the investor paying him or her monthly installments—as well as maintenance, insurance and taxes—over an agreed-upon period to provide the seller with continued monthly income.

HOW TO CUT PROPERTY TAXES
■ ■ ■ ■ ■

Valuing property is a subjective science at best. While most assessors do a professional job, they can make mistakes.

Stanley Sprayberry, president of the Noel Company, says his experts found that 57% of the properties they evaluated for corporate clients were overassessed by as much as 100%.

In Arlington County, VA, for example, 20% of all challenges are successful. Mistakes are probably fewer on residential properties, but there are still enough to make it worth your time to check. Here's how:

- *Talk to neighbors whose property has been reassessed.* Even if their residences aren't strictly comparable to yours, calculate their percentage hikes and see if they're in line with yours.
- *Ask for justification.* If you think your assessment is too high, go to your local assessor and ask to see the property record card for your home.

Don't go in angry. A genial attitude will get you courteous attention. To avoid delay, be ready to furnish your property's tax account, lot and block numbers.

- *Look for disparities* between what the assessor has listed and the actual materials used in your home and attendant buildings.

Assessors sometimes muff important details about a building. They may mistake plastic shingles for wooden ones, which are worth three times more, for instance, or confuse wallpaper for much costlier wood paneling. Sometimes, they make a major gaffe, such as listing a swimming pool, shed, or garage that actually belongs to a neighbor. If your house has defects, such as inadequate plumbing, ask if the assessor considered them.

- *Be sure you're getting the benefit of any special rate deductions that might apply.* For example, in some places, owner-occupied homes qualify for lower rates than rentals. Or there may be a senior citizen discount.

If you find mistakes, calmly call them to the attention of the assessor. Most are conscientious and don't mind having their mistakes corrected.

Be prepared for the possibility that the assessor's valuation may be fully justified, however. Property assessment is a complex task, and subtle details can be important. While one house may be similar to a neighboring one in floor and backyard space, it may have certain structural particulars that make it far more valuable.

If you and the assessor disagree, go to your municipal governing body. If this fails, you can still go to court to seek a reduction.

REAL ESTATE INVESTMENTS STILL GET GOOD TAX BREAKS
■ ■ ■ ■ ■ ,

The 1986 tax law didn't take away all the tax benefits of owning real estate. Property investments are no longer highly favored but they're not disfavored either, because the law has left plenty of tax breaks still standing.

TAX BREAKS STILL AVAILABLE

■ **Depreciation deductions on buildings that don't depreciate.** The theory of depreciation is that the asset deteriorates as it is used, and eventually you'll have to junk it and buy a new one. That's usually true of business equipment or a car, say, but rarely true of real estate.

The depreciation deduction is smaller than it used to be for property bought after 1986. But a real estate investor can still take write-offs of over 3% a year on an asset whose value may increase by 5% or more annually over the long term. The depreciation period is 27.5 years for residential property and 31.5 years for commercial holdings.

■ **Avoiding or delaying capital gains tax.** There are several ways to postpone or avoid capital gains tax on real estate profits:

• *Trading investment properties.* If you hold property for investment or use in your business, you can delay the capital gains tax by trading for another property instead of selling. You can do this as often as you wish.

And if you keep the last property, your heirs will avoid income tax on the capital gains on all the properties.

• *Installment sales to delay capital gains tax.* If you sell real estate and take back an installment note, you're taxed on the profit only as you collect the payments. Your money is tied up, but your taxes are postponed too. Holding a second mortgage on real estate that you sell at a profit might be a good investment.

Tax law changes have reduced the appeal of installment sales, however. You must pay tax on all the depreciation recaptured in the year of sale. This could be expensive if you've held property for a long time and you've sharply reduced your cost basis through large amounts of depreciation.

● N O T E :

You will lose the installment-sale tax postponement if you sell the installment paper or use it as collateral to secure loans. And if you take back over $5 million of installment sales paper in any year, you'll owe the IRS interest on the amount of income tax delayed on amounts exceeding $5 million.

■ **Silver lining on the passive loss rules.** If your adjusted gross income is $100,000 or less, you may write off up to $25,000 of real estate losses per year. As AGI increases above $100,000, this allowance declines by $1 for every $2 up to $150,000, then disappears.

Wealthier investors can't use real estate losses to offset a current year's earned and other taxable income. But you can carry forward losses you can't use now to offset future passive income from real estate or other activities. And when you sell real estate, you can use any unused passive losses to offset either capital gains or other taxable income.

For real estate investments made by 1986, there is still a break on passive loss write-offs. But it's nearly dried up: In 1990, you can use 10% of such losses; in 1991, none.

■ **Owners of profitable business corporations can avoid the passive loss rules.** By putting your real estate investments into the corporation, real estate losses can be used to offset business operating profits, along with "portfolio" income such as dividends and interest in some cases.

■ **Tax credits are still available.** Two types of investments qualify: rehabilitation of certified historic buildings or those built before 1936; and low-income housing. You can't use the credits in any year your AGI exceeds $250,000, and they're cut back in the $200,000–$250,000 range.

EQUITY SHARING: TWO CAN PROFIT FROM ONE HOME

. . . . .

Would-be home buyers who can afford healthy mortgage payments often can't afford the required down payment on the home they want. That's one reason a new opportunity for investors and home buyers is surfacing around the country. It's called a "shared equity" purchase.

HOW IT WORKS

An investor puts up the down payment and the home buyer pays the mortgage. At the end of an agreed time, usually three years, the property is appraised and the home buyer repays the investor's down payment and pays him his share of appreciation.

> **EXAMPLE:**
>
> Say the investor put up $30,000 for the down payment on a $110,000 home. Three years later the home is worth 10% more ($121,000). The investor will receive $35,500 (the return of his $30,000 investment plus his half of the $11,000 appreciation). He has gained about 37%—a good 12% a year.

In most such arrangements, the real estate broker who's selling the house matches investor and home buyer.

PROS AND CONS

• **As an investor,** you have to hope that property values will rise at a reasonably brisk pace, giving you a better return on your money than you could get elsewhere.

• **As a buyer,** you have to adjust to the fact that sooner or later you'll have to either come up with a payment to buy out the investor, or sell the house, divvy up the profits, and use the cash as a down payment elsewhere.

Because there are so many variables to consider, firms that specialize in shared equity deals employ an agreement form that investors and buyers can use to be sure every contingency is covered.

Typically, the agreement calls for the investor to put up all the down payment money and to receive half of any gain. Agreements generally say that no decision to sell the house has to be made for at least three years. On the agreed date, buyer and investor must come to some decision, even if it's to let the money run.

• **When either party wants to sell,** the other has the right of first refusal, which can be a mixed blessing. For the investor who wants to hold on, it can mean smaller-than-anticipated profits. For the buyer who wants to stay, it means coming up with a substantial payment to the investor.

As for upkeep costs, such routine items as plumbing, electrical and furnace repairs are usually paid by the buyer. Capital improvements generally are shared.

WHEN 'USED' IS BETTER: REAL ESTATE LIMITED PARTNERSHIPS

■ ■ ■ ■ ■

The best time to buy real estate is when prices are down and the conventional wisdom sees little hope in sight. Buying at a discount is the surest way to generate excellent returns over the long term.

When you own a single property, you're heavily exposed to a local area. You could do well or not so well, but the result might have little to do with broad real estate trends.

An alternative to consider is a "used" limited partnership. You'll probably get more for your money than if you buy "new" in an unproven venture.

ADVANTAGES OF LIMITED PARTNERSHIPS

• You get a partnership that's been in operation for several years; so there's already a performance record to evaluate.

• Prices are negotiable, and sometimes you can buy a partnership at a low price. Although the overwhelming majority of partnership investors holds on until the partnership winds up, there are always some

who want to cash out early.

• The later in a partnership's cycle you buy, the fewer years you'll have to wait until the properties are sold and any profits are distributed.

For example, suppose you bought into a partnership with a modest debt of 36% that's distributing cash flow to investors at a 5.4% rate. Say the partnership units, originally priced at $1,000 each, were offered for $780 on the National Partnership Exchange (NAPEX). Assuming you bought the units for $750, your cash flow would be 7.2%.

NAPEX publishes price information on used limited partnerships in its quarterly *Trade Price Reporter* ($55 for the year-end issue, or $160 per year). Performance information, including estimated total returns, is available for 195 real estate partnerships for $35 from Robert A. Stanger & Co., P.O. Box 7490, 1129 Broad St., Shrewsbury, NJ 07702; 1-800-631-2291, 201-389-3600 in NJ.

CAUTION

Discounted partnership units aren't always a bargain. Sometimes the best properties have been sold. Or there may be little equity left in the real estate because of heavy mortgage loans or declines in property values.

GETTING A MORTGAGE FOR A VACATION HOME

■ ■ ■ ■ ■

Start shopping for a mortgage before you sign a purchase contract. Before making your mortgage application, contact a credit-clearing house to find out if you have any faults or errors in your records that can be corrected. A personal credit history is available from TRW's Personal Credit Department if you send $16.20 with your full name, current and last five addresses, Social Security number, date of birth and your spouse's first name to the company's nearest office, listed in the *White Pages*. Also, have whatever documentation the lender requires ready when you apply.

GET TAX BREAKS WHEN YOU SELL YOUR HOME
. . . . .

Prices of most homes have soared over the years, so slicing your tax liability on a sale can mean a large dollar saving.

■ **The rollover residential replacement rule defers all capital gains tax.** Within two years before or after the sale, you must buy and occupy another principal residence of equal or greater value.

EXAMPLE:
You bought a house in 1975 for $50,000. You sell it now for $200,000 (after deducting selling expenses and improvement costs). Now you have to buy another home worth $200,000 or more. If the new home is less expensive—$170,000, say—you pay current tax only on the price difference of $30,000. Tax on the rest stays deferred.

The deferral continues to the extent that the price of each new home at least equals the sale price of the property it replaces. If you own the house when you die, your heirs won't have to pay income tax on the accrued profits because the property will be included in your estate. If you become a renter, you must pay the deferred gain from all previously owned homes, aside from use of the one-time exclusion (explained below).

OBSERVATION:
To reduce tax under the replacement-value rule, you can boost the new home's effective cost by making capital improvements—modernizing a kitchen or adding a bathroom, say—within the two-year replacement period.

● *Special situations.* If you sell more than one home in a 24-month period, you can defer the gain you've earned on each sale if it's made because of a job-related move for which you can deduct moving expenses. Otherwise, the last residence is considered the replacement.

What if two people each sell a home and buy a new one jointly? Say you bought a home for $90,000 and sell it for $135,000, and your new spouse's property cost $60,000 and sells for $95,000. To defer tax on the combined $80,000 profit, you buy a home for at least $230,000 (the two homes' total sales price). The deferral also applies on the sale of a jointly owned home when a couple splits up and each purchases a separate home.

■ **People 55 and older can exclude up to $125,000 of profit on the sale of a principal residence.** You can use the exclusion just once, even if the profit is under $125,000. Saving the exclusion means paying tax now on any portion you don't defer.

Suppose you sell your house for a $50,000 profit. If potential home changes lie ahead, you may do better to either pay tax now or buy a new home costing as much as the sale price of the old one. You'll be able to use the exclusion when your profit may be much larger.

You can combine the exclusion and deferral breaks if you sell a home at a profit greater than $125,000. This may come in handy if you want to move to a smaller home after retirement.

> **EXAMPLE:**
> You sell for $200,000, seeing a $145,000 profit. After excluding $125,000, you can postpone tax on the remaining $20,000 if you buy a new home costing at least $75,000—the old property's sale price less the excluded gain.

• *Exclusion qualifications and exceptions.* You must have owned and lived in your home for three of the five years before the sale. For a married couple, one spouse must meet the age, ownership and residence tests.

Married couples are considered a unit and get only one exclusion. So if two homeowners who qualify for the exclusion plan to marry, sell their properties and look for a new home jointly, each should probably sell before the marriage and take advantage of their individual exclusions.

Once a couple has used the one exclusion they're entitled to, it's gone for life, even if they divorce or one spouse dies. And if the divorced party, widow, or widower remarries, the new spouse may not use the exclusion either.

A widow(er) not meeting the three tests of age, residence and ownership on an inherited home can still qualify for an exclusion if the late spouse would have met the tests on the home sale date and had not used the exclusion.

If a divorcing couple who has not used the exclusion holds a home jointly until after the divorce, each person becomes eligible for the exclusion of up to $125,000 on his or her interest. Unmarried seniors selling a jointly owned home also can qualify for separate exclusions if they meet the other requirements.

OBSERVATION:
By filing an amended tax return, a taxpayer can elect or revoke the $125,000 exclusion at any time within three years after the tax return deadline for the year of sale.

■ **When you have a home office.** Normally, you can defer capital gains tax only on a home's residential portion. Say you take annual write-offs for a home office that uses 15% of your house. Sell the property for a $100,000 profit and you'll have to pay tax on $15,000.

But you qualify for the full deferral tax break if you're not entitled to deduct a home office in the year the home is sold. So you can avoid the home office tax if you convert the office to personal use before the year of sale.

With the $125,000 exclusion, if you used the office for two of the five years before the sale, you must prorate the exclusion to cover only the residential portion. But you can keep the entire exclusion if your use was less.

RECOMMENDATION:
The home-sale tax breaks can be extremely complicated in certain situations. Carefully plan any home sale and subsequent purchase.

SELLING YOUR HOME IN A SLOW MARKET

· · · · ·

In a buyers' market, sellers have to work extra hard to get a good price for their homes. Getting the best price possible, though, requires three vital steps: Make sure your property is in excellent cosmetic condition, price the house realistically and use a top real estate broker.

CAUTION

Don't buy another home until you sell yours. Otherwise, you could be forced into a distress sale if you are burdened with heavy carrying costs.

FIX UP YOUR HOME

A house you want to sell should look bright and clean. Correct all conspicuous flaws, such as faulty plumbing, sticking doors and windows, and crumbling caulking in bathrooms. Replace peeling paint and wallpaper or threadbare carpet, using quiet colors such as off-white or beige. Make your home look as spacious as possible by keeping rooms uncluttered, rearranging furniture and storing what you don't need. Keep pets out of the way, and eliminate any lingering odors. The lawn should be in good shape too.

CAUTION

Don't make major improvements—installing a new bathroom or kitchen, for instance—because you won't get all your money back in the sale (see "Investing in your home," page 328).

SET YOUR PRICE

Regardless of what you think your home is worth, a realistic asking price is based on the recent sales prices of comparable homes—those close to yours in location, size, age, style and condition.

Information on sales is available at the county courthouse or local deeds office. But it's easier to consult local real estate brokers, who will be glad to provide this information in the hope of signing you up as a client. Free appraisals of your house by three agents will also help. However, these appraisals can be colored by an eagerness to list your property. Hiring a professional appraiser is another alternative. Your cost can be added to other selling expenses for tax purposes.

Tack on a modest amount to your home's fair value—5% or so—as a cushion, because a buyer probably will bargain for a reduction. Starting off with an excessive price usually backfires. It turns off both serious buyers and brokers, who will concentrate on realistically priced properties instead. Your home may sit too long and become "damaged goods," so you could end up selling it below market value.

Setting too low a price happens less frequently, usually because the seller is ignorant of the local home market. Occasionally, though, an owner deliberately sets a below-market price to sell the property quickly—after a divorce, to settle an estate or to raise cash, for instance.

Another reason to move the property quickly is if the market is in a rapid decline; your home will be worth less in several months anyway.

OBSERVATION:

One approach is to determine the average selling time in your area, then deduct your estimated carrying costs for that period and lop the total off your asking price.

Consider dropping your asking price 5% if you get no serious interest within six weeks of putting your home on the market.

Or, offer prospective buyers a cash rebate—to help with closing costs, say. If you are financially comfortable, consider partial financing for the right buyer (see below).

SELECT A GOOD BROKER

To save a large commission—$9,000 on a $150,000 sale at 6%, say—you may be tempted to sell your home yourself. But this strategy usually pays off only in a strong market—unless your home is in top condition and you're sure it's priced to sell. Your sales skills and how much time you have to sell the home are other key factors.

Get broker recommendations from successful home sellers. At local real estate offices, request the names of the top brokers in dollar sales. Then ask at least three agents to make listing presentations, along with a written analysis of your home's estimated value.

FINANCE THE SALE OF YOUR HOME
· · · · ·

Sluggish housing markets are making it increasingly difficult for owners to sell their homes at a high price in many parts of the country. To avoid sharply lowering your price, consider helping to finance the purchase of your home. Giving a buyer a mortgage at a below-market interest rate may even make the difference between a quick sale and none at all.

HOW IT WORKS

Most home sellers understandably aren't interested in becoming mortgage lenders. Yet you may be an ideal candidate if you don't need all your home equity now and you would welcome high-interest income from a loan secured by your former residence.

To a buyer, seller financing provides a loan at below-market rates, and eliminates or reduces the amount paid in costly "points" and other closing charges to a conventional lender. Even partial financing can help a buyer get a regular mortgage.

Most sellers carry loans for five, seven or 10 years, with monthly payments set as if the loan carried a 30-year term. The full loan amount—a "balloon" payment—is due when the loan expires. The buyer usually may prepay the loan with no penalty by either selling the home or refinancing with a conventional mortgage.

HOW TO PROTECT YOURSELF

The biggest risk is that the buyer will default on the mortgage or miss some payments. Thus, it is essential to make a thorough credit and character check on a prospective buyer. If the buyer defaults and you hold a second mortgage, you won't get your money back until the first-mortgage lender had gotten its share.

• *Get a decent down payment.* The higher, the better. It should be at least 10% on a second mortgage, and 20% if a conventional lender isn't involved. This will make it harder for the borrower to walk away from your property.

• *Specify that the mortgage is non-assumable* if your buyer later sells the home. You'll avoid being stuck with a new borrower you didn't choose.

• *Consider insuring the loan.* Several companies offer mortgage insurance on seller financing. Coverage is available through approved lenders, who prepare and manage the plan. The buyer usually pays for the insurance and the seller handles servicing expenses.

SHOULD YOU HOLD OR SELL THE MORTGAGE?

If you're getting a good return, it may not pay to sell the mortgage unless you need the cash. The loan probably would be sharply discounted, and there's a good chance you'd get all your money back before the term is up anyway because of a sale or refinancing. Owners remain in the same home for only seven years on average.

• *Possible reasons to sell.* You're moving away from the area; you think interest rates will climb sharply, thereby depressing the value of the mortgage; you want the capital to use for other purposes; or you're having several problems collecting your monthly payments.

You may be able to structure the mortgage so that it can be easily sold in the secondary market. The Federal National Mortgage Association (Fannie Mae) buys seller loans according to stringent guidelines. Information and loan forms are available through the nearest Fannie Mae office and some local mortgage bankers or mortgage brokers.

Other investors might be interested in buying your mortgage. But mortgage-purchase companies usually insist on deep discounts—typically 60%–75% of the loan's unpaid balance. Their resulting return is exceptionally lucrative, especially consider-

ing the typical homeowner's short stay in their home. A good source is local real estate agents who often know private investors who may offer a better deal than a financial institution will provide.

• *A better way.* Offer the home buyer a financial incentive to close out the loan—a 10% discount off the unpaid balance, say. Or agree to pay his refinancing expenses. Another reason to contact the buyer: You might learn that the house will go on the market soon. By waiting awhile, you'll get all your money out.

◆ ALTERNATIVE:

Take out a loan using the mortgage as collateral, and apply your mortgage income directly toward the payments. Even if your payments are higher than your mortgage income, your net cost will probably be far less than if you sell the mortgage.

TAX IMPLICATIONS

Seller-financed mortgages are considered an installment sale. Any taxable capital gains earned on the mortgage are spread over the life of the loan as principal is paid, rather than fully taxed in the current year.

If you sell the loan, the difference between the unpaid balance and the amount you receive is a capital loss. This can offset capital gains and up to $3,000 a year of ordinary income, depending on how the loan is structured.

RECOMMENDATION:

If you decide to offer financing when selling your home (or any other property), be sure to seek competent professional assistance.

THESE REAL ESTATE SCAMS COULD COST YOU A BUNDLE

· · · · ·

Be on your guard against these scams:

• *The phantom assumption.* Suppose you own a house that needs work, has been empty for three months, has mortgage payments of $700 and would rent for $600 a month.

A buyer offers to assume your mortgage. He gives you a second mortgage for your equity in the property, with the first payment due in a year. You will receive no cash up front, but you'd get relief from your mortgage payment and rid of a house you don't like.

All is well until 10 months later, when you receive a notice from the holder of the first mortgage that a foreclosure action is underway. You find that the house is rented to some folks you'd never rent to and still needs repairs. The new "owner" has collected a security deposit and rent for 10 months. You're about to get back a house with 10 back payments (plus late fees and attorney's costs) and bad tenants.

If you still have personal liability on the first loan, either you must make up the back payments or possibly be sued and lose other assets. If you have no personal liability, you can walk away from the property, but you'll lose your equity in the second mortgage.

■ LESSONS:

If you're anxious to sell and if you don't want your property back again, lower your price to attract a buyer who will refinance and pay off the loan. If you want a higher price, offer a lease with an option to buy, and continue to make the loan payments yourself. Make sure you get a cash down payment that's large enough to cover all your expenses in case you have to foreclose.

• *The subordinated second mortgage.* The Smiths got full price for their $100,000 house, with $50,000 cash down. The buyer gave them a second mortgage for $50,000 at 9% interest.

After a year, the payments stopped. The Smiths couldn't find the buyer. The house was rented, but the tenants didn't know the owner. The Smiths discovered that there were two other loans on the house, both in default: one for $75,000 and another for $10,000. All told, the buyer had borrowed $135,000 on $100,000 property. What's more, the Smiths' second mortgage had never been recorded. The Smiths' money will never be recovered.

■ LESSONS:

If you accept a second mortgage when you sell a property, never allow it to be subordinated to a loan from which the buyer takes the proceeds. Otherwise, he can borrow too much money against the property, then walk away. It's your responsibility to have the second mortgage recorded.

• *Double-sell caper.* Bob was happy when he found a tenant for a recently remodeled house. The tenant even offered to prepay the first six months' rent. Bob let the tenant move in that day, Saturday, although the banks were closed and Bob couldn't find out if the check for the rent and security deposit was good.

A week after Bob deposited the check in the bank, it was returned to him marked "insufficient funds." Bob drove directly to the house, but no one was home and there was no furniture in any of the rooms.

Then Bob received several telephone calls from people asking about the closing on the house. The callers had signed contracts to buy the house for $90,000 over the weekend and given the "owner" cash deposits ranging from $500 to $3,000. The "owner" had given them Bob's telephone number to call.

Bob told the callers there must be some mistake. First, the house was worth at least $150,000. Second, he owned the house and it wasn't for sale. Bob never saw the tenant again, and the "buyers" never saw their cash.

■ LESSONS:

1. Never give a renter possession of a property before the check for the first month's rent and deposit clears. 2. Never give a seller a cash deposit. Always pay by check and make the check payable to a title company or attorney acting as an escrow agent.

RECOMMENDATION:

To protect yourself, you should have some form of legal representation in any type of real estate deal in which you're not an expert.

EXECUTIVE INVESTMENT: RENTAL REAL ESTATE
· · · · ·

While rental real estate may not be the perfect investment, for many executives it's the next best thing. Buy in a good location and take care of the property, and you're sure to find that values will increase substantially. Meanwhile, the rent you receive

can go toward the monthly payments and, if you've bought well, it will generate a positive cash flow early in your ownership.

TAX DEDUCTIONS

Mortgage interest, depreciation, property taxes, and improvement and maintenance expenses are tax deductible. In some cases, those costs could exceed your rental income, especially when you're just starting out. The IRS characterizes these as *passive losses*, which means you can only offset them with *passive income*, such as from another rental property or a limited partnership.

♦ EXCEPTION:

If your adjusted gross income is no more than $100,000, you can deduct as much as $25,000 of passive losses from your *active income* (from wages and the like), *as long as you actively manage the property*. Above that amount, the break gradually phases out. It ends at $150,000. On income above that figure, you must take your deductions against rental income.

IT PAYS TO FIX IT UP

Smart deals can be found in slightly run-down places in up-and-coming neighborhoods. Acting as your own general contractor and subcontracting all or most of the work can save you a fair amount on repairs. You and your agent will have to work up figures that estimate initial costs, projected earnings, expenses and profits based on your down payment, mortgage costs and taxes.

It can pay to hire a qualified inspector to look for large repairs, such as a new roof or heating system. And you can use that in negotiating a lower sales price.

RECOMMENDATION:
Before you sign, check state laws and local regulations affecting landlords and tenants—everything from how much you can raise the rent to how you're required to treat security deposits.

HOW TO BE A LANDLORD

. . . . .

Be businesslike in all your dealings with tenants, repair persons, tax collectors and the myriad of others you may have to deal with.

THE LEASE

A lease must conform to state and local requirements, but it should also be a "landlord" lease—one that's written to protect *you*.

The lease should go into detail on everything you and a good real estate lawyer can think of: penalties for late payment, charges for lost keys, costs of repairs resulting from carelessness or neglect, where parking is allowed, whether basement storage is permitted, when television and stereo sets should be turned off (or at least played softly). In short, it should try to anticipate everything that could possibly happen, because it might.

> EXAMPLE:
> A tenant installs a window air conditioner incorrectly, so that the unit leaks water and causes major damage. You'll have trouble collecting if the lease doesn't mention damages of this type.

You might find that a tenant is operating a business, complete with inventory piled in the hallways and customers trouping in and out at all hours, if no ban against such activity is in the lease.

CHOOSING TENANTS

Sizing up prospective tenants is difficult. Once they're in it's very hard to evict them. Even if they don't pay the rent, it can take months to get them out.

Check references and credit if you can, but ultimately, use your best judgment. Here, experience is a good teacher.

You should also check the rental unit's interior from time to time.

Chapter   7

RETIREMENT/PENSIONS

BEING GENEROUS NOW CAN HELP YOU RETIRE COMFORTABLY

· · · · ·

Most of us make some charitable contributions, so a charitable remainder trust (CRT) is worth considering as a basic retirement plan alternative.

You don't have to be a philanthropist or a millionaire to set up a CRT. It can pay off if you can put at least $20,000 into it, either all together or over a period of years. You can set up a CRT for just a few hundred dollars and maintain it with minimal ongoing fees.

HOW CRTs WORK

You establish a CRT by donating property or money to a trust. The CRT, which is tax exempt, sells the property, if necessary, and invests the proceeds for you. High-yield vehicles are usually emphasized with this type of trust.

Income from the trust is paid outright to you and/or to others you previously designate for either a specified term or for the rest of your life. After that, the assets remaining in the trust go to one or more charities of your choosing.

Even though the charity probably won't get anything for several years, you get an immediate tax write-off for your donation. The deduction is a percentage of your donation, based on the IRS actuarial tables. The smaller the income you want and the shorter the charity's expected waiting period, the greater the financial deduction. The larger the income and the longer the wait, the smaller the up-front write-off you can declare.

355

EXAMPLE:

You and your spouse are each 55 years old. Your joint life expectancy is about 25 years. Assuming you want a 5% annual payout, your deduction would be about 25%, or $2,500 per $10,000 donation. If you and your wife are 60, the write-off is over 30%.

• **Charitable remainder annuity trust.** You receive a fixed amount periodically from the trust. The minimum is 5% of the net fair market value of property placed in the trust.

• **Charitable remainder unitrust.** You get a fixed percentage of the assets, at least 5% per year. The unitrust is becoming the more popular choice because it provides growth potential.

EXAMPLE:

You ask for a 6% annual payout, while the trust actually earns 8% per year. The trust assets grow because the excess 2% stays reinvested in the trust. Thus your 6% "yield" grows over the years.

HOW TO USE A CRT

• **As a retirement plan.** You may make annual contributions either to supplement your present retirement plan or as your sole plan. Using a CRT as a supplement may help executives with large pension plans (over $600,000, say) avoid the 15% excise tax on "excess distributions," which was created by the 1986 tax law.

With an ongoing CRT, you may donate as little or as much as you want, when you want. You can even elect a "catch-up" provision: You take little or nothing from the trust while you're still working and making donations; then, you make up the shortfall by receiving more after you retire.

• **Donating assets that have risen dramatically in value.** Under normal circumstances, the sale of such assets would trigger a tax at your highest federal marginal rate, up to 33%, plus state and local income taxes. If you donate these appreciated assets to charity, including a CRT, you can avoid all capital gains tax.

In addition, your charitable contribution to the CRT will be based on the assets' full value. You can convert a no-yield asset into steady income and save tax rather than pay it.

For example, say you bought a parcel of land for $10,000 years ago. The land is now in the path of suburban development, and you've had an offer of $100,000 for it. If you sell, you'll have a $90,000 gain and could owe at least $25,200 (28%) in tax. If you donate the land to a CRT, you'll owe no income tax. What's more, your donation will be valued at $100,000. Assuming a 30% deduction, you get an immediate $30,000 write-off and save $8,400 in taxes in the 28% bracket. In addition, the CRT can sell the land for $100,000 and owe no tax. So it will have the full $100,000 to invest, from which to distribute income to you.

CRTs AND ESTATE PLANNING

If your estate is over $600,000 ($1.2 million for a couple), it could be subject to steep estate tax. Counting real estate and pension plans, such sums are within reach of many executives these days.

Transferring assets to a CRT gets assets out of your estate and reduces estate taxes. Yet you can enjoy income from those assets for the rest of your life (and your spouse's, if desired).

Your heirs, of course, won't get the assets you've given away. If that's a concern, you may be able to use either the immediate tax savings, the ongoing income or both to buy a life insurance policy. When you (or you and your spouse) die, your heirs will get life insurance proceeds, free of income tax.

DRAWBACKS

CRTs are irrevocable. Once you donate an appreciated asset to the trust, it probably will be sold, and further appreciation will be lost forever. Life insurance may not make up the full difference to your heirs. In some cases, you may be subject to alternative minimum tax or annual limits on charitable deductions.

CRTs also require careful, precise planning, so it's vital that you have good legal and tax advice. In the case of real estate or securities that aren't publicly traded, you will need an appraisal.

KEOGHS AND SEPs OFFER BIG TAX BREAKS
· · · · ·

If you're self-employed, be sure to make the most of a major tax break: retirement plans. You can make large, tax-deductible contributions that grow tax free until you withdraw the assets.

If your full-time or part-time business venture is unincorporated, you can open either a Keogh plan or a Simplified Employee Pension (SEP) plan as a tax shelter for income from fees, retainers and royalties—anything except salary, wages or

investments. If you're an employee covered by a corporate retirement plan, you can keep a Keogh or SEP if you also have a profitable self-employed enterprise.

Keogh plans offer more flexibility than SEPs, but the latter require less paperwork and may carry lower administrative costs. In both cases, you must make tax-deductible contributions for all employees meeting contrasting age and minimum service requirements.

KEOGHS

These plans come in four varieties. Your best choice depends on your age when you start the plan, when you plan to retire, your expected self-employment income and the rate of return you think the plan will achieve.

Most Keoghs are *defined-contribution plans,* which can take three forms. In a defined-contribution plan, the amount you will have at retirement will depend upon how much you have contributed and the plan's investment performance.

• *In a profit-sharing Keogh,* you may vary the contribution each year, or make none at all if you'd rather use the cash elsewhere. This lets you put aside more in high-profit years, and little or nothing in bad years.

The trade-off for this flexibility is that your annual contribution is relatively low: up to 13.043% of net self-employment income (or 15% after subtracting the contribution), with a top of $30,000 per plan participant. Thus, if you're a sole proprietor who earns $60,000 this year, you can put $7,826 into your Keogh.

• *With a money-purchase Keogh,* your annual contribution can total up to 20% of net earned income or $30,000, whichever is less. So, with $60,000 of self-employed income, you can contribute $12,000. This alternative may be your best choice if you still have many years until retirement. The drawback is that you must put a specified percentage of annual net income into your Keogh each year, regardless of how your business does, unless you get the IRS approval to vary it.

• *A "paired" Keogh plan* may provide the best package of flexibility and tax breaks. It combines a money-purchase segment and a profit-sharing portion, which varies from zero to 15% depending on that year's income. The paired plan carries a 20%/$30,000 top.

• *A defined-benefit Keogh* usually is better than a defined-contribution plan if you have less time to build retirement assets because you can dramatically boost your tax-deductible plan contributions. By selecting the annual pension benefit you want to receive in retirement, you then work backwards to an annual contribution. On $100,000 of income, for instance, you might be allowed a $50,000 annual write-off if you plan to work a relatively short time. The contribution changes over time, depending on the plan's investment results.

At retirement, you can collect up to $98,000, or 100% of your average annual self-employment income over your three highest consecutive earning years, whichever is less. However, you can set a $10,000 minimum pension even if your highest earnings averaged less than that, enabling you to make larger deductible contributions.

SEPs

Take a close look at the simplified employee benefit plan (SEP). It's ideal for business owners who feel that setting up a regular pension plan is just too difficult and expensive.

The SEP is also a good way for sole proprietors and "moonlighting" employees to shelter income and build up a retirement nest egg. Here's how it works:

An SEP is actually an individual retirement account, or a group of IRAs, set up by an employer for himself and his employees. Unlike a regular IRA, however, contributions to an SEP aren't limited. Not only does the contribution reduce your taxable income, but the SEP fund grows, tax-deferred, until you start making withdrawals at retirement.

These plans are easy to set up. Just fill out the one-page Form 5305-SEP and keep it on file. You don't even have to send a copy to the IRS. Then you and your employees open accounts at the financial institution each chooses.

The SEP contribution formula is the same formula as for computing profit-sharing Keoghs, including the 15%/$30,000 limit. The contribution percentage generally must be the same for all employees, but you can vary it every year.

KEOGH/SEP COMPARISONS

• A Keogh must be established by December 31, but it may be funded at any time until you file your tax return the following year. An SEP may be set up as late as April 15 of the following year, when it must be funded.

• Investment options for Keoghs and SEPs are largely the same. You can be the trustee of your own Keogh plan and still invest in areas not open to SEPs, such as a direct investment in real estate. While you have the authority to make Keogh investment decisions for your employees, you should delegate that thankless task to a major financial institution. A defined-benefit Keogh can carry significant administrative costs because it must be designed by a pension consultant or an actuary. A plus for SEPs: Employees make their own investment decisions.

INCLUDING EMPLOYEES IN THE PLANS

• To qualify for Keogh coverage, employees must be 21 or older, and have worked at least 1,000 hours annually for two years. Vesting can be phased in over several years, which gives employees an incentive to stay with you, or you can choose other options. Note that your Keogh may also be subject to other rules regarding top-heavy pension plans.

In an SEP, you must cover all employees 21 or older who earned at least $300 a year in each of the last five years. Employees in an SEP get full, immediate vesting, so they take their SEP money with them if they quit.

• Elective salary deferral is easily available in an SEP, and may reduce your current taxable income. Total employer/employee contributions may not exceed 15% of salary or $30,000, whichever is less. A 401(k) plan allows participants in a Keogh to fund pensions with deferred salary.

• At retirement, Keogh payouts qualify for five-year averaging, which means you can have a lump-sum distribution taxed as if it occurred over five years. SEPs have no provision for averaging distributions. In either case, distributions generally can begin between ages 59 1/2 and April 1 of the year after you turn 70 1/2, even if you're still working. You can continue making contributions while you get distributions.

WATCH THE TIMING OF PENSION CONTRIBUTIONS
• • • • •

A Cleveland doctor's attempt to make the funding of his pensions more or less automatic was well-intentioned but illegal, the Tax Court said.

Here's what happened: After Dong Lee incorporated himself, he set up two pension plans. He relied on a pension consultant to tell him when and how much to pay into the plans, which the consultants generally did at the last minute.

The doctor, therefore set up an interest-bearing checking account in the corporate name from which to transfer funds to the plans when needed. He applied for an extension to file the plans' annual returns for 1982, but did not make the payments until a month past the deadline.

The IRS wanted to hit the doctor with an excise tax for underfunding the plans. He said the money had been put in the special account in time. Not good enough, the court said. He still controlled the money. A "contribution" must be set aside irrevocably. (*D.J. Lee, M.D., Inc., v. Commissioner,* 92 T.C. No 16, Feb. 7, 1989)

CONSIDER STATE TAXES BEFORE YOU RETIRE
• • • • •

Although they're often overlooked in retirement planning, where you live will directly affect how much you'll pay in taxes over the years. So be sure to look at income-tax rates among the states, along with taxes on real estate, personal property and estates when making retirement decisions. Counties and cities may levy additional taxes.

WHAT TO CONSIDER BEFORE SETTLING DOWN

■ **Income taxes.** State taxes are deductible on federal returns, thereby reducing the effective state tax rate—for instance, from 7% to 5% if you're in the 28% federal bracket. Ten states—Alaska, Connecticut, Florida, Nevada, New Hampshire, South Dakota, Tennessee, Texas, Washington and Wyoming—don't tax personal income.

A state's entire tax-rate schedule is worth a hard look, not just the top rate. A couple with taxable income under $30,000 might pay less income tax in a state with a 9% rate on taxable income over $100,000 than in a state that collects 6% on all taxable income over $10,000. Most states offer a modest tax break for those 65 and over, such as a larger personal exemption or standard deduction.

Here's how your income might be affected by other income-tax laws:

• *If you'll be getting Social Security and/or pension income.* Social Security benefits are tax free in 28 states, regardless of your other income. Payouts from a private pension are at least partially tax free in 18 states, from a state public pension plan in 28 states, and from a federal public pension plan in 31. Where pension plan income is taxed, it may be at a lower rate than on earned income. Also, find out how distributions from Individual Retirement Accounts, profit-sharing plans and 401(k) plans are taxed in the states you're considering.

• *If you'll have significant investment income.* Some states charge a higher tax on unearned income than on earned income.

Among the states that don't tax earned income, Connecticut, New Hampshire and Tennessee tax investment income.

• *If you own municipal bonds.* You may want to adjust your portfolio if you move: 40 states tax interest on out-of-state municipal bonds, but not on in-state bonds. Illinois and a few others tax all municipal-bond interest.

■ **Real estate taxes.** You'll pay property taxes if you own your retirement home. You might want to settle in an area where property taxes are going up slowly. But the likely trade-off is that good schools, which tend to require higher taxes, are a major factor in the long-term appreciation of property values.

Other special tax features that may benefit retired homeowners include:

• *Homestead exemptions.* Most states, including Arizona and Florida, reduce the real estate taxes on your principal residence.

• *Income tests.* Real estate taxes in some areas can be significantly reduced for people with moderate incomes.

• *Tax postponements.* In 18 states, older homeowners can delay paying real estate taxes until the home is sold or death. Interest usually is charged at a fairly low rate—6%, say. This break may be available only if you're disabled or you have a low income.

■ **Other taxes.** Florida and several others levy an annual tax on the fair market value of stocks and bonds. In a few states, personal property taxes apply to costly cars and artworks.

• *Estate taxes.* Federal estate tax applies only to estates valued at $600,000 or more, excluding assets left to a surviving spouse. Half the states levy estate taxes, but their tax formula generally tracks the federal tax, so that it offsets federal estate tax. Some states—Massachusetts, New York, Ohio and four others—do levy an additional tax.

▲ IMPORTANT:

Establish residence in only one state. Sometimes two or more states may try to collect income tax (and even estate tax). This can happen if you don't make it perfectly clear where your principal residence is.

EXAMPLE:

You've owned a home for many years in the Northeast or Midwest. Then you decide to retire and buy a place in the sun, where you spend seven months a year. But you keep your old house to live in the rest of the year. You leave one car up north, and take a new one south and register it there. You carry drivers' licenses in both states.

As enticing as this scenario may sound, don't follow it. You've paid income taxes for years in one state, which wants you to keep paying because you keep a principal residence there. But the tax collector will come after you down south too, and he'll have a strong case if you spend six months or more there.

To avoid that and other potential tax problems that may arise, establish your true home in one state. Register to vote there, register your cars there, use one driver's license and file all required tax returns there. If possible, also spend more than six months a year there. Some states, including Florida, allow you to declare domicile with a special form.

You may even want to get rid of property in the other state—either through sale, by putting it in trust for your heirs, or by giving them a remainder interest while you keep a life interest.

RECOMMENDATION:

Before you move to another state, check with a lawyer in the new state to see whether your will and other legal documents need to be changed, either to comply with, or take advantage of, that state's laws.

ROLLING OVER YOUR 401(k) PLAN: DO IT WITH CARE

There's one item that many managers forget to check when they're changing jobs: how they can roll their 401(k) plan money into the plan run by their new employer.

If you don't get all the details of the new plan from the person who's in charge, you can run into serious and expensive trouble.

EXAMPLE:

A manager routinely turned over the check from his old 401(k) plan to the new one. But after more than 60 days—the legal time limit for all tax-deferred rollovers—had passed, he found to his dismay that he wasn't eligible to join the new plan for at least a year. As a result, he discovered that all the money he had accumulated suddenly was taxable as ordinary income.

• If you can't join your new company's plan right away, you can always roll your pension money over into an IRA account. But make sure you do so within 60 days, and you'll continue to get tax deferral on the money.

A TRIPLE ROLLOVER GETS IRS OK

■ ■ ■ ■ ■

A triple rollover of a taxpayer's pension into an Individual Retirement Account has been approved by the IRS.

Here's how the deal worked: The taxpayer, whom we'll call Smith, had pension benefits from a prior job before he joined a firm as a partner in 1984. That same year Smith also formed a separate new company, which, in turn, took over his partnership interest.

The following year, Smith transferred his account balance from the pension plan to the partnership's plan.

Now the IRS has approved his request to transfer the pension from the partnership to his new company's plan and roll it over from there directly to an IRA account within 60 days.

PENSION RIGHTS AND DIVORCE

■ ■ ■ ■ ■

Divorce courts must look beyond the value of a person's pension at the time of divorce in figuring how to divide its future benefits, the New Jersey Supreme Court ruled. The justices followed the lead of most other states that have looked at the question.

The divorce case in question involved a husband whose pension plan provided for periodic cost-of-living increases. The wife has a claim on those increases just as she does to the basic pension payouts, the ruling says.

■ REASON:

The right to increases was earned during the years of the marriage, just like any other future benefits that can be traced to the joint marital effort. (*Moore v. Moore*, No. A-67)

THE LEAST TAXING WAYS TO TAKE RETIREMENT FUNDS

■ ■ ■ ■ ■

If you're among the many people who receive a lump-sum distribution or who plan to withdraw cash from a retirement plan, it's vital that you do some careful tax planning first. Sooner or later, you must pay income tax on all funds in the retirement plan except for any aftertax contributions you've made. It's up to you whether the tax bite will prove very painful or barely worth noticing.

ROLLOVER YOUR RETIREMENT FUNDS

If you're in good health and you can live comfortably on other income, you should probably take as little as possible from your retirement plan now.

■ REASON:

You'll postpone income tax on current holdings, and account assets will continue to grow tax-free.

To avoid tax on a lump-sum distribution, you must put all the money into an Individual Retirement Account (IRA), a Keogh plan or any other qualified retirement plan within 60 days. This deadline is strict: If you miss it, you'll be taxed on the whole amount, even if the delay was beyond your control.

One disadvantage of a rollover is that you cannot later use forward averaging (explained below). But sheltering the rollover and all future earnings from tax for many years before withdrawals begin is probably more valuable.

As an example, suppose you're a 55-year-old who receives $100,000 from your pension plan. If you roll over the money into an IRA earning 10%, the account will generate 20 annual aftertax payments of $20,772 if you're in a 25% federal/state tax bracket. This is $3,358 more per year than if you pay tax immediately under 10-year averaging, then invest the rest at 8% after tax. To justify taking the money now, your tax rate on withdrawals would have to jump from 25% to 37.5%, or the aftertax return on your portfolio from 8% to 9.2%.

RECOMMENDATION:

If you already have an IRA, set up a separate one for a pension plan rollover. You may want to roll it over again later into a company retirement plan if you take another job, or into a Keogh plan in case you're self-employed in the future.

LUMP-SUM DISTRIBUTION

If you want access to all the money now, you may face a large tax bill. But a key tax break will help lower it. *Forward averaging* lets you pay tax on a lump-sum distribution as if you received the money over five or 10 years, rather than all at once. You can use averaging only after age 59 1/2. And you can use it just once—unless you used it before 1986, when the rule took effect; then you can use it once more.

If you were born before 1936, you can use either 10-year forward averaging at 1986 tax rates of as high as 50%, or five-year averaging at lower current rates (a 33% top). The 10-year option is better if the taxable amount is $475,000 or less. Calculate both ways.

Say, you need only some of your retirement plan money now. You're allowed a partial rollover if you're leaving your job or you're disabled, so long as you roll over at least 50%. Note, though, that you're not eligible for forward averaging on the portion that is not rolled over.

ANNUAL DISTRIBUTIONS

Many people assume that distributions before age 59 1/2 from all retirement plans are subject to a 10% penalty. In fact, there's no penalty in some situations. The most important is if you take annual payouts as an annuity, based on your own life expectancy, or that of yourself and a beneficiary. The formulas are set forth in the IRS tables.

At age 56, you could withdraw, at no penalty, 3.73% of what remains in your IRA, based on your own life expectancy. Because a person's life expectancy changes as he gets older, you have to recalculate the withdrawal percentage each year.

If you turned 50 before 1986, any pension assets earned before 1974 are entitled to a special capital gains break—a top rate of 20%, compared with today's 28% or 33%—no matter when your pension distributions begin. For younger individuals, the break applies to 75% of the pre-1974 balance this year, 50% in 1990, 25% in 1991, then none.

WHEN WITHDRAWALS MUST BEGIN

The first deadline for taking out cash

from retirement plans is April 1 of the year following the year you turn 70 $\frac{1}{2}$. A second distribution must occur by that year's end.

If you wish to minimize annual withdrawals and lengthen the payout period, you can name a young beneficiary. The life expectancy of a 71-year-old is 15.3 years, and the first required annual distribution from a $100,000 retirement plan pension account is $6,536. If a 62-year-old spouse is named beneficiary, the joint life expectancy rises to 24.7 years and the minimum withdrawal drops to $4,049. You can't name a three-year-old as beneficiary, though; the IRS imputes a 10-year maximum difference in age for all but spouses.

RECOMMENDATION:
Coordinate withdrawals with Social Security payments, part of which become taxable when a married couple's income, with certain adjustments, exceeds $32,000 ($25,000 for singles). Professional guidance is advisable if your plan assets are large or your situation is complicated.

Chapter 8

TAXES/TAX STRATEGIES

RENT YOUR CONDO TO THE KIDS
. . . . .

Buying your parent or college-student child a condominium to live in can save you money. You can buy a condo for a relative to use and deduct mortgage interest and property taxes on your tax return for a second home.

Or you can buy a place as a rental property, rent it to the relative at fair market value, and write off depreciation, condo fees, utilities, insurance and repairs, as well. Here are some tips to keep in mind if you decide to treat the property as a rental:

• *Handle the money transaction carefully.* The rent cannot come directly from your pocket. However, your child, say, could use earnings from a summer job to pay the rent, or you might give him or her a lump sum at the beginning of the school year to cover living expenses, including rent.

It's also smart to set up a separate account where you can deposit the rent and write checks for repairs. It shows a businesslike approach to the operation.

• *Visits.* You may be able to write off at least a portion of the cost of trips taken to inspect the property. The key is your dominant purpose for the trip. If the IRS sees it as predominantly familial, the expense may not pass muster.

• *Deductions.* If your adjusted gross income is $100,000 or less, and you actively manage the condo, you can deduct up to $25,000 in losses on the property, against "active" income, such as wages. The deduction phases out as income exceeds this level, until it disappears entirely at $150,000.

• *The rent.* While you must charge your relative a reasonable market rent in order to take a rental deduction, you can discount it if the family member agrees to maintain the place, saving you the cost of hiring an agent or property manager.

• *Your purchase.* Like any other real estate investment, location, price and market conditions are crucial to your decision to buy. Since you will likely hold the property for a relatively short time if you're buying to house a college-student child, it's particularly important not to overpay. If the college and its community are expanding, though, a reasonable price today might spell a profit four years down the line.

OBSERVATION:

Even if your relative handles the day-to-day management and maintenance of the condominium, you can still qualify as an active investor. Simply make sure you take an active role in approving new tenants, setting rents, and agreeing to all major repairs or improvements.

SAVE TAXES ON A VACATION HOME
· · · · ·

Money you save from tax write-offs on a vacation home can help subsidize your expenses. A second home may offer a badly needed tax shelter, particularly if your first is largely paid off.

HOW YOU USE IT DETERMINES TAX BREAKS

If your second home is a residence, you can write off mortgage interest and property taxes, just as you do on your first home. A residence is a place you use for more than 14 days a year or 10% of the number of days

it's rented, whichever is greater. (A home not rented out is considered a residence.) A boat or mobile home qualifies if it has basic living accommodations—sleeping space, a toilet and cooking facilities.

Included as personal use is occupancy by family members, a part owner, anyone who rents your place for below fair-market rent or someone with whom you barter home use. Days spent on repairs and maintenance don't count as either personal or rental use.

You can earn unreported, tax-free income if you rent out any residence for 14 days or less each year. You can't take any write-offs for the rental period, but you can deduct mortgage interest and taxes.

HOW TO ALLOCATE EXPENSES

If your vacation home doubles as a rental, you must prorate all expenses between rental use and personal use. Your rental income probably won't be taxed because you can usually allocate enough deductible expenses to the rental activity so that it won't show a taxable profit.

At the same time, though, you can't show a tax loss on a residence. So you must take write-offs in this order: mortgage interest, real estate taxes, casualty losses, operating expenses (including utilities, insurance, maintenance and repairs) and depreciation. Unused property tax and mortgage interest expenses can be taken as personal itemized deductions. (Mortgage interest deductions are limited to two homes.)

■ **Tax break.** The courts have given vacation home owners a tax break on write-off allocations for taxes and mortgage interest. Say you use your vacation spot for two months, rent it out for two months and it's vacant for eight. The IRS wants a 50% allocation of mortgage interest and taxes to the rental period, since this is half the time the house is used.

But the courts have decided that, since interest and tax payments are spread over the entire year, you need allocate only one-sixth (two months out of twelve) of interest and taxes to the rental period (*Bolton v. Commissioner,* T.C. 104). This treatment enables you to more fully use depreciation and other deductions that aren't deductible on your personal return, thus boosting your total deductions.

IF YOUR PROPERTY IS A RENTAL

You may be able to take a tax loss, provided your vacation home is rented out most of the season and personal use is no more than 14 days or 10% of the number of rental days.

• Losses on a rental are considered "passive." If your adjusted gross income (AGI) is under $100,000, you can write off up to $25,000 of passive losses against earned or investment income. This deduction is phased out up to AGI of $150,000.

Above $150,000 AGI, deductions for rental expenses are limited to rental income. But you can use them to offset other passive income—from another rental property or a limited partnership, for instance—in the current or future years. When you sell the property, any unused losses can offset your profit or any other income. Note that if your property qualifies as a rental, the interest allocated to personal use becomes personal interest.

RECOMMENDATION:
For the best tax breaks, you may want to either increase or reduce the amount of

time you spend at your second home, or the amount of time you rent it out. For instance, you might not be able to write off all of a rental's mortgage interest if doing so would result in a passive loss for which you are ineligible.

The solution is to change your property from a rental to a residence by increasing personal use to 15 days or more than 10% of the number of rental days. Then you can write off all home mortgage interest. Or you may want to convert from residence to rental use so you can take a tax loss. If so, cut back family use to 14 days or less than 10% of rental days.

TAX-SMART HOME CONSTRUCTION LOANS
· · · · ·

Borrow the money for your new home the right way and the interest will be fully deductible. Do it wrong and you'll lose out on any breaks.

A construction loan must be secured by the land itself to qualify for the full interest deduction. As a loan secured by the land will rarely cover the cost of building a house, the regulations force you to "eat" some of the interest cost on additional loans until you can get permanent financing.

This makes speedy construction and quick refinancing a must. Once you have a regular home mortgage, all your interest on it is deductible.

● NOTE:

On a renovation loan, you can get the full interest deduction by securing it against the house. (*IRS Notice 88-74*)

EXTRA PAYMENTS MEAN BIGGER TAX WRITE-OFFS

■　■　■　■　■

You can accelerate mortgage interest and property tax payments before year-end in order to boost your income-tax deductions. The IRS allows you to make one extra payment of monthly interest and to pay up to 20 months of property taxes in one year. For the extra property tax payment, determine how much you normally pay each month and multiply it by up to eight. Payments must be received and processed before Dec. 31. Then verify that your lender has reported them correctly to the IRS.

● N O T E :

An extra write-off this year will mean smaller-than-normal deductions in the following year, unless you prepay again next year.

MAILING IN TAX RETURNS

■　■　■　■　■

Don't try to save money when you mail your tax return to the IRS. That stern message came out of the Tax Court recently in a case involving a tax return that was lost in the mail.

Paul Walden and his wife had been given a two-month extension and mailed their completed form on June 13, two days before the extended deadline.

Unfortunately, they sent it by regular mail, and the IRS said it never received the return. But it wasn't until the following February that the agency notified the couple that it was missing.

Months later, the Waldens sent in an unsigned copy of their return and, still later, signed a paper specifying that it was their joint return for the year. The IRS then hit them with a tax bill and a late filing penalty.

When the Waldens went to trial, the Tax Court said the return wasn't filed until they signed the return they gave the IRS, adding that by failing to use certified or registered mail, they assumed the risk of nondelivery.

HOW TO HANDLE AN AUDIT

■　■　■　■　■

The odds are roughly 100 to 1 that you won't be called for a tax audit. But if you're among the chosen few, you have little to fear if you can support most of your deductions.

TYPES OF AUDITS

● **The correspondence audit.** You're asked to send receipts or other information about one or a few specific items. Make copies rather than sending original papers.

● **Office audit.** You're required to visit the IRS district office. Specific matters the auditor wants to review are noted in the notification letter. Although your entire return may be subject to examination, it's necessary to bring documentation only for the specified items.

● **Field audit.** An IRS agent comes to your home or business to examine a wider range of records. Have a tax accountant or lawyer represent you. You can also ask that the audit be conducted at your representative's office or the IRS office.

WHAT TO DO AT THE AUDIT

You have the burden of proving that the numbers you provided are accurate. So good preparation is essential. Be ready to cooperate—up to a point:

- *Provide as much documentation as possible on the specified areas.* Arrange papers so you can quickly present them to the auditor and he or she can examine them easily. But don't bring in more than you've been asked for. You'll just make it easier for the auditor to go on a fishing expedition.
- *Don't volunteer information.* When you answer the questions, be brief and direct. Stay on your guard at all times: The auditor is trained to regard even idle conversation as a means of eliciting additional information from you.
- *Maintain a businesslike attitude.* If you show you're serious and honest, you may receive the benefit of any doubts. But if you play games with the auditor, he may make a more detailed examination or become unwilling to compromise.
- *Don't concede immediate defeat even if you lack full documentation.* The auditor may accept a reasonable explanation of how you came up with a figure even if you can't fully support it. Accept the agent's challenges only if you're convinced he's right. If you disagree, say so and why. Quick agreement may even raise suspicions that your return deserves closer examination.
- *Don't "give away the store."* Agents often make trades by giving in on some items while you compromise on others. But too many concessions could result in a large tax deficiency being assessed against you. Try to negotiate a total dollar amount for the audit as a whole. Also, be leery of compromises on write-offs you deduct every year.
- *Don't allow yourself to be rushed, con-*

fused, intimidated or insulted. If you're having numerous problems with an auditor, you have the right to demand another one.

WHEN YOU DISAGREE WITH THE AUDIT

Many taxpayers are so intimidated that they quickly settle for whatever amount they're told is due. The best place for negotiation rests with the initial examiner. But if you disagree, the stakes may be high enough to justify an appeal.

- *Ask for a meeting with the auditor's supervisor.* At that point, the agent may agree to reduce or eliminate a proposed assessment. If not, the supervisor may do so.
- *If necessary, you may appeal formally within the IRS or go to court.* Within the IRS, when the dispute centers on a factual issue, you should be able to cite IRS regulations or rulings that have led to favorable settlements in similar cases. When the dispute is over a legal issue, the outlook is fuzzier.

The IRS appeals officer often considers the chances of the IRS winning the case in court, and proposes a settlement accordingly. Feel free to make or seek an offer.

OBSERVATION:

Any appeal within the IRS involves the risk that your entire return will be reexamined and your potential tax deficiency increased. If your return contains vulnerable areas involving larger sums, weigh the odds before appealing.

- *You can go to Tax Court,* District Court or the Court of Claims. In Tax Court, the most common choice, you must show that the IRS is wrong, but you needn't specify exact figures or prove you owe no money at all. The judge will determine any deficiency. Sessions are held in some 80 cities. Once you file a petition, you may want to pay the tax deficiency to stop the interest accumulation. The court will order a refund if you win.

• *Small case division.* If the amount at stake is under $10,000, you can cut down on time and legal expense by going to the Tax Court's Small Case Division. This is an informal court that follows informal rules of evidence, and you can present your own case if you wish. The court's decision is final.

WHEN TO HIRE EXPERT ASSISTANCE

Whether you should have an advisor with you depends on two main factors:

• *The nature of the information required.* Most audits cover only facts and documentation, so it may simply be a matter of supplying back-up material. If you don't agree with the auditor's findings, consult your advisor later or bring him to another session. But if tax law interpretations are involved, you'll probably want a pro with you.

• *How much money is involved.* The larger the sum, the more useful help may be. An experienced practitioner may be adept at bargaining with the auditor and generally can keep the discussion on safe ground.

RECORD YOUR AUDIT

■ ■ ■ ■ ■

One of the protections taxpayers are getting from the Taxpayer Bill of Rights is the right to make a sound recording of any interview with an IRS employee involving the assessment or collection of a tax.

There are some procedural hoops to jump through, however. You have to give the IRS 10 days' notice that you want to record the interview. You also have to supply your own recording equipment, permit the agency to make its own recording, and present yourself at a location, usually an IRS office, where the agency can make its own recording.

If the IRS chooses to record the session, you can get a transcript or a copy of its recording, if you ask for it within 30 days, and pay the cost of copying or transcription.

WHEN TO SETTLE OUT OF COURT

■ ■ ■ ■ ■

You may be better off settling out of court in a dispute with the IRS over valuation of a piece of property for tax purposes. That's the advice from the Tax Court, struggling to divine the true value of an historic preservation facade easement.

The court explained that the parties involved and their experts have a better grasp of the facts than do the courts which rely on "a cold record and dry briefs."

Litigation, the court added, "is an inefficient, wasteful and inherently imprecise method of resolving these disputes."

At issue was the valuation of an historic preservation easement on a building near Dupont Circle in Washington, DC. The taxpayers' expert said the gift was worth $235,000, while the government's representative put it at $70,000. The court came up with a value of $130,000.

Not only did the taxpayers have to pay more taxes but higher rates of interest for "substantial underpayments attributable to tax motivated transactions," a reference to their 165% overstatement of the property's value. (*Losch v. Commissioner*)

IRS CAN'T ALWAYS DEMAND RECORDS

If you're a sole proprietor, the rules against self-incrimination apply to an IRS summons demanding your tax records, even if the papers are for a civil investigation.

This ruling comes from the federal District Court of Maryland in a case involving a self-employed doctor who hadn't filed a processable tax return since 1979. The doctor objected on grounds of self-incrimination when an IRS agent ordered him to produce W-2 and 1099 forms, along with employee earnings statements and bank deposit records.

The IRS claimed the documents were for a civil proceeding, so his fear of incrimination was based on speculation.

▲ DECISION:

The court didn't buy this argument, pointing out that "routine" tax investigations often lead to criminal prosecutions. Production of the records involved the doctor's Fifth Amendment rights, the court said. (*U.S. v. Cates*)

ESTATE LEGAL FEES

Legal bills run up by an estate may not be deductible expenses as far as the tax laws go, the Tax Court held. It said that when litigation deals with how much the estate is to receive for selling off part of its assets, the cost of pressing the suit must be capitalized, resulting in a bigger tax bite.

The underlying dispute is not uncommon in a family business. In this case, two brothers owned a business and had entered a buy-sell agreement, which gave the firm itself the right to buy from the heirs of a deceased partner the stock he owned.

After one brother died, the survivor found a buyer for the entire business, one who would pay much more than the per-share price outlined in the buy-sell agreement.

The widow—and executrix—of the deceased brother sued and eventually won the higher price for the estate-owned shares.

The $250,000 spent on the legal action was a legitimate estate expense, the opinion says, but does not allow a deduction. It simply must be deducted from the amount paid for the stock in figuring the capital gain on the sale. (*Estate of Block v. Commissioner*, No. 1988-159)

DEDUCTING LAWYER'S FEES FOR A LAWSUIT

By applying a new wrinkle from an IRS ruling, you may be able to save taxes on damages won in a lawsuit.

A man injured in an accident received an award for damages plus interest. To bring and win the case he had to pay attorney's fees. The IRS ruled that no taxes were due on the award itself, though the interest was taxable income. Thus, the part of the attorney's fee that was attributable to the recovery of interest on the award was deductible.

■ LESSON:

While attorney's fees that pertain to the recovery of purely "personal" damages aren't deductible, fees that relate to the production, preservation or recovery of income are deductible. (*LTR 8918038*)

SIDELINE BUSINESSES CAN EARN TAX BREAKS

· · · · ·

Extra income and tax breaks are two compelling reasons for you to start a sideline business. Low tax rates—no more than 28% (or 33% in some cases)—and significant write-offs will boost the aftertax value of that new income.

TAX-SAVING OPPORTUNITIES

■ **Boost your retirement plan deductions.** You can set up a Keogh or self-employment pension (SEP) even if you're already covered by a retirement plan at your full-time job. You may contribute up to 25% of earned income to a Keogh or 15% to an SEP. Employed family members can open Individual Retirement Accounts for a write-off of another $2,000 each.

■ **Open a home office.** Deducting the cost of space used for business is like found money because you already own or rent your home. To take this write-off, you must use the home office regularly and exclusively for business, either as your principal place of business or as a place where you meet customers or clients.

• Your deduction depends on the home office's proportionate space in your entire home. Use one room of an eight-room home and you can write off one-eighth of your basic housing cost. Or you can use the office's square footage as a percentage of the house's total footage. Part of a room qualifies if it is physically separated from the rest.

You can amortize depreciation over 31.5 years, based on how much office space you use. Say, for example, that your office takes up 12% of the space in a home costing $200,000; $24,000 divided by 31.5 equals an annual deduction of $762. You get to write off a portion of your home's utility, maintenance, repair and insurance costs, in addition to the cost of work done in the office itself.

• Also deductible is a similar percentage of mortgage interest and property tax payments. True, they're already deductible on your personal tax return. But earmarking them as business expenses instead cuts your sideline profit, which may be subject to self-employment tax, depending on your other earned income. This allocation also reduces your adjusted gross income (AGI), which determines how much of your medical/dental and miscellaneous expenses are deductible.

● N O T E :

You can't use a home office deduction to create a tax loss. To prevent this, you are required to subtract expenses from gross income in a specific order. The order of write-offs isn't important if your business is profitable.

■ **Hire family members.** Many forms of family income shifting have disappeared through the years because of several tax law changes. But you can hire your spouse and children to work for you, paying them reasonable wages that you deduct as a business expense. Each child's earnings are taxed at low rates.

If you're not incorporated, children under 18 don't have to make Social Security payments, and you needn't make payments for them. You must withhold income tax on their wages, however, until they reach the required age.

The IRS scrutinizes family employee arrangements carefully. Make sure you can prove that the work is legitimate and the pay reasonable.

■ **Entertain clients.** When you're in business for yourself, your friends may become clients, and vice versa. When you meet for dinner, say, the expense may be a legitimate write-off.

You can deduct 80% of the cost of meals and entertainment expenditures if business is discussed before, during or afterward. Keep a business diary listing all expenses, their business purpose and whom you were with. Hold on to receipts for expenses exceeding $25.

■ **Maximize travel deductions.** Business-related travel costs, such as transportation and lodging, are fully deductible. If your spouse provides substantial business services during the trip, you can also write off his or her expenses. However, business, not pleasure, must be the primary purpose of the trip. Take brief vacations or trips after business trips instead of so-called working vacations.

■ **Save on equipment.** Every year, you can deduct as much as $10,000 of the purchase price immediately, instead of depreciating it over several years. For a car or more costly equipment, leasing may be more attractive than buying from a tax standpoint.

■ **Take miscellaneous deductions.** For most people, such items as accountants' fees, professional dues and subscriptions are now deductible only to the extent they exceed 2% of AGI. But you can include many of those expenses on your business

return without having to fully satisfy the 2% requirement.

MAKE SURE YOUR VENTURE QUALIFIES AS A BUSINESS

If it does, you can write off all business expenses and use the losses to directly offset any other income. The best way to pass IRS muster is to make sure you earn a profit in at least three of five consecutive years in most cases.

Another way is to show that your activity is profit-oriented. Proof of a profit motive can depend on such factors as whether you run your venture in a businesslike manner, your expertise, how much time you put in, whether the operation's asset value is likely to appreciate, how much your activity resembles recreation, and your income from other sources.

● N O T E :

If your venture is considered just a hobby, you can deduct expenses only up to the amount of gross income—with a big catch. Hobby write-offs are considered personal itemized deductions, and are subject to the 2% annual floor on miscellaneous deductions.

E X A M P L E :

Your hobby generates $5,000 in gross income and you want to take $5,000 in deductions. Your adjusted gross income is $75,000 and you have no other miscellaneous deductions. Your actual hobby expense deduction drops to $3,500 (2% of $75,000 is $1,500, which is subtracted from $5,000).

AN OFFICE FOR ONLY ONE CLIENT

• • • • •

A transportation consultant whose only client was the Department of Energy is entitled to take a deduction for his home office, the Tax Court has ruled.

The consultant, Samuel Ewer Eastman, spent about half of his time in his home office and the rest at the DOE or in the field, reviewing a large computer simulation of coal supplies and the transportation industry.

At the DOE he used the office's computers and conferred with programmers and other employees. He researched and wrote his reports at home.

Nonetheless, the IRS tried to disallow his deductions for his home office and for travel and entertainment, claiming that he was an independent contractor whose principal place of business was the DOE.

Eastman won his home office deduction in Tax Court, but lost the decision on his travel and entertainment expenses because he didn't have enough documentation, another illustration of the importance of keeping records and receipts. (Eastman v. Commissioner)

MEDICAL FEES AT RETIREMENT COMMUNITIES

• • • • •

Part of the entrance and monthly fees paid by residents of a retirement community is deductible as a medical expense, the IRS has ruled.

The ruling involves a residential retirement facility that offers three levels of care: independent living, assisted living care and nursing care.

Those under independent and assisted living care are guaranteed 10 free days of care. Days over that are charged at 90% of the normal rate. Fees increase when nursing care is necessary.

The IRS said that any part of the entrance and monthly fees that isn't covered by insurance and that is properly attributed to medical care is deductible as a medical expense. The agency noted that it doesn't have any published position on how expenses should be allocated, and said that medical expenses are a question of fact that falls under the jurisdiction of the IRS district director, leaving the deductible amounts open to various interpretations.

DEDUCTING YOUR TAX PREPARER

• • • • •

If you have a sideline business, you may be missing a deduction that could cut your tax bill by a fair amount.

That's the fee you pay to the tax professional who prepares your business return, and probably takes care of your personal return as well.

For work on the business part of your return, such as Schedule C, all fees would be a deduction against the profits of your trade or business. This would also apply to rents and royalties, which you would file on Schedule E. Thus, they wouldn't be subject to the 2% floor on miscellaneous itemized deductions, which is where the fees for preparing your personal return would go.

RECOMMENDATION:
Ask your adviser to separate the costs of preparing your business and personal returns and schedules, so you can make maximum use of the deduction.

WHEN EDUCATION COSTS ARE NOT DEDUCTIBLE

· · · · ·

Deducting the cost of college courses you take to improve your job skills can be a tricky business. The IRS tends to take a narrow view of what education is necessary to maintain or improve the skills of your present job, thus deductible, and what qualifies you for a new job.

For example, a New York woman got a college degree in order to qualify for a teaching certificate. The IRS ruled, and the Tax Court agreed, that the cost of getting the degree wasn't deductible—even though she had been a teacher prior to a hiatus for raising a family. The specifics:

Janice Baist taught fourth grade at a Catholic parochial school for three years, and then left the work force for several years to raise a family. When she was teaching, the diocese didn't require its teachers to be state-certified, and she wasn't.

When she sought to resume her teaching career in the late 1970's, she found that she had to be certified and needed a degree to qualify. She took college courses for three years while working as a teaching assistant, a position that didn't require a degree. She deducted $3,000 on her 1983 tax return as employment-related educational expenses.

The Tax Court nixed the deduction. To the argument that being a teaching assistant

and being a teacher were both part of the general teaching profession, the court replied that the jobs were qualitatively different. Teaching assistants have no authority to plan lessons, evaluate students or issue grades. In fact, a certified teacher has to be present in the classroom at all times.

As a certified special education teacher, however, Ms. Baist did all these things, even to the extent of preparing individual education plans for each of her learning-impaired students. This was a markedly different job from being a teaching assistant, the court decided. (*Baist v. Commissioner,* T.C. Memo. 1988-554, Dec. 6, 1988)

ALL IN THE FAMILY: CHILD-CARE CREDIT

· · · · ·

An unusual but perfectly legal way to use the child care credit to cut the family tax bill has been approved by the Tax Court. Earl and Penny Langlois both worked outside the home, as did their 20-year-old daughter, Wendy Ann. However, her hours were from 3:00 p.m. to 11:00 p.m., so she could take care of the family's younger children during the early part of the day.

Though Wendy Ann was living with her own family, the Langloises didn't take her on as a dependent. Instead, they claimed a 20% child-care credit on their tax return, based on their estimate of the value of the free room and board they openly provided their daughter in return for her babysitting services.

The IRS opposed this reasoning, but the Tax Court found it persuasive, at least in part. Although they didn't produce specific data on the value of Wendy Ann's services, room and board, they spent something on child care, it said. The court awarded them a reduced credit on that basis.

The court said that the relationship between daughter and parents doesn't preclude claiming a child-care credit. But it did caution in a footnote that the free room and board given Wendy Ann are income to her. (*Langlois v. Commissioner*)

OBSERVATION:

If this applies to you, make the arrangement in a businesslike way, with a written agreement stating the value of the services exchanged. This will give you a defensible position, if the IRS attacks.

IRS PAYS LEGAL FEES
. . . . .

Try as it might, the IRS couldn't avoid paying legal costs to a couple whose tax return the agency had questioned at length.

The couple seemingly had reported only part of a $95,000 rental payment on their tax return. Questioned by the IRS, their attorney pointed out that the remainder had been reported on a trust in the wife's name, and sent additional documentation.

The agency sent a tax bill, anyway, so the couple contacted a problem resolution officer. But it wasn't until they petitioned the Tax Court four months later that the IRS service center sent them a notice saying their return would be accepted as filed.

About this time, the couple said they were going to ask for legal fees. Then the IRS began raising a series of issues that basically had been settled at the administrative level, a situation that dragged on for months.

After the couple submitted still more documents, the IRS finally settled the case, and the couple asked the Tax Court for legal costs. The court came down on their side, saying the IRS had refused to concede in hopes that the couple would stop asking for remuneration. (*Wilbourn v. Commissioner*)

HOW YOU WORD A SETTLEMENT CAN SAVE YOU MONEY
. . . . .

Word that lawsuit settlement right and your tax bill might be zero. The trick is to have as much as possible labeled as compensation for "personal injuries."

As an example, Michael Matray was a real estate developer in Ohio. Charles and Joseph Iannis went into partnership with him on one of his developments, and Matray managed the property.

One day a friend of the Iannis brothers, John Terlep, asked to be allowed to participate in the management of that property and another. Matray turned him down, and pretty soon Terlep told the Iannises that Matray was mismanaging the property. The brothers, in turn, spread the word that Matray was a bad manager.

Eventually, the Iannis brothers settled with Matray for $400,000. Of this, $100,000 was allocated to buying Matray's stock. The rest was in settlement of "all claims and cause of action relating to personal injury, termination of employment, and damage to business reputation."

Matray claimed that $224,000 of the settlement should be excluded from income, as payment for personal injuries.

The Tax Court judge agreed that at least

some of the settlement was attributable to payment for personal injuries. The judge ruled that $100,000 was for termination of employment, and allocated another $15,000 to settling a contract claim. The remaining $109,000 was excludable, the court said. (*Matray v. Commissioner*)

OBSERVATION:

If the settlement document had spelled out exactly how much was for redress of personal injuries, Matray might have been able to shelter more of it from taxation.

INJURY TO PROFESSIONAL REPUTATION
· · · · ·

A $300,000 settlement in a malicious prosecution case is entirely tax free. The Tax Court handed down the ruling and an appeals court upheld it.

Part of the money was for damages to the professional reputation of James E. Threlkeld. His sale of a piece of real estate had resulted in the dispute.

The IRS finally agreed that most of the money was tax free, but wanted to tax the part attributable to damages to Threlkeld's professional reputation.

The Tax Court said there wasn't any valid distinction between injury to personal and professional reputation. And under Tennessee law damages received in settlement of a claim for malicious prosecution in a civil proceeding are for personal injury.

The Sixth Circuit agreed, saying the injury to Threlkeld's reputation was just as much a personal injury as a physical one. (*Threlkeld v. Commissioner*)

DISABILITY PAYMENTS MAY NOT BE DEDUCTIBLE
· · · · ·

Income payments under your company's disability insurance plan may or may not be taxable. It all depends on the wording of the policy.

For example, a corporate executive was left totally and permanently disabled from injuries suffered in a horse-riding accident. For partial or total disability lasting longer than six months, his employment contract said, the company would pay his full salary for six months, then 75% of it for the balance of the contract term.

The executive paid the taxes on the income, but later filed refund claims, contending the payments were exempt from tax under Code Sec. 105(c). The U.S. district court bought the argument, but it was not accepted in the 4th Circuit Court of Appeals.

The appeals court said that, to be exempt, payments must be made under an accident- or health-insurance plan for the permanent loss of a body part or function, and must be based on the nature of the injury, regardless of the period the employee was away from work.

The payments met the first test but not the others, the appeals court said in their ruling, pointing out that under case law, permanency of injury alone isn't enough to qualify a payment.

Instead, the court said, the amount paid must vary according to the kind and severity of the injury. The disability plan didn't do that and, further, the length of absence from work affected the amount paid. (*Rosen v. United States*)

DO YOU QUALIFY FOR TAX-FREE HOUSING?

· · · · ·

Suppose then that you own and live in a house on or adjacent to the land where your business stands. If you must be there constantly to see that machinery runs properly, that vandals don't damage the equipment, etc., you might also enjoy "free" housing.

You could first sell your house to your business corporation. The corporation then could require you to live there as a condition of employment.

Others have successfully defended such arrangements for a variety of businesses. For example, a U.S. district court has ruled that a school district supervisor doesn't have to pay income tax on the value of the free housing given to him as part of his job. The court found that the house was furnished for the convenience of the employer, was located on the business premises of the employer and that the employer required him to occupy it as a condition of employment. (*Erdelt v. U.S.*)

▲ I M P O R T A N T :

To support your bid for tax-free housing, you have to be able to prove that your presence really is necessary to the operation of the business.

DEDUCTING ROUTINE LEGAL FEES

· · · · ·

Some legal fees can be deducted immediately. Others must be amortized over the years, wait until a property is sold, or be nondeductible. Here are the rules:

• You can deduct the fee in the current year if your lawyer represents you in an everyday business matter, such as collecting a bill, drawing up a contract or handling a contract dispute.

• If the legal work secures a benefit that extends beyond the current year, the fee is deductible only gradually. For example, if the fee for negotiating and preparing a three-year lease is $600, you can write off $200 a year for three years.

• If the property isn't depreciable—your home or raw land, say—the fee is deductible only when the property is sold.

R E C O M M E N D A T I O N :
Make sure that your lawyer itemizes all your bills.

TAX SOFTWARE SAVES TIME AND MONEY

· · · · ·

Today's computerized tax-preparation programs can make filing your return easier than it's ever been. The better programs provide simple, step-by-step guides as you work your way through the screens. You may not even need to use the manual to get the job done.

Basically, tax-preparation programs are very user-friendly spreadsheet tools. Plug in a number here, and your software instantly calculates what you owe or what Uncle Sam owes you. When you're finished, they print out the full tax return. On that basis alone, they're well worth their modest cost because of the time and tedium they eliminate.

• The good programs give you the opportunity to play the "what-if" game. After entering the basic data, you can quickly recalculate your taxes under countless alternative scenarios.

EXAMPLE:

What if you treated your second home as a rental property? You'll know immediately whether you'll come out ahead using a "what if" and by how much. Then, if you decide to use a particular "what if," the program adjusts all the numbers on all the appropriate forms.

• Some programs also contain an extra feature: content-sensitive help screens. When queried by pressing a special key, they give you the basic information about the tax form line you're at.

The programs begin with a question-and-answer section. You answer basic questions about your tax status. Then the software programs determine which tax forms are necessary, present them in the correct sequence and prompt you to supply the necessary information.

For example, suppose you say you have a sideline business. Your program will advise you to fill out Schedule C. Then it will prompt you on how to enter the data, including such areas as equipment depreciation, listing expenses and so on. It will automatically determine your self-employment tax and carry that number to the appropriate line on the 1040.

To be sure, these programs can't offer sophisticated counsel on the nuances of such areas as the alternative minimum tax or which depreciation method is best for your circumstances. You'll have to make those decisions yourself and/or consult a tax professional.

SAVINGS FOR YOU

A tax expert charges anywhere from $50 to $300 an hour. Some of that time is spent providing cogent advice on tax strategy. But most is probably spent sorting the tax receipts you've saved and inputting the information into a computer.

If you sort out the receipts and you plug the raw data into your computer, you can then print out a preliminary return and review it with your expert. What might otherwise be a $300–$1,500 bill can be cut by 50%–75%.

The two best programs on the market: *TaxCut* ($79.95 from Meca Ventures Inc., 203-222-9150) and *TurboTax* ($75 from ChipSoft, 1-800-782-1120). Both are discounted by many software retailers to $50–$60. Be sure that you get the latest versions of each. Lower-cost allied software for your state tax return is also available.

TaxCut, which incorporates the well-regarded *Ask Dan About Your Taxes* preparation program, can be used with the popular *Managing Your Money* personal finance program by "importing" data into *TaxCut* at the touch of a button.

ORGANIZE YOUR FINANCIAL PAPERS
▪ ▪ ▪ ▪ ▪

As tax season draws near, most people look with dismay at the mounting piles of bills, receipts, and canceled checks they've accumulated over the past 12 months.

What should you keep? What should you throw away? Neil Barnes, chairman emeritus of the International Association for Financial Planners in Atlanta, GA, offers some pointers:

SORTING IT OUT

■ **Tax records.** Keep prior returns plus documentation (bills, 1099s, W2s) for deductions for seven years. For audit or review, the IRS can ask you to produce records going back three years. In cases of suspected fraud, the statute of limitations for producing documentation is seven years.

Receipts to keep include:

• *Charitable contributions.* You can deduct charitable contributions only if you itemize deductions.

• *Medical and drug receipts.* It's a deduction if it exceeds 7 1/2% of your adjusted gross income.

• *Bills for home improvement* should be kept permanently because they can reduce any capital gains tax a homeowner might have to pay on profits from home sales over the years.

• **If you are making nondeductible contributions to Individual Retirement Accounts,** keep permanent records relating to those contributions, in order to determine how money withdrawn from the account will be taxed. Accurate records will enable you to separate the deductible and nondeductible contributions.

■ **Bank records.** Keep statements, and canceled checks for at least seven years. Deposit and withdrawal slips, however, can be thrown away once they are checked against your monthly statement to make sure the account was correctly credited or debited.

■ **Utility bills.** No need to keep them. However, hold them for seven years if they are for an investment property or represent an expense of a side business in which you're taking a percentage of the bill.

■ **Telephone bills.** Throw them away, unless you are claiming home office deductions on your tax return. Telephone bills must be kept if they are proof that calls qualify for either business or charitable deduction.

■ **Credit card receipts.** Unless you have a side business, and you're taking some or all of it as a deduction, they need not be kept. Hold your current bill for one month to check to see that it is accurate and has recorded your most recent payment. Credit card interest deductions will be phased out in 1991; 10% of such interest is deductible in 1990.

■ **Insurance documentation.** Each year you get a new declaration page on your auto and homeowner policies. Once the new one is in effect, throw away the old one. For life insurance, keep annual premium notices, even though you may pay for your policy on a quarterly basis. Annual notices list additional information, such as cash value balances, dividends, etc.

■ **Pay stubs.** You only need your year-end stub, which lists the cumulative balance for all the categories of deductions and payments. Ideally, you should have one for each year, going back five years.

■ **Investments.** If you have a mutual fund, for example, keep only the year-end statement in order to establish your cost basis. Reinvested dividends and capital gains distributions are taxable each year. When you sell the fund, you should total all the distributions and add them to your cost, so that you're not taxed twice. You should only pay tax on the distributions in excess of the cost. For all investments, keep records of your original cost basis, plus any dividends that are reinvested.

■ **Sales receipts.** Since the sales tax deduction has been eliminated, there is no reason to hold on to them. Receipts not needed as proof for specific purposes (substantiating a tax deduction, property-insurance claim, warranty repair or to return defective merchandise) can be thrown away. Receipts for everyday purchases such as cosmetics, perishables and nonprescription drugs, which account for the majority of most people's sales slip collection, can be discarded once you are sure none of the items have to be returned.

DEDUCT MORE OF YOUR BUSINESS EXPENSES

■　■　■　■　■

If you're an employee, you can only deduct unreimbursed expenses that exceed 2% of your adjusted gross income (AGI).

So, if you have an AGI of $50,000, you'd have to rack up a total of $1,000 in miscellaneous expenses for such things as mileage, tax advice, and investment-related costs before you could deduct a single dollar. And you couldn't deduct any of the first $1,000.

One way to keep from having to eat those business-related expenses is to convince your employer to reimburse you. This is something some companies are reluctant to do because it would be a cost to them, albeit mostly deductible.

Another way out won't cost the company any money, but can save you plenty. Ask your employer to reduce your salary by the amount you're spending and reimburse you for your costs instead. This way, you avoid that "floor" and also cut your tax bill because your adjusted gross income is smaller.

CAUTION

Before taking the second course, check how it could affect your future pension and Social Security benefits. It won't affect the latter if your salary after the cut is at least equal to Social Security's maximum taxable earnings for the year ($51,300 in 1990).

Note that if you use the pay-cut method, you must regularly turn over to your employer the logs and records you now keep for your expenses, so that the company has a backup record for the IRS.